# CORPORATION PARTNERSHIP FIDUCIARY

## Filled-In Tax Return Forms

### 2006 EDITION

CCH Editorial Staff Publication

**Editorial Staff**

Revision Editor: Susan Flax Posner, J.D., LL.M.
Production: Craig Arritola, Domenic Fosco

ISBN 0-8080-1413-7

# Table Of Contents

# What's New for 2005 Returns

This publication contains the basic 2005 income tax returns to be filed in 2006 by corporations (Form 1120, Form 1120-A, and Form 1120-W for estimated tax), partnerships (Form 1065), S corporations (Form 1120S), and estates and trusts (Form 1041).

CCH Explanations are coordinated with the official instructions for these filled-in forms, cover the separate items and schedules of each return, and are keyed to the actual illustrative figures. For more detailed information, refer to the 2006 CCH federal tax reporters.

The building-block Form 1040 for individuals, along with its many schedules, is filled in with illustrative figures and published in the separate companion CCH publication, "Individuals' Filled-In Tax Return Forms—2006 Edition."

Among the important items for 2005 are:

(1) **Domestic Production Activities Deduction— New Line 25 on Form 1120.** Beginning January 1, 2005, the corporation may be able to deduct up to 3 percent of its "qualified production activities income" from the following activities:

a. manufacturing, production, growth or extraction of certain tangible personal property, computer software, films and videotapes, sound recordings (such as discs, tapes, or other phonorecordings), electricity, natural gas, or potable water produced by the taxpayer;

b. construction performed in the United States; and

c. engineering or architectural services performed in the United States for construction projects in the United States [Code Sec. 199]. See Form 8903, Domestic Production Activities Deduction, for further discussion.

(2) **Code Sec. 1202 Exclusion Increased for Gain from Empowerment Zone Business Stock.** A taxpayer other than a corporation can generally exclude up to 50 percent of gain on the sale or trade of qualified small business stock held for more than 5 years. This is called the Code Sec. 1202 exclusion. Beginning in 2005, the exclusion is increased to as much as 60

percent of the taxpayer's gain if the taxpayer meets the following additional requirements:

a. the taxpayer sells or trades stock in a corporation that qualifies as an empowerment zone business during substantially all of the time the stock was held; and

b. the taxpayer acquired the stock after December 21, 2000.

The part of the gain that is included in income is 28 percent rate gain.

(3) **Capital Gain Treatment Applies to Outright Sales of Timber.** Outright sales of timber by landowners after December 31, 2004, will qualify for capital gains treatment if the timber was held for more than 1 year before the date of disposal.

(4) **Electing S Corporation Status.** For tax years beginning after December 31, 2004, the number of shareholders an S corporation may have increases from 75 to 100. For purposes of the 100-shareholder limit, members of a family are no longer required to make an election to be treated as one shareholder as a result of the Gulf Opportunity Zone Act of 2005.

(5) **Increase to Withholding on Supplemental Wage Payments Exceeding $1 Million.** For payments made after 2004, the flat withholding rate on supplemental wage payments that exceed $1million increased to 35 percent.

(6) **Employment Taxes on Employee Stock Options.** Wages for social security, Medicare, and federal unemployment tax purposes do not include remuneration from exercising an incentive stock option or employee stock purchase plan option or from any disposition of stock acquired by exercising such an option. Therefore, Federal income tax withholding is not required on these items.

(7) **Increase to FUTA Tax Deposit Requirement.** The deposit threshold for FUTA tax has been increased from $100 to $500. The $500 threshold applies to FUTA tax deposits required for taxes reported on Form 940, 940-EZ, or 940-PR, Employer's Annual Federal Unemployment (FUTA) Tax Return, for tax periods beginning January 1, 2005.

(8) **Temporary suspension of 10 percent limitation.** The charitable contribution deduction for a corporation is generally limited to 10 percent of its taxable income for the year in which the contribution was made A corporation may elect to deduct qualified cash contributions without regard to the general 10 percent limit if the contributions were made after August 27, 2005, and before January 1, 2006, to a qualified charitable organization for Hurricane Katrina relief efforts. The total amount claimed cannot be more than 100 percent of the corporation's taxable income through the end of 2005. Excess contributions are carried over 5 years. Taxpayers should attach a statement to the return, substantiating that the contributions are for Hurricane Katrina relief efforts and indicating the amount of qualified contributions for which the election is made.

(9) **Donations of food.** Any taxpayer, including C corporations, S corporations and partnerships may claim an enhanced deduction for contributions of food inventory to charitable organizations that are: (1) used in a manner consistent with the donee's exempt purpose solely for the care of the ill, needy or infants; (2) not transferred in exchange for money, other property, or services; and (3) substantiated by a written statement that their use will be consistent with such requirements. Donated property that meets these requirements is deductible in an amount that is the lesser of: (1) the basis of the property, plus one half of the excess of fair market value over the basis; or (2) two times the basis. For taxpayers other than C corporations, the total deduction for food inventory contributions in a tax year generally may not exceed 10 per cent of the taxpayer's net income for such tax year for all trades or businesses, including sole proprietorships, S corporations, partnerships, or other entities, from which such contributions were made. The deduction for contributions of food inventory applies only to "food that is apparently wholesome" defined as food intended for human consumption that meets all quality and labeling standards imposed by applicable law, even though it may not be readily marketable for various reasons. This provision for food inventory applies to contributions made on or after August 28, 2005 and before January 1, 2006.

(10) **Donations of books.** C corporation may claim an enhanced deduction equal to the lesser of: (1) the basis of the property, plus one half of the excess of fair market value over the basis; or (2) two times the basis. A qualified book contribution is a chari-table contribution of books to a public school that provides elementary education or secondary education (kindergarten through grade 12) and that is an educational organization that normally maintains a regular faculty and curriculum and normally has a regularly enrolled body of pupils or students in attendance at the place where its educational activities are regularly carried on. The deduction is only allowed if the donee school certifies in writing that: (1) the books are suitable, in terms of currency, content, and quantity for use in the school's educational programs, and (2) the school will use the books in its educational programs. The enhanced deduction applies to contributions made after August 27, 2005, and before January 1, 2006.

(11) **Enhanced Work Opportunity Tax Credit.** The Work Opportunity Tax Credit (WOTC) encourages employers to hire economically-challenged individuals. The credit generally equals 40 percent of the first $6,000 of wages ($3,000 for summer youth employees) paid to each targeted group member during the first year of employment. The Katrina Emergency Tax Relief Act (KETRA) creates a new target group for the WOTC, "Hurricane Katrina employees." A Hurricane Katrina employee is an individual whose principal place of abode was in the core disaster area on August 28, 2005. If a business employed a particular worker on August 28, however, it is ineligible for a WOTC for that worker. Under the new law, employers can take the credit for an individual hired to work in a core disaster area by August 27, 2007; employers can claim the credit for a displaced individual hired by December 31, 2005, regardless of where the employee works. The December 31, 2005, expiration date of the WOTC is waived for these employees.

(12) **New employee retention tax credit.** A new tax credit is available to encourage employers to retain employees on their payrolls. The credit is affected by Hurricanes Katrina, Rita and Wilma 40 percent of the first $6,000 in wages paid to each eligible employee after August 28, 2005 (Hurricane Katrina) September 23, 2005 (Hurricane Rita), and October 23, 2005 (Hurricane Wilma), and before January 1, 2006, by employers located in the core disaster area, for the period the business is rendered inoperable as a result of damage caused by Hurricane Katrina, Rita and Wilma. See Form 5884-A.

(13) **Extended Deadlines.** KETRA extended deadlines for filing tax returns and making payments

for income, estate and gift, excise, and employment taxes until February 28, 2006 for both victims and volunteers. In addition, the IRS is required to abate interest and late filing, late payment or failure to deposit penalties that would otherwise apply. The extension to file and pay does not apply to information returns in the W-2, 1098, 1099 or 5498 series, or to Forms 1042-S or 8027.

(14) **Automatic extensions.** Most businesses that cannot file by the due date can get an automatic six-month extension of time to file by submitting Form 7004, Application for Automatic 6-Month Extension of Time To File Certain Business Income tax, Information, and Other Returns. Extension will be granted if the business taxpayer completes Form 7004 properly, makes a proper estimate of the tax, files the form by the due date of the return and pays any tax that is due. Form 7004 replaces the following extension forms: Form 2758, Application for Extension of Time to File Certain Excise, Income, Information, and Other Returns; Form 8736, Application for Automatic Extension of Time to File U.S. Return for a Partnership, REMIC, or for Certain Trusts; and Form 8800, Application for Additional Extension of Time to File U. S. Return For a Partnership, REMIC, or for Certain Trusts. Taxpayers can use Form 7004 for any return with a tax year which ends on or after December 31, 2005.

(15) **Increased Code Sec. 179 Expensing Deduction Amount.** For tax years beginning in 2005, the maximum Code Sec. 179 expense deduction is $105,000 ($140,000 for qualified enterprise zone, renewal community, and New York Liberty Zone property). This limit is reduced by the amount by which the cost of Code Sec. 179 property placed in service during the tax year exceeds $420,000. The Gulf Opportunity Zone Act of 2005 increased the expensing limitation by the lesser of $105,000, or the cost of qualified GO Zone property. It also increases the $420,000 investment limitation by the lesser of $600,000, or the cost of qualified Code Sec.179 GO Zone property placed in service during the tax year. Property purchased on or after August 28, 2005 qualifies. Expensing on property that ceases to be GO Zone property (that is, property moved out of the area) must be recaptured. GO Zone property is property located in affected counties in Alabama, Louisiana, and Mississippi.

(16) **Increased depreciation allowance for automobiles.** The special depreciation allowance and the increased limits on depreciation for passenger automobiles do not apply to most property placed in service in 2005 or later. Taxpayers can only claim the special allowance for certain aircraft, certain property with a long production periods, and qualified Liberty Zone property.

(17) **Gas Gathering Lines – 7-Year MACRS Property.** Certain natural gas gathering lines placed in service after April 11, 2005, are treated as 7-year property under the Modified Accelerated Cost Recovery System (MACRS).

(18) **Electric Transmission and Natural Gas Distributions lines – 15-year MACRS Property.** Certain electric transmission property and natural gas distributions lines placed in service after April 11, 2005, are treated as 15-year property under MACRS.

(19) **Pollution Control Facilities Eligible for 84-month Amortization.** Taxpayers can elect to amortize certain atmospheric pollution control facilities placed in service after April 11, 2005, over an 84-month period.

(20) **Geological and Geophysical Expenses Eligible for 24-month write-off.** For tax years beginning after August 8, 2005, taxpayer can elect to amortize certain geological and geophysical expenses over a 24-month period.

# 2005 Tax Rate Tables

## Corporations

The corporate tax rates for tax years beginning in 2005 are as follows:

| Taxable Income Over | | But Not Over | Pay | + | % on Excess | Of the Amount Over— |
|---|---|---|---|---|---|---|
| $ 0 | — | $ 50,000 | $ 0 | + | 15% | $ 0 |
| 50,000 | — | 75,000 | 7,500 | + | 25 | 50,000 |
| 75,000 | — | 100,000 | 13,750 | + | 34 | 75,000 |
| 100,000 | — | 335,000 | 22,250 | + | 39* | 100,000 |
| 335,000 | — | 10,000,000 | 113,900 | + | 34 | 335,000 |
| 10,000,000 | — | 15,000,000 | 3,400,000 | + | 35 | 10,000,000 |
| 15,000,000 | — | 18,333,333 | 5,150,000 | + | 38** | 15,000,000 |
| 18,333,333 | — | ......... | 0 | + | 35 | 0 |

* A 5% additional tax rate applies to phase out the benefits of the graduated rates between $100,000 and $335,000 of taxable income.

** A 3% additional tax applies to phase out the benefits of the graduated rates between $15,000,000 and $18,333,333 of taxable income.

Members of a controlled group of corporations must apportion each of the applicable brackets among themselves.

A personal holding company is subject to an additional tax on all undistributed personal holding company income at a 15% tax rate. The accumulated earnings tax is 15% on accumulated taxable income exceeding the $250,000 ($150,000 for certain personal service corporations) minimum accumulated earnings credit. Taxable income of personal service corporations is taxed at a flat rate of 35%.

## Estates and Nongrantor Trusts

For tax years beginning in 2005, the tax rates for estates and nongrantor trusts are as follows:

| Taxable Income Over | | But Not Over | Pay | + | % on Excess | Of the Amount Over— |
|---|---|---|---|---|---|---|
| $ 0 | — | $1,950 | $ 0 | + | 15% | $ 0 |
| 1,950 | — | 4,600 | 292.50 | + | 25 | 1,950 |
| 4,600 | — | 7,000 | 955.00 | + | 28 | 4,600 |
| 7,000 | — | 9,550 | 1,627.00 | + | 33 | 7,000 |
| 9,550 | — | ..... | 2,468.50 | + | 35 | 9,550 |

If an estate or trust has both a net capital gain and any taxable income its tax should be computed on Part V of Form 1041 Schedule D (see ¶82).

# General Rules for Corporate Returns

## ¶1  WHO MUST FILE

Unless the corporate entity is exempt from tax under Code Sec. 501, all domestic corporations (including corporations in bankruptcy) must file an income tax return whether or not they have taxable income. Most domestic corporations—so-called "C corporations"—must generally file Form 1120, "U.S. Corporation Income Tax Return." Smaller C corporations may be eligible to file an abbreviated return on Form 1120-A, U.S. Short-Form Corporation Income Tax Return. The purpose of Form 1120 and Form 1120-A is to report the income, gains, losses, deductions, credits, and to figure the income tax liability of a corporation.

## ¶2  SPECIAL RETURNS FOR CERTAIN ORGANIZATIONS

- **Limited liability companies (LLCs).**
- **LLC with more than one owner.** If an entity with more than one owner was formed under state law as a limited liability company (LLC), it is generally treated as a partnership for federal income tax purposes and files Form 1065, U.S. Partnership Return of Income. The LLC is an attractive entity for conducting a wide variety of businesses because the LLC offers the best of both the corporate and partnership worlds and has fewer restrictions than the S corporation. The LLC combines the limited liability benefit of conducting a business in the corporate form with the major tax benefits associated with doing business as a partnership. Like a partnership, the LLC avoids tax at the entity level and passes through taxable income, losses and credits to the "member" level. In addition, since the LLC is taxed like a partnership, it may specially allocate items of income or expense provided the allocations have substantial economic effect. In the LLC context, a *member* is the person who owns an interest in the LLC and is the functional equivalent of a partner or shareholder. The members of an LLC have the discretion to decide how they want to share profit and losses provided the agreement is reflected in the operating agreement or the articles of incorporation, which are filed with the state.

- **Single-member LLC.** Generally a single-member LLC is disregarded as an entity separate from its owners and reports its income and deductions on its owner's federal income tax return. The LLC can file a Form 1120 or Form 1120-A only it if has filed Form 8832, Entity Classification Election, and made an election to be treated as an associated taxable as a corporation

**Corporations engaged in farming.** Any corporation that engages in farming should use Form 1120, or if they qualify Form 1120-A, to report income (loss) from such activities.

**Ownership in a Financial Asset Securitization Investment Trust.** Special rules apply to a FASIT in existence on October 22, 2004, to the extent that regular interests issued by the FASIT before October 22, 2004, continue to remain outstanding in accordance with their original terms. If a corporation holds an ownership interest in a FASIT to which these special rules apply, it must report all items of income, gain, deductions, losses, and credits. Show a breakdown of the items on an attached schedule. If a corporation holds an ownership interest in a financial asset securitization investment trust (FASIT), it must report all items of income, gain, deductions, losses and credits on the corporation's income tax return. Taxpayers must show a breakdown of the items on an attached schedule. The special rules for FASITs generally do not apply after 2004. However, the rules do apply to any FASIT in existence on October 22, 2004, to the extent that regular interests issued by the FASIT before October 22, 2004, continue to remain outstanding in accordance with their original terms.

**Corporations Participating in Tax Shelters.** Corporations that participate directly or indirectly in a "reportable" tax shelter must file Form 8886, Reportable Transaction Disclosure Statement. Taxpayers must disclose on their tax returns certain information regarding each *reportable transaction* in which the taxpayer participates [Reg. §1.6011-4]. There are six categories of reportable transactions as follows:

1. Listed transaction, which is any transaction that is the same as (or substantially similar) a transaction that is specified by the IRS as a tax avoidance transaction and whose tax benefits may be disallowed [Reg. §1.6011-4(b)(2)].

2. Any transaction that is offered under conditions of confidentiality. These conditions are satisfied if the advisor who is paid a minimum fee places a limitation on disclosure by the taxpayer of the tax treatment or tax structure of the transaction, and the limitation on disclosure protects the confidentiality of that advisor's tax strategies (irrespective if such terms are legally binding) [Reg. §1.6011-4(b)(3)].

3. Any transaction for which (a) the taxpayer has the right to a full or partial refund of fees if the intended tax consequences from the transaction are not sustained or (b) the fees are contingent on the intended tax consequences from the transaction being sustained [Reg. §1.6011-4(b)(4)].

4. Any transaction resulting in a taxpayer claiming a loss of at least (a) $10 million in any single year or $20 million in any combination of years by a corporate taxpayer or a partnership with only corporate partners; (b) $2 million in any single year or $4 million in any combination of years by all other partnerships, S corporations, trusts, and individuals; or (c) $50,000 in any single year for individuals or trusts if the loss arises with respect to foreign currency translation losses [Reg. §1.6011-4(b)(5)].

5. Any transaction done by certain taxpayers in which the tax treatment of the transaction differs (or is expected to differ) by more than $10 million from its treatment for book purposes (using generally accepted accounting principles) in any year [Reg. §1.6011-4(b)(6)].

6. Any transaction that results in a tax credit exceeding $250,000 (including a foreign tax credit) if the taxpayer holds the underlying asset for less than 45 days [Reg. §1.6011-4(b)(7)].

A penalty will be imposed on a corporation that fails to include with any return or statement any required information with respect to a reportable transaction. The penalty applies without regard to whether the transaction ultimately results in an understatement of tax, and applies in addition to any accuracy-related penalty that may be imposed. The penalty for failure to disclose a reportable transaction is $50,000 for each failure to file Form 8886. The amount increases to $200,000 if the failure involves a listed transaction. The penalty cannot be waived with respect to a listed transaction. The IRS can rescind (or abate) the penalty only if rescinding the penalty would promote compliance with the tax laws and effective tax administration. In making this determination, the IRS should consider: (1) whether the person on whom the penalty is imposed has a history of complying with the tax laws, (2) whether the violation is due to an unintentional mistake of fact, and (3) whether imposing the penalty would be against equity and good conscience.

**Material Advisors Involved in Reportable Transactions.** Each material advisor to any reportable transaction (including any listed transaction) must timely file Form 8264, Application for Registration of a Tax Shelter, with the IRS and include on the form the following:

1. Information identifying and describing the transaction,

2. Information describing any potential tax benefits expected to result from the transaction, and

3. Other information requested by the IRS.

Form 8264 must be filed within 30 days after the date on which a person becomes a material advisor. A person will be treated as becoming a material advisor when all of the following events have occurred: (1) the material advisor makes a tax statement; (2) the material advisor receives (or expects to receive) the minimum fees; and (3) the transaction is entered into by the taxpayer [Notice 2005-22, 2005-12 IRB 756].

A *material advisor* is defined as any person who:

1. Provides material aid, assistance, or advice with respect to organizing, managing, promoting, selling, implementing, or carrying out any reportable transaction,

2. Provides material aid, assistance, or advice with respect to insuring any reportable transaction (and who derives gross income for such assistance or advice), and

3. Directly or indirectly derives gross income for such assistance or advice in excess of $250,000 ($50,000 in the case of a reportable transaction substantially all of the tax benefits from which are provided to natural persons).

A $50,000 penalty is imposed on any material advisor who fails to file an information return, or who files a false or incomplete information return, with respect to a reportable transaction (including a listed transaction). In the case of a listed transaction, the amount of the penalty is increased to the greater of:

1. $200,000 or

2. 50 percent of gross income received by the material advisor for any aid, assistance, or advice provided before the date the information return is filed. The penalty is increased to 75 percent of gross income for intentional disregard by a material advisor of the requirement to disclose a listed transaction.

The penalty cannot be waived for a listed transaction. As to reportable transactions, the penalty can be rescinded (or abated) only if rescinding the penalty would promote compliance with the tax laws and effective tax administration. The decision to rescind a penalty must be accompanied by a record describing the facts and reasons for the action and the amount rescinded. There will be no right to judicially appeal a refusal to rescind a penalty.

**Small Corporations - Form 1120-A.** Small corporations may be able to file Form 1120-A, U.S. Corporation Short-Form Income Tax Return, if all of the following requirements are satisfied:

- The corporation's gross receipts, income, and total assets are under $500,000.

- All dividend income is from domestic corporations qualifying for the 70 percent dividends-received deduction, and none of the dividend income is from debt-financed securities. Subchapter T co-operatives can include patronage dividends on Form 1120-A.

- It does not owe any AMT on Form 4626, Alternative Minimum Tax - Corporations.

- The corporation's only nonrefundable credit is either the general business credit.

- The corporation is not a member of a controlled group, a personal holding company, filing a consolidated return, electing to forego the entire carryback period for any NOL, or required to file one of the returns listed under **Forms Required from other Organizations** listed below.

- The corporation does not have any ownership in a foreign corporation, foreign partnership, or foreign shareholders that directly or indirectly own 25 percent or more of its stock or any ownership in, or transactions with, a foreign trust.

**Forms Required from Other Organizations.** Instead of filing Form 1120 or Form 1120-A, certain organizations, as shown below, have to file special returns.

| If the organization is a : | File Form |
|---|---|
| • Farmer's cooperative (Code Sec. 1381) | 990-C |
| • Exempt organization with unrelated trade or business income | 990-T |
| • Religious or apostolic organization exempt under Code Sec. 501(d) | 1065 |
| • Entity formed as a limited liability company under state law and treated as a partnership for federal income tax purposes | 1065 |
| • Entity that elects to be treated as a real estate mortgage investment conduit (REMIC) under Code Sec. 860D | 1066 |
| • Interest charge domestic international sales corporation (Code Sec. 992) | 1120-IC-DISC |
| • Foreign corporation (other than life and property and casualty insurance company filing Form 1120-L or Form1120-PC) | 1120-F |
| • Foreign sales corporation (Code Sec. 922) | 1120-FSC |
| • Condominium management, residential real estate management, or timeshare association that elects to be treated as a homeowners association under Code Sec. 528 | 1120-H |
| • Life insurance company (Code Sec. 801) | 1120-L |
| • Fund set up to pay for nuclear decommissioning costs (Code Sec. 468A) | 1120-ND |
| • Property and casualty insurance company (Code Sec. 831) | 1120-PC |
| • Political organization (Code Sec. 521) | 1120-POL |
| • Real estate investment trust (Code Sec. 856) | 1120-REIT |
| Regulated investment company (Code Sec. 851) | 1120-RIC |
| • S corporation (Code Sec. 1361) | 1120S |
| • Settlement fund (Code Sec. 468B) | 1120-SF |

## FILING REQUIREMENTS

- **Return Due Date:**

Corporations must generally file their federal income tax returns by the 15th day of the third month following the close of the tax year. Calendar year corporations must file the 2005 return by March 15, 2006. If the due date falls on a Saturday, Sunday or legal holiday, the corporation may file on the next business day.

**Private Delivery Services.** Corporations may file their return at the last minute using certain qualifying private delivery services (PDS) other than the U.S. Postal Service and still qualify under the rule that a return or payment mailed on time is considered to be filed or received on time. Only the following PDS will qualify:

- DHL Express (DHL); DHL "Same Day" Service, DHL Next Day 10:30 am, DHL Next Day 12:00 pm, DHL Next Day 3:00pm, and DHL 2nd Day Service.

- Federal Express (FedEx); FedEx Priority Overnight, FedEx Standard Overnight, FedEx 2Day, FedEx International Priority, and Fed Ex International First; and

- United Parcel Service (UPS); UPS Next Day Air, UPS Next Day Air Saver, UPS 2nd Day Air, UPS 2nd Day Air A.M., UPS Worldwide Express Plus, and UPS Worldwide Express.

A delivery service not listed above does not qualify for the timely mailing rule. Note also that a registered mail date is treated as the postmark date, and registration is proof of delivery.

**Automatic 6-Month Extension –Form 7004.** Most businesses that cannot file by the due date can get an automatic six-month extension of time to file by submitting Form 7004, Application for Automatic 6-Month Extension of Time To File Certain Business Income tax, Information, and Other Returns. Extension will be granted if the business taxpayer completes Form 7004 properly, makes a proper estimate of the tax, files the form by the due date of the return and pays any tax that is due.

> **Practice Tip:** The IRS will no longer be sending notifications that the extension has been allowed.

> **New:** Form 7004 replaces the following extension forms: Form 2758, Application for Extension of Time to File Certain Excise, Income, Information, and Other Returns; Form 8736, Application for Automatic Extension of Time to File U.S. Return for a Partnership, REMIC, or for Certain Trusts; and Form 8800, Application for Additional Extension of Time to File U. S. Return For a Partnership, REMIC, or for Certain Trusts. Taxpayers can use Form 7004 for any return with a tax year which ends on or after December 31, 2005.

All the returns shown at the bottom of Form 7004 are eligible for an automatic 6-month extension of time to file from the due date of the return.

**Practice Pointer:** Filing Form 7004 does not extend the time for payment of tax. Generally, payment of any balance due on Line 8 of Form 7004 is required by the due date of the return for which the extension is filed. Domestic corporations must deposit all income tax payments by using the Electronic Federal Tax Payment System (EFTPS) or with Form 8109, Federal Tax Deposit Coupon, by the due date of the return. If Form 7004 is filed electronically, the taxpayer can pay by Electronic Funds Withdrawal. See Form 8878-A. If the corporation expects to have a net operating loss carryback, the corporation can reduce the amount to be deposited to the extent of the overpayment resulting from the carryback, provided all other prior year tax liabilities have been fully paid and Form 1138, Extension of Time for Payment of Taxes by a Corporation Expecting a Net Operating Loss Carryback, is filed with Form 7004. *Important:* Payment should *not* be mailed with the Form 7004.

**Penalty for Late Filing of Return.** Generally, a penalty is charged if the return is filed after the due date (including extensions) unless the taxpayer can show reasonable cause for not filing on time. The penalty is usually 5 percent of the amount due for each month or part of month that the return is late. Generally, the maximum penalty is 25 percent. If the return is more than 60 days late, the minimum penalty is $100 or the balance due on the return, whichever is smaller. If the taxpayer has reasonable cause for not filing on time, a statement explaining the reasons should be attached to the return.

**Penalty for Late Payment of Tax.** Generally, a penalty of ½ of 1 percent of any tax not paid by the due date is charged for each month or part of a month that the tax remains unpaid. The penalty cannot exceed 25 percent of the amount due. The penalty will not be charged if the taxpayer can show reasonable cause for not payment on time. If the corporation is granted an extension of time to file a corporation income tax return after filing Form 7004, it will not be charged a late payment penalty if the amount of tax paid by the regular due date of the return is at least 90 percent of the total tax due as shown on Form 7004 and the balance due on Form 7004 is paid by the extended due date.

**Electronic Filing (Form 1120 Only).** Corporations have the option to file Form 1120 and related forms,

| | |
|---|---|
| Form **7004** | **Application for Automatic 6-Month Extension of Time To File** |
| (Rev. December 2005) | **Certain Business Income Tax, Information, and Other Returns** |
| Department of the Treasury Internal Revenue Service | ► **File a separate application for each return.** |

OMB No. 1545-0233

**Type or Print**

File by the due date for the return for which an extension is requested. See instructions.

Name

Taxpayer identification number

Number, street, and room or suite no. If P.O. box, see instructions.

City, town, state, and ZIP code (If a foreign address, enter city, province or state, and country (follow the country's practice for entering postal code)).

**Caution: Carefully complete all items. Incorrect information may cause delay or rejection.**

**1**   Enter only one code for type of return that this automatic 6-month extension is for (see below) . . . . . . . [ ][ ]

**2**   If the foreign corporation does not have an office or place of business in the United States, check here . . . ► [ ]

**3**   If the organization qualifies under Regulations section 1.6081-5 (see instructions), check here . . . . . . . ► [ ]

**4a**   For calendar year 20......, or other tax year beginning ............... , 20......, and ending ............... , 20......

  **b**   **Short tax year.** If this tax year is less than 12 months, check the reason:

     [ ] Initial return      [ ] Final return      [ ] Change in accounting period      [ ] Consolidated return to be filed

**5**   If the organization is a corporation and is the common parent of a group that intends to file consolidated, check here . ► [ ]
     Also, you must attach a schedule, listing the name, address, and EIN for each member covered by this extension.

**6**   Tentative total tax (see instructions) . . . . . . . . . . . . . . . . . . . . . . **6**

**7**   **Total** payments and credits (see instructions) . . . . . . . . . . . . . . . . . **7**

**8**   **Balance due.** Subtract line 7 from line 6. **Generally, you must deposit this amount using the Electronic Federal Tax Payment System (EFTPS), a Federal Tax Deposit (FTD) Coupon, or Electronic Funds Withdrawal (EFW)** (see instructions for exceptions) . . . . . . . . . . **8**

| Extension Is For: | Form Code | Extension Is For: | Form Code |
|---|---|---|---|
| Form 706-GS(D) | 01 | Form 1120-L | 18 |
| Form 706-GS(T) | 02 | Form 1120-ND | 19 |
| Form 990-C | 03 | Form 1120-ND (section 4951 taxes) | 20 |
| Form 1041 (estate) | 04 | Form 1120-PC | 21 |
| Form 1041 (trust) | 05 | Form 1120-POL | 22 |
| Form 1041-N | 06 | Form 1120-REIT | 23 |
| Form 1041-QFT | 07 | Form 1120-RIC | 24 |
| Form 1042 | 08 | Form 1120-S | 25 |
| Form 1065 | 09 | Form 1120-SF | 26 |
| Form 1065-B | 10 | Form 3520-A | 27 |
| Form 1066 | 11 | Form 8612 | 28 |
| Form 1120 | 12 | Form 8613 | 29 |
| Form 1120 (subchapter T cooperative) | 13 | Form 8725 | 30 |
| Form 1120-A | 14 | Form 8804 | 31 |
| Form 1120-F | 15 | Form 8831 | 32 |
| Form 1120-FSC | 16 | Form 8876 | 33 |
| Form 1120-H | 17 | | |

**For Paperwork Reduction Act Notice, see instructions.**      Cat. No. 13804A      Form **7004** (Rev. 12-2005)

¶ **2**

schedules, and attachments electronically. The following returns may not be filed electronically:

- Amended returns,
- Bankruptcy returns,
- Final returns,
- Returns with a name change,
- Returns with precomputed penalty and interest,
- Returns with reasonable cause for failing to file timely,
- Returns with reasonable cause for failing to pay timely,
- Returns with request for overpayment to be applied to another account.

**Mandatory Electronic Filing.** Large corporations with total assets of $50 million or more that file at least 250 returns a year are required to electronically file Form 1120. However, these corporations can require a waiver of the electronic filing requirements. When certain taxpayers required to file over 250 returns fail to file electronically as required, those taxpayers may be liable for failure to file penalties, unless the taxpayer can establish that the failure to file the return electronically was due to reasonable cause and not due to willful neglect. The IRS may waive the electronic filing requirement if the taxpayer demonstrates that undue hardship would result if it were required to file its return electronically. The IRS will approve or deny requests for a waiver of the electronic filing requirement based on each taxpayer's particular facts and circumstances. In determining whether to approve or deny a waiver

request, the IRS will consider the taxpayer's ability to timely file its return electronically without incurring an undue economic hardship. The IRS will generally grant waivers for filing returns electronically where the taxpayer can demonstrate the undue hardship that would result by complying with the electronic filing requirement, including any incremental costs to the filer. Mindful of the software and technological issues in filing electronically, the IRS will also generally grant waivers for filing returns electronically where technology issues prevent the taxpayer from filing its return electronically. Guidance on situations in which deviations or exclusions from the electronic filing requirement can be made without a waiver request ( *e.g.,* amended returns) is available in IRS Publication 4163 and IRS Publication 4206. See Notice 2005-88, 2005-48 IRB 1060.

- **Where to File**

File the corporation's return at the applicable IRS address listed below:

## Where To File

File the corporation's return at the applicable IRS address listed below.

| If the corporation's principal business, office, or agency is located in: | And the total assets at the end of the tax year (Form 1120, page 1, item D) are: | Use the following Internal Revenue Service Center address: |
|---|---|---|
| Connecticut, Delaware, District of Columbia, Illinois, Indiana, Kentucky, Maine, Maryland, Massachusetts, Michigan, New Hampshire, New Jersey, New York, North Carolina, Ohio, Pennsylvania, Rhode Island, South Carolina, Vermont, Virginia, West Virginia, Wisconsin | Less than $10 million | Cincinnati, OH 45999-0012 |
| | $10 million or more | Ogden, UT 84201-0012 |
| Alabama, Alaska, Arizona, Arkansas, <u>California</u>, Colorado, Florida, Georgia, Hawaii, Idaho, Iowa, Kansas, Louisiana, Minnesota, Mississippi, Missouri, Montana, Nebraska, Nevada, New Mexico, North Dakota, Oklahoma, Oregon, South Dakota, Tennessee, Texas, Utah, Washington, Wyoming | Any amount | Ogden, UT 84201-0012 *General* |
| A foreign country or U.S. possession (or the corporation is claiming the possessions corporation tax credit under sections 30A and 936) | Any amount | Philadelphia, PA 19255-0012 *Mutual* |

**15**

• **Required Signatures**

The return must be signed and dated by the company president, vice president, treasurer, assistant treasurer, chief accounting officer, or any other corporate officer (for example, the tax officer) authorized to sign on behalf of the company. Receivers, trustees, or assignees must also sign and date any return filed on behalf of a corporation.

If the return is prepared by a paid preparer (other than officers and employees of the corporation), the paid preparer must complete the required preparer information and must sign by hand in the space provided for the preparer's signature. Note that signature stamps and labels are not acceptable.

**Paid preparer authorization.** Form 1120 includes a box where the taxpayer may check either "Yes" or "No" in response to the question whether the IRS may discuss the return with the paid preparer shown on the return. If the corporation wants to allow the IRS to discuss its tax return with the paid preparer who signed it, the corporation should check the "Yes" box in the signature area of the return. This authorization applies only to the individual whose signature appears in the "Paid Preparer's Use Only" section of the corporation's return. If the "Yes" box is checked, the taxpayer is authorizing the IRS to call the paid preparer to answer any questions that may arise during the review and processing of the return. This includes giving the IRS any information that is missing from the return, calling the IRS for information regarding the processing of the return or the status of any related refund or payment and responding to any IRS notices that the corporation has shared with the preparer about math errors, offsets, and return preparation.

The paid preparer is not authorized to receive any refund check, bind the corporation to anything (including any additional tax liability), or otherwise represent the corporation before the IRS. The authorization granted to the paid preparer cannot be revoked. However, the authorization will automatically end no later than the due date (excluding extensions) for filing the corporation's 2006 tax return.

**Assembling the return.** Attach all schedules and forms after Form 1120 in the following order:

1. Schedule N (Form 1120)
2. Form 8050
3. Form 4136
4. Form 4626
5. Form 851
6. Additional schedules in alphabetical order
7. Additional forms in numerical order.

## ACCOUNTING METHODS

A corporation must select an accounting method that clearly reflects its taxable income. Generally, a corporation will use either the cash method or the accrual method. However, some corporations may use a hybrid method (combinations of the cash and accrual methods). For example, a corporation may use the accrual method to account for sales, cost of goods sold, inventories, receivables and payables, and the cash method to account for other items of income and expense.

**Cash method:** When the cash method is used, income is reported in the year that it is actually or constructively received. Checks received but not cashed are included in income. Expenses are generally deducted when paid. However, prepaid expenses are generally deductible only in the year to which they apply. If the corporation is a qualifying taxpayer or a qualifying small business taxpayer, it may be able to adopt or change to the cash method of accounting to account for inventoriable items in the same manner as materials and supplies that are not incidental. A qualifying taxpayer is a taxpayer whose average annual gross receipts for the 3 prior tax years are $1 million or less and whose business is not a tax shelter. A qualifying small business taxpayer is a taxpayer whose average annual gross receipts for the 3 prior tax years are more than $1 million but not more than $10 million, and whose principal business activity is not an ineligible business.

**Accrual method:** Under the accrual method, income is generally reported when earned, even if payment is not received until a later year. All events that fix the right to payment must have occurred and you must be able to determine the amount of income with reasonable accuracy.

Expenses are deducted when all events that fix the liability have occurred and the amount of the liability can be reasonably estimated. As a further restriction, expenses accrued for services or property are generally not deductible until economic performance has occurred [Reg. §1.461-4]. Generally, a corporation (other than a qualified personal service corporation) must use the accrual method of accounting if its average annual gross receipts exceed $5 million for the three years pro-ceeding the current tax year. A corporation engaged in farming operations also must use the accrual method unless it has gross receipts of $1 million or less ($25 million for a family farming corporation).

*Recurring items:* Corporations can elect a special rule for "recurring items." Under this rule, regularly recurring expenses can be deducted in the tax year before economic performance occurs, provided economic performance takes place by the earlier of 8½ months or a reasonable period of time after the close of the tax year.

*Note:* A corporation can get IRS consent to change to the recurring item exception method.

**Limitations on the cash method.** Businesses that sell inventory to customers must use the accrual method to report their sales and cost of goods sold. If otherwise eligible, they may use the cash method to report other items of income and expenses.

C corporations generally may not use the cash method of accounting unless they meet one of the following exceptions:

- The corporation's average annual gross receipts from the past three years (or the period of time in existence, if shorter) are $5 million or less. Generally, a corporation (other than a qualified personal service corporation) must use the accrual method of accounting if its average annual gross receipts exceed $5 million.

- The corporation is engaged in the trade or business of farming or timber with gross receipts of $1 million or less ($25 million if a family farm corporation). A corporation engaged in farming operations must use the accrual method.

- The corporation is a qualified personal service corporation.

*Important:* This is not the same definition as a personal service corporation for the calendar year restrictions. For purposes of the cash method exception, a "qualified" personal service corporation is: (1) a corporation that provides services in the specified personal service fields; (2) at least 95 percent of the employee hours are spent on the specified service activities, including support activities; and (3) at least 95 percent of the fair market value of the stock is owned directly or indirectly by employees, retired employees, or estates or heirs of former employees (for up to two years after

death). The attribution rules are very narrowly applied for purposes of this test. In general, stock owned by relatives is not attributable to employees.

**Mark-to-Market Accounting Method.** A securities dealer is required to maintain an inventory of all securities held for sale to customers. They are also required to use the mark-to-market accounting method to value this inventory. This means that any securities held by the dealer as inventory must be valued at their fair market value. Any security that is not an inventory item and that is held by the dealer at the end of the tax year is treated as if it were sold by the dealer for its fair market value on the last business day of the taxable year and any gain or loss must be taken into account by the dealer as ordinary gain or loss. When the security is subsequently sold, the gain or loss that is realized is adjusted for the gain or loss that was recognized earlier as a result of the mark-to-market rules. Once elected, the mark-to-market treatment will be effective for the taxable year for which it is made and all subsequent taxable years, unless revoked with the consent of the IRS.

**Commodities dealers and traders and securities traders.** Commodities dealers and traders and securities traders are eligible to make an election to use the mark-to-market accounting method. Gain or loss with respect to electively marked-to-market securities will be ordinary. Thus, if an electing trader disposes of a security before the close of the tax year, the gain or loss would be ordinary. Note that the mark-to-market accounting rules are mandatory for securities dealers but may be elected by securities traders and commodities traders and dealers. If a securities trader elects application of mark-to-market, all securities held in connection with his business generally (with one specified exception) are subject to mark-to-market treatment. As a result of the election made by the trader to use the mark-to-market accounting rules, all gain and loss will be treated as capital gain or loss and not as ordinary income.

**Change in accounting method:** A change in accounting method includes a change from the cash method to the accrual method, or vice versa, and a change in the method or basis used for valuing inventories. But correction of a mathematical error, adjustment for items included in income or deducted in the wrong period, and adjustment in the useful life of a depreciable asset are examples of changes that are not considered changes in accounting methods. IRS approval is not needed for these changes.

If consent is necessary for the change in accounting method, Form 3115, Application for Change in Accounting Method, must be filed within the first 180 days of the tax year for which the change is requested. A fee must also be paid. In general, an accounting change needs to be requested if it alters a consistent pattern of treatment of a material item that has been used in preparing two or more conventionally filed returns. When a method is changed, an adjustment must be made to avoid duplicating or omitting income or deduction items—a so-called Code Sec. 481 adjustment. The timing of the change and the adjustment period depends on who initiates the change. For example, if the corporation initiates it, the change can generally be made starting with the current year. Any adjustments to income required by the change can generally be spread over several years. Less favorable treatment is afforded if the change is requested within a 90-day period after an IRS contact is made to begin an audit.

## TAX COMPUTATION

### CORPORATE INCOME TAX RATES

For tax years beginning after December 31, 1992, the corporate tax rates are as follows:

Taxable Income

| over | but not over | the tax is | of the amount over: |
|---|---|---|---|
| 0 | $50,000 | 15% | 0 |
| $50,000 | 75,000 | $7,500 + 25% | $50,000 |
| 75,000 | 100,000 | 13,750 + 34% | 75,000 |
| 100,000 | 335,000 | 22,250 + 39% | 100,000 |
| 335,000 | 10,000,000 | 113,900 + 34% | 335,000 |
| 10,000,000 | 15,000,000 | 3,400,000 + 35% | 10,000,000 |
| 15,000,000 | 18,333,333 | 5,150,000 + 38% | 15,000,000 |
| 18,333,333 | ......... | 6,416,667 + 35% | 18,333,333 |

### PERSONAL HOLDING COMPANY

In addition to the regular corporate income taxes, a special tax is imposed on any personal holding company. For 2005, the additional tax is 15 percent of undistributed personal holding company income.

### REGULATED INVESTMENT COMPANY

The regular corporate tax rates apply to a company's taxable income. In the case of regulated investment companies, the corporate tax rates apply to investment company taxable income.

### ACCUMULATED EARNINGS TAX

There is imposed, for each tax year, a tax on the accumulated taxable income of each corporation. For 2003 through 2008, the rate is 15 percent. Beginning in 2009, accumulated taxable income is taxed at the highest individual rate. The tax (payable in addition to the regular tax payable by a corporation) is imposed on accumulated taxable income exceeding the $250,000 minimum accumulated earnings credit ($150,000 for personal service corporations engaged in the fields of health, law, engineering, architecture, accounting, actuarial science, performing arts, or consulting).

### FOREIGN CORPORATION

A foreign corporation's income that is effectively connected with a U.S. trade or business is taxed at the rates that apply to domestic corporations. U.S. source income that is not effectively connected with the conduct of the U.S. trade or business is taxed at a flat 30-percent rate or lower treaty rate.

### PERSONAL SERVICE CORPORATIONS

The taxable income of a personal service corporation that engages in activities involving the performance of services in the fields of health, law, engineering, architecture, accounting, actuarial science, performing arts, or consulting and substantially all of the stock of which is held by employees performing services for the corporation, retired employees, or the estates of employees or retired employees is taxed at a flat rate of 35 percent.

### ESTATES AND TRUSTS
#### FOR TAX YEARS BEGINNING IN 2005

| If taxable income is: Over – | but not over – | The tax is: | of the amount over – |
|---|---|---|---|
| $ 0 | 2,000 | 15 % | $0 |
| 2,000 | 4,700 | $300 + 25% | 2,000 |
| 4,700 | 7,150 | 975 + 28% | 4,700 |
| 7,150 | 9,750 | 1,661 + 33% | 7,150 |
| 9,750 | ....... | 2,519 + 35% | 9,750 |

## ¶3   FORM 1120, ITEMS A–E

### • Item A, Line 1: Consolidated Return

If a consolidated return is filed, the parent corporation must attach Form 851, Affiliations Schedule (a list of the companies included in the return), to the consolidated return. Each subsidiary, for the first year a consolidated return is filed, must attach Form 1122, Authorization and Consent of Subsidiary Corporation to be Included in a Consolidated Income Tax Return, consenting to the return and the application of the regulations under Code Sec. 1502. Supporting schedules for each corporation included in the consolidated return must be filed. The schedules must be in columnar form and show, both before and after adjustments, the items of gross income and deductions, a computation of taxable income, balance sheets as of the beginning and end of the tax year, a reconciliation of retained earnings, and a reconciliation of income per books with income per return. Consolidated balance sheets and a reconciliation of consolidated retained earnings must also be attached.

> **Practice Pointer:** The corporation need not include the following if its total receipts and its total assets at the end of the tax year are less then $250,000: (1) balance sheets as of the beginning and end of the year; (2) a reconciliation of income per books and income per return; and (3) a reconciliation of retained earnings.

### • Item A, Line 2: Personal Holding Company

Where the corporation is a personal holding company within the meaning of Code Sec. 542, a separate Schedule PH must be filed with Form 1120.

### • Item A, Line 3: Personal Service Corporation

The box on Line 3 should be checked by a personal service corporation. This is a corporation the principal activity of which during a test period (generally the preceding tax year) is the performance of personal services in the fields of health, law, engineering, architecture, accounting, actuarial science, performing arts, or consulting, that are substantially performed by employee-owners who own more than 10% of the fair market value of the corporation's outstanding stock as of the last day of the test period. Personal services are considered substantially performed by employee-owners if more than 20% of the corporation's compensation cost for the test period attributable to the performance of personal services is attributable to their services.

### • Item A, Line 4: Schedule M-3 (Form 1120)

A corporation must file Schedule M-3. Schedule M-3 is required in place of Schedule M-1 if the total assets of the corporation (or consolidated group) are $10 million or more on the last day of the day year. See ¶36.01.

### • Item B, C, and D: Employer ID Number • Date of Incorporation • Total Assets

The employer identification number, date of incorporation, and total assets of the corporation at the end of the tax year are indicated in Items B, C, and D, respectively.

Item D, Total Assets, is from Schedule L, Line 15, column (d). If there are no assets at the end of the year, enter total assets at start of year from Line 15, column (b).

### • Item E: Initial or Final Return • Name Change or Change of Address

For an initial return, a final return, a name change, or a change of address, box 1, 2, 3, or 4 of Item E, respectively, should be checked.

## ¶4   FORM 1120-A, ITEMS A–F AND PART II

A personal service corporation must check the box in Item A. The employer identification number, date of incorporation, and total assets at the end of the tax year are indicated in Items B, C, and D, respectively. An initial return, a final return, a change of name, or a change of address is indicated by checking box 1, 2, 3, or 4 of Item E. The method of accounting is indicated in Item F.

Part II of Form 1120-A requests additional information. The principal business activity code number, business activity, and product or service are entered on Lines 1a, 1b, and 1c, respectively. Information regarding controlled corporations is entered on Line 2. Tax-exempt interest received or accrued is entered on Line 3. The amount of cash distributions and the book value of property (other than cash) distributions made during the tax year are entered on Line 4 of Part II, Form 1120-A. If an amount for cost of goods sold is entered on Line 2 of page 1, Form 1120-A, Line 5a of Part II should be completed to show the amount of purchases, additional costs subject to the uniform capitalization rules, and other costs (a schedule should be attached), and the appropriate box on

Line 5b should be checked to indicate whether the uniform capitalization rules apply to the corporation regarding property produced or acquired for resale. Control over foreign financial accounts is indicated on Line 6.

Line 7 asks whether the corporation's total receipts for the tax years and its total assets at the end of the tax year are less than $250,000. If the corporation answers yes, then it doesn't need to complete Part III (Balance Sheet per Books) or Part IV dealing with the reconciliation of taxable and book income.

## INCOME

When calculating a corporation's income, the following exceptions should be noted:

- **Extraterritorial income.** Gross income generally does not include extraterritorial income that is qualifying foreign trade income. The extraterritorial income exclusion is reduced by 20 percent for transactions in 2005 (40 percent for transactions in 2006), unless made under a binding contract with an unrelated person in effect on September 17, 2004, and at all times therefore. Use Form 8873, Extraterritorial Income Exclusion, to figure the exclusion. Include the exclusion in the total for Other Deductions on Line 26, Form 1120 or Line 22, Form 1120-A.

- **Income from qualifying shipping activities.** Gross income does not include income from qualifying shipping activities if the corporation makes an election under Code Sec. 1354 to be taxed on its notional shipping income at the highest corporate tax rate. If the election is made, the corporation generally may not claim any loss, deduction, or credit with respect to qualifying shipping activities. A corporation making this election may also elect to defer gain on the disposition of a qualifying vessel. Use Form 8902, Alternative Tax on Qualifying Shipping Activities, to compute the tax. Include the alternative tax on Schedule J, line 10.

- **Gross Receipts or Sales- Line 1a.**

Most gross receipts and sales are entered on Line 1a of Form 1120 or Form 1120-A. Corporations must report *gross* sales and receipts from all business operations, including fees for services. Only final sales are reported, however. Sales that are made on approval or consignment are not included until finalized. This information is generally readily available from the corporation's books and records. Sales returns and allowances are deducted from gross sales. Only the amounts that have actually been paid can be deducted as sales returns, allowances and discounts.

- **How to Handle Special Income Items**

There are a number of special situations that require special handling for tax purposes. These special rules generally apply to transactions that span more than one tax year.

**1. Advance Payments:**

Cash-basis businesses must report advance customer payments in the year of receipt. Accrual-basis businesses may be able to defer the reporting of prepaid income from sales or services until the year the income is actually earned.

> **For services:** Accrual-basis taxpayers can defer recognition of advance payments for services until the year earned if the service is to be performed by the end of the tax year following the year of receipt. However, no deferral is allowed if any part of the service is to be performed or might be performed in the second year after the year of receipt [Rev. Proc. 71-21, 1971-2 CB 549].

> **For goods:** Accrual-basis taxpayers can generally elect to defer reporting advance payments for goods if the same accounting method is used for both tax and financial reporting [Reg. Sec. 1.451-5(b)]. In this case, the income is generally reported in the year earned. If the goods to be sold are normally held as inventory, however, advances generally can't be deferred more than two tax years. The estimated cost of the goods should be deducted in the same year the sale is reported.

**2. Refundable deposits:**

The U.S. Supreme Court has decided that refundable deposits are not currently taxable advance payments if the corporation does not have "complete dominion" over the payments at the time received [*Indianapolis Power & Light Co.*, 493 U.S. 203, 110 S. Ct. 589].

**3. Long-Term Contracts:**

A long-term contract is a contract for building, installing, constructing or reconstructing property that will not be completed within one tax year. A manufacturing contract is a long-term contract only if it involves manufacturing a unique item not usually found in the company's finished goods inventory or an item that takes over 12 months to complete [Code Sec. 460(f)].

Generally, for construction contracts, taxpayers must use the percentage-of-completion method. However, there are certain exceptions, where either the completed-contract method or the percentage-of-completion capitalized cost method may be used. To determine the proper method to apply, it may be necessary to refer to the contract.

### 4. Percentage-of-completion method:

Under this method, a company calculates each year's income from a contract by multiplying the estimated contract price by the percentage of the contract completed that year. The percentage of completion is calculated by dividing contract costs incurred during the year by total estimated contract costs.

## SPECIAL ELECTION

A corporation can elect not to recognize income or take deductions related to a contract in any year that less than 10 percent of the estimated contract costs have been incurred at the end of the tax year. All prior revenues and costs are reported in the first year in which the 10 percent test is met [IRC Sec. 460(b)(5)].

At the completion of the contract, the corporation must "look back" and compare actual revenues and costs with income and deductions that were reported under the percentage-of-completion method. The corporation pays or receives interest on the amount of tax it "overpaid" or "underpaid" [IRC Sec. 460(b)(2)].

## ON THE RETURN

The look-back interest is reported on Form 8697, "Interest Computation Under the Look-Back Method for Completed Long-Term Contracts."

*Key exceptions:* The completed contract method may be used for (1) home construction contracts or (2) other construction contracts if the estimated completion period is less than two years from the date of the contract and the corporation's average annual gross receipts for the three years prior to the contract are less than $10 million.

In addition, no "look back" is required for contracts completed within two years if the contract's gross price (at completion) does not exceed the lesser of (1) $1 million or (2) 1 percent of the taxpayer's average annual gross receipts for the three years prior to the contract.

A taxpayer may elect not to apply the "look back" method with respect to a long-term contract if for each contract year, the cumulative taxable income (or loss) recognized is within 10 percent of the actual cumulative taxable income (or loss) computed at the completion of the contract.

### 5. Installment Sales:

An installment sale is a sale of property where one or more payments are to be received after the close of the tax year. Under the installment method, gain from a sale is reported only as payments are received. Each payment is treated as composed of three elements: return of investment in the property (basis), gain on the sale, and interest.

> **Dealer sales:** Dealers generally cannot defer tax by using the installment method of reporting sales profits. A dealer sale is any sale of (1) personal property by a person who regularly sells or otherwise disposes of personal property of the same type on the installment plan or (2) real property held for sale to customers in the ordinary course of the taxpayer's sale or business.

*Exceptions:* Installment sale reporting can be used for: (1) Dispositions of property used or produced in the trade or business of farming. (2) Dealer sales of timeshares and residential lots. Interest must be paid on any tax deferred on timeshares and residential lots [Code Sec. 453(l)].

## ON THE RETURN

Enter on Line 1 (Form 1120) and carry to Line 3 (Form 1120) the gross profit on collections from installment sales for any of the following: (1) dealer dispositions of property before March 1, 1986, (2) dispositions of property used or produced in the trade or business of farming, (3) certain dispositions of timeshares and residential lots reported under the installment method. Any interest payable with respect to installment sales of timeshares or residential lots is reported on Schedule J of Form 1120.

> **Nondealer installment sales:** Nondealer installment sales *must* be reported on the installment method, unless the corporation "elects out" of installment sale treatment.

## TAX PLANNING TIP

A corporation may want to elect out of installment treatment for sales if it has offsetting capital losses.

The election out must be made by the due date for the corporation's return for the year the sale is made. Making the election out is simple: The corporation simply reports the sale according to its normal method of accounting.

## ON THE RETURN

Installment sale gain is reported on Form 6252, Installment Sale Income, which should be attached to the corporation's return for each year the corporation receives payment on the sale. The interest portion of any installment payment is not reported on Form 6252; instead, it is reported as interest on Form 1120.

### 6. Nonaccrual experience method.

Accrual method corporations are not required to accrue fees that are uncollectible, if:

- The fees result from the performance of services in the fields of health, law, engineering, architecture, accounting, actuarial science, performing arts, or consulting, or

- The corporation's average annual gross receipts for the 3 prior tax years do not exceed $5 million.

This provision does not apply to any amount if interest must be paid on the amount or if there is any penalty for failure to pay the amount on time.

A corporation that has not used the nonaccrual experience method before can adopt the method only in the first year that it earns eligible receivables (new business) or after it receives permission from the IRS to change its method by filing Form 3115, Application for Change in Accounting Method. The filing deadline for Form 3115 is 180 days after the beginning of the year for which the change is requested.

## ON THE RETURN

A corporation that qualifies to use the nonaccrual experience method should report only the net amount of service fees on Form 1120. A schedule must be attached showing total gross receipts from services, the estimated uncollectible fees not being reported, and the net amount of fees that are being reported.

## COST OF GOODS SOLD- SCHEDULE A (FORM 1120)

**Line 2**. The cost of goods sold is entered on Line 2, page 1 of Form 1120 or Form 1120-A. Corporations that make or buy goods they sell are allowed to deduct the cost of those goods from gross receipts. This cost is determined by either (1) specifically identifying the cost of goods sold, or (2) by taking beginning inventory, adding purchases (including all costs of producing or obtaining inventory), and deducting ending inventory. In general, corporations that have inventories must account for sales and purchases using the accrual basis of accounting. For corporations that qualify, the cash basis may be used to report other transactions.

**Special exception for qualifying small business taxpayers.** If the corporation is a qualifying taxpayer or a qualifying small business taxpayer, it may be able to adopt or change to the cash method of accounting to account for inventoriable items in the same manner as materials and supplies that are not incidental (unless its business is a tax shelter).

- A qualifying taxpayer is a taxpayer whose average annual gross receipts for the 3 prior tax years are $1 million or less and whose business is not a tax shelter.

- A qualifying small business taxpayer is a taxpayer whose average annual gross receipts for the 3 prior tax years are more than $1 million but not more than $10 million, and whose principal business activity is not an ineligible business. Under this accounting method, inventory costs for raw materials purchased for sue in producing finished goods and merchandise purchased for resale are deductible in the year the finished goods or merchandise are sold (but not before the year the corporation paid for the raw materials or merchandise, if it is also using the cash method).

- Ineligible businesses include manufacturers, wholesalers, retailers, miners, certain publishers, and sound recorders unless they are principally a service business or perform certain kinds of custom manufacturing.

- **Schedule A – Form 1120 Cost of Goods Sold**

**Line 1 – Schedule A.** Inventories at the beginning and end of each tax year are generally required if a corporation's production, purchase, or sale of merchandise is an income-producing factor. Inventory includes all finished or partially finished goods. Raw materials and supplies are included in inventory if they are acquired for sale or will physically become part of the merchandise intended for sale. The value of inventories at the beginning and end of each tax year is required to determine the cost of goods sold.

## ON THE RETURN

On Line 1 of Schedule A enter the businesses inventory at the beginning of the year. The cost of goods sold is computed on Schedule A of Form 1120. The total is subtracted from the corporation's Gross Receipts to determine the corporation's Gross Profit. There is no comparable schedule if Form 1120-A is filed, but a worksheet is provided in the Form 1120 instructions for determining that amount.

**Line 2, Purchases, Schedule A:** Per Worksheet, Falcon Machinery Corp. purchased $422,133 of raw materials for direct use in its production activities and enters this amount on Line 2, Schedule A.

**Line 3, Cost of Labor, Schedule A:** This is where Falcon Machinery Corp's direct labor costs are entered. Labor costs of employees with more than one function are allocated according to estimated time spent on each function. Payroll taxes are allocated according to the related labor costs. Falcon enters factory wages of $149,613 on this line. Total officer's compensation is entered on Schedule E (Form 1120).

**Line 4, Additional Section 263A Costs, Schedule A, UNICAP:** Line 4 is where the total additional Code Sec. 263A costs required to be included in the inventory calculation under UNICAP are added. An entry is only required on this line if the corporation has elected a simplified method of accounting.

## ON THE RETURN

Falcon Machinery Corp. does not elect the simplified production method and enters on Schedule A Line 5 all of its indirect UNICAP costs. Falcon's Line 5 indirect costs are $424,441. The costs entered on Line 5 (but not lines 2 and 3) are reflected in Falcon's books (p.8) in the account entitled "Costs attributable to inventory." Examples of indirect inventory costs that must be allocated to inventory and included on Line 5 include administrative expenses, taxes, depreciation, insurance, utilities, repairs and maintenance, compensation paid to officers, rework labor,

contributions to pension, stock bonus, and certain profit-sharing, annuity, or deferred compensation plans. See Reg. §1.263A-1(e)(3). Falcon's indirect costs include (but are not limited to) $211,754 of depreciation (see Form 1120 Line 21), officer's salaries of $8,444 (see Form 1120 Schedule E), and repair expenses.

Corporations (retailers and producers) that elect a simplified method of accounting for allocating indirect costs under Code Sec. 263A must include on Line 4, Schedule A, of Form 1120, the Code Sec. 263A costs paid or incurred during the tax year which are not reported in purchases or the cost of labor on Lines 2 and 3, respectively, or on Line 5 for other costs paid or incurred during the tax year.

There are two simplified methods—the simplified production method and the simplified resale method.

The simplified production method, which is described in Reg. §1.263A-2(b), provides a simplified method for determining additional section 263A costs properly allocable to ending inventory produced by the corporation. This method may also be used for other types of eligible property specified in the regulations. If the simplified production method was elected, the additional Code Sec. 263A costs entered on Line 4 are costs, other than interest, that were not capitalized under the corporation's method of accounting immediately prior to the effective date of the UNICAP rules but that are now required to be capitalized under those rules.

The simplified resale method is generally available only to a corporation that is engaged exclusively in resale activities, subject to an exception for de minimis production activities. See Reg. §1.263A-3(d). Under the simplified resale method, additional 263A costs are generally those costs incurred with respect to: (1) off-site storage or warehousing; (2) purchasing and handling, such as processing, assembling, repackaging, and transporting; and (3) mixed service costs (general and administrative costs).

*Line 9.*—Line 9 contains six questions that pertain to inventory valuation. On Line 9a, the corporation must specify by checking one of three boxes whether it has valued its ending inventory by using the cost method, lower of cost or market method, or another method to value its ending inventory (attach explanation if the last box is checked). The corporation indicates on Line 9b whether there was a writedown of subnormal goods. Lines 9c and 9d deal with whether or not the LIFO inventory method is being used. On Line 9e, the corporation indicates whether or not the rules of Code Sec. 263A apply if property is produced or acquired for resale. A corporation must also specify on Line 9f whether or not it has changed any element in computing the beginning and ending inventories.

**Inventory Valuation Methods.** To determine the value of inventories the corporation must have (1) a method of identifying the items in inventory and (2) a method for valuing those items. There are three methods of identifying items in inventory—specific identification, last-in first-out (LIFO), and first-in first-out (FIFO).

*Specific identification:* To use this method, the corporation must match each item with its cost of acquisition and other allocable costs (e.g., labor and transportation).

*First-in first-out:* The FIFO method assumes that the items the company purchased or produced first were the ones it sold (or otherwise disposed of) first.

*Last-in first-out:* The LIFO method, on the other hand, assumes the company sold (or otherwise disposed of) first the last items it produced or purchased. There are basically two methods of valuing inventories: (1) cost or (2) lower of cost or market. A corporation that uses FIFO can use either method. Corporations using LIFO must value inventories at cost (subject to special rules).

*Cost:* Under the cost method, the cost of goods bought during the year is the invoice price, less any discounts. Freight or other charges to get the goods are added to the price.

The cost of goods manufactured by a company includes the cost of raw materials and supplies consumed in the manufacturing process, direct labor costs, and indirect production costs (including a reasonable portion of management expenses, but excluding selling expenses).

*Lower of cost or market:* Under this method, the company compares the market value of each inventory item (i.e., the price the company would have to pay for the item on the valuation date) with the item's cost and uses the lower value as its inventory cost. The method applies to purchased goods bought and to the elements of cost (e.g., materials, labor and overhead) of manufactured goods.

## ON THE RETURN

A corporation must indicate the method used for valuing its inventories on Schedule A. It must also indicate whether it has adopted the LIFO method for any goods during the year. A corporation that adopted LIFO or expanded its use of the LIFO method during the year should attach Form 970, "Application to Use LIFO Inventory Method," to its return. (A statement may be attached in lieu of Form 970, provided it contains the same information.) Corporations using the LIFO method of inventory identification must give the percentage of the closing inventory that was computed using LIFO. Estimates are acceptable.

Taxpayers are permitted to use estimates of inventory shrinkage to adjust ending inventories based on inventory counts taken at other than year-end.

**Uniform Capitalization Rules:**

The uniform capitalization (UNICAP) rules generally require taxpayers to capitalize or include in inventory direct costs and an allocable portion of most indirect costs that benefit or are incurred because of production or resale activities [Code Sec. 263A(a)]. Capitalized costs are generally treated in one of two ways. Costs allocable to goods included in inventory become part of the inventory's value and the costs are recovered when the inventory is sold. Other capitalized costs are included in the basis of property produced, rather than being claimed as a current deduction. These costs are recovered annually through depreciation or amortization deductions.

The UNICAP rules generally required corporation to capitalize certain costs incurred in connection with: (1) the production of real or tangible personal property held in inventory or held for sale in the ordinary course of business, or (2) real property or personal property (tangible or intangible) acquired for resale, and (3) the production of real property and tangible personal property by a corporation for use in a trade or business in an activity engaged in for profit.

**When do taxpayers produce property?** Taxpayers produce property if they construct, build, install, manufacture, develop, improve, create, raise, or grow the property. Producers must capitalize direct and indirect costs without regard to whether those costs are incurred before, during, or after the production period. Property produced under a contract is treated as produced by a taxpayer to the extent that the taxpayer makes payments or otherwise incurs costs in connection with the property. Tangible personal property produced by a corporation includes intellectual or creative property such as films, sound records, videotapes, books, artwork, photographs, or similar property containing words, ideas, concepts, images or sounds. Tangible personal property does not include stocks, securities, debt instruments, mortgages or loans.

**Property Excluded From Capitalization Rules.**

The uniform capitalization rules do not apply to the following types of property:

- Personal property acquired for resale if the corporation's average annual gross receipts for the 3 prior tax years were $10 million or less;

- Timber;

- Most property produced under a long-term contract;

- Certain property produced in a farming business;

- Research and experimental costs under Code Sec. 174

- Geological and geophysical costs amortized under Code Sec. 167(h);

- Intangible drilling costs for oil, gas, and geothermal property.

- Mining exploration and development costs.

- Inventoriable items accounts for in the same manner as materials and supplies that are not incidental..

- **Costs Subject to UNICAP Rules.**

Corporations subject to the UNICAP rules are required to capitalize:

1. Direct costs; and

2. An allocable part of most indirect costs (including taxes) that:

   (a) benefit the assets produced or acquired for resale, or

   (b) are incurred by reason of the performance of production or resale activities.

- **Direct Material Costs.**

Direct material costs include the costs of the materials that become an integral part of specific property

produced and those materials that are consumed in the ordinary course of production and that can be identified or associated with particular units or groups of units of property produced.

**How to allocate direct material costs.** Direct material costs must be allocated to the property produced or acquired to resell using your method of accounting for materials such as specific identification, FIFO, LIFO, or any other reasonable allocation method.

- **Direct Labor Costs.**

Direct labor costs include the costs of labor that can be identified or associated with particular units or groups of units of specific property produced. For this purpose, labor encompasses full-time and part-time employees, as well as contract employees and independent contractors. Direct labor costs include all elements of compensation other than employee benefit costs. Elements of direct labor costs include basic compensation, overtime pay, vacation pay, holiday pay, sick leave pay, shift differential, payroll taxes, and payments to a supplemental unemployment benefit plan.

**How to allocate direct labor costs.** Direct labor costs are generally allocated to property produced or acquired to resell using a specific identification method, standard cost method or any other reasonable allocation method. All elements of compensation, other than basic compensation, may be grouped together and then allocated in proportion to the charge for basic compensation. You will not be treated as using an erroneous method of accounting if direct labor costs are treated as indirect costs under your allocation method, provided such costs are capitalized as required under the UNICAP rules.

- **Indirect Costs.**

Indirect costs include all costs other than direct material costs and direct labor or acquisition costs. You must capitalize all indirect costs allocable to property produced or acquired for resale when the costs directly benefit or are incurred because of production or resale activities. Indirect costs may be allocable to both production and resale activities, as well as to other activities that are not subject to the UNICAP rules. If a corporation is subject to the UNICAP rules, the corporation must make a reasonable allocation of indirect costs between production, resale and other activities.

Examples of indirect costs that must be capitalized to the extent they are properly allocable to property produced or acquired for resale include the following:

- Indirect labor costs;

- Officers' compensation;

- Pension and other related costs;

- Employee benefit expenses;

- Indirect material costs;

- Purchasing costs;

- Handling costs such as attaching wheels and handlebars to a bicycle acquired for resale;

- Storage costs;

- Cost recovery such as depreciation and amortization;

- Depletion;

- Rent includes the cost of renting equipment, facilities or land;

- Taxes attributable to labor, materials, supplies, equipment, land, or facilities used in production or resale activities;

- Insurance includes the cost of insurance on plant or facility, machinery, equipment, materials, property produced or property acquired for resale;

- Utilities include the cost of electricity, gas and water;

- Repairs and maintenance of equipment or facilities;

- Engineering and design costs such as expenses incurred prior to the beginning of production;

- Spoilage includes the cost of rework labor, scrap, and spoilage;

- Tools and equipment;

- Quality control and inspection;

- Bidding costs incurred in the solicitation of contracts;

- Licensing and franchise costs;

- Interest incurred during the production period; and

- Capitalizable service costs. Service costs that must be capitalized include general and administrative costs that may be identified specifically with, or

directly benefit, a service department or function. Service departments are administrative, service, or support departments including the personnel, purchasing operations, materials handling, accounting, data processing, security and legal services departments.

- **Indirect Costs Excluded From Capitalization.**

The following indirect costs need not be capitalized and thus may be deducted currently:

- Selling and distribution costs such as marketing, selling, advertising, and distribution costs;

- Research and experimental expenditures;

- Code Sec. 179 costs (the election to expense certain depreciable business assets);

- Code Sec. 165 losses;

- Cost recovery allowances on temporarily idle equipment and facilities;

- Taxes assessed on the basis of income including only state, local, foreign income and franchise taxes;

- Strike expenses associated with hiring employees to replace striking personnel (but not the wages of replacement personnel), costs of security, and legal fees associated with settling strikes;

- Warranty and product liability costs incurred in fulfilling product warranty obligations for products that have been sold and costs incurred for product liability insurance;

- On-site storage and warehousing costs; and

- Unsuccessful bidding expenses incurred in the solicitation of contracts not awarded to the taxpayer.

Deductible service costs that do not directly benefit or are not incurred because of production or resale activities. Examples are costs incurred in conjunction with overall management, policy guidance, general financial planning, personnel policy, quality control policy, and marketing.

- **Interest Capitalization Rules.**

Interest incurred in producing property must be capitalized as an indirect cost of production under the UNICAP rules [Code Sec. 263A(f)]. The interest capitalization rules do not apply unless the property is produced for use in a trade or business or for an activity engaged in for profit. The "avoided cost method" is used to determine the amount of capitalized interest. This method requires the capitalization of interest to the extent that it would not have been incurred during the production period if the money had been spent on production expenditures to pay down outstanding indebtedness. The capitalized interest will be recovered through depreciation deductions or through cost of sales. If a property consists of a depreciable component and a nondepreciable component, such as a building and the lot on which it is located, any interest that must be capitalized with respect to the property must be added to the basis of the depreciable component.

**Designated property.** Only "designated property" is subject to the interest capitalization rules. Designated property includes:

(1) All real property (land, buildings, and permanent structures) produced by the taxpayer;

(2) Tangible personal property produced by or for the taxpayer if it either has a class life of 20 years or more, an estimated production period of more than 1 year and total estimated production costs of more than $1 million, or an estimated production period of more than 2 years. Property with a production period of 90 days or less and total production expenditures that do not exceed $1 million divided by the number of days in the production period will not be considered designated property. The production period of a property, generally, begins on the date production begins and ends on the date the property is ready to be placed in service or is ready to be held for sale.

In the case of real property, designated property may be divided into units that could consist of individual apartments, condominiums, offices, or spaces in a shopping mall if the units are expected to be separately placed in service or sold.

The amount of interest that must be capitalized under the avoided cost method is determined separately for each unit of "designated" property produced by or for you.

**Traced debt.** Indebtedness directly allocable to production expenditures is considered *traced debt*. Interest on traced debt is capitalized first and is referred to as the *traced debt amount* [Reg. §1.263A-9(b)]. If the production expenditures exceed the amount of traced debt, interest on other debt (nontraced debt) is capitalized to the extent this interest could have been reduced if production expenditures had not been

incurred. This second category of capitalized interest is referred to as the "excess expenditure amount." A traced debt amount and excess expenditure amount are calculated for each tax year, or shorter computation period, during which production of the unit takes place. The corporation may elect an annual computation period that corresponds to the corporation's tax year or divide the tax year into two or more computation periods of equal length.

- **Alternative Minimum Tax**

Corporations compute their alternative minimum tax (AMT) on Form 4626. Form 4626 must be filed by a corporation (other than a qualifying small corporation as defined below) if its taxable income (or loss) before the NOL deduction plus its adjustment and preference items are greater than the smaller of $40,000 or its allowable exemption amount. Also, if a corporation (other than a qualifying small corporation) claims a general business credit, qualified electric vehicle credit, nonconventional fuel source credit, or credit for a prior year's minimum tax liability, it must file Form 4626.

## ON THE RETURN

The alternative minimum tax is computed on Form 4626 and is entered on Line 4, Schedule J, Form 1120. Form 1120A may not be filed by a corporation which owes alternative minimum tax.

Corporations (other than qualifying "small corporations" described below) are subject to an alternative minimum tax (Line 14 of Form 4626) equal to the excess of the tentative minimum tax (Line 12) over the regular tax (as defined in Code Sec. 55(c)) (Line 13). The tentative minimum tax is determined by multiplying the excess of alternative minimum taxable income (AMTI) over an exemption amount by 20% for corporations and then reducing the product by a limited amount of alternative minimum tax foreign tax credit.

Taxable income (before the net operating loss deduction) computed with certain adjustments and preferences on Lines 2a–2o of Form 4626 equals preadjustment AMTI on Line 3. Preadjustment AMTI is increased by any adjusted current earnings (ACE) adjustment and entered on Line 5. The ACE adjustment is calculated on the worksheet found in the Form 4626 instructions and then entered on Line 4a (see discussion below). The adjustment is 75% of the excess of ACE (as defined by Code Sec. 56(g)) over the preadjustment AMTI. A negative adjustment is allowed for 75% of any excess preadjustment AMTI over ACE to the extent of the net positive adjustments for ACE in prior tax years. The alternative tax net operating loss deduction (ATNOL), Line 6, is subtracted from Line 5 to arrive at alternative minimum taxable income on Line 7.

Generally, the deduction for an ATNOL (Line 6) is limited to 90 percent of alternative minimum taxable income. The AMT exemption amount of $40,000 is reduced by 25% of the excess of AMTI over $150,000 and is entered on Line 8c, Form 4626. A controlled group of corporations must allocate one exemption amount equally among the component members of the group unless all members consent to an unequal allocation.

The adjustment on Line 2a, Form 4626, reflects the excess of the MACRS deduction claimed for regular tax purposes over the amount allowed for AMT tax purposes. Depreciation adjustments attributable to a tax shelter farm activity or a passive activity are not included on Line 2a but, rather, are included on Line 2i or 2j, as appropriate. If depreciation is included in inventory under the uniform capitalization rules, the inventory must be refigured based on the depreciation adjustment.

Adjusted depreciation deductions must be used to calculate the amount of gain or loss from the sale of depreciable property. The difference between the gain or loss reported for regular tax purposes and the recomputed amount is entered on Line 2e.

Loss limitations (such as the amount at risk or the amount of a partner's basis) are affected by alternative minimum tax adjustments and tax preference items. Accordingly, the difference between the recomputed allowable loss for alternative minimum tax purposes and the loss reported for regular tax purposes is reported on Line 2k.

Personal service corporations and closely held C corporations that are subject to the passive activity loss rules may not use passive activity losses to offset AMTI. The difference between the recomputed passive activity loss for alternative minimum tax purposes and such loss used for regular tax purposes is entered on Line 2j.

A personal service corporation that has a gain or loss from a tax shelter farm activity that is *not* a passive activity, completes Line 2i. For passive tax shelter farm

activities, all gains and losses reported for regular tax purposes must be recomputed by taking into account alternative minimum tax adjustments and tax preference items. These are included in Line 2j (see above). Recomputed gains from passive tax shelter farm activities may be used to offset recomputed losses from other passive activities, but recomputed losses from passive tax shelter farm activities may not be used to offset recomputed gains from other passive activities.

A corporate beneficiary of an estate or trust should enter on Line 2o of Form 4626 the amount included on Line 9, Schedule K-1, Form 1041. Negative amounts are entered on Line 2o for income eligible for the possessions tax credit or the alcohol fuel credit and included in income for regular tax purposes. Also entered on Line 2o are deductions based on an income limit (e.g., charitable contributions) refigured because of AMT adjustments to income; and net AMT adjustments from an electing large partnership (from box 6, Schedule K-1, Form 1065-B and, unless the corporation is closely held or a personal service corporation, from box 5, Schedule K-1, Form 1065-B).

*ACE worksheet.*—The adjusted current earnings (ACE) adjustment attempts to more accurately recreate current earnings and profits so that the AMT tax base is expanded to include much of a corporation's income that is neither claimed in regular taxable income nor covered by the AMT adjustments and preferences. For ACE purposes, an item must be included in ACE if it is income for purposes of earnings and profits. Thus, many items on the ACE worksheet will not appear on Form 4626.

In determining ACE, the corporation begins with pre-adjustment AMTI (Line 3 of Form 4626 is carried over to Line 1 of the ACE worksheet). A depreciation adjustment is made if depreciation under AMT still overstates the deduction. Property is reclassified into one of six categories and depreciation is recalculated under the ACE method, generally the straight-line method under ADS, which should result in a lower depreciation amount than the AMT depreciation amount (Line 2b). This adjustment does not apply to property placed in service after 1993. (ACE depreciation is the same as AMT depreciation.) Also, any items taken into account for earnings and profits, but not AMTI, are added (Line 3). Such items include some tax-exempt interest income and distributions or inside buildup of life insurance contracts. Next, any items not taken into account for earnings and profits, but deducted from AMTI, are added (Line 4). Various types of dividends fall into this category. Then, adjustments are made for additional items not included in AMTI such as intangible drilling costs, circulation expenses, organizational expenses, LIFO inventory adjustments, and installment sales (Line 5). Finally, adjustments are made for disallowance of loss on exchange of debt pools (Line 6), acquisition expenses of life insurance companies for qualified foreign contracts (Line 7), depletion (Line 8), and a basis adjustment for gain or loss from sale or exchange of pre-1994 property (Line 9).

*Small corporations exempt from AMT.*—A corporation that meets certain gross receipts tests is considered to be a small corporation and will not be liable for the AMT for as long as it remains a small corporation. For tax years beginning in 2005, a corporation qualifies as a small corporation if: (1) for all prior tax years beginning after 1997 it was exempt from the AMT as a small corporation and (2) its average annual gross receipts for the 3-tax-year period ending before its tax year beginning in 2005 did not exceed $7.5 million ($5 million if the corporation had only one prior year).

If the alternative minimum tax was paid in a previous tax year or if there is a carryforward of the credit for a prior year's minimum tax, see Form 8827, Credit for Prior Year Minimum Tax - Corporations.

*Eg.* *ON THE RETURN.*—For illustrative purposes, the Form 4626 and ACE worshee are completed for XYZ, Inc., which is unrelated to Falcon Machinery Corporation. In 2005, XYZ has ordinary taxable income of $200,000, adjusted current earnings of $350,000, regular tax liability of $61,250, and the various adjustments and tax preference items indicated on Form 4626.

XYZ, Inc. must use the worksheet to compute the ACE adjustment for Line 4a of Form 4626. Preadjustment AMTI of $308,000 is adjusted by various items as the worksheet attempts to recreate XYZ, Inc.'s earnings and profits for the year to more accurately reflect and tax its income. XYZ, Inc. claimed AMT depreciation of $25,000 for various pieces of property on Line 2a of Form 4626. However, depreciation must be recalculated for purposes of the ACE worksheet and Line 2c of the worksheet indicates the adjustment amount of $10,000—the excess of AMT depreciation over ACE depreciation. XYZ,

Inc. reported tax-exempt bond interest of $34,000 on Line 2m of Form 4626; however, it had an additional $20,000 of tax-exempt income that was not included in pre-adjustment AMTI. This amount is reported on Line 3a of the worksheet. XYZ, Inc. also had $9,000 of preferred stock dividends from public utilities which is reported on Line 4b of the worksheet. Finally, XYZ, Inc. claims a $3,000 basis adjustment on Line 9, stemming from the sale of property reported on Line 2e of Form 4626. These adjustment amounts are totaled to obtain the $350,000 adjusted current earnings amount.

- **Credits Against Tax**

*Nonrefundable credits.*—Nonrefundable credits against tax are claimed on Lines 6a–6f on Schedule J of Form 1120. The credits claimed are:

- **Line 6a of Schedule J - Foreign tax credit:**

The foreign tax credit allows a corporation to reduce its U.S. tax by the amount of tax it paid to foreign countries. The amount of the credit may be subject to an overall foreign tax credit limitation or to one of several separate limitations. A corporation claiming the credit must attach Form 1118, "Computation of Foreign Tax Credit—Corporations."

## ANOTHER OPTION

Instead of claiming a credit, the corporation may take a deduction for foreign taxes.

- **Line 6b of Schedule J - Possessions tax credit:**

The possession tax credit was repealed for possession business income, except for corporations qualifying as existing credit claimants. For corporations that are existing credit claimants that use the wage credit method, the credit attributable to business income continues to apply for tax years beginning before January 1, 2006. A cap exists on the credit based on the claimant's adjusted base period income. An existing credit claimant is a corporation that was actively conducting a business in a possession on October 13, 1995, and that had a Section 936 election in effect for the corporation's tax year, which includes October 13, 1995.

- **Line 6c of Schedule B - Nonconventional source fuels credit.**

For tax years ending on December 31, 2005, use Form 8907, Nonconventional Source Fuel Credit, to figure the credit for the sale of qualified fuels produced from a nonconventional source. Include the amount from line 23 in the total for Line 6c, Form 1120. Beginning in 2006, the nonconventional source fuel credit is a general business credit included on Form 3800.

- **Line 6c of Schedule J- Qualified electric vehicle credit:**

A 10 percent credit ($4,000 maximum per vehicle) is allowed for qualified electric vehicles placed in service before 2006. The credit is computed on Form 8834, Qualified Electric Vehicle Credit, and entered on Schedule J.

- **Line 6d of Schedule J- General business credit:**

The general business credit is also claimed on Schedule J. Complete Form 3800 if the corporation has two or more of these credits. This credit is actually composed of a number of different credits as follows:

- Investment Credit, which is composed of (a) the rehabilitation credit, (b) the energy credit, (c) the reforestation credit, and (d) the regular credit for transition property (Form 3468);

- Work Opportunity Credit (Form 5884);

- Welfare-to-work Credit (Form 8861);

- Increased Research Credit (Form 6765);

- Low-Income Housing Credit (Form 8586);

- Enhanced Oil Recovery Credit (Form 8830);

- Disabled Access Credit (Form 8826);

- Renewable Electricity Production Credit (Form 8835);

- Indian Employment Credit (Form 8845);

- Credit for Employer Social Security and Medicare Taxes Paid on Certain Employee Tips (Form 8846);

- Orphan Drug Credit (Form 8820);

- New Markets Tax Credit (Form 8874) (Code Sec. 45D);

- Credit for Contributions to Selected Community Development Corporations (Form 8847);

- Small Employer Pension Plan Start-up Cost Credit (Form 8881) (Code Sec. 45E); and

- Employer-Provided Child Care Credit (Form 8882) (Code Sec. 45F)

- Biodiesel Fuels Credit (Form 8864) (Code Sec. 40A); and Renewable Diesel

- Low Sulfur Diesel Fuel Production Credit (Form 8896) (Code Sec. 45H).

- Qualified Railroad Track Maintenance Credit (Form 8900).

- **Line 6e – Credit for prior year minimum tax**

–Corporations must Form 8827, Credit for Prior Year Minimum Tax – Corporations, to figure the minimum tax credit, if any, for AMT incurred in prior tax years and to figure any minimum tax credit carryforward. Form 8827 should be filed by corporations that had

- An AMT liability in 2004,

- A minimum tax credit carryforward from 2004 to 2005, or

- A nonconventional source fuel credit or qualified electric vehicle credit not allowed for 2004.

- **Line 6f-Qualified zone academy bond credit -QZAB credit:**

A QZAB credit may be claimed on Line 6f of Schedule J for financial institutions such as banks, insurance companies, and corporations that hold qualified zone academy bonds. The financial institutions are entitled to a nonrefundable tax credit in an amount equal to a credit rate multiplied by the face amount of the bond. The credit rate applies to all QZABs purchased in each month. A taxpayer holding a QZAB will be entitled to a credit for each year that the bond is held. The credit is includible in gross income, but may be claimed against regular income tax and AMT liability. The Treasury Department establishes the credit rate each month so that the bonds can be issued without discount and without any interest cost to the issuer. The maximum term of the bond issued in a given month also is determined by the Treasury Department so that the present value of the obligation to repay the bond is 50 percent of the face value of the bond. Present value will be determined by using a discount rate equal to the average annual interest rate of tax-exempt obligations with a term of 10 years or more issued during the month.

QZABs are defined as any bond issued by a State or local government, provided that:

1. 95 percent of the proceeds are used for the purpose of renovating, providing equipment to, develop-

ing course materials for use at, or training teachers and other school personnel in a "qualified zone academy," and

2. Private entities have promised to contribute to the qualified zone academy certain equipment, technical assistance or training, employee services, or other property or services with a value equal to at least 10 percent of the bond proceeds.

## ON THE RETURN

Enter on Line 6f the amount of any credit from Form 8860, Qualified Zone Academy Bond Credit or From Form 8912, Clean Renewable Energy Bond Credit. Check the applicable box(es) and include the amount of the credit in the total for Line 6f.

- **Line 9 - Schedule J - Personal holding company tax:**

A corporation classified as a personal holding company (PHC) must pay a surtax on undistributed PHC income. Personal holding company status, which is determined on an annual basis, is applied only if both a stock ownership and income test are met. The stock ownership test is met if five or fewer individuals own, either directly or constructively, 50 percent of the stock of the corporation at any time during the last half of the tax year. The income test is met if at least 60 percent of the corporation's adjusted ordinary gross income (generally, gross income less capital and 1231 gains, leasing income, interest, royalties) is personal holding company income [Code Sec. 543]. The personal holding company tax rate is 15 percent of a corporation's undistributed personal holding company income.

## ON THE RETURN

All companies that are classified as personal holding companies must file Schedule PH with Form 1120, whether or not they owe PHC tax. If the tax is owed, it is calculated on Form PH and entered on Schedule J.

- **Line 10 - Schedule J - Recapture taxes:**

When property for which a tax credit was taken is disposed of early, a part or all of that credit may be subject to recapture.

**Recapture of Investment Credit.** The investment credit was repealed for property placed in service after 1985, and most investment credit property was three-or five-year property. So most corporations should not have an investment credit recapture. A more likely recapture situation may concern the low-income housing credit. If such property is disposed of or fails to qualify for the credit during the 15-year credit period, there is recapture. If there is investment credit recapture, the recapture amount is calculated on Form 4255, Recapture of Investment Credit, and entered on Schedule J.

**Recapture of Low-Income Housing Credit.** If the corporation disposed of property (or there was a reduction in the qualified basis of the property) for which it took the low-income housing credit, it may owe tax. Use Form 8611, Recapture of Low-Income Housing Credit, to calculate the recapture, and attach the completed form to Form 1120. The recapture amount is entered on Schedule J.

**Interest due under the look-back methods.** If the corporation used the look-back method for certain long-term contracts, see Form 8697, Interest Computations Under the Look-Back Method for Completed Long-Term Contracts, for information on figuring the interest the corporation may have to include. The corporation may also have to include interest due under the look-back method for property depreciated under the income forecast method.

**Alternative tax on qualifying shipping activities.** Enter any alternative tax on qualifying shipping activities from Form 8902.

**Recapture of Qualified Electric Vehicle Credit.** A corporation may have to pay recapture tax if it claimed a qualified electric vehicle credit in a prior year and if, within 3 years of the date the vehicle was placed in service, it ceased to qualify for the credit. See Reg. Sec. 1.30-1 for details on how to figure the recapture. Include the amount of the recapture in the total for Line 10, Schedule J, Form 1120. Check the box marked "Other" and on the dotted line next to the entry space, write "QEV recapture" and the amount.

**Recapture of Indian Employment Credit.** If an employer terminates the employment of a qualified employee less than 1 year after the date of initial employment, any Indian employment credit allowed for a prior tax year because of wages paid or incurred to that employee must be recaptured. See Form 8845. Include the amount of the recapture in the total for Line 10, Schedule J, Form 1120. On the dotted line next to the entry space, write "Form 8845" and the amount.

**Recapture of New Markets Credit (Form 8874).** Include the amount of the recapture in the total for Line 10, Schedule J, Form 1120. On the dotted line next to the entry space, write "Form 8874" and the amount.

**Recapture of Employer-Provided Childcare Facilities and Services Credit (Form 8882)** Include the amount of the recapture in the total for Line 10, Schedule J, Form 1120. On the dotted line next to the entry space, write "Form 8882" and the amount.

**Tax and interest on a nonqualified withdrawal from a capital construction fund.** Include the amount of the tax and interest in the total for Line 10, Schedule J, Form 1120. On the dotted line next to the entry space, write "Section 7518" and the amount. Attach a schedule showing the computation of the amount.

**Interest on deferred tax attributable to (a) installment sales of certain timeshares and residential lots and (b) certain nondealer installment obligations.** Include the amount of the interest in the total for Line 10, Schedule J, Form 1120. On the dotted line next to the entry space, write "section 453A(C)" and the amount. Attach a schedule showing the computation of the amount.

**Interest due on deferred gain** Include the amount of the interest in the total for Line 10, Schedule J, Form 1120. On the dotted line next to the entry space, write "Section 1260(b)" and the amount. Attach a schedule showing the computation of the amount.

## ON THE RETURN

*Filled-in Form 3800.*—Falcon Machinery Corporation, is not required to file Form 3800.

For illustrative purposes, a Form 3800 is completed for an unrelated corporation, the CXX Corporation, Inc. The filled-in form is based on the following facts for 2005: (1) the corporation's tax, as entered on Line 3 of Schedule J, Form 1120, is $75,000; (2) the corporation files Form 6765 (not reproduced) and has a research credit of $6,350; and (3) the corporation files Form 5884 (not reproduced) and has a $3,000 work opportunity credit.

## ¶8    DIVIDENDS RECEIVED – Schedule C

### • Dividends and Special Deductions

Dividends are reported on Line 4, page 1, of Form 1120 or Form 1120-A. If Form 1120 is filed, Schedule C on page 2 must be completed and the amount from Line 19 of Schedule C is reported on Line 4, page 1. There is no comparable schedule if Form 1120-A is filed because use of that form is restricted to corporations that received dividends only from domestic corporations qualifying for the 70% dividends-received deduction (dividends that are not from debt-financed stock).

Corporations that own less than 20% of the voting power and value of the stock of the distributing corporation may deduct 70% of dividends received or accrued. An 80% deduction is allowed if ownership is at least 20% of the distributing corporation.

Schedule C of Form 1120 breaks down dividends into those received from:

(1)  domestic corporations subject to the 70% dividends-received deduction;

(2)  domestic corporations subject to the 80% dividends-received deduction;

(3)  debt-financed stock;

(4)  certain preferred stock of public utilities less than 20% owned;

(5)  certain preferred stock of public utilities at least 20% owned;

(6)  foreign corporations (and certain foreign sales corporations) subject to the 70% dividends-received deduction;

(7)  foreign corporations (and certain foreign sales corporations) subject to the 80% dividends-received deduction

(8)  wholly owned foreign subsidiaries subject to the 100% dividends-received deduction;

(9)  domestic corporation dividends received by small business investment companies;

(10) foreign sales corporations subject to the 100% dividends-received deduction;

(11) other members of a controlled corporate group subject to the 100% deduction,

(12) other foreign corporations (including ordinary earnings of a qualified electing fund from Part I, Line 1c of Form 8621, Return by a Shareholder of a Passive Foreign Investment Company or Qualified Electing Fund), and

(13) any distribution of a passive foreign investment company from Line 10e of Form 8621), an IC-DISC or former DISC, and any other dividends.

Also, Line 14 of the schedule calls for Subpart F income from controlled foreign corporations (as computed on Schedule 1, Form 5471) and Line 15 calls for the foreign dividend gross-up required by Code Sec. 78 for taxes deemed paid under Code Secs. 902 and 960.

The dividends-received and dividends-paid deductions are entered on Lines 1 through 12 and Line 18, respectively, of column (c) on Schedule C. The total of such deductions is entered on Line 20 and is carried to Line 29b, page 1, of Form 1120. The dividends-received deductions are determined by multiplying the dividends received in column (a) of Schedule C by the percentage indicated in column (b) and entering the product in column (c). The special deduction for dividends paid on preferred stock of public utilities is determined according to the instructions for Line 18. Qualified dividends received from a regulated investment company (mutual fund) are reported on Line 1, column (a), of Schedule C unless they pertain to debt-financed stock, in which case they are reported on Line 3, column (a).

Dividends received on debt-financed stock acquired after July 18, 1984, reported on Line 3, column (a), Schedule C, are not entitled to the full 70% or 80% dividends-received deduction. The deduction is reduced by a percentage that is related to the amount of debt incurred to acquire the stock. This reduction does not apply to dividends that are eligible for the 100% dividends-received deduction for qualifying dividends received from a member of an affiliated group that includes the corporate taxpayer or dividends received from a small business investment company (Code Sec. 246A).

A dividends-received deduction is not available if the dividend paying stock is not held at least 46 days in a 90-day period beginning 45 days before the stock's ex-dividend date. Special rules may apply to preferred stock dividends.

The total deductions for dividends received cannot exceed a specified percentage of the taxable income computed without regard to the deductions for dividends received, dividends paid to a public utility, any Code Sec. 1059 gain resulting from the basis adjustment for the nontaxed portion of extraordinary dividends, or net operating loss and capital loss carrybacks. However, this limitation does not apply for any tax year in which the deduction for dividends received results in a net operating loss. The limitation is applied first regarding any 80% deductible dividends and then separately for 70% deductible dividends (after reducing taxable income by the 80% deductible dividends). A worksheet for this computation is provided on page 19 of the Form 1120 instructions. Members of an affiliated corporate group not filing a consolidated return may elect to deduct 100% of the qualifying dividends received from the same group (including wholly owned foreign subsidiaries).

- **Property Dividends**

Where dividends are received in kind by a corporate shareholder, the amount of the distribution is the fair market value of the property received. In the filled-in return, the fair market value of property received from Dunbar Steel, Inc. (less than 20% ownership) is $6,850, which is included in the total dividends of $8,730 on Line 1, column (a), of Schedule C. Other cash dividends received from a domestic corporation totaled $1,880. Dividends of $240 from the foreign corporation are not reflected in the special deductions because the foreign corporation had no income (or predecessor domestic corporation's accumulated earnings) from United States sources.

## ¶9   INTEREST

Line 5, Page 1 (Form 1120) Interest on obligations of the United States and on loans, notes, mortgages, bonds bank deposits, corporate bonds, tax refunds, etc. is reported on Line 5, page 1, of the return. Do not offset interest expense against interest income. Accrued interest credited on the books and matured interest coupons not cashed should be included.

Interest on most state and municipal bonds and obligations is exempt from federal income tax. If such bonds are acquired at a premium, the premium must be included in the basis of the bond and amortized from acquisition to maturity of the bond. This bond premium amortization is not deductible. However, taxpayers may elect to amortize and deduct the premium on U.S. obligations. Interest on arbitrage bonds issued by state and local governments after October 9, 1969, is taxable.

Interest on loans, notes, mortgages, bonds, bank deposits, corporate bonds, and tax refunds is also entered on Line 5.

If a taxpayer acquires a taxable bond at a premium, the taxpayer may elect either to treat the premium as part of the cost of the bond or to amortize the premium over the remaining life of the bond.

## ON THE RETURN

The Falcon Machinery Corporation has acquired such a bond and has elected to amortize the premium under the yield to maturity method. The bond was purchased on July 1, 2004, for $23,875, matures on December 31, 2012, has a face value of $22,400, pays interest at 7%, and is expected to yield an effective rate of return of 6% (3% every six months for 17 periods). Amortization for 2005 is $142, and the carrying value of the bond at the beginning of 2005 is $23,807. The $142 bond premium amortization is claimed by Falcon as an offset to interest income received on such bond and included on Line 5 of Form 1120.

Generally, for bonds issued after September 25, 1985, amortization of bond premium is calculated under a constant yield method (amortizable bond premium is computed on the basis of the taxpayer's yield to maturity, using the taxpayer's basis for the bond, and compounding at the close of each accrual period).

If the above election to amortize the premium is made, the taxpayer must amortize the premium on all wholly taxable bonds. A statement must be attached to the return, showing the computation of the amortizable portion of the premium deductible in the current year. Amortizable bond premium is treated as an offset to interest income from the bond (Line 5 on Form 1120), rather than an interest expense deduction, for taxable bonds generally acquired after 1987. A reduction in the basis of the bond is required for such offset.

*Amortized Discount is included in income*

If a corporate or government bond with a maturity exceeding one year is originally issued after July 1, 1982, at a discount, the holder of the bond must include in income the sum of the daily portion of original issue discount (OID) determined for each day during the tax year the bond is held. The OID is allocated over the life of the bond through a series of adjustments to the issue price for each accrual period. The increase in the adjusted issue price for any accrual period is allocated ratably to each day in the accrual period.

For bonds with a maturity of one year or less, gain on the sale or redemption is treated as interest to the extent of the amount that would have been accrued OID.

For (1) market discount bonds issued after July 18, 1984, and (2) market discount bonds issued before July 19, 1984, that are purchased after April 30, 1993 (bonds purchased at a discount that were originally issued at face value), gain on disposition is treated as interest to the extent of the accrued market discount. Alternatively, an election may be made to include the accrued market discount in income as interest annually (Code Sec. 1278(b)). Accrued market discount may be determined either (1) under the ratable accrual method (Code Sec. 1276(b)(1)), or (2) at the taxpayer's option, accrued on the constant-interest method under the OID rules (Code Sec. 1276(b)(2)). Obligations that mature within one year of issuance, tax-exempt obligations purchased before May 1, 1993, installment obligations, and U.S. Savings Bonds are not subject to the market discount bond rule. However, certain holders are required to include acquisition discount on short-term obligations in income on a level straight-line basis (accrual basis taxpayers, dealers, banks, regulated investment companies, common trust funds, and certain pass-through entities (Code Sec. 1281)). For short-term obligations other than government obligations, current inclusion is made under the OID rules rather than the market discount rules unless the holder elects the latter method (Code Sec. 1283).

Special rules apply to interest income from certain below-market-rate loans (Code Sec. 7872).

## ¶10  INCOME FROM RENTS

Line 6, page 1 (Form 1120) - The entire amount received as gross rents should be entered on Line 6 of Form 1120. Deductions for related expenses such as repairs, interest, taxes, and depreciation are claimed on the appropriate "deduction" lines.

## ¶11  ROYALTIES RECEIVED

Line 7, page 1 (Form 1120) - Gross royalties are ordinarily entered at Line 7 of Form 1120, and amounts claimed as expenses or reductions of royalty income are entered at appropriate items under "Deductions."

Where timber, coal, or domestic iron ore is disposed of under a contract by virtue of which the owner retains an economic (depletable) interest in the timber, coal, or iron ore, it may be appropriate to treat the royalties or other income received under the contract as the proceeds of a sale or exchange. In this case, the proceeds or income would be shown on Schedule D of Form 1120 instead of at Line 7. See Code Secs. 631 and 1231.

The retained economic interest requirement will not apply to sales of timber after December 31, 2004 (Code Sec. 631(b)).

## ¶12 GAINS AND LOSSES FROM SCHEDULE D AND FORM 4797

See ¶39 and ¶40.

## ¶13 OTHER INCOME

Line 10, page 1 (Form 1120) - All miscellaneous taxable income not covered by other items should be entered at Line 10 of Form 1120. A separate schedule explaining the income must be attached unless the "other income" consists of only one item, in which case an explanation is described at Line 10. Examples of the type of income reported here include:

- Recoveries of bad debts deducted in prior years under the specific charge-off method;

- The amount included in income from Form 6478, Credit for Alcohol Used as Fuel.

- The amount included in income from Form 8864, Biodiesel and Renewable Diesel Fuels Credit.

- Refund of taxes deducted in prior years to the extent they reduced income subject to tax in the year deducted. Do not offset current year taxes against tax refunds.

- The amount of any deduction previously taken under Code Sec. 179A that is subject to recapture. The corporation must recapture the benefit of any allowable deduction for clean-fuel vehicle property (or clean-fuel refueling property) if the property later ceases to qualify.

- Ordinary income from trade or business activities of a partnership [from Schedule K-1 (Form 1065 or 1065-B)]. Do not offset ordinary losses against ordinary income. Instead, include the losses on Line 26, Form 1120. Show the partnership's name, address, and EIN on a separate statement attached to this return. If the amount entered is from more than one partnership, identify the amount from each partnership.

- Any LIFO recapture amount under Code Sec. 1363(d). The corporation may have to include a LIFO recapture amount in income if it (a) used the LIFO inventory method for its last tax year before the first tax year for which it elected to become an S corporation or (b) transferred LIFO inventory assets to an S corporation in a nonrecognition transaction in which those assets were transferred basis property.

- Any net positive Code Sec. 481(a) adjustment. The corporation may have to make an adjustment to prevent amounts of income or expense from being duplicated or omitted.

## DEDUCTIONS

## ¶14 COMPENSATION OF OFFICERS

Line 12, page 1 (Form 1120) - Compensation of officers is reported on Line 12 of Form 1120 or Form 1120-A. Schedule E, Form 1120, must be completed if total receipts (Line 1a, plus Lines 4 through 10 of page 1, Form 1120) are $500,000 or more. The information on Line 1, columns (a) through (f), of Schedule E must be furnished for all officers and totaled on Line 2 of Schedule E. This amount is reduced by compensation claimed elsewhere on the return, such as compensation included in the cost of goods sold, elective contributions to a Code Sec. 401(k) cash or deferred arrangement, or amounts contributed under a salary reduction SEP agreement, or a SIMPLE IRA retirement plan. For discussing of directors' fees, see ¶28.

**Disallowance of deduction for employee compensation in excess of $1 million.** Publicly-held corporations may not deduct compensation exceeding $1 million (reduced by amounts that are disallowed as excess parachute payments under Code Sec. 280G) paid to certain officers (Code Sec. 162(m)). For this purpose, compensation does not include exempt benefits or income from certain employee trusts, annuity plans, or pensions. The deduction limit does not apply to commissions based on individual performance, qualified performance-based compensation, and income payable under a written, binding contract in effect on February 17, 1993.

## ¶15 OTHER SALARIES AND WAGES

Line 13, page 1 (Form 1120) - Compensation for personal services, to the extent that such compensation is not deducted elsewhere on the return, is deducted on Line 13. Reduce total salaries and wages by the amount claimed for the following credits: Work Opportunity Credit (Form 5884), Hurricane Katrina Employee Retention Credit (Form 5884-A), Empowerment Zone and Renewal Community Employment Credit (Form 8844), Indian Employment Credit (Form 8845), Welfare-to-Work Credit (Form 8861), the salary and wage deduction must be reduced by the amount of the credit. Falcon Machinery does not claim these credits.

*Pensions.*—In regard to contributions or additions to pension trusts, etc., see ¶**27**.

## ¶16  REPAIRS AND MAINTENANCE

Line 14, page 1 (Form 1120) - Repairs generally include maintenance and replacement expenses that do not increase the value or usability of equipment or buildings, and that do not add to their useful life. Such repairs that are not reported elsewhere on the return are included on Line 14, page 1. Expenses that do not meet this test are ordinarily depreciable capital expenditures. Falcon includes its repair expenses in inventory in Schedule A as a UNICAP expense.

## ¶17  BAD DEBTS

Line 15, page 1, (Form 1120) - This deduction, on Line 15, usually covers only debts that have become worthless in whole or in part within the tax year. If a business debt became only *partially* worthless during the tax year or an earlier year, the amount that is *charged off* during the tax year may be deducted.

A cash basis taxpayer may not claim a deduction unless the amount was previously included in income.

## ¶18  RENT PAID ON BUSINESS PROPERTY

Line 16, page 1, (Form 1120) - Rent paid or accrued for business property in which the corporation has no equity is deducted on Line 16, page 1. The rental expense deduction for cars leased for a term of 30 days or more is reduced by an inclusion amount based on the price of the car if it would be subject to the luxury car depreciation caps if it were owned by the corporation rather than leased (Code Sec. 280F(c)).

## ¶19  TAXES AND LICENSES

Line 17, page 1, (Form 1120) – Enter taxes paid or accrued during the tax year. Real and personal property taxes, state franchise taxes, income and capital stock taxes, federal and state employment taxes, and the corporation's portion of social security taxes are examples of the types of taxes that are deducted on Line 17. The deduction can be computed on the basis of taxes paid or accrued during the year. Do not include on Line 17 the following:

- Federal income taxes,

- foreign and U.S. possession income taxes for which a foreign tax credit is being claimed,

- taxes not imposed on the corporation

- taxes including state or local sales taxes that are paid or incurred in connection with an acquisition or disposition of property (these taxes must be treated as part of the cost of acquired property or that reduce the amount realized upon disposition of property),

- taxes deducted elsewhere on the return, and

- taxes assessed against local benefits that increase the value of the property assessed are not deductible.

Falcon's Line 17 deduction ($38,631) is the sum of the following taxes that are also reflected in its books on the worksheet appearing on p.65 of this publication: Capital stock ($520); franchise ($300); property ($8,000); employment ($25,491) and state income tax ($4,320). Falcon does not claim a deduction on this line for $93 foreign income tax it paid, but instead claims a credit on Schedule J. The Line 17 deduction does not include taxes that were allocable to inventory and reflected on line 5 of Schedule A.

## ¶20  INTEREST EXPENSE

Line 18, page 1, (Form 1120) - Enter on Line 18 the deductible interest paid or accrued which is not deductible elsewhere (e.g., Schedule A).

**Nondeductible interest:** The following interest may not be deducted:

- Interest paid or accrued on indebtedness incurred or continued to purchase or hold tax-exempt securities.

- For cash basis taxpayers, prepaid interest allocable to years following the current tax year. For example, a cash basis calendar year taxpayer who in 2005 prepaid interest allocable to any period after 2005 can deduct only the amount allocable to 2005.

- Interest and carrying charges on straddles. Generally, these amounts must be capitalized.

- Interest on debt allocable to the production of designated property by a corporation for its own use or for sale. The corporation must capitalize this interest.

- Interest paid or incurred on any portion of an underpayment of tax that is attributable to an understatement arising from an undisclosed listed transaction or an undisclosed reportable avoidance transaction (other than a listed transaction) entered into in tax years beginning after October 22, 2004.

- The interest deduction is limited when the corporation is a policyholder or beneficiary with respect to a life insurance, endowment, or annuity contract issued after June 8, 1997.

## ¶21 CHARITABLE CONTRIBUTIONS OR GIFTS

Line 19, page 1 (Form 1120) - Corporations may deduct on Line 19 contributions or gifts to charitable, etc., organizations *actually paid* within the tax year in an amount not in excess of 10%* of their taxable income. Taxable income is computed without regard to the following:

- Any deduction for contributions

- Any net operating loss or capital loss carryback

- The limited deduction for convertible bond premium on repurchase, or

- The special deduction allowed for dividends received.

**\*Temporary suspension of 10 percent limitation.** A corporation may elect to deduct qualified cash contributions without regard to the general 10 percent limit if the contributions were made after August 27, 2005, and before January 1, 2006, to a qualified charitable organization for Hurricane Katrina relief efforts. The total amount claimed cannot be more than taxable income as computed above substituting 100 percent for 10 percent. Excess contributions are carried over 5 years. Taxpayers should attach a statement to the return, substantiating that the con-

tributions are for Hurricane Katrina relief efforts and indicating the amount of qualified contributions for which the election is made.

A schedule attached to Form 1120 would show the following contributions made by Falcon Machinery Corp.:

| | |
|---|---|
| United Charities, Chicago | $ 750 |
| Boy Scouts, Chicago | 500 |
| Red Cross, Chicago | 250 |
| Community Fund, Chicago | 750 |
| Total contributions | $2,250 |

Carryover Contributions exceeding 10% of taxable income may be carried over to the succeeding five tax years, subject to the 10% maximum limitation. A contributions carryover will not be allowed to the extent it increases a net operating loss carryover. An attached statement must show the amount of the carryover and how it is computed.

- **Contribution of Property other than Cash**

Corporations, other than closely held and personal service corporations, that make total noncash contributions exceeding $500 must attach a schedule describing the property contributed and the method used in determining its fair market value. Closely held corporations and personal service corporations must file Form 8283 (Noncash Charitable Contributions) to report such contributions if the total claimed value of the donated property exceeds $500. Other corporations must file Form 8283 for noncash contributions if the total value of the donated property exceeds $5,000.

- **Substantiation Requirements**

Generally, no deduction is allowed for a charitable contribution of $250 or more unless it is substantiated by a contemporaneous written acknowledgement from the donee. Charitable deductions are also denied for amounts contributed to an organization that conducts certain lobbying activities.

- **Larger Reduction**

An increased deduction is available to a corporation that contributes the following:

- Inventory and other property to certain organizations for use in the care of the ill, needy, or infants, including contributions after August 27, 2005 and before January 1, 2006 of "apparently wholesome food" and qualified book contributions [Code Sec. 170(e)(3)(D)];

- Scientific equipment used for research to institutions of higher learning or to certain scientific research organizations (other than by personal service companies and service organizations); and

- Computer technology and equipment for educational purposes [Code Sec. 170(e)(6)].

# ¶23 DEPRECIATION

- **Line 20, page 1 Form 1120.**

The tax law permits an annual deduction for the wear and tear on assets with a useful life of over one year that are used in a trade or business or for the production of income. The cost of the asset is recovered by depreciating or amortizing it over a period of several years. The period and method used are determined by the type of asset and the year it was placed in service. Tangible assets are usually depreciated and intangible assets are usually amortized.

Depreciation starts in the year that an asset is *placed in service*. This may be later than the year of acquisition. Property is deemed placed in service when it is first placed in a condition or state of readiness and availability for a specially assigned function [Reg. Sec. 1.167(a)-11(e)(1)(i)]. The asset is depreciated until its basis is recovered, it is sold or it is no longer used for business or investment purposes. Assets that are temporarily idle continue to be depreciated.

## ON THE RETURN

Depreciation and amortization of property is computed on Form 4562, Depreciation and Amortization and then entered on Line 20 (Form 1120). Also included on Line 20 is the cost of property that the corporation elected to expense under Code Sec. 179.

Form 4562 must be completed if the taxpayer is claiming any of the following:

- Depreciation for property placed in service during the tax year.

- A Code Sec. 179 expense deduction for certain tangible property (which may include a carryover from a previous year).

- Depreciation on any vehicle or other *listed property** regardless of when it was placed in service.

- Any depreciation on a corporate income tax return (other than Form 1120S).

- Amortization of costs that begins during the tax year.

   **Special Note.** A separate Form 4562 must be filed for each business activity and the total depreciation deduction is entered on Line 20 of the **Deductions** section of Form 1120.

   **Listed property* includes the following:

- Passenger automobiles weighing 6,000 pounds or less.

- Any other property used for transportation if the nature of the property lends itself to personal use, such as motorcycles, pick-up trucks, sport utility vehicles.

- Any property used for entertainment or recreational purposes (such as photographic, phonographic, communication, and video recording equipment).

- Cellular telephones (or similar telecommunications equipment).

- Computers or peripheral equipment.

**Exception.** *Listed* property does not include:

1. Photographic, phonographic, communication, or video equipment used exclusively in your trade or business or at the taxpayer's regular business establishment;

2. Any computer or peripheral equipment used exclusively at a regular business establishment and owned or leased by the person operating the establishment; or

3. An ambulance, hearse, or vehicle used for transporting persons or property for hire.

- **Form 4562- Part 1 – Election to Expense Certain Property Under Section 179.**

The expensing deduction is computed in Part I of Form 4562. In lieu of depreciation deductions over time, a corporation may elect a current write-off for some or all of the cost of the depreciable equipment and other personal property placed in service in a trade or business in 2005. This is known as the "expensing" or Section 179 deduction. The dollar limit on the expensing deduction is $105,000 in 2005 ($140,000 for qualified enterprise zone, renewal community, and New York Liberty Zone property). The $105,000 maximum can be allocated among two or more assets in any combination. Of course, if less than $105,000 worth of property are placed in service during the year, the taxpayer cannot expense more than the cost of the property.

> **Practice Pointer:** An estate or trust cannot make this election.

If the combined cost of items placed in service during the year exceeds $105,000, the excess can be written off through depreciation deductions. To do this, subtract the amount expensed from the basis for each item. This reduced basis is the amount used to compute your depreciation deduction.

The $105,000 maximum expensing deduction is reduced (but not below zero) by the amount by which the cost of qualifying property placed in service during the year exceeds $420,000. For a partnership (other than an electing large partnership) these limitations apply to the partnership and each partner. For an electing large partnership, the limitations apply only to the partnership. For an S corporation, these limitations apply to the S corporation and each shareholder. For a controlled group, all component members are treated as one taxpayer.

*Eligible property:* The expensing deduction is available for property acquired for use in the active conduct of your trade or business and that is either:

1. Tangible personal property.

2. Other tangible property (except buildings and their structural components) used as: (a) an integral part of manufacturing, production, or extraction or of furnishing transportation, communications, electricity, gas, water, or sewage disposal services; (b) a research facility used in connection with any of the activities in (a) above; or (c) a facility used in connection with any of the activities in (a) above for the bulk storage of fungible commodities.

3. Single purpose agricultural (livestock) or horticultural structures.

4. Storage facilities (except buildings and their structural components) used in connection with distributing petroleum or any primary product of petroleum.

5. Off-the-shelf computer software. Computer software is defined as software that:

a. Is readily available for purchase by the general public,

b. Is subject to a nonexclusive license, and

c. Has not been substantially modified.

Computer software does not include any database or similar item unless it is in the public domain and is incidental to the operation of otherwise qualifying computer software.

*Property ineligible for expensing deduction.* The following types of property do not qualify for the expensing deduction:

- Property used 50 percent or less in a trade or business.

- Property held for investment .

- Property used mainly outside the United States.

- Property used for lodging or for furnishing the lodging.

- Property used by a tax-exempt organization unless the property is used mainly in a taxable unrelated trade or business.

- Property used by a governmental unit or foreign person or entity (except for property used under a lease with a term of less than 6 months).

- Air conditioning or heating units.

The expensing election must be made by the due date (including extensions) of the return for the tax year in which the property was first placed in service. A taxpayer may revoke an election without IRS consent. To qualify for the expensing break, the property must be depreciable, have a useful life of at least three years, and be purchased (generally, acquired from a non-related party and not a gift). In addition, the property must be used over 50 percent in a trade or business. Property used in an activity to produce income that is not a trade or business (e.g., rental property) cannot be expensed.

The amount expensed is subtracted from the property's basis, which thereby reduces the depreciation deduction.

If expensed property is disposed of (or business use falls below 51 percent of total use) before the end of the property's depreciation period, the tax benefit from expensing is recaptured.

## CARRYFORWARD

Unused expensing deductions can be carried over to future years only if caused by the taxable-income limitation.

- **Form 4562—Part II. Special Depreciation Allowance and Other Depreciation (Do not include listed property.) - Lines 14 - 16**

**Lines 14 – 16.** The taxpayer may be able to claim an additional first-year depreciation deduction equal to 50 percent (or 30 percent) of the adjusted basis of most types of new capital assets (other than buildings) acquired after May 5, 2003, and before January 1, 2005. The 30 percent special allowance applies to qualified property for which the 50 percent allowance does not apply (or for property for which the taxpayer has elected the 30 percent allowance for property that would otherwise qualify for the 50 percent allowance). To claim the 30 percent bonus depreciation, the taxpayer must have acquired the property after September 10, 2001 and before January 1, 2005. If a binding contract to acquire the property existed before September 11, 2001, the property does not qualify.

The amount of the deduction is computed by multiplying the depreciable basis of the property by 50 percent (or 30 percent, if applicable). To figure the depreciable basis, subtract from the business/investment portion of the cost or other basis of the property the total of the following amounts allocable to the property: (1) Code Sec. 179 expense deduction; (2) deduction for removal of barriers to the disabled and the elderly; (3) disabled access credit; (4) enhanced oil recovery credit; (5) credit for employer-provided childcare facilities and services; and (6) basis adjustment in investment credit property under Code Sec. 50(c).

The basis of the property and the depreciation allowances in the year of purchase and later years are appropriately adjusted to reflect the additional first-year depreciation deduction. The additional first-year depreciation deduction is allowed for both regular tax and alternative minimum tax (AMT) purposes for the year in which the property is placed in service.

The following property qualifies for the additional 30 percent or 50 percent first-year depreciation deduction:

- MACRS property with a recovery period of 20 years or less;

- Computer software depreciated under Code Sec.

167(f)(1);

- Water utility property;

- Qualified leasehold improvement property, which is any interior improvements made under a lease to commercial property (such as an office building or warehouse), and placed in service more than 3 years after the building was first placed in service. Qualified leasehold improvement does not include expenditures for enlargement of a building; any elevator or escalator; any structural component benefiting a common area; or the internal structural framework of the building. The following kinds of improvements would qualify as leasehold improvements if they benefit the tenant's space only rather than a common area: (a) electrical or plumbing systems (including sprinkler system), (b) permanently installed lighting fixtures, (c) heating equipment, cooling equipment, air conditioners and other air handling equipment, and (d) ceiling and doors; or

- Qualified Liberty Zone property other than qualified Liberty Zone leasehold improvement property, not otherwise treated as qualified property. Liberty Zone property is defined as property located on or south of Canal Street, East Broadway (east of its intersection with Canal Street), or Grand Street (east of its intersection with East Broadway) in the Borough of Manhattan in the City of New York, New York.

*Property ineligible for bonus first-year depreciation.* . The additional first -year depreciation is unavailable for the following types of property: (1) listed property used 50% or less in a qualified business; (2) property that must be depreciated under the alternative depreciation system; (3) qualified Liberty Zone leasehold improvement property; and (4) property for which you make an election out.

*Election out.* If the taxpayer makes an election out, the property may be subject to an AMT adjustment for depreciation. To make the election, attach a statement to a timely filed return indicating that an election is being made not to claim the additional allowance and the class of property for which the election is being made.

- **Line 15: Property subject to Section 168(f)(1) election.**

Report on this line depreciation for property that you elect, under IRC Sec. 168(f)(1) to depreciate by the unit-of-production method, or any other method not based on a term of years, other than the retirement-replacement-betterment method, which has its own rules. Attach a separate sheet showing:

- A description of the property and the depreciation method you elect that excludes the property from MACRS or ACRS; and

- The depreciable basis (cost or other basis reduced, if applicable, by salvage value, any IRC Sec. 79 expense deduction, deduction for removal of barriers to the disabled and the elderly, disabled access credit, enhanced oil recovery credit, credit for employer-provided childcare facilities and services, and any special depreciation allowance. See Code Sec. 50(c) to determine the basis adjustment for investment credit property.

- **Line 16: ACRS and other depreciation.**

Enter the total depreciation you are claiming for the following types of property (except listed property and property subject to an Code Sec. 168(f)(1) election):

- Accelerated cost recovery system (ACRS) property (pre-1987 rules).

- Property placed in service before 1981.

- Certain public utility property, which does not meet certain normalization requirements.

- Certain property acquired from related persons.

- Property acquired in certain nonrecognition transactions.

- Certain sound recordings, movies, and videotapes.

- Property depreciated under the income forecast method. The use of the income forecast method is limited to motion picture films, videotapes, sound recordings, copyrights, books, and patents. For property placed in service in 2005, you can either include certain participations and residuals in the adjusted basis of the property in the year the property is placed in service or deduct these amounts when paid. You cannot use this method to depreciate any amortizable Code Sec. 197 intangibles. If you use the income forecast method for any property placed in service after September 13, 1995, you may owe or be entitled to a refund for the third and tenth tax years beginning after the tax year the property was placed in service. See Form 8866, "Interest

Computation Under the Look-Back Method for Property Depreciated Under the Income Forecast Method."

- Intangible property, other than Code Sec. 197 intangibles including: (1) computer software which is written off over 36 months using the straight line method; (2) any right to receive tangible property or services under a contract or granted by a governmental unit (not acquired as part of a business); (3) any interest in a patent or copyright not acquired as part of a business; and (4) residential mortgage servicing rights. Use the straight line method over 108 months. (5) Other intangible assets with a limited useful life that cannot be estimated with reasonable accuracy. Generally, use the straight line method over 15 years.

Note that prior years' depreciation, plus current year's depreciation, can never exceed the depreciable basis of the property. The basis and amounts claimed for depreciation should be part of your permanent books and records. There is no need to attach these records to your tax return.

> **Practice Pointer:** Taxpayers who elect the Code Sec. 179 expense deduction or take the special depreciation allowance for computer software, must reduce the amount on which they figure their regular depreciation deduction by the amount deduction.

- **Form 4562- Part III. MACRS Depreciation.**

Most tangible business property placed in service after 1986 is depreciated under the Modified Accelerated Cost Recovery System (MACRS). There are two basic MACRS depreciation systems: the General Depreciation System (GDS) and the Alternative Depreciation System (ADS). Generally MACRS is used to depreciate any tangible property placed in service after 1986. However, MACRS does not apply to films, videotapes, and sound recordings.

- **Line 17: MACRS depreciation for past years.**

For tangible property placed in service before 2005 and depreciated under MACRS, enter the deductions for the current year. You do not have to tell the IRS how you figured your depreciation deduction. Taxpayers should apply the applicable rules for each property, total the results, and enter the total amount on Line 17.

- **Line 18:**

If you are making the election to group any assets placed in service during 2005 into one or more general asset accounts, check the box on Line 18. You must make this election no later than the due date for the tax year (including extensions) for the tax year in which the assets were placed in service. Once made, the election is irrevocable and applies to the tax year for which the election is made and all later tax years. Assets are grouped in this fashion to simplify the computation of MACRS depreciation. The assets in each general asset account are depreciated under MACRS as a single asset. Each account must include only assets that were placed in service during the same tax year with the same asset class, depreciation method, recovery period and convention. However, an asset cannot be included in a general asset account if the asset is used both for personal purposes and business/investment purposes. When an asset in an account is disposed of, the amount realized generally must be recognized as ordinary income. The unadjusted depreciable basis and depreciation reserve of the general asset account are not affected as a result of a disposition.

- **Line 19: Section B - Assets Placed in Service During 2005 Tax Year Using the General Depreciation System.**

To figure MACRS depreciation under the GDS, taxpayers must know the following:

(a) The type of property you are depreciating;

(b) The date you placed each property in service;

(c) The cost basis of each property;

(d) The recovery period of each property;

(e) How to handle depreciation for the first and last years you use the property; and

(f) The depreciation method you are using.

Taxpayer will provide this information for each asset in columns (a) through (f) of Line 15 before they enter the amount of depreciation allowable in column (g).

*Column (a): Property type.* Column (a) lists all the types of MACRS property. You enter information about each property placed in service during the year on the line corresponding to that type of property. For example, if you purchased an asset classified as "residential rental property," you would provide all the information requested about that asset in columns (b) through (g) of Line 19g on Form 4562. A property's "type" generally depends on its class life, as listed in the IRS Table of Class Lives and Recovery Periods. The types of MACRS property are:

- **Line 19a:**

3-year property includes a race horse that is more than 2 years old at the time it is placed in service, any horse (other than a race horse) that is more than 12 years old at the time it is placed in service, and any qualified rent-to-own property. Generally, qualified rent-to-own property is tangible personal property of a type used within the home for personal use and held by a dealer for lease to customers under a rent-to-own agreement.

- **Line 19b:**

5-year property includes cars, light-duty purpose trucks, computers or peripheral equipment, calculators, typewriters, copiers, duplicating equipment, semi-conductor manufacturing equipment, trailers and cargo containers, appliances, carpet, furniture, etc. used in a residential rental real estate activity, and equipment used in connection with research and experimentation. In addition, any qualified Liberty Zone leasehold improvement property is classified as 5-year property.

- **Line 19c:**

7-year property includes any motorsports entertainment complex, office furniture and equipment, railroad track, any natural gas gathering line placed in service after April 11, 2005, and any property not assigned to another class.

- **Line 19d:**

10-year property includes water transportation vessels such as barges and tugs, any single purpose agricultural or horticultural structure, and any tree or vine bearing fruit or nuts.

- **Line 19e:**

15-year property includes any municipal wastewater treatment plant, telephone distribution plant and similar communication equipment used for 2-way exchange of voice and data communication, any IRC Sec. 1250 property that is a retail motor fuels outlet (whether or not food or other convenience items are sold there), any qualified leasehold improvement property placed in service before January 1, 2006, any qualified restaurant property placed in service before January 1, 2006, initial clearing and grading land improvements for gas utility property, certain electric transmission property placed in service after April 11, 2005, and any natural gas distribution line placed in service after April 11, 2005.

• **Line 19f:**

20-year property includes initial clearing and grading land improvements for electric utility transmission and distribution plants, **farm** buildings (other than single purpose agricultural or horticultural structures) and municipal sewers not classified as 25-year property.

• **Line 19g:**

25-year property includes water utility property that is an integral part of the gathering, treatment, or commercial distribution of water that without regard to this classification would be 20-year property, and municipal sewers.

• **Line 19h:**

Residential rental property has a recovery period of 27.5 years. It includes buildings that generate more than 80 percent of their income from dwelling units—but not buildings that mainly provide short-term housing, such as hotels.

• **Line 19i:**

Nonresidential real property, including almost all depreciable real estate other than residential rental property, has a recovery of 39 years.

• **50-year property:**

50-year property includes any improvements necessary to construct or improve a roadbed or right-of-way for railroad track that qualifies as a railroad grading or tunnel bore. There is no separate line to report 50-year property. Therefore, attach a statement showing the same information required in columns (a) through (g). Include the deduction in the Line 22 total and write "See attachement" in the bottom margin of the form.

*Column (b): Date placed in service.* For real property placed in service in 2005 (reported on Lines 19h and 19i), you must enter the month and year you placed the property in service in column (b). *Reason:* Depreciation on real property is calculated from the middle of the month it is actually placed in service.

*Column (c): Cost basis.* Your cost basis for an asset is generally the amount you paid for it, reduced by any depreciation deduction claimed in a prior year. You must also reduce your cost basis by any expensing you claim in Part I.

*Column (d): Recovery period.* How quickly you can write off property depends on its MACRS recovery period. For personal property, the recovery period is the same as the property type. In other words, 3-year property has a three-year recovery period.

The recovery period for residential rental property is 27.5 years and 39 years for nonresidential real property.

*Column (e): Convention.* The convention you use affects how much depreciation you can claim for the year you place property in service (and sometimes the year you dispose of the property). There are three types of conventions: half-year convention; mid-quarter convention; and mid-month convention.

**Half-year convention.** This convention applies to all property reported on line 19a through 19g, unless the mid-quarter convention applies. It does not apply to residential rental property, nonresidential real property and railroad gradings and tunnel bores. It treats all property placed in service during the tax year as placed in service on the midpoint of that year. You enter "HY" in column (e). With the half-year convention, you get a half-year's worth of depreciation in the first year you place personal property in service, regardless of when during the year it is actually placed in service. Likewise, if you dispose of property before the end of the recovery period, a half-year of depreciation is allowed for the disposition year.

**Mid-quarter convention.** If the total depreciable bases of MACRS property placed in service during the last 3 months of the tax year exceed 40 percent of the total depreciable bases of MACRS property placed in service during the tax year, the mid-quarter, instead of the half-year, convention generally applies. In determining whether the mid-quarter convention applies, do not take into account the following: (1) property that is being depreciated under a method other than MACRS; (2) any residential rental property, nonresidential real property, or railroad grading and tunnel bores; (3) property that is placed in service and disposed of within the same tax year. The "mid-quarter" (MQ) convention property treats all property placed in service (or disposed of) during any month as placed in service (or disposed of) in the middle of the quarter of the year when it was actually placed in service. Instead of deducting half of a full year's depreciation (as you would under the half-year convention), the mid-quarter convention allows you to claim 87.5% for property placed in service during the first quarter of the year, 62.5% for property placed in service in the second quarter, 37.5% for third-quarter property and 12.5% for fourth-quarter property. Enter "MQ" in column (e).

**Mid-month convention.** This convention applies only to residential rental property, nonresidential real property and railroad gradings and tunnel bores. It treats all property placed in service (or disposed of) during any month as placed in service (or disposed of) on the midpoint of that month. Enter "MM" in column (e).

*Column (f): Method.* To figure your depreciation for the year, you multiply your basis in each (column (c)) by a certain percentage. MACRS uses three methods to figure the percentage of your basis you can depreciate each year: 200% declining balance; 150% declining balance; or S/L for straight line.

For personal property, you can start out using either the "150% declining balance" method (for 15-year and 20-year property) or the "200% declining balance" method (for all other MACRS property). But you switch to the "straight line" method when that would produce a larger result. For real property, you must always use the straight-line method to figure your depreciation deduction.

You indicate the method you are using on Form 4562 by entering "200 DB," "150 DB" or "S/L" in column (f).

*Special elections:* Instead of the 150%/200% declining balance methods, you can elect to use a less accelerated method of depreciation. The tax rules permit the use of (1) straight line depreciation over the regular MACRS recovery period, or (2) 150% declining balance switching to straight line over the "class life" of the property. You make the election by entering "150 DB" or "S/L" in column (f). In addition, you must attach a sheet to your return, stating that an election is being made under IRC section 168(b)(5) and indicate which items are covered by the election.

*Column (g): Depreciation deduction.* You enter the depreciation deduction you are allowed for each property in column (g). There are two ways of figuring your depreciation deduction: the long way, where you compute the deduction yourself; and the short way, using the IRS optional tables. They should both give you the same results.

*The long way:* You figure your MACRS declining balance deduction by (1) determining the depreciation rate, according to the appropriate method (column (f)) and then (2) multiplying the depreciation rate by the property's adjusted basis (column (c)). For the year the property is placed in service (or if the property is disposed of before the recovery period is over), you must then reduce your deduction by applying the appropriate convention (column (e)). Once you have figured your deduction for this year, you must reduce your basis in the property before you figure your deduction for next year.

- **Form 4562 - Line 20 Section C - Assets Placed in Service During 2005 Using the Alternative Depreciation System.**

Most tangible business property placed in service after 1986 is depreciated under the Modified Accelerated Cost Recovery System (MACRS). There are two basic MACRS depreciation systems: the General Depreciation System (GDS) and the Alternative Depreciation System (ADS).

You will probably depreciate all the property you place in service in 2005 under the GDS system. However, you may elect to use the ADS system if you wish. Also, in some unusual situations, the use of ADS is mandatory. For example, tangible property used predominantly outside of the U.S. must use ADS. Your depreciation deduction for ADS property is figured on Line 20.

The following property must be depreciated under ADS:

- Tangible property used predominately outside the United States.

- Tax-exempt use property.

- Tax-exempt bond financed property.

- Imported property covered by an executive order of the President of the United States.

- Property used predominantly in a farming business and placed in service during any tax year in which you made an election under Code Sec. 263A(d)(3) not to have the uniform capitalization rules apply.

Rather than depreciating property under GDS (Line 15), you may make an irrevocable election with respect to any classification of property for any tax year to use ADS. For residential rental and nonresidential real property, you may make this election separately for each property.

## HOW TO ELECT

You elect ADS by entering the ADS depreciation deduction on Line 20. Use Line 20a for personal property with a class life, Line 20b for 12-year property that does not have a class life, and Line 20c for residential rental and nonresidential real property that is classified as 40-year property. You must also attach a sheet to your return, stating that you are making an election under Code Sec. 168(g)(7) and listing the items covered by the election.

## FORM 4562, PART IV. SUMMARY

## ON THE RETURN

- **MACRS Deduction for Post-1986 Assets**

The Falcon Machinery Corporation in the filled-in form placed into service machinery (7-year property) in August 2005 at a cost of $300,000. The machinery qualified as a long production period asset. The company makes the MACRS straight-line election and uses a 7-year recovery period. The bonus depreciation deduction is $150,000 ($300,000 × 50%). This amount is entered on Part II, line 14 of Form 4562. The first-year depreciation deduction is $10,710 (($300,000 - $150,000) × 7.14%), which is entered on line 19c.

Construction of a factory building (39-year property) is completed during June 2005 at a cost of $250,000 and is depreciated under the MACRS straight-line method. The current-year deduction is $3,478 ($250,000 × 1.391%) and is entered on line 19i.

For machinery (7-year property) purchased in July 2004, at a cost of $134,892, the company uses the regular MACRS method and a 7-year recovery period. Because the machinery was used, it did not qualify for bonus depreciation. MACRS depreciation claimed on such property in 2004 was $19,276 ($134,892 × 14.29%). The rate for the current year is 24.49%. The current-year deduction is $33,035 ($134,892 × 24.49%).

For office furniture and fixtures (7-year property) purchased in 2002, at a cost of $30,629, the company uses the regular MACRS method and a 7-year recovery period. Bonus depreciation claimed in 2003 was $9,189 ($30,629 × 30%). Regular depreciation was $3,064 (($30,629 - $9,189) × 14.29%). Regular depreciation in 2003 was $5,251 (($30,629 - $9,189) × 24.49%)). Total

depreciation claimed in 2003 and 2004 was $17,504 ($9,189 + $3,064 + $5,251). The MACRS rate for the current year is 17.49%. The current-year deduction (2005) is $3,750 (($30,629 - $9,189) × 17.49%).

For trucks (5-year property not subject to Code Sec. 280F) purchased in April 2004, at a cost of $45,264, the company uses the regular MACRS method and a 5-year recovery period. MACRS depreciation claimed on such property in 2004 was $6,337 (($45,264 – $13,579 bonus depreciation) × 20%). Bonus depreciation was $13,579 ($45,264 × 30%) The rate for the current year is 32%. The current-year deduction (2005) is $10,139 (($45,264 - $13,579) × 32%).

The total current-year MACRS depreciation deduction for the pre-2005 machinery, office furniture and fixtures, and trucks is $46,924 ($33,035 + $3,750 + $10,139), which is entered on Part III, Line 17 of Form 4562.

- **ACRS Deduction for Post-1980 and Pre-1987 Assets**

A shed placed in service on January 2, 1986 (19-year real recovery property for which the ACRS straight-line election over a 35-year recovery period was made), is destroyed by fire in February 2005. The ACRS deduction claimed in previous years was $5,200, and the rate for the current year is 2.9%. The property cost $10,000, and there is no insurance. The current-year deduction is $36 ($10,000 × 2.9% × 1.5/12).

- **CLS Deduction for Pre-1971 Assets**

The total cost of buildings in a single account at the beginning of 2005 was $420,500. Depreciation on these buildings is $9,344–$420,500 unadjusted basis at the end of the year times 2 2/9% straight-line class life rate.

The total ACRS and CLS depreciation deduction is $9,380 ($36 + $9,344). This amount is entered on Line 16 of Form 4562.

- **Depreciable Assets and Reserves for Schedule L**

Here is an analysis of the beginning and ending balances shown in Schedule L, Form 1120, for depreciable assets (Line 10a) and accumulated depreciation (Line 10b):

- **Form 4562—Part V: Listed property—automobiles, certain other vehicles, cellular telephones, certain computers and property used for entertainment, recreation, or amusement.**

If you claim the standard mileage rate, actual vehicle expenses (including depreciation), or depreciation on other listed property, you must provide the information requested in Part V, regardless of the tax year the property was placed in service.

*Recapture:* If property meets the 50 percent test in the first year and fails to meet it in a subsequent year, then ADS must be used in the later year. In addition, the corporation must include in income in that year the "excess depreciation" claimed in prior years. Excess depreciation is (1) the amount of depreciation (including expensing) claimed during the prior years, less (2) the amount of depreciation that would have been allowed using straight-line depreciation under ADS.

- **Line 24:**

This line asks whether there is evidence to support the business use claimed for the listed property (Box 24a) and if this evidence is written (Box 24b).

- **Line 25:**

Enter on Line 25 your total special depreciation allowance for all listed property. For discussion of the bonus 30 percent and 50 percent depreciation deduction allowed for qualified property placed in service during the tax year, see instructions for Line 14.

- **Line 26:**

Property used more than 50 percent in a qualified business use. In column (a) of Lines 26 and 27 depending on your percentage of qualified business use for each property, list on a property-by-property basis all your listed property in the following order: (1) automobiles and other vehicles; and (2) other listed property (computers and peripheral equipment, etc.).

## DOLLAR LIMITS FOR AUTO WRITEOFFS

The instructions to Form 4562 list dollar limits that are imposed on depreciation (plus expensing) deductions for passenger automobiles. For any passenger automobile (including an electric passenger automobile) listed on Lines 26 and 27, the total of columns (h) and (i) on Line 26 or 27 and column (h) on Line 25 for that automobile cannot exceed the applicable limit shown in Table 1, 2, 3, or 4 found in the instructions to Form 4562.

**These tables are reproduced in the 2006 CCH Federal Tax Reporters.**

If the business/investment use percentage for the automobile is less than 100 percent, you must reduce the applicable limit to an amount equal to the limit multiplied by that percentage.

For purposes of the limits for passenger automobiles, the following apply:

- Passenger automobiles are 4-wheeled vehicles manufactured primarily for use on public roads that are rated at 6,000 pounds unloaded gross vehicle weight or less (for a truck or van, gross vehicle weight is substituted for unloaded gross vehicle weight).

- Electric passenger automobiles are vehicles produced by an original equipment manufacturer and designed to run primarily on electricity.

**Exceptions:** The following vehicles are not considered passenger automobiles:

- An ambulance, hearse, or combination ambulance-hearse used in your trade or business

- A vehicle used in your trade or business of transporting persons or property for compensation or hire.

- Any truck or van placed in service after July 6, 2003, that is a qualified nonpersonal use vehicle. A truck or van is a qualified nonpersonal use vehicle only if it was specially modified so that it is not likely to be used more than a de minimis amount for personal purposes. For example, a van that has only a front bench for seating, in which permanent shelving has been installed, that carried merchandise or equipment, and that has been specially painted with advertising or the company's name, is a vehicle not likely to be used more than a de minimis amount for personal purposes.

- The limits for passenger automobiles placed in service after August 5, 1997, and before January 1, 2006, do not apply to the cost of any qualified clean fuel property (such as retrofit parts and components) installed on a vehicle to permit that vehicle to run on a clean-burning fuel.

- The business use requirement and the limits for passenger automobiles generally do not apply to passenger automobiles leased or held by anyone regularly engaged in the business of leasing passenger automobiles.

### Total Assets

| Assets | Balance 1-1-05 | Additions | Retirements | Balance 12-31-05 |
|---|---|---|---|---|
| Buildings: | | | | |
| Pre-1971 | $420,500 | ........ | ........ | $ 420,500 |
| Shed | 10,000 | ........ | $10,000 | 0 |
| 2004 | ........ | $250,000 | ........ | 250,000 |
| Machinery: | | | | |
| 2004 | 134,892 | ........ | ........ | 134,892 |
| 2005 | ........ | 300,000 | ........ | 300,000 |
| Office furniture and fixtures | 30,629 | ........ | ........ | 30,629 |
| Trucks | 45,264 | ........ | ........ | 45,264 |
| Totals | $641,285 | $550,000 | $10,000 | $1,181,285 |

### Total Accumulated Depreciation

| Accumulated Depreciation for — | Balance 1-1-05 | Additions | Retirements | Balance 12-31-05 |
|---|---|---|---|---|
| Buildings | $315,456 | $ 9,344 | ........ | $ 324,800 |
| Shed | 5,200 | 36 | $5,236 | 0 |
| 2005 building | 0 | 3,478 | ........ | 3,478 |
| Machinery: | | | | |
| 2004 | 19,276 | 33,035 | ........ | 52,311 |
| 2005 | 0 | 160,710 | ........ | 160,710 |
| Office furniture and fixtures | 17,504 | 3,750 | ........ | 21,254 |
| Trucks | 19,916 | 10,139 | ........ | 30,055 |
| Totals | $377,352 | $220,492 | $5,236 | $ 592,608 |
| Depreciation for 2005–per Form 4562 | | $220,492 | | |

- **Depletion (Form 1120 only)**

Taxpayers involved in mining, timber, oil and gas, or other natural resources may qualify for depletion deductions. Depletion may be based either on the cost of the resources (cost depletion), or a percentage of gross revenues (percentage or statutory depletion).

### ON THE RETURN

The depletion deduction is entered directly in the Deductions section of Form 1120 on Line 21. Attach Form T (Timber) if depletion of timber resources is deducted.

## ¶26 ADVERTISING

- **Line 22, page 1 (Form 1120).**

Reasonable costs of advertising are deducted on Line 22, page 1, of Form 1120 (Line 22 of Form 1120-A). Various forms of advertising may be used by a taxpayer to keep its name or products before the public, so long as they bear a reasonable relation to the business activities in which the corporation is engaged.

## ¶27 PENSION AND EMPLOYEE BENEFIT PLAN CONTRIBUTIONS

- **Line 23, page 1 (Form 1120).**

Deductible contributions made by a corporation to qualified pension, profit-sharing, and other types of deferred compensation plans are entered on Line 23 of Form 1120 (Line 22 of Form 1120-A). Generally, except for simplified employee pension plans, a Form 5500 must be filed for each plan. One-participant plans, however, should generally file Form 5500-EZ, Annual Return of One-Participant Pension Benefit Plan. These forms are filed separately and are due by the last day of the 7th month following the close of the plan year unless extensions have been granted. Contributions to other types of employee benefit programs—such as insurance, health or welfare programs—that are not an incidental part of a pension, profit-sharing plan, etc. are deducted on Line 24 of Form 1120 (Line 22 of Form 1120-A).

## ¶28 OTHER DEDUCTIONS

- **New Line 25 page 1 (Form 1120) –
  Domestic Production Activities Deduction
  (Attach Form 8903):**

Beginning January 1, 2005 the corporation may deduct up to 3 percent of their "qualified production activities income" from the following activities:

a. Manufacturing, production, growth or extraction of certain tangible personal property, computer software, films and videotapes, sound recordings (such as discs, tapes, or other phonorecordings), electricity, natural gas, or potable water produced by the taxpayer;

b. Construction performed in the United States; and

c. Engineering or architectural services performed in the United States for construction projects in the United States.

See Code Sec. 199 and Form 8903, Domestic Production Activities Deduction for further discussion.

Eligible taxpayers may claim a manufacturing deduction equal to the lesser of a phased-in percentage of taxable income (or an individual's adjusted gross income) or qualified production activities income. In applying these rules, only items that are attributable to the actual conduct of a trade or business are taken into account. The deduction does not apply to income derived from (1) the sale of food and beverages prepared at a retail establishment; (2) property leased, licensed or rented for use by an related person; or (3) the transmission or distribution of electricity, natural gas, or potable water. This new manufacturing deduction replaces the benefits of the repealed exclusion for extraterritorial income and is intended to provide tax relief that is economically equivalent to a three-percent reduction in taxes applicable to U.S.-based manufacturing.

- **Line 26, page 1 (Form 1120).**

There should be included on Line 26 of Form 1120 (Line 22 of Form 1120-A) any authorized deductions not included in the deductible items above. Attach a schedule listing by type and amount, all allowable deductions not deductible else where on the return. Examples of other deductions include the following:

- Amortization. See Form 4562

- Certain costs of qualified film or television productions

- Certain business start-up and organizational costs that the corporation elects to deduct.

- Reforestation costs-The corporation can elect to deduct up to $10,000 of qualified reforestation expenses for each qualifying timber property. The corporation can elect to amortize over 84 months any amount not deducted.

- Insurance premiums

- Legal and professional fees

- Supplies used and consumed in the business

- Utilities

- Ordinary losses from trade or business activities of a partnership from Schedule K-1 (Form 1065 or 1065-B).

- Extraterritorial income exclusion

- Deduction for clean-fuel vehicle and certain refueling property placed in service before January 1, 2006

- Any negative Code Sec. 481(a) adjustment

- Deduction for certain energy efficient commercial building property placed in service after December 31, 2005.

- Dividends paid in cash on stock held by an employee stock ownership plan provided the dividends are: (a) paid in cash directly to the plan participants or beneficiaries; (b) paid to the plan participants or their beneficiaries no later than 90 days after the end of the plan year in which the dividends are paid; or (c) at the election of the participants or their beneficiaries payable as provided in (a) or (b) above or paid to the plan and reinvested in qualifying employer securities; or (d) used to make payments on an IRC Sec. 404(a)(9) loan.

Do **not** deduct fines or penalties paid to a government for violating any law or any amount that is allocable to a class of exempt income.

- **Travel and Entertainment Expenses:**

Generally, a corporation may deduct ordinary and necessary travel and entertainment expenses that are business related as "Other Deductions." Travel expenses must be incurred while an employee is "away from home overnight." Away from home overnight must be substantially longer than an ordinary day's work and must require rest or sleep. Expenses that are deductible as travel expenses include cost of transportation, lodging, meals (provided they aren't lavish or extravagant), entertainment, laundry and other business-related expenses. In addition, entertainment expenses that are either "directly related" or "associated with" business are deductible.

Deductions for meals and entertainment expenses are generally limited to 50 percent of the cost.

A corporation can deduct only 50 percent of the expenses reimbursed to an employee if the employee makes an adequate accounting. If, however, the reimbursement is included in the employee's wages subject to withholding and FICA, the full amount is generally deductible as compensation.

## RECORDS A MUST

The corporation must keep records reflecting the amount of the expense, the date, time, and place of the expense, the business purpose and the business relationship. A receipt must be kept for expenditures of $75 or more. Any disallowed travel and entertainment expense will require a book-tax adjustment on Schedule M-1.

Employers who reimburse employee travel expenses by providing a per diem allowance for either lodging and meals and incidental expenses (M&IE) or M&IE only under an accountable plan can satisfy the IRS's onerous substantiation requirements by reimbursing employees using either the federal per diem allowances for the locality of travel or by using the high-low substantiation method for travel within the continental U.S.

> **Special rules:** Special restrictions apply to gifts, skybox rentals, tickets to entertainment events, travel outside of North America, and certain entertainment facilities [Code Sec. 274].

**Membership dues.** Corporations may deduct membership dues paid to join civic or public service organizations, professional organizations (such as bar and medical associations), business leagues, trade associations, chambers of commerce, boards of trade, and real estate boards. However, no deduction is allowed if a principal purpose of the organization is to entertain, or provide entertainment facilities for members or their guests. In addition, no deduction is allowed for membership dues in any club organized for business, pleasure, recreation, or other social purpose. This includes country clubs, golf and athletic clubs, airline and hotel clubs, and clubs operated to provide meals under conditions favorable to business discussion. In addition, no deduction is allowed for expenses paid or incurred for entertainment or recreational facilities including yacht or hunting lodges.

## ON THE RETURN

The schedule attached to the filled-in Form 1120 would show the following:

| | |
|---|---|
| Legal and accounting fees. | $ 12,500 |
| Service guaranties | $ 8,252 |
| Amortized bond issue expense | $ 700 |
| Heat and light—office | $ 9,720 |
| Printing, mailing, etc. | $ 5,115 |
| Travel expense | $ 6,850 |
| Total entered in Line 26 (Form 1120) | $ 43,137 |

## ¶29 TAXABLE INCOME BEFORE NOL DEDUCTION AND SPECIAL DEDUCTIONS AT-RISK RULES

The at-risk rules of Code Sec. 465 apply to closely held C corporations that are engaged in any activity as a trade or business or for the production of income. These corporations may have to adjust the amount on Line 28 Form 1120 or Line 24, Form1120-A as a result of the at-risk rules. The at-risk rules do not apply to:

- Holding real property (excluding mineral property) placed in service by the taxpayer before 1987;

- Equipment leasing if 50 percent or more of the corporation's gross receipts are from such leasing;

- Certain active closely held C corporations (other than personal holding companies and personal service corporations determined by using a 5 percent shareholder test) engaged in a qualifying business.

If a corporation has a net loss in any activity covered by the at-risk rules, the loss is limited to the amount that the corporation has at risk in the activity at the close of the tax year. The amount at risk is generally the sum of (1) cash contributions to the activity, (2) the adjusted basis of any property contributed to the activity, and (3) any amounts borrowed for use in the activity if the taxpayer is personally liable for the borrowed amounts or has pledged other assets as security for the borrowed amounts. This amount is increased by income from the activity and is decreased by losses (Code Sec. 465(b)).

Where a corporation is engaged in more than one activity and more than one activity incurs a loss for the year, the losses must be reported separately and Form 6198, At-Risk Limitations, should be filed. In determining whether an activity has incurred a loss, gains and losses from the sales or dispositions of assets used in the activity and from sales or dispositions of interests (either partial or total) are combined with the profit or loss from the activity.

If the at-risk limitation applies, a corporation must reduce the amount otherwise entered on Line 28 of Form 1120 (Line 24 of Form 1120-A) by the difference between the loss for the activity and the amount that the corporation has at risk in the activity at the end of the tax year. This means that the corporation cannot claim deductions for the amount of the excess loss. However, the corporation can claim a deduction in the next tax year for the excess (subject, again, to the at-risk rules).

## ¶30 PASSIVE ACTIVITY LOSSES AND CREDITS

Closely held C corporations and personal service corporations may use losses and credits from passive activities only to offset income and tax, respectively, from passive activities. A passive activity subject to the Code Sec. 465 at-risk rules must first be tested under such rules before applying the passive activity rules.

The corporate passive activity loss and credit limitations are determined in Part I and Part II, respectively, of Form 8810, Corporate Passive Activity Loss and Credit Limitations. Several worksheets are provided in the instructions for Form 8810 for computing such limitations. Income, gains, deductions, losses, prior-year unallowed passive activity losses, and overall gain or loss are determined for each activity. Amounts disallowed under this rule in the current year may be carried forward. A similar procedure is used for determining credit limitations. Special rules apply to corporate interests in publicly traded partnerships.

For an activity with an overall gain, all deductions and losses (including prior-year unallowed losses) for such activity are allowed and are entered on the ap-

propriate line of Form 1120, Schedule D of Form 1120, or Form 4797, Sales of Business Property, whichever is applicable. A notation should be made identifying prior-year unallowed passive activity losses.

For an activity with an overall loss, deductions and losses are separated into unallowed and allowed categories and the latter are allocated among Form 1120 deductions, Schedule D losses, and Form 4797 losses.

Closely held corporations are allowed to increase: (1) the limitation on losses from passive activities by the amount of net active income, and (2) the limitation on passive activity credit by the tax attributable to net active income. Net active income is taxable income determined without regard to (1) income, expense, gain, or loss from a passive activity, or (2) portfolio income, expense, gain, or loss (Code Sec. 469(e)(2)).

Passive activity losses do not include casualty and theft losses if such losses do not recur regularly in an activity. Reimbursements of casualty and theft losses included in income to recover a prior year loss deduction are not passive income if the loss deduction was nonpassive.

Rental activity is not considered a passive activity for a closely held C corporation that derives more than 50% of its gross receipts from a real property trade or business in which it materially participates (Code Sec. 469(c)(7)(D)).

## ¶31 NET OPERATING LOSS DEDUCTION

- **Line 29, page 1 (Form 1120).**

The net operating loss deduction entered on Line 29a of Form 1120 (Line 25a of Form 1120-A) is the sum of the net operating loss carryovers and carrybacks to the tax year. For a net operating loss arising in a tax year ending during 2001 or 2002, the carryback period is five years. For net operating losses that occur in tax years (1) beginning after August 5, 1997 and ending before 2001 and (2) ending in 2003 and later, the carryback period is two years. The carryforward period for an NOL arising in a tax year beginning after August 5, 1997 is 20 years. The carryforward period for earlier NOLs is 15 years. Special rules apply to farming losses, specified liability losses, excess interest losses, and capital losses.

A corporation may elect to forgo the entire carryback period and to apply the loss during the carryforward period. The irrevocable election to forgo the entire carryback period is made by checking the box on Line 11 of Schedule K, Form 1120, on a timely filed return (including extensions). If the corporation is filing a consolidated return, an election statement must be attached to the return or the election will not be valid. The amount of available NOL carryover from previous tax years is entered on Line 12 of Schedule K. If a corporation claims a net operating loss deduction, a detailed schedule showing the computation of the deduction must be attached to Form 1120.

## ON THE RETURN

The taxpayer (Falcon) on the filled-in return had no net operating loss deduction for 2005.

Generally, for corporate equity reduction transactions (major stock acquisitions and excess distributions), C corporations may be limited in the amount of net operating loss deductions that may be carried back to prior years for interest deductions of one million dollars or more that are allocable to such transactions (Code Sec. 172(b)(1)(E)) and (h)). Limitations also exist on (1) the amount of taxable income of a new loss corporation that may be offset by NOL carryovers from an old loss corporation (Code Sec. 382); and (2) the use of preacquisition losses of one corporation to offset recognized built-in gains of another corporation (Code Sec. 384).

Personal service corporations may not carry back a net operating loss to or from any tax year for which there is an election of a tax year other than a required tax year under Code Sec. 444 (Code Sec. 280H (e)).

- **Schedule K, Other Information**
- **Line 1: Method of Accounting**

The method of accounting used by a corporation is indicated on Schedule K, Line 1, page 3, of Form 1120. Generally, corporations (other than qualified personal service corporations) are required to use the accrual method of accounting if their average annual gross receipts exceed $5 million. Dealers in securities must use the mark-to-market accounting method of Code Sec. 475. For tax years ending after August 5, 1997, dealers in commodities and traders in securities and commodities may elect to use the mark-to-market accounting method.

- **Line 2: Business Classification Activity**

On Line 2a, Schedule K, Form 1120, the principal business activity "code" number is indicated. These are found in the schedule on pages 20-22 of the official instructions for Form 1120. The principal business activity and the product or service are entered on Schedule K, Lines 2b and 2c, respectively.

- **Lines 3, 4, and 5: "Controlled" Corporations**

These lines are intended to help identify related groups of corporations so that they can be audited as a group. The yes box for Line 4, Schedule K should only be checked if the corporation is a subsidiary in an affiliated group but is not filing a consolidated return with that group, or if the corporation is a subsidiary in a parent-subsidiary controlled group.

- **Line 6: Excess Dividends**

The corporation must indicate on Line 6, Schedule K whether it paid dividends in excess of its current and accumulated earnings and profits. If so, Form 5452 (Corporate Report of Nondividend Distributions) must be filed.

- **Line 7: Foreign Ownership**

The corporation must indicate on Line 7, Schedule K whether, at any time during the tax year, one foreign person owned at least 25% of the total voting power of all classes of stock entitled to vote or the total value of all classes of stock. If there is more than one 25%-foreign owner, Line 7 should be completed for the foreign owner with the highest ownership percentage. The percentage owned must be reported as well as the owner's country of residence or incorporation. Form 5472, Information Return of a 25% Foreign-Owned U.S. Corporation or a Foreign Corporation Engaged in a U.S. Trade or Business, may be required.

- **Line 8: Original Issue Discount Debt Instruments**

A corporation that issued publicly offered debt instruments with original issue discount must check the box on Line 8, Schedule K, and may be required to file Form 8281, Information Return for Publicly Offered Original Issue Discount Instruments.

- **Line 9: Tax-Exempt Interest**

Tax-exempt interest received or accrued by a corporation is reported on Line 9, Schedule K. This amount includes any exempt-interest dividends received by a corporation as a shareholder in a mutual fund or other regulated investment company.

- **Line 10: Shareholders**

Corporations that have 100 or fewer shareholders must enter the number of shareholders at the end of the tax year on Line 10, Schedule K.

• **Line 11: Election to Forgo NOL Carryback**

The corporation must indicate on Line 11, Schedule K if it is making an election under Code Sec. 172(b)(3) to forgo the entire carryback period for a net operating loss. A corporation that checks the box is not required to file an election statement that is otherwise required and described by Temp. Reg. §301.9100-12T(d). However, a corporation filing a consolidated return must attach the statement required by Temp. Reg. §1.1502-21T(b)(3)(i) or (ii) or the election will not be valid. Line 11 specifically mentions this requirement for consolidated return filers.

• **Line 12: NOL Carryover**

The corporation must indicate on Line 12, Schedule K the amount of available NOL carryover from prior tax years.

• **Line 13: Exemption from Completing Schedules L, M-1, and M-2**

If a corporation's total receipts (line 1a plus lines 4 through 10 on page 1 of Form 1120 or 1120A) for the tax year and its total assets at the end of the tax year are less than $250,000, line 13 is checked "yes" and Schedules L, M-1, and M-2 do not need to be completed. Instead, the total amount of cash distributions and the book value of property distributions are entered on line 13.

## ¶32 Schedule J - TAX COMPUTATION

The tax of a corporation filing Form 1120 is computed on Form 1120, Schedule J, Tax Computation, which is on page 3 of the return. The tax as computed on this schedule is based on the "taxable income" as reported on Line 30, page 1. The tax as computed on Schedule J, Line 11, is then entered on Line 31, page 1, of Form 1120.

The tax for a corporation that files Form 1120-A is computed in Part I on page 2 of that form, using the "taxable income" on Line 26, page 1, and then entered on Line 27.

A corporation cannot file Form 1120-A if it has any of the "write-in" additions to tax that are reported on Schedule J, Line 3 (income tax) or Line 11 (total tax) of Form 1120.

The method of computing the tax on Schedule J depends on whether the corporation is a member of a controlled group of corporations or a qualified personal service corporation. If a corporation is not a member of a group of controlled corporations and is not a qualified personal service corporation, the tax is computed by applying the corporate tax rates to the amount of taxable income as reported on Line 30, page 1. The resulting tax is then entered on Line 3 of Schedule J.

• **Members of Controlled Groups**

The members of a controlled group of corporations are entitled, in the aggregate, to the benefit of only one amount in each taxable income bracket. The term "controlled group" means any parent-subsidiary group, brother-sister group, or combined group. Therefore, if the members of such a group do not file a consolidated return, they must apportion each income tax bracket amount among themselves for income tax computation purposes. The apportionment can be made in amounts agreed to by the members pursuant to an apportionment plan, or, if no such plan is adopted, the bracket amounts are apportioned equally among the members. A corporation must signify whether it is a member of a controlled group on Line 1 of Schedule J. In addition, a member of a controlled group must enter its portion of each income tax bracket amount on Line 2a of Schedule J.

Members of a controlled group of corporations are entailed to one $50,000, and one $25,000, and one $9,925,000 taxable income bracket amount (in that order) on Line 29. If the additional tax applies, each member of the controlled group must pay that tax based on the portion of the taxable income bracket amount that is used in each taxable income bracket to reduce that member's tax. Each member of the group must enter its share of the additional tax on Line 2b of Schedule J and attach to its tax return a schedule that shows how its portion of the additional tax was computed and that indicates the taxable income of the entire group. Each member of a controlled group should complete the tax computation worksheet that appears on page 16 of the Form 1120 instructions to determine the income tax entered on line 3 of Schedule J.

Members of a controlled group cannot file Form 1120-A.

*Personal service corporations.*—A qualified personal service corporation is taxed at a flat rate of 35% on its taxable income and the box on Line 3 of Schedule J (Line 1, Part 1 of Form 1120-A) should be checked.

*Deferred tax under Code Sec. 1291.*—The tax-deferred amount under Code Sec. 1291(c)(2) of a corporate shareholder in a passive foreign investment company (PFIC) that received an excess distribution or disposed of an investment in such entity during the year (attach Form 8621) is included in the total on Line 3 of Schedule J. Enter "Section 1291" and the amount on the dotted line next to Line 3. Any Code Sec. 1291(c)(3) interest charge is reported as such in the bottom margin of Form 1120, page 1, and not on Line 3, Schedule J.

*Tax on sale of intangibles.*—A corporation that elects to pay tax on the gain from the sale of an intangible under the related person exception to the Code Sec. 197 anti-churning rules (Code Sec. 197(f)(9)(B)) includes any additional tax on Line 3 and should indicate "Section 197" and the amount on the dotted line next to Line 3.

## ¶33 FORM 1120, SCHEDULE L— BALANCE SHEETS

• **Comparative Balance Sheets**

Schedule L, M-1, and M-2 do not need to be completed if the corporation's total receipts for the tax year (Line 1a plus Lines 4 through 10 on page 1 of Form 1120 or 1120A) and its total assets at the end of the tax year (Line 15, column (d) of Schedule L) are less than $250,000. See question 13 on Schedule K.

The taxpayer must show a balance sheet for the first day of the taxable period, January 1 (on a calendar-year basis), and for the last day of the taxable period, December 31 (on a calendar-year basis). The balance sheets should agree with the books. Any differences between the two should be reconciled and explained. It is not necessary to revise the books to state the amount of taxable income. Reconciliation between book income and taxable income may be made as suggested in the Work Sheet on pages 7 and 8 and reflected in Schedule M-1 (see ¶34).

Tax-exempt state and local government securities and stock in a mutual fund or other regulated company that distributed exempt-interest dividends are reported on Line 5 of Schedule L.

For various groups of assets and liabilities in the balance sheet, schedules should be attached to the return. From the Work Sheet on pages 65 and 66, the schedule for "Other Investments," Line 9, would show the following at the end of the tax year:

| | |
|---|---|
| Corporate bonds | $ 22,400 |
| Domestic corporation stock | 97,500 |
| Foreign corporation stock | 8,000 |
| Total | $127,900 |

For an analysis of Lines 10a and 10b for depreciable assets, see ¶24.

The schedule for "Other Assets," Line 14, at the end of the tax year would show:

| | |
|---|---|
| Sinking fund—Bond retirement | $ 50,000 |
| Goodwill, nominal value | 1 |
| Insurance on officers' lives (surrender value) | 8,150 |
| Unamortized bond premium | 1,265 |
| Unamortized bond issue expense | 8,875 |
| Prepaid expenses and supplies | 2,215 |
| Total | $ 70,506 |

The schedule for Line 18, "Other Current Liabilities," for the end of the tax year would show:

| | |
|---|---|
| Accrued interest | $ 2,925 |
| Accrued payroll | 3,328 |
| Accrued vacation pay | 18,910 |
| Accrued capital stock tax (state) | 520 |
| Accrued franchise tax (state) | 300 |
| Accrued state income tax | 135 |
| Accrued federal income tax | 1,230 |
| Accrued foreign income tax | 93 |
| Accrued property taxes (local) | 8,000 |
| Accrued employment taxes | 1,048 |
| Withheld payroll taxes | 3,062 |
| Total | $39,551 |

Similar schedules should be furnished for the beginning balance sheet.

The appropriated retained earnings at the end of 2005 (Line 24, Schedule L) consist of a reserve of $50,000 for sinking fund requirements, $2,544 to cover the cost of treasury stock, and a reserve of $15,000 for contingencies. A schedule should be attached. Adjustments to shareholder equity would be reported on Line 26 (Line 22, Form 1120-A). Examples of these adjustments include: unrealized gains and losses on securities held available for sale, foreign currency translation adjustments, the excess of additional pension liability over unrecognized prior service cost, guarantees of employee stock (ESOP) debt, and compensation related to employee stock award plans. The $2,544 cost of treasury stock is subtracted on Line 27, Schedule L.

## ¶34 FORM 1120-A, PART III, BALANCE SHEETS

A corporation that files Form 1120-A must complete Part III, Balance Sheets unless its total receipts and total assets are less than $250,000. See the discussion for Schedule L of Form 1120, above.

## ¶35 FORM 1120, SCHEDULE M-1— RECONCILIATION OF INCOME PER BOOKS WITH INCOME PER RETURN

Schedule M-1 reconciles book and taxable income; it does not have to be completed if the corporation's total receipts for the tax year (Line 1a plus Lines 4 through 10 on page 1 of Form 1120) and its total assets at the end of the tax year (Line 15, column (d) of Schedule L) are less than $250,000. See question 13 on Schedule K. The items entered on Schedule M-1 are derived from the "Tax Adjustments" column of the Work Sheet at pages 65 and 66.

### ON THE RETURN

On Schedule M-1, the $788 amount on Line 7 of Schedule M-1 represents tax-exempt interest income.

The income tax liability for 2005 is $41,230.

Those expenses that are recorded on the books in computing the profit or loss for the year and that are not deducted or that may not be deducted in arriving at a corporation's taxable income are entered on Line 5 of Schedule M-1. Examples of such items include:

- life insurance premiums paid by the corporation on policies of which the corporation is the beneficiary,
- excess charitable contributions, expenses attributable to earning tax-exempt income, and
- charges that give rise to a foreign tax credit and that were recorded on the books as an expense. The work opportunity credit salary reductions (see ¶15), the "at risk" reduction (see ¶29), and the passive activity loss limitation adjustment on Line 28 of Form 1120 (Line 24 of Form 1120-A) (see ¶30) should be reported on Line 5.

### ON THE RETURN

Falcon Machinery has recorded two items on this line: (1) the $93 foreign tax credit claimed on Line 4a of Schedule J; and (2) $2,573 in life insurance premiums paid on policies covering the lives of the company officers and of which the corporation was the beneficiary.

Certain meal and entertainment amounts entered on Line 5c of Schedule M-1 include:

- the 50% portion of such expenses that are nondeductible (Code Sec. 274(n));
- expenses for the use of an entertainment facility;
- the portion of business gifts exceeding $25;
- cruise ship convention expenses exceeding $2,000 per individual;
- employee achievement awards exceeding $400;
- the cost of entertainment tickets exceeding face value (also subject to the 50% disallowance);
- the cost of skyboxes exceeding the face value of nonluxury box seat tickets;
- the disallowed portion of the cost of luxury water travel;
- expenses for travel as a form of education;
- and other nondeductible travel and entertainment expenses.

All tax deductions that are not recorded in a company's books are entered on line 8a. For example, any differences between book depreciation and tax depreciation is entered here.

### ON THE RETURN

The $100 on Line 8 for Falcon represents the $100 capital loss carryover claimed on its Schedule D. Note that no adjustment is made for the dividends received deduction ($6,111) on line 29b of Form 1120 since Schedule M-1 is used to reconcile taxable income as shown on line 28 of Form 1120.

## ¶36 FORM 1120-A, PART IV— RECONCILIATION OF INCOME PER BOOKS WITH INCOME PER RETURN

A corporation that files Form 1120-A is not required to complete Part III (Balance Sheet per Books) or Part IV (Reconciliation of Income (Loss) per Books With Income per Return) if its total receipts for the tax year (Line 1a plus Lines 4 through 10 on page 1 of Form 1120-A) and its total assets at the end of the tax year (Line 15, column (d) of Schedule L) are less than $250,000.

## ¶37 FORM 1120, SCHEDULE M-2— ANALYSIS OF UNAPPROPRIATED RETAINED EARNINGS PER BOOKS

The figure on Line 1 of Schedule M-2 is the same as the unappropriated retained earnings figure shown for the beginning of the tax year on Schedule L, Line 25, column (b). Any changes should be explained in full. Schedule M-2 need not be completed if the corporation's total receipts for the tax year (Line 1a plus Lines 4 through 10 on page 1 of Form 1120) and its total assets at the end of the tax year (Line 15, column (d) of Schedule L) are less than $250,000. See question 13 on Schedule K.

### ON THE RETURN

The corporation distributed a cash dividend of $26,000 on its common stock, and dividends of 7% ($3,500) were paid on the outstanding preferred stock of $50,000. These are shown on Line 5a, Schedule M-2.

During 2005, retained earnings were appropriated to the sinking fund reserve for bond retirement ($10,000) and the reserve for contingencies ($3,000). The total of $13,000 is entered on Line 6 of Schedule M-2, and a schedule is attached to the return. Beginning year retained earnings shown on Schedule L line 24 column (b) ($54,544) are increased by $13,000 to $67,544 (Line 24 column (d)).

The unappropriated retained earnings reported on Line 8 of Schedule M-2 on page 4 of the return should be the same as the ending balance sheet figure on Line 25(d), Schedule L.

## ¶38 FORM 1120, SCHEDULE M-3—NET INCOME (LOSS) RECONCILIATION FOR CORPORATIONS WITH TOTAL ASSETS OF $10 MILLION OR MORE

Effective for tax years ending on or after December 31, 2004, certain corporations that file Form 1120 are required to complete Schedule M-3, Net Income (Loss) Reconciliation for Corporations With Total Assets of $10 Million or More, in place of Schedule M-1. Schedule M-3 is a 3 page form which includes 18 pages of detailed instructions. Numerous lines require the attachment of explanatory schedules. This Schedule is filed by any corporation (or U.S. consolidated tax group) with total (consolidated) assets of $10 million or more at the end of the corporation's (or U.S. consolidated group's) tax year on Schedule L. A corporation not otherwise required to file Schedule M-3 may do so. A Corporation that files Schedule M-3 should not also file Schedule M-1.

The schedule requires corporations to disclose detailed information about book-tax differences as part of their tax return that will help the IRS identify corporations that may have engaged in abusive tax transactions.

Part I asks questions about the type of financial statement maintained by the corporation and reconciles financial statement net income or loss with the income or loss reported on the income statement for the corporate tax return (or consolidated tax group). Parts II and III reconcile financial statement net income or loss to taxable income reported on Form 1120. Income and loss items, as reported for financial and tax purposes, are identified on Part II, in columns (a) and (d), respectively. Temporary and permanent differences between the two amounts are shown in columns (b) and (c), respectively. Part III, column (a), is used to report expenses shown on the financial statement. The corresponding deduction claimed on the tax return is shown in column (d). Temporary and permanent differences in the amounts are reported in columns (b) and (c), respectively.

For the first tax year that Schedule M-3 is filed, a corporation is not required to complete columns (a) or (d) for Parts II and III.

In the case of a consolidated tax group, multiple Schedule M-3s are prepared and attached to the parent's return. These include: (1) Parts I, II, and II of a Schedule M-1 reflecting Part I information for the entire consolidated group and the parent's activity on Parts II and III; (2) Parts II and III prepared separately for each subsidiary; (3) Parts II and III of a consolidating Schedule M-3 to account for items such as differences between financial statement net income and taxable income related to intercompany transactions and adjustments made at the consolidated group level that are not attributable to any specific member of the group; and (4) one consolidated Schedule M-3 with Parts I, II, and III resulting from consolidating the preceding Schedule M-3s.

| SCHEDULE M-3<br>(Form 1120)<br><br>Department of the Treasury<br>Internal Revenue Service | **Net Income (Loss) Reconciliation for Corporations<br>With Total Assets of $10 Million or More**<br>▶ Attach to Form 1120.<br>▶ See separate instructions. | OMB No. 1545-0123<br><br>20**05** |
|---|---|---|

| Name of corporation (common parent, if consolidated return) | Employer identification number |
|---|---|

**Part I**    **Financial Information and Net Income (Loss) Reconciliation**

**1a** Did the corporation file SEC Form 10-K for its income statement period ending with or within this tax year?

    ☐ **Yes.** Skip lines 1b and 1c and complete lines 2a through 11 with respect to that SEC Form 10-K.

    ☐ **No.** Go to line 1b.

 **b** Did the corporation prepare a certified audited income statement for that period?

    ☐ **Yes.** Skip line 1c and complete lines 2a through 11 with respect to that income statement.

    ☐ **No.** Go to line 1c.

 **c** Did the corporation prepare an income statement for that period?

    ☐ **Yes.** Complete lines 2a through 11 with respect to that income statement.

    ☐ **No.** Skip lines 2a through 3c and enter the corporation's net income (loss) per its books and records on line 4.

**2a** Enter the income statement period:   Beginning  \_\_\_\_\_/\_\_\_\_/\_\_\_\_\_    Ending  \_\_\_\_\_/\_\_\_\_/\_\_\_\_\_

 **b** Has the corporation's income statement been restated for the income statement period on line 2a?

    ☐ **Yes.** (If "Yes," attach an explanation and the amount of each item restated.)

    ☐ **No.**

 **c** Has the corporation's income statement been restated for any of the five income statement periods preceding the period on line 2a?

    ☐ **Yes.** (If "Yes," attach an explanation and the amount of each item restated.)

    ☐ **No.**

**3a** Is any of the corporation's voting common stock publicly traded?

    ☐ **Yes.**

    ☐ **No.** If "No," go to line 4.

 **b** Enter the symbol of the corporation's primary U.S. publicly traded voting common stock . . . . . . . . . . . . . . . . . . . . . . . . . . . .

 **c** Enter the nine-digit CUSIP number of the corporation's primary publicly traded voting common stock . . . . . . . . . . . . . . . . . . . .

| | | |
|---|---|---|
| **4** | Worldwide consolidated net income (loss) from income statement source identified in Part I, line 1 | **4** |
| **5a** | Net income from nonincludible foreign entities (attach schedule) . . . . . . . . . . . | **5a** (       ) |
| **b** | Net loss from nonincludible foreign entities (attach schedule and enter as a positive amount) . . | **5b** |
| **6a** | Net income from nonincludible U.S. entities (attach schedule) . . . . . . . . . . | **6a** (       ) |
| **b** | Net loss from nonincludible U.S. entities (attach schedule and enter as a positive amount) . . . . | **6b** |
| **7a** | Net income of other includible corporations (attach schedule) . . . . . . . . . . | **7a** |
| **b** | Net loss of other includible corporations (attach schedule) . . . . . . . . . . | **7b** (       ) |
| **8** | Adjustment to eliminations of transactions between includible corporations and nonincludible entities (attach schedule) . . . . . . . . . . . . . . . . . . . . . . | **8** |
| **9** | Adjustment to reconcile income statement period to tax year (attach schedule) . . . . . . . | **9** |
| **10** | Other adjustments to reconcile to amount on line 11 (attach schedule) . . . . . . . . . | **10** |
| **11** | **Net income (loss) per income statement of includible corporations.** Combine lines 4 through 10 . . . . . . . . . . . . . . . . . . . . . . . . . . . . . . . | **11** |

For Privacy Act and Paperwork Reduction Act Notice, see the Instructions for Forms 1120 and 1120-A.     Cat. No. 37961C     **Schedule M-3 (Form 1120) 2005**

Schedule M-3 (Form 1120) 2005                                                      Page **2**

| Name of corporation (common parent, if consolidated return) | Employer identification number |
|---|---|

If consolidated return, check applicable box: **(1)** ☐ Consolidated group **(2)** ☐ Parent corporation **(3)** ☐ Consolidated eliminations **(4)** ☐ Subsidiary corporation

| Name of subsidiary (if consolidated return) | Employer identification number |
|---|---|

**Part II** — **Reconciliation of Net Income (Loss) per Income Statement of Includible Corporations With Taxable Income per Return**

| Income (Loss) Items | (a) Income (Loss) per Income Statement | (b) Temporary Difference | (c) Permanent Difference | (d) Income (Loss) per Tax Return |
|---|---|---|---|---|
| 1 Income (loss) from equity method foreign corporations | | | | |
| 2 Gross foreign dividends not previously taxed | | | | |
| 3 Subpart F, QEF, and similar income inclusions | | | | |
| 4 Section 78 gross-up | | | | |
| 5 Gross foreign distributions previously taxed | | | | |
| 6 Income (loss) from equity method U.S. corporations | | | | |
| 7 U.S. dividends not eliminated in tax consolidation | | | | |
| 8 Minority interest for includible corporations | | | | |
| 9 Income (loss) from U.S. partnerships (attach schedule) | | | | |
| 10 Income (loss) from foreign partnerships (attach schedule) | | | | |
| 11 Income (loss) from other pass-through entities (attach schedule) | | | | |
| 12 Items relating to reportable transactions (attach details) | | | | |
| 13 Interest income | | | | |
| 14 Total accrual to cash adjustment | | | | |
| 15 Hedging transactions | | | | |
| 16 Mark-to-market income (loss) | | | | |
| 17 Cost of goods sold | | | | |
| 18 Sale versus lease (for sellers and/or lessors) | | | | |
| 19 Section 481(a) adjustments | | | | |
| 20 Unearned/deferred revenue | | | | |
| 21 Income recognition from long-term contracts | | | | |
| 22 Original issue discount and other imputed interest | | | | |
| 23a Income statement gain/loss on sale, exchange, abandonment, worthlessness, or other disposition of assets other than inventory and pass-through entities | | | | |
| 23b Gross capital gains from Schedule D, excluding amounts from pass-through entities | | | | |
| 23c Gross capital losses from Schedule D, excluding amounts from pass-through entities, abandonment losses, and worthless stock losses | | | | |
| 23d Net gain/loss reported on Form 4797, line 17, excluding amounts from pass-through entities, abandonment losses, and worthless stock losses | | | | |
| 23e Abandonment losses | | | | |
| 23f Worthless stock losses (attach details) | | | | |
| 23g Other gain/loss on disposition of assets other than inventory | | | | |
| 24 Disallowed capital loss in excess of capital gains | | | | |
| 25 Utilization of capital loss carryforward | | | | |
| 26 Other income (loss) items with differences (attach schedule) | | | | |
| 27 **Total income (loss) items.** Combine lines 1 through 26 | | | | |
| 28 **Total expense/deduction items** (from Part III, line 36) | | | | |
| 29 Other income (loss) and expense/deduction items with no differences | | | | |
| 30 **Reconciliation totals.** Combine lines 27 through 29 | | | | |

**Note.** Line 30, column (a), must equal the amount on Part I, line 11, and column (d) must equal Form 1120, page 1, line 28.

Schedule M-3 (Form 1120) 2005

¶ **38**

Schedule M-3 (Form 1120) 2005                                                                        Page **3**

| Name of corporation (common parent, if consolidated return) | Employer identification number |
|---|---|
| | |

If consolidated return, check applicable box: **(1)** ☐ Consolidated group **(2)** ☐ Parent corporation **(3)** ☐ Consolidated eliminations **(4)** ☐ Subsidiary corporation

| Name of subsidiary (if consolidated return) | Employer identification number |
|---|---|
| | |

**Part III**    **Reconciliation of Net Income (Loss) per Income Statement of Includible Corporations With Taxable Income per Return—Expense/Deduction Items**

| Expense/Deduction Items | (a) Expense per Income Statement | (b) Temporary Difference | (c) Permanent Difference | (d) Deduction per Tax Return |
|---|---|---|---|---|
| 1  U.S. current income tax expense | | | | |
| 2  U.S. deferred income tax expense | | | | |
| 3  State and local current income tax expense | | | | |
| 4  State and local deferred income tax expense | | | | |
| 5  Foreign current income tax expense (other than foreign withholding taxes) | | | | |
| 6  Foreign deferred income tax expense | | | | |
| 7  Foreign withholding taxes | | | | |
| 8  Interest expense | | | | |
| 9  Stock option expense | | | | |
| 10  Other equity-based compensation | | | | |
| 11  Meals and entertainment | | | | |
| 12  Fines and penalties | | | | |
| 13  Judgments, damages, awards, and similar costs | | | | |
| 14  Parachute payments | | | | |
| 15  Compensation with section 162(m) limitation | | | | |
| 16  Pension and profit-sharing | | | | |
| 17  Other post-retirement benefits | | | | |
| 18  Deferred compensation | | | | |
| 19  Charitable contribution of cash and tangible property | | | | |
| 20  Charitable contribution of intangible property | | | | |
| 21  Charitable contribution limitation/carryforward | | | | |
| 22  Domestic production activities deduction | | | | |
| 23  Current year acquisition or reorganization investment banking fees | | | | |
| 24  Current year acquisition or reorganization legal and accounting fees | | | | |
| 25  Current year acquisition/reorganization other costs | | | | |
| 26  Amortization/impairment of goodwill | | | | |
| 27  Amortization of acquisition, reorganization, and start-up costs | | | | |
| 28  Other amortization or impairment write-offs | | | | |
| 29  Section 198 environmental remediation costs | | | | |
| 30  Depletion | | | | |
| 31  Depreciation | | | | |
| 32  Bad debt expense | | | | |
| 33  Corporate owned life insurance premiums | | | | |
| 34  Purchase versus lease (for purchasers and/or lessees) | | | | |
| 35  Other expense/deduction items with differences (attach schedule) | | | | |
| 36  **Total expense/deduction items.** Combine lines 1 through 35. Enter here and on Part II, line 28 | | | | |

Schedule M-3 (Form 1120) 2005

 Printed on recycled paper

¶ **38**

A corporation that files Schedule M-3 is deemed to satisfy disclosure obligations under Reg. §1.60111-4(b)(6) for transactions with a significant book-tax difference (that is, transactions involving a book-tax difference in excess of $10 million) (Rev. Proc. 2004-45).

# ¶39 SCHEDULE D—SALES OR EXCHANGES OF CAPITAL ASSETS

Gains and gains on distributions to shareholders of appreciated capital assets and losses from the sale or exchange of capital assets are reported in Parts I and II of separate Form 1120 Schedule D, to the extent that they are recognized for federal income tax purposes. If the net result of Code Sec. 1231 transactions is a gain on Line 7 or 9, Part I, Form 4797, Sales of Business Property, it is carried to Line 7, Part II, Schedule D of Form 1120 and added to the long-term capital gains and losses. See ¶40.

Previously unrecognized gain or loss on a like-kind exchange of property between related persons is generally recognized if either party disposes of the property received within two years (Code Sec. 1031(f)). Certain exchanges of like-kind property are also reported on Schedule D or on Line 16, Part II, Form 4797, whichever applies, even though no gain or loss is recognized.

Form 8824, Like-Kind Exchanges, must be filed for each like-kind exchange. On Schedule D, Form 1120, a short-term gain or loss is entered on Line 3, while a long-term gain or loss is entered on Line 9. If there is a related-party like-kind exchange, a note to that effect is to be made in the top margin.

Gain on the disposition of market discount bonds issued after July 18, 1984, is generally treated as interest income.

An employer may elect not to recognize gain from the sale of certain stock of the employer-corporation to an employee stock ownership plan if such stock was held for at least three years (Code Sec. 1042).

A corporation that sells publicly traded securities at a gain may elect to postpone all or part of the gain if the seller buys stock or a partnership interest in a specialized small business investment company during the 60-day period that begins on the date the securities are sold (Code Sec. 1044).

The basis of stock held by a corporation must be reduced by the nontaxed portion of any extraordinary dividend received with respect to the stock, unless the corporation has held the stock for more than two years. If the aggregate nontaxed portions of the extraordinary dividends exceed the corporate shareholder's basis, the excess is treated as gain from the sale or exchange of such stock. Dividends on certain disqualified preferred stock are treated as extraordinary dividends that require a reduction in stock basis (Code Sec. 1059).

The portion of the load charge incurred to purchase mutual fund shares is not included in the purchaser's basis in computing gain or loss on the sale of the mutual fund shares within 90 days of their purchase if a second acquisition of mutual fund shares is made at a reduced charge under reinvestment rights received in the original purchase (Code Sec. 852(f)).

The required holding period for the treatment of gain or loss on the sale or exchange of a capital asset as long-term capital gain or loss is more than one year (Code Sec. 1222).

- **Short Sales**

Gains or losses from a short sale of property are capital gains or losses if the property used to close the short sale is a capital asset (Code Sec. 1233). Hedging transactions in futures, however, result in ordinary income or ordinary loss (Reg. §1.1221-2). Special rules apply for determining gains and losses on straddles and regulated futures contracts marked to market and reported on Form 6781, Gains and Losses from Section 1256 Contracts and Straddles.

- **Installment Sales**

Form 6252, Installment Sale Income, is used to report gains from the casual sale of real property or personal property (other than inventory) on the installment method. Gains from trade or business property are carried to Form 4797 and gains from capital assets are carried to Schedule D of Form 1120, Line 2 or 8. A corporation may elect out of the installment method by reporting the full amount of the gain from the sale on Schedule D or Form 4797, whichever is applicable.

The installment method may not be used for sales of stock or securities traded on an established securities market or for sales under revolving credit plans (Code Sec. 453(k)).

A special interest charge may apply to installment obligations arising from nondealer dispositions of real or personal property having a sales price of over $150,000 (Code Sec. 453A). If such obligations are outstanding at the close of a tax year, an interest charge is imposed on the tax deferred under the installment method to the extent that the face amount of deferred payments arising from all dispositions of such property during any year exceeds $5 million. The interest charge does not apply to dispositions of farm property. The interest is separately stated on Line 11 of Schedule J, Form 1120 and also included as part of the total tax shown on that line. A corporation must attach a schedule to its return showing how the interest was computed. The interest is deductible by the corporation.

### • Passive Activity Gains and Losses

A closely held or personal service corporation that has a gain or loss from a passive activity may be required to complete Form 8810, Corporate Passive Activity Loss and Credit Limitations, before completing Schedule D.

A capital gain on the sale or exchange of an entire interest in a passive activity in a fully taxable disposition to an unrelated party is reported on Schedule D. The gain (reduced by any current year operating loss from that activity) is also included on Form 8810 if the corporation has other passive activity losses.

Capital losses from a fully taxable disposition of an entire interest in a passive activity to an unrelated party are allowed in full under the passive activity loss rules, but may be subject to capital loss limitations. Such losses are entered on Schedule D and not on Form 8810.

Capital gains and losses from a disposition of less than an entire interest in a passive activity are treated the same as any other passive activity gain or loss. The gain is entered on Schedule D and also on Form 8810 as passive activity income if the corporation has other passive activity losses. The loss is not entered on Schedule D until the passive activity loss allowed is determined on Form 8810.

Allowed losses determined on worksheet 4 in the instructions for Form 8810 are reported as separate short-term or long-term losses in column (f) of Schedule D. A description should be included in column (a) stating that such loss is from Form 8810.

### • Capital Loss Carryovers

Net capital losses sustained by a corporation in a given year are not deductible against the corporation's ordinary income and, accordingly, net capital losses are not reflected in the computation of a corporation's taxable income in the year of the loss. Instead, the amount of capital loss in excess of capital gain may be carried back to the three preceding years and over to the five succeeding years and applied against the capital gains of these years. The carrybacks are limited to an amount which does not cause or increase a net operating loss in the carryback year. All carryovers and carrybacks are treated as short-term capital losses. Carryovers are entered on Line 4, Part I, of Schedule D.

## ¶40 PROPERTY OTHER THAN CAPITAL ASSETS

Gains and losses from the sale or exchange of business property other than capital assets are reported on Form 4797, Sales of Business Property, to the extent that they are recognized for federal income tax purposes. Form 4797 should be used by taxpayers to report:

- The sale or exchange of:
  1. Property used in a taxpayer's trade or business;
  2. Depreciable and amortizable property;
  3. Oil, gas, geothermal, or other mineral properties; and
  4. Code Sec. 126 property.

- The involuntary conversion (from other than casualty or theft) of property used in your trade or business and capital assets held in connection with a trade or business or a transaction entered into for profit.

- The disposition of noncapital assets (other than inventory or property held primarily for sale to customers in the ordinary course of a taxpayer's trade or business).

- The disposition of capital assets not reported on Schedule D

- The gain or loss (including any related recapture) for partners and S corporation shareholders from certain Code Sec. 179 property dispositions by partnerships (other than electing large partnerships) and S corporation.

- The computation of recapture amounts under Code Secs 179 and 280F(b)(2) when the business use of Code Sec. 179 or listed property decreases to 50 percent or less.

Gains and losses from thefts and casualties are reported on Form 4684, Casualties and Thefts.

The amount of loss allowable on an asset used in a passive activity is determined on Form 8810 before it is entered on Form 4797. Gains from assets used in a passive activity are reported on Form 4797 and also on Form 8810 to offset losses from other passive activities.

Gross proceeds from the sale or exchange of real estate that are indicated on Form 1099-S are entered on Line 1, Part I, of Form 4797.

- **Gain from Disposition of Recapture Property**

Where Sec. 1231 business or farm properties are disposed of or involuntarily converted at a gain, part or all of the gain may be recaptured as ordinary income under the following provisions:

- Sec. 1245 (depreciation recapture on tangible personal property),

- Sec. 1250 (depreciation recapture on realty),

- Sec. 1252 (recapture of farmland expenditures),

- Scc. 1254 (recapture of intangible drilling and development costs, expenditures for development of mines and other natural deposits, and mining exploration costs),

- or Sec. 1255 (gain from disposition of cost-sharing payments property). Any such transaction is reported in Part III of Form 4797.

In determining the amount of gain from a disposition on Line 24 of Form 4797, the cost or other basis entered on Line 21 should not reflect deductions for depreciation, amortization, depletion or preproduction expenses; the Code Sec. 179 expense deduction; the investment credit basis reduction; the deduction for qualified clean-fuel vehicle or refueling properly; or deductions claimed under Code Secs. 190 (for removing architectural and transportation barriers), 193 (for tertiary injectant expenses of oil and gas drillers), or former 1253(d)(2) or (3) (as in effect before the enactment of P.L. 103-66) (for payments made in connection with the grant of a franchise, trademark, or trade name). However, the cost or other basis of property should be reduced by the amount of any qualified electric vehicle credit, diesel-powered highway vehicle credit, enhanced oil recovery credit or disabled access credit. The cost or other basis is increased by any qualified electric vehicle recapture amount.

To calculate the amounts reported on Line 22, Form 4797, add (1) preproductive expenses, depreciation, depletion and amortization deductions, (2) Code Sec. 179 expense deduction, (3) the investment credit downward basis adjustment, (4) the deduction for qualified clean-fuel vehicle property or refueling property, (5) deductions claimed under Code Secs. 190, 193, and former 1253(d)(2) or (3), (6) commercial reutilization deduction, (7) basis reduction for the qualified electric vehicle comittee, and (8) basis reduction for employer-provided childcare facility credit.

From this, subtract (1) any investment credit recapture amount, if the basis of the property was reduced when placed in service, (2) any Code Sec. 179 or 280F recapture amount included in gross income in a prior year because the business use of the property dropped to 50% or less, (3) any qualified clean-fuel vehicle property or refueling property deduction required to be recaptured because property became ineligible for the deduction (4) any basis increase for qualified electric vehicle credit recapture, and (5) any basis increase for recapture of the employer-provided child care facility credit. .

For installment sales of personal or real property, all depreciation recapture under Code Secs. 1245 and 1250 (including the recapture of amounts regarding Code Secs. 179 and 291) must be included in income in the year of disposition (Code Sec. 453(i)). Complete Part III of Form 4797 and enter the gain from the installment sale on Lines 30 and 31. The amount entered on Line 31 of Form 4797 is entered on Line 12 of Form 6252, Installment Sale Income, and on Line 13 of Form 4797. Generally, Code Sec. 1245 recaptures depreciation as ordinary income up to the amount of gain.

The amount recaptured when the business use of Sec. 179 property is reduced to 50% or less is determined in column (a), Lines 33 through 35, of Part IV of Form 4797. The Sec. 179 expense previously deducted is entered on Line 33 of Part IV. The depreciation deduction that would have been allowed on the Sec. 179 amount from the time it was placed in service until the current year is entered on Line 34 of Part IV and is subtracted from the amount on Line 33. The remainder, which represents the amount recaptured as ordinary income, is reported on Line 35 of Part IV and on Line 10 of Form 1120 or Form 1120-A.

The amount recaptured under Code Sec. 280F when the business use of property subject to Sec. 280F drops to 50% or less during the current year is determined in column (b), Lines 33 through 35 of Part IV of Form 4797. The recovery deduction previously allowed on Sec. 280F property is entered on Line 33 of Part IV. The depreciation that would have been allowed in previous years if the property had not been predominantly used in a trade or business is entered on Line 34 of Part IV and is subtracted from the amount on Line 33. The remainder, which represents the amount recaptured as ordinary income, is reported on Line 35 of Part IV and on Line 10 of Form 1120 or Form 1120-A.

Generally, Code Sec. 1250 recaptures accelerated depreciation as ordinary income up to the amount of gain. For corporations subject to the Sec. 291 reductions, and where there is a disposition of Sec. 1250 property depreciated under an accelerated method, the amount subject to recapture as ordinary income is 20% of the excess, if any, of the amount that would be treated as ordinary income if such property was Sec. 1245 property, over the amount treated as ordinary income under Sec. 1250. If the straight-line method of depreciation was used, the ordinary income under Sec. 291 subject to recapture is 20% of the amount figured under Sec. 1245. The appropriate amount is then entered on Line 26(f) of Form 4797.

The total recapture on Line 31, Part III, page 2, of Form 4797 is entered on Line 13, Part II, page 1, of Form 4797 and treated as ordinary income.

Where the gain exceeds the recapture under Sec. 1245, 1250, 1252, 1254, or 1255, the excess gain is treated as a Sec. 1231 gain and is included with other Sec. 1231 transactions in determining whether there is a net gain or loss from them. See the discussion below on Sec. 1231 transactions.

## ON THE RETURN

Falcon Machinery Corp. had no dispositions of either Sec. 1245 or Sec. 1250 property in 2005. Accordingly, Part III, page 2, of Form 4797 is not reproduced. However, a filled-in Part III, Form 4797, is illustrated for an S corporation. Also, Falcon Machinery Corp. did not have any nonrecaptured net Sec. 1231 losses from previous tax years.

- **Gains and Losses from Casualties and Thefts**

Gains or losses that are realized or sustained on thefts of or casualties involving Code Sec. 1231 property can be reported on Form 4797, Sales of Business Property, on Form 4684, Casualties and Thefts, and in many cases, on both forms. Casualty and theft losses of personal assets (those not held in a trade or business or for investment) are excluded from the operation of Code Sec. 1231.

If the property is recapture property of the types discussed above and a gain results, the casualty or theft is first reported in Part III of Form 4797. The portion of the gain from the theft or casualty that qualifies for capital gain treatment under Code Sec. 1231, as determined on Line 32, Part III, Form 4797, is carried over to Form 4684 where it is entered on Section B, Part II, Line 33. This gain is combined with other casualty or theft gains and losses from business property on Form 4684.

In all other cases, gains or losses from thefts and casualties are reported on Form 4684 on an item-by-item basis in Section A for personal use property or in Section B, Part I, for business and income-producing property. This rule applies to gains and losses realized or sustained on Code Sec. 1231 business property, other than gains realized on recapture property and losses sustained on recapture property. The gain or loss from each business or income-producing property is computed in Section B, Part I.

Once determined, the gains and losses are carried over to Section B, Part II, of Form 4684 and separated into those involving short-term property (Lines 32–35) and those involving long-term property (Lines 36–42). Losses from thefts and casualties are further broken down into those involving (1) trade or business, rental or royalty property and (2) income-producing property. Gains are not similarly separated.

Gains and losses from casualties or thefts of short-term property are listed on Line 33 of Section B, Part II of Form 4684, totaled on Line 34, and combined or netted on Line 35 by applying the total losses from business property against total gains. The net gain or loss from Line 35, Form 4684, is then carried over to Form 4797, where it is entered on Line 14 of Part II. However, if Form 4797 does not otherwise have to be filed, then the net gain or loss can be entered on Form 1120, page 1, Line 9, with the notation "Form 4684." Such a net gain or loss is an ordinary gain or loss.

Gains and losses from casualties and thefts of long-term property are listed in Section B, Part II on Line 37 of Form 4684, the gains from recapture property as determined on Form 4797 are reported on Line 36, the losses are totalled on Line 38 and the combined losses are further reported on Line 40, and the total gains are reported on Line 39. The total gains are then netted against the total losses from business, etc., property. If this produces a net loss, the loss is entered on Line 41a of Form 4684 and is carried over and reported on Form 4797, Part II, Line 14 as an ordinary loss. If Form 4797 is not otherwise required, the loss is reported on Form 1120, page 1, Line 9, with the notation "Form 4684." If a net gain is produced, it is reported on Line 42 of Form 4684 and is carried over and reported on Form 4797, Part I, Line 3 as a gain from a Sec. 1231 asset held for more than one year which is eligible for long-term capital gain treatment.

A disaster loss may, at the election of the taxpayer, be deducted for the tax year immediately before the disaster if it occurred in a federal disaster area (Code Sec. 165(i)).

## ON THE RETURN

Falcon Machinery Corp. sustained a loss from the destruction of a shed by fire in February 2005. This loss is computed on Form 4684 (page 2) and would be carried over to Form 4797.

### • Amount of Casualty or Theft Loss

The amount of the loss from a complete destruction of or damage to business or income-producing property is the basis of the property, adjusted for depreciation and other items up to the date of the loss, minus any insurance or other compensation received for the property.

If there is only a partial destruction or taking, the amount of the loss that is deductible is limited to the difference between the value of the property immediately preceding the casualty and its value immediately thereafter, but not in excess of the adjusted basis of the property, and is further reduced by any insurance or other compensation received.

If the property is covered by insurance, a timely claim for reimbursement must be filed. Otherwise, this loss cannot be deducted as a casualty or theft loss. However, the portion of the loss that is not covered by insurance remains deductible.

Reconstruction or repairs generally do not affect the computation of the loss. The procedure is to subtract from the old adjusted basis the insurance (or other

compensation) and the amount of the loss deduction, and then increase this new basis to reflect the cost of restoration.

If the insurance or other compensation received exceeds the basis, there is a taxable gain. The taxpayer may elect, however, to replace the property and have the gain not recognized under Code Sec. 1033. Special rules apply to property damaged in Presidentially-declared disasters (Code Sec. 1033(h)).

### • Gains and Losses from Section 1231 Transactions

Real property and depreciable personal property used in a trade or business and held more than one year are Sec. 1231 assets, not capital assets. If a net gain results from the sale, exchange, or involuntary conversion of Sec. 1231 assets, the gains and losses are treated as long-term capital gains and losses. If a net loss results, they are treated as ordinary gains and losses.

The determination of whether a net Code Sec. 1231 gain or loss results is made in Part I, Form 4797. Net gains arising from casualties and thefts, as computed on Form 4684, Section B, Line 39, are entered on Line 3, Part I, Form 4797. The net gains, if any, from dispositions of recapture property from Line 32, Part III, Form 4797, are entered on Line 6 of Part I.

If there is a net Code Sec. 1231 gain on Line 7, Part I, Form 4797, any nonrecaptured net Sec. 1231 losses for the previous five tax years that are reported on Line 8 are recaptured as ordinary income to the extent of such net Sec. 1231 gain. The losses are recaptured on a first-in, first-out basis, and the amount recaptured is carried over to Line 12, Part II, Form 4797. Nonrecaptured net Sec. 1231 losses do not include the excess of recognized losses over gains arising from casualty, theft or involuntary conversions of business property or long-term capital gain assets used in a business or for the production of income. Any remaining net Sec. 1231 gain is treated as long-term capital gain and entered on Line 9, Form 4797 and Line 7, Schedule D, Form 1120.

If there is a net Code Sec. 1231 gain on Line 7, Part I, Form 4797, and there are no prior year net Sec. 1231 losses, the gain is entered on Line 7 of Schedule D of Form 1120 as a long-term capital gain (see ¶39 above). If there is a net Code Sec. 1231 loss on Line 7, it is entered as an ordinary loss on Line 11, Part II, Form 4797.

## ON THE RETURN

Falcon Machinery Corp. had only one Code Sec. 1231 transaction—a $17,288 gain realized on the sale of land. This would be reported on Line 2 of Part I, Form 4797, totaled on Line 7 of Part I, Form 4797, and then carried to Line 7, Part II, Schedule D, Form 1120, as a long-term capital gain. Form 4797 is not reproduced here.

- **Ordinary Gains and Losses**

If a gain or loss results from the sale, exchange or involuntary conversion of property other than a capital asset or Sec. 1231 property, it is reported in Part II, Form 4797. This includes short-term gains and losses on sales, exchanges, and involuntary conversions (other than thefts and casualties) of property used in a trade or business.

These gains and losses are combined with (1) any net casualty and theft losses and gains carried from Lines 31 and 38a, Section B, of Form 4684, (2) any net Sec. 1231 gain or loss brought from Line 7, Part I, Form 4797, (3) any ordinary income recaptures transferred from Line 31, Part III, Form 4797, (4) ordinary gain from installment sales from Line 25 or 36 of Form 6252, (5) any recapture of prior years' nonrecaptured net Sec. 1231 losses from Line 8, Part I, Form 4797, and (6) any recapture income from like-kind exchanges from Line 21, Part III, Form 8824. The net ordinary gain or loss resulting on Line 18, Part II, Form 4797, is entered on Line 9, page 1, Form 1120 or Line 9, page 1, Form 1120-A.

## ON THE RETURN

Falcon Machinery Corp. would report its casualty loss from Form 4684 on Form 4797, Part II, Line 18 and Form 1120, Line 9. Form 4797 is not reproduced here.

WORKSHEET—Falcon Machinery Corp.—Calendar year 2005

| Account | Balances (per books) Dr. | Cr. | Tax Adjustments (Schedules M-1, M-2) Dr. | Cr. | Taxable Net Income Dr. | Cr. | Balance Sheet (Schedule L) Dr. | Cr. |
|---|---|---|---|---|---|---|---|---|
| Cash | 196,180 | | | | | | 196,180 | |
| Accounts receivable | 61,159 | | | | | | 61,159 | |
| Notes receivable | 11,100 | | | | | | 11,100 | |
| Inventories | 333,894 | | | | | | 333,894 | |
| Corporate bonds | 22,400 | | | | | | 22,400 | |
| State and municipal bonds | 30,000 | | | | | | 30,000 | |
| Treasury bonds | 48,000 | | | | | | 48,000 | |
| Stock: | | | | | | | | |
|     Domestic corporations | 97,500 | | | | | | 97,500 | |
|     Foreign corporations | 8,000 | | | | | | 8,000 | |
| Land | 25,500 | | | | | | 25,500 | |
| Buildings | 670,500 | | | | | | 670,500 | |
| Machinery | 434,892 | | | | | | 434,892 | |
| Office furniture | 30,629 | | | | | | 30,629 | |
| Trucks | 45,264 | | | | | | 45,264 | |
| Sinking fund—Bond retirement | 50,000 | | | | | | 50,000 | |
| Goodwill | 1 | | | | | | 1 | |
| Insurance on officers' lives | 8,150 | | | | | | 8,150 | |
| Prepaid expenses | 2,215 | | | | | | 2,215 | |
| Unamortized bond premium | 1,265 | | | | | | 1,265 | |
| Unamortized bond issue expense | 8,875 | | | | | | 8,875 | |
| Accounts payable | | 36,075 | | | | | | 36,075 |
| Notes payable (short-term) | | 30,000 | | | | | | 30,000 |
| Accrued interest | | 2,925 | | | | | | 2,925 |
| Accrued payroll | | 3,328 | | | | | | 3,328 |
| Accrued vacation pay | | 18,910 | | | | | | 18,910 |
| Accrued taxes: | | | | | | | | |
|     Capital stock (state) | | 520 | | | | | | 520 |
|     Franchise (state) | | 300 | | | | | | 300 |
|     Income (state) | | 135 | | | | | | 135 |
|     Income (Federal) | | | (8) 1,230 | | | | | 1,230 |
|     Income (foreign) | | 93 | | | | | | 93 |
|     Property (state) | | 8,000 | | | | | | 8,000 |
|     Employment | | 1,048 | | | | | | 1,048 |
| Withheld payroll taxes | | 3,062 | | | | | | 3,062 |
| Bonds payable (long-term) | | 552,403 | | | | | | 552,403 |
| Reserves: | | | | | | | | |
|     Depreciation | | 592,608 | | | | | | 592,608 |
| Capital stock: | | | | | | | | |
|     7% Preferred | | 50,000 | | | | | | 50,000 |
|     Common | | 435,000 | | | | | | 435,000 |
| Surplus—Paid-in | | 20,000 | | | | | | 20,000 |
| Sales | | 1,646,691 | | | | 1,646,691 | | |
| Returns and allowances | 36,395 | | | | 36,395 | | | |
| Purchases (net) | 422,133 | | | | 422,133 | | | |
| Inventory variation (decrease) | 21,346 | | | | 21,346 | | | |
| Factory wages | 149,613 | | | | 149,613 | | | |

*WORKSHEET—Falcon Machinery Corp.—Calendar year 2005 (page 2)*

| Account | Balances (per books) Dr. | Cr. | Tax Adjustments (Schedules M-1, M-2) Dr. | Cr. | Taxable Net Income Dr. | Cr. | Balance Sheet (Schedule L) Dr. | Cr. |
|---|---|---|---|---|---|---|---|---|
| Depreciation | 8,738 | | | | 8,738 | | | |
| Advertising | 25,815 | | | | 25,815 | | | |
| Bad debts | 3,923 | | | | 3,923 | | | |
| Heat, light (office) | 9,720 | | | | 9,720 | | | |
| Insurance (officers' lives) | 2,573 | | | (1) 2,573 | | | | |
| Office salaries | 82,392 | | | | 82,392 | | | |
| Officers' compensation | 126,000 | | | | 126,000 | | | |
| Pensions | 10,000 | | | | 10,000 | | | |
| Travel expense | 6,850 | | | | 6,850 | | | |
| Salesmen's compensation | 91,703 | | | | 91,703 | | | |
| Legal and accounting fees | 12,500 | | | | 12,500 | | | |
| Service guaranties | 8,252 | | | | 8,252 | | | |
| Interest expense | 22,000 | | | | 22,000 | | | |
| Printing, mailing, etc. expense | 5,115 | | | | 5,115 | | | |
| Amortized bond issue expense | 700 | | | | 700 | | | |
| Health plan costs | 20,700 | | | | 20,700 | | | |
| Costs attributable to inventory | 424,441 | | | | 424,441 | | | |
| **Taxes:** | | | | | | | | |
|     Capital stock (state) | 520 | | | | 520 | | | |
|     Franchise (state) | 300 | | | | 300 | | | |
|     Property (state) | 8,000 | | | | 8,000 | | | |
|     Employment | 25,491 | | | | 25,491 | | | |
|     Income (foreign) | 93 | | | (2) 93 | | | | |
|     Income (state) | 4,320 | | | | 4,320 | | | |
|     Income (Federal) | 40,000 | | | (8) 40,000 | | | | |
| **Interest income:** | | | | | | | | |
|     Corporate bonds | | 1,426 | (7) 142 | | | 1,284 | | |
|     State and municipal bonds | | 788 | (3) 788 | | | | | |
|     Treasury bonds | | 7,125 | | | | 7,125 | | |
|     Notes receivable | | 2,300 | | | | 2,300 | | |
|     Trade accounts | | 770 | | | | 770 | | |
| Dividends received (domestic) | | 8,730 | | | | 8,730 | | |
| Dividends received (foreign) | | 240 | | | | 240 | | |
| Rental income | | 15,000 | | | | 15,000 | | |
| Sale of scrap | | 411 | | | | 411 | | |
| Securities sales (net) | | 1,758 | (6) 100 | | | 1,658 | | |
| Real estate and equipment sales (net) | | 17,288 | | | | 17,288 | | |
| Worthless stocks | 12,500 | | | | 12,500 | | | |
| Fire loss | 4,764 | | | | 4,764 | | | |
| Amortized bond premium | 142 | | | (7) 142 | | | | |
| Contributions | 2,250 | | | | 2,250 | | | |
| Appropriated retained earnings | | 67,544 | | | | | | 67,544 |
| Unappropriated retained earnings | | 182,379 | (1) 2,573 | (3) 788 | | | | 264,887 |
| | | | (2) 93 | (5) 155,016 | | | | |
| | | | (4) 29,500 | (6) 100 | | | | |
| | | | (8) 41,230 | | | | | |
| Treasury stock | 2,544 | | | | | | 2,544 | |
|     Common stock dividends | 3,500 | | | (4) 3,500 | | | | |
|     Preferred stock dividends | 26,000 | | | (4) 26,000 | | | | |
| Taxable income (line 30, page 1, Form 1120) | | | (5)155,016 | | 155,016 | | | |
| Totals | $3,706,857 | $3,706,857 | $229,442 | $229,442 | $1,701,497 | $1,701,497 | $2,088,068 | $2,088,068 |

Form **1120** Department of the Treasury Internal Revenue Service

# U.S. Corporation Income Tax Return

For calendar year 2005 or tax year beginning .............., 2005, ending .............., 20 ....
▶ See separate instructions.

OMB No. 1545-0123 **2005**

A Check if:
1 Consolidated return (attach Form 851) ☐
2 Personal holding co. (attach Sch. PH) ☐
3 Personal service corp. (see instructions) ☐
4 Schedule M-3 required (attach Sch. M-3) ☐

Use IRS label. Otherwise, print or type.

Name: **Falcon Machinery Corp**
Number, street, and room or suite no. If a P.O. box, see instructions.: **271 Beaumont Street**
City or town, state, and ZIP code: **Chicago, Il 60612**

B Employer identification number: **35:081630**
C Date incorporated: **07/01/74**
D Total assets (see instructions): $ **1,492,916 00**

E Check if: (1) ☐ Initial return (2) ☐ Final return (3) ☐ Name change (4) ☐ Address change

| | Line | Description | | Amount |
|---|---|---|---|---|
| Income | 1a | Gross receipts or sales 1,646,691 00 b Less returns and allowances 36,395 00 c Bal ▶ | 1c | 1,610,296 00 |
| | 2 | Cost of goods sold (Schedule A, line 8) | 2 | 1,017,533 00 |
| | 3 | Gross profit. Subtract line 2 from line 1c | 3 | 592,763 00 |
| | 4 | Dividends (Schedule C, line 19) | 4 | 8,970 00 |
| | 5 | Interest | 5 | 11,479 00 = 11621 - 142 (Int. Inc.; Premium Amort.) |
| | 6 | Gross rents | 6 | 15,000 00 |
| | 7 | Gross royalties | 7 | |
| | 8 | Capital gain net income (attach Schedule D (Form 1120)) | 8 | 6,446 00 |
| | 9 | Net gain or (loss) from Form 4797, Part II, line 17 (attach Form 4797) | 9 | (4,764) 00 |
| | 10 | Other income (see instructions—attach schedule) | 10 | 411 00 |
| | 11 | **Total income.** Add lines 3 through 10 ▶ | 11 | 630,305 00 |
| Deductions (See instructions for limitations on deductions.) | 12 | Compensation of officers (Schedule E, line 4) | 12 | 126,000 00 |
| | 13 | Salaries and wages (less employment credits) | 13 | 174,095 00 |
| | 14 | Repairs and maintenance | 14 | |
| | 15 | Bad debts | 15 | 3,923 00 |
| | 16 | Rents | 16 | |
| | 17 | Taxes and licenses | 17 | 38,631 00 |
| | 18 | Interest | 18 | 22,000 00 |
| | 19 | Charitable contributions (see instructions for 10% limitation) | 19 | 2,250 00 |
| | 20a | Depreciation (attach Form 4562) — 20a 220,492 00 | | |
| | b | Less depreciation claimed on Schedule A and elsewhere on return — 20b 211,754 00 | 20c | 8,738 00 |
| | 21 | Depletion | 21 | |
| | 22 | Advertising | 22 | 25,815 00 |
| | 23 | Pension, profit-sharing, etc., plans | 23 | 10,000 00 |
| | 24 | Employee benefit programs | 24 | 20,700 00 |
| | 25 | Domestic production activities deduction (attach Form 8903) | 25 | |
| | 26 | Other deductions (attach schedule) | 26 | 43,137 00 |
| | 27 | **Total deductions.** Add lines 12 through 26 ▶ | 27 | 475,289 00 |
| | 28 | Taxable income before net operating loss deduction and special deductions. Subtract line 27 from line 11 | 28 | 155,016 00 |
| | 29 | **Less:** a Net operating loss deduction (see instructions) — 29a | | |
| | | b Special deductions (Schedule C, line 20) — 29b 6,111 00 | 29c | 6,111 00 |
| Tax and Payments | 30 | **Taxable income.** Subtract line 29c from line 28 (see instructions if Schedule C, line 12, was completed) | 30 | 148,905 00 |
| | 31 | **Total tax** (Schedule J, line 11) | 31 | 41,230 00 |
| | 32 | **Payments:** a 2004 overpayment credited to 2005 — 32a | | |
| | b | 2005 estimated tax payments — 32b 40,000 00 | | |
| | c | Less 2005 refund applied for on Form 4466 — 32c ( ) d Bal ▶ 32d 40,000 00 | | |
| | e | Tax deposited with Form 7004 — 32e | | |
| | f | Credits: (1) Form 2439 (2) Form 4136 — 32f | 32g | 40,000 00 |
| | 33 | Estimated tax penalty (see instructions). Check if Form 2220 is attached ▶ ☐ | 33 | |
| | 34 | **Tax due.** If line 32g is smaller than the total of lines 31 and 33, enter amount owed | 34 | 1,230 00 |
| | 35 | **Overpayment.** If line 32g is larger than the total of lines 31 and 33, enter amount overpaid | 35 | |
| | 36 | Enter amount of line 35 you want: **Credited to 2006 estimated tax** ▶ **Refunded** ▶ | 36 | |

**Sign Here** Under penalties of perjury, I declare that I have examined this return, including accompanying schedules and statements, and to the best of my knowledge and belief, it is true, correct, and complete. Declaration of preparer (other than taxpayer) is based on all information of which preparer has any knowledge.

Signature of officer ____ Date ____ Title: **Secretary-Treasurer**

May the IRS discuss this return with the preparer shown below (see instructions)? ☑ Yes ☐ No

**Paid Preparer's Use Only**
Preparer's signature ▶ Date ____ Check if self-employed ☑ Preparer's SSN or PTIN: **311-62-4121**
Firm's name (or yours if self-employed), address, and ZIP code ▶ **John Service**, **1510 Steward Bldg., Chicago, IL 60072** EIN ____ Phone no. ( **847** ) **012-0612**

For Privacy Act and Paperwork Reduction Act Notice, see separate instructions. Cat. No. 11450Q Form **1120** (2005)

Form 1120 (2005)          Page **2**

### Schedule A — Cost of Goods Sold (see instructions)

| # | | Amount | |
|---|---|---:|---|
| 1 | Inventory at beginning of year | 355,240 | 00 |
| 2 | Purchases | 422,133 | 00 |
| 3 | Cost of labor | 149,613 | 00 |
| 4 | Additional section 263A costs (attach schedule) | | |
| 5 | Other costs (attach schedule) | 424,441 | 00 |
| 6 | **Total.** Add lines 1 through 5 | 1,351,427 | 00 |
| 7 | Inventory at end of year | 333,894 | 00 |
| 8 | **Cost of goods sold.** Subtract line 7 from line 6. Enter here and on page 1, line 2 | 1,017,533 | 00 |

**9a** Check all methods used for valuing closing inventory:

(i) ☐ Cost

(ii) ☑ Lower of cost or market

(iii) ☐ Other (Specify method used and attach explanation.) ▶ --------------------------------------------

**b** Check if there was a writedown of subnormal goods . . . . . . . . . . . . . . . . ▶ ☐

**c** Check if the LIFO inventory method was adopted this tax year for any goods (if checked, attach Form 970) . . . . . . ▶ ☐

**d** If the LIFO inventory method was used for this tax year, enter percentage (or amounts) of closing inventory computed under LIFO . . . . . . . . . . . . . . . |9d| |

**e** If property is produced or acquired for resale, do the rules of section 263A apply to the corporation? . . . . . ☑ Yes ☐ No

**f** Was there any change in determining quantities, cost, or valuations between opening and closing inventory? If "Yes," attach explanation . . . . . . . . . . . . . . . . . . . . . . . ☐ Yes ☑ No

### Schedule C — Dividends and Special Deductions (see instructions)

| # | | (a) Dividends received | (b) % | (c) Special deductions (a) × (b) |
|---|---|---:|---:|---:|
| 1 | Dividends from less-than-20%-owned domestic corporations (other than debt-financed stock) | 8,730 | 70 | 6,111 |
| 2 | Dividends from 20%-or-more-owned domestic corporations (other than debt-financed stock) | | 80 | |
| 3 | Dividends on debt-financed stock of domestic and foreign corporations | | see instructions | |
| 4 | Dividends on certain preferred stock of less-than-20%-owned public utilities | | 42 | |
| 5 | Dividends on certain preferred stock of 20%-or-more-owned public utilities | | 48 | |
| 6 | Dividends from less-than-20%-owned foreign corporations and certain FSCs | | 70 | |
| 7 | Dividends from 20%-or-more-owned foreign corporations and certain FSCs | | 80 | |
| 8 | Dividends from wholly owned foreign subsidiaries | | 100 | |
| 9 | **Total.** Add lines 1 through 8. See instructions for limitation | | | 6,111 |
| 10 | Dividends from domestic corporations received by a small business investment company operating under the Small Business Investment Act of 1958 | | 100 | |
| 11 | Dividends from affiliated group members and certain FSCs | | 100 | |
| 12 | Dividends from controlled foreign corporations (attach Form 8895) | | 85 | |
| 13 | Dividends from foreign corporations not included on lines 3, 6, 7, 8, 11, or 12 | 240 | | |
| 14 | Income from controlled foreign corporations under subpart F (attach Form(s) 5471) | | | |
| 15 | Foreign dividend gross-up | | | |
| 16 | IC-DISC and former DISC dividends not included on lines 1, 2, or 3 | | | |
| 17 | Other dividends | | | |
| 18 | Deduction for dividends paid on certain preferred stock of public utilities | | | |
| 19 | **Total dividends.** Add lines 1 through 17. Enter here and on page 1, line 4 ▶ | 8,970 | | |
| 20 | **Total special deductions.** Add lines 9, 10, 11, 12, and 18. Enter here and on page 1, line 29b . . . . . ▶ | | | 6,111 |

### Schedule E — Compensation of Officers (see instructions for page 1, line 12)

**Note:** *Complete Schedule E only if total receipts (line 1a plus lines 4 through 10 on page 1) are $500,000 or more.*

| (a) Name of officer | (b) Social security number | (c) Percent of time devoted to business | (d) Common | (e) Preferred | (f) Amount of compensation |
|---|---|---|---|---|---:|
| 1 F.L. Davis | 252-67-8315 | 100 % | 15 % | % | 54,000 |
| B.L. West | 269-40-7222 | 100 % | 10 % | % | 41,500 |
| T.N. Dorst | 307-31-3433 | 100 % | 10 % | % | 38,944 |
| | | % | % | % | |
| | | % | % | % | |

| # | | Amount |
|---|---|---:|
| 2 | Total compensation of officers | 134,444 |
| 3 | Compensation of officers claimed on Schedule A and elsewhere on return | 8,444 |
| 4 | Subtract line 3 from line 2. Enter the result here and on page 1, line 12 | 126,000 |

Form **1120** (2005)

Form 1120 (2005)     Page **3**

## Schedule J   Tax Computation (see instructions)

| | | | | |
|---|---|---|---|---|
| 1 | Check if the corporation is a member of a controlled group . . . . . . . . . . . ▶ ☐ | | | |
| | **Important:** Members of a controlled group, see instructions. | | | |
| 2a | If the box on line 1 is checked, enter the corporation's share of the $50,000, $25,000, and $9,925,000 taxable income brackets (in that order): | | | |
| | (1) $ \_\_\_\_\_    (2) $ \_\_\_\_\_    (3) $ \_\_\_\_\_ | | | |
| b | Enter the corporation's share of: (1) Additional 5% tax (not more than $11,750) $ \_\_\_\_\_ | | | |
| | (2) Additional 3% tax (not more than $100,000) $ \_\_\_\_\_ | | | |
| 3 | Income tax. Check if a qualified personal service corporation (see instructions) . . . . ▶ ☐ | **3** | 41,323 | 00 |
| 4 | Alternative minimum tax (attach Form 4626) . . . . . . . . | **4** | 0 | |
| 5 | Add lines 3 and 4 . . . . . . . . . . . . . . . . | **5** | | |
| 6a | Foreign tax credit (attach Form 1118) . . . . | 6a | | |
| b | Possessions tax credit (attach Form 5735) . . . . | 6b | | |
| c | Credits from: ☐ Form 8834   ☐ Form 8907, line 23 . . . . | 6c | | |
| d | General business credit. Check box(es) and indicate which forms are attached: ☐ Form 3800   ☐ Form(s) (specify) ▶ \_\_\_\_\_ | 6d | | |
| e | Credit for prior year minimum tax (attach Form 8827) . . . . | 6e | | |
| f | Bond credits from: ☐ Form 8860   ☐ Form 8912 . . . . | 6f | | |
| 7 | **Total credits.** Add lines 6a through 6f . . . . . . . . | **7** | 93 | 00 |
| 8 | Subtract line 7 from line 5 . . . . . . . | **8** | 41,230 | 00 |
| 9 | Personal holding company tax (attach Schedule PH (Form 1120)) . . . . | **9** | | |
| 10 | Other taxes. Check if from: ☐ Form 4255 ☐ Form 8611 ☐ Form 8697 ☐ Form 8866 ☐ Form 8902 ☐ Other (attach schedule) . . | **10** | | |
| 11 | **Total tax.** Add lines 8 through 10. Enter here and on page 1, line 31 . . . . . . | **11** | 41,230 | 00 |

## Schedule K   Other Information (see instructions)

| | | Yes | No |
|---|---|---|---|
| 1 | Check accounting method:   a ☐ Cash   b ☑ Accrual   c ☐ Other (specify) ▶ \_\_\_\_\_ | | |
| 2 | See the instructions and enter the: | | |
| a | Business activity code no. ▶ \_\_\_\_ 339990 \_\_\_\_ | | |
| b | Business activity ▶ **Manufacturing** | | |
| c | Product or service ▶ **Office Supplies** | | |
| 3 | At the end of the tax year, did the corporation own, directly or indirectly, 50% or more of the voting stock of a domestic corporation? (For rules of attribution, see section 267(c).) . . . . . . . . . | | ✔ |
| | If "Yes," attach a schedule showing: (a) name and employer identification number (EIN), (b) percentage owned, and (c) taxable income or (loss) before NOL and special deductions of such corporation for the tax year ending with or within your tax year. | | |
| 4 | Is the corporation a subsidiary in an affiliated group or a parent-subsidiary controlled group? . . . . . . | | ✔ |
| | If "Yes," enter name and EIN of the parent corporation ▶ \_\_\_\_\_ | | |
| 5 | At the end of the tax year, did any individual, partnership, corporation, estate, or trust own, directly or indirectly, 50% or more of the corporation's voting stock? (For rules of attribution, see section 267(c).) . . . . . . | | ✔ |
| | If "Yes," attach a schedule showing name and identifying number. (Do not include any information already entered in 4 above.) Enter percentage owned ▶ \_\_\_\_\_ | | |
| 6 | During this tax year, did the corporation pay dividends (other than stock dividends and distributions in exchange for stock) in excess of the corporation's current and accumulated earnings and profits? (See sections 301 and 316.) . . | | ✔ |
| | If "Yes," file **Form 5452,** Corporate Report of Nondividend Distributions. | | |
| | If this is a consolidated return, answer here for the parent corporation and on **Form 851,** Affiliations Schedule, for each subsidiary. | | |

| | | Yes | No |
|---|---|---|---|
| 7 | At any time during the tax year, did one foreign person own, directly or indirectly, at least 25% of (a) the total voting power of all classes of stock of the corporation entitled to vote or (b) the total value of all classes of stock of the corporation? . . . . . . . . . . | | ✔ |
| | If "Yes," enter: (a) Percentage owned ▶ \_\_\_\_\_ and (b) Owner's country ▶ \_\_\_\_\_ | | |
| c | The corporation may have to file **Form 5472,** Information Return of a 25% Foreign-Owned U.S. Corporation or a Foreign Corporation Engaged in a U.S. Trade or Business. Enter number of Forms 5472 attached ▶ \_\_\_\_\_ | | |
| 8 | Check this box if the corporation issued publicly offered debt instruments with original issue discount . ▶ ☐ | | |
| | If checked, the corporation may have to file **Form 8281,** Information Return for Publicly Offered Original Issue Discount Instruments. | | |
| 9 | Enter the amount of tax-exempt interest received or accrued during the tax year ▶ $ \_\_\_\_\_ | | |
| 10 | Enter the number of shareholders at the end of the tax year (if 100 or fewer) ▶ \_\_\_\_\_ | | |
| 11 | If the corporation has an NOL for the tax year and is electing to forego the carryback period, check here ▶ ☐ | | |
| | If the corporation is filing a consolidated return, the statement required by Temporary Regulations section 1.1502-21T(b)(3) must be attached or the election will not be valid. | | |
| 12 | Enter the available NOL carryover from prior tax years (Do not reduce it by any deduction on line 29a.) ▶ $ \_\_\_\_\_ | | |
| 13 | Are the corporation's total receipts (line 1a plus lines 4 through 10 on page 1) for the tax year **and** its total assets at the end of the tax year less than $250,000? . . . | | ✔ |
| | If "Yes," the corporation is not required to complete Schedules L, M-1, and M-2 on page 4. Instead, enter the total amount of cash distributions and the book value of property distributions (other than cash) made during the tax year. ▶ $ \_\_\_\_\_ | | |

**Note:** *If the corporation, at any time during the tax year, had assets or operated a business in a foreign country or U.S. possession, it may be required to attach* **Schedule N (Form 1120),** *Foreign Operations of U.S. Corporations, to this return. See Schedule N for details.*

Form **1120** (2005)

¶ **40**

Form 1120 (2005)      Page **4**

**Note:** *The corporation is not required to complete Schedules L, M-1, and M-2 if Question 13 on Schedule K is answered "Yes."*

## Schedule L — Balance Sheets per Books

| | | Beginning of tax year | | End of tax year | |
|---|---|---|---|---|---|
| | **Assets** | **(a)** | **(b)** | **(c)** | **(d)** |
| 1 | Cash | | 230,532 | | 196,180 |
| 2a | Trade notes and accounts receivable | 63,115 | | 72,259 | |
| b | Less allowance for bad debts | ( 0 ) | 63,115 | ( 0 ) | 72,259 |
| 3 | Inventories | | 355,240 | | 333,894 |
| 4 | U.S. government obligations | | 30,000 | | 48,000 |
| 5 | Tax-exempt securities (see instructions) | | 10,000 | | 30,000 |
| 6 | Other current assets (attach schedule) | | | | |
| 7 | Loans to shareholders | | | | |
| 8 | Mortgage and real estate loans | | | | |
| 9 | Other investments (attach schedule) | | 96,700 | | 127,900 |
| 10a | Buildings and other depreciable assets | 641,285 | | 1,181,285 | |
| b | Less accumulated depreciation | ( 377,352 ) | 263,933 | ( 592,608 ) | 588,677 |
| 11a | Depletable assets | | | | |
| b | Less accumulated depletion | ( ) | | ( ) | |
| 12 | Land (net of any amortization) | | 17,500 | | 25,500 |
| 13a | Intangible assets (amortizable only) | | | | |
| b | Less accumulated amortization | ( ) | | ( ) | |
| 14 | Other assets (attach schedule) | | 61,225 | | 70,506 |
| 15 | Total assets | | 1,128,245 | | 1,492,916 |
| | **Liabilities and Shareholders' Equity** | | | | |
| 16 | Accounts payable | | 39,456 | | 36,075 |
| 17 | Mortgages, notes, bonds payable in less than 1 year | | 40,000 | | 30,000 |
| 18 | Other current liabilities (attach schedule) | | 71,410 | | 39,551 |
| 19 | Loans from shareholders | | | | |
| 20 | Mortgages, notes, bonds payable in 1 year or more | | 225,000 | | 552,403 |
| 21 | Other liabilities (attach schedule) | | | | |
| 22 | Capital stock:   a Preferred stock | 50,000 | | 50,000 | |
| |       b Common stock | 435,000 | 485,000 | 435,000 | 485,000 |
| 23 | Additional paid-in capital | | 20,000 | | 20,000 |
| 24 | Retained earnings—Appropriated (attach schedule) | | 54,544 | | 67,544 |
| 25 | Retained earnings—Unappropriated | | 195,379 | | 264,887 |
| 26 | Adjustments to shareholders' equity (attach schedule) | | | | |
| 27 | Less cost of treasury stock | | ( 2,544 ) | | ( 2,544 ) |
| 28 | Total liabilities and shareholders' equity | | 1,128,245 | | 1,492,916 |

## Schedule M-1 — Reconciliation of Income (Loss) per Books With Income per Return (see instructions)

| 1 | Net income (loss) per books | 112,008 | 7 | Income recorded on books this year not included on this return (itemize): | |
|---|---|---|---|---|---|
| 2 | Federal income tax per books | 41,230 | | Tax-exempt interest $ ............ 788 | |
| 3 | Excess of capital losses over capital gains | | | | |
| 4 | Income subject to tax not recorded on books this year (itemize): ................ | | | | 788 |
| | ................................ | | 8 | Deductions on this return not charged against book income this year (itemize): | |
| 5 | Expenses recorded on books this year not deducted on this return (itemize): | | | a Depreciation . . . $ ........... | |
| a | Depreciation . . . . $ ............ | | | b Charitable contributions $ ........ | |
| b | Charitable contributions $ ........ | | | ................................ | |
| c | Travel and entertainment $ 2,573 + 93 | | | | 100 |
| | (Insurance + Foreign Tax Credit) | 2,666 | 9 | Add lines 7 and 8 | 888 |
| 6 | Add lines 1 through 5 | 155,904 | 10 | Income (page 1, line 28)—line 6 less line 9 | 155,016 |

## Schedule M-2 — Analysis of Unappropriated Retained Earnings per Books (Line 25, Schedule L)

| 1 | Balance at beginning of year | 195,379 | 5 | Distributions:   a Cash | 29,500 |
|---|---|---|---|---|---|
| 2 | Net income (loss) per books | 112,008 | |       b Stock | |
| 3 | Other increases (itemize): ............ | | |       c Property | |
| | ................................ | | 6 | Other decreases (itemize): ......... | 13,000 |
| | ................................ | | 7 | Add lines 5 and 6 | 42,500 |
| 4 | Add lines 1, 2, and 3 | 307,387 | 8 | Balance at end of year (line 4 less line 7) | 264,887 |

Form **1120** (2005)

¶40

| **SCHEDULE D**<br>(Form 1120)<br><br>Department of the Treasury<br>Internal Revenue Service | **Capital Gains and Losses**<br><br>► Attach to Form 1120, 1120-A, 1120-F, 1120-FSC, 1120-H,<br>1120-IC-DISC, 1120-L, 1120-ND, 1120-PC, 1120-POL, 1120-REIT,<br>1120-RIC, 1120-SF, 990-C, or certain Forms 990-T. | OMB No. 1545-0123<br><br>20**05** |
|---|---|---|

| Name<br>Falcon Machinery Corp. | Employer identification number<br>35 : 0816830 |
|---|---|

### Part I  Short-Term Capital Gains and Losses—Assets Held One Year or Less

| (a) Description of property<br>(Example: 100 shares of Z Co.) | (b) Date acquired<br>(mo., day, yr.) | (c) Date sold<br>(mo., day, yr.) | (d) Sales price<br>(see instructions) | (e) Cost or other<br>basis (see<br>instructions) | (f) Gain or (loss)<br>(Subtract (e) from (d)) |
|---|---|---|---|---|---|
| **1** 100 shares of XYZ Corp.<br>common stock | 05-26-04 | 02-03-05 | 20,500 | 18,487 | 2,013 |
| 200 shares of ABC preferred<br>stock | 04-14-04 | 01-26-05 | 4,400 | 4,755 | (355) |
| | | | | | |

| | | | |
|---|---|---|---|
| **2** Short-term capital gain from installment sales from Form 6252, line 26 or 37 . . . . . . . . | **2** | | |
| **3** Short-term gain or (loss) from like-kind exchanges from Form 8824 . . . . . . . . . | **3** | | |
| **4** Unused capital loss carryover (attach computation) . . . . . . . . . . . . . | **4** ( | 100 | ) |
| **5** Net short-term capital gain or (loss). Combine lines 1 through 4 . . . . . . . . . . | **5** | | 1,558 |

### Part II  Long-Term Capital Gains and Losses—Assets Held More Than One Year

| (a) | (b) | (c) | (d) | (e) | (f) |
|---|---|---|---|---|---|
| **6** 6 U.S. Treasury Bonds | 06-09-99 | 05-14-05 | 15,100 | 15,000 | 100 |
| Zero Corp. stock (worthless) | 01-30-91 | 12-31-05 | 0 | 12,500 | (12,500) |
| | | | | | |

| | | | |
|---|---|---|---|
| **7** Enter gain from Form 4797, line 7 or 9 . . . . . . . . . . . . . . . . | **7** | 17,288 | |
| **8** Long-term capital gain from installment sales from Form 6252, line 26 or 37 . . . . . . . | **8** | | |
| **9** Long-term gain or (loss) from like-kind exchanges from Form 8824 . . . . . . . . . | **9** | | |
| **10** Capital gain distributions (see instructions) . . . . . . . . . . . . . . . | **10** | | |
| **11** Net long-term capital gain or (loss). Combine lines 6 through 10 . . . . . . . . . . | **11** | | 4,888 |

### Part III  Summary of Parts I and II

| | | |
|---|---|---|
| **12** Enter excess of net short-term capital gain (line 5) over net long-term capital loss (line 11) . . . | **12** | 1,588 |
| **13** Net capital gain. Enter excess of net long-term capital gain (line 11) over net short-term capital<br>loss (line 5) . . . . . . . . . . . . . . . . . . . . . . . . . . | **13** | 4,888 |
| **14** Add lines 12 and 13. Enter here and on Form 1120, page 1, line 8, or the proper line on other<br>returns . . . . . . . . . . . . . . . . . . . . . . . . . . . | **14** | 6,446 |

**Note:** *If losses exceed gains, see* **Capital losses** *on page 2.*

## General Instructions

*Section references are to the Internal Revenue Code unless otherwise noted.*

### Purpose of Schedule

Use Schedule D to report sales and exchanges of capital assets and gains on distributions to shareholders of appreciated capital assets.

Generally report every sale or exchange of a capital asset (including like-kind exchanges) on this schedule even if there is no gain or loss.

**Note:** *For more information, see Pub. 544, Sales and Other Dispositions of Assets.*

## Other Forms the Corporation May Have To File

Use Form 4797, Sales of Business Property, to report the following.

● The sale or exchange of:

  1. Property used in a trade or business;

  2. Depreciable and amortizable property;

  3. Oil, gas, geothermal, or other mineral property; and

  4. Section 126 property.

● The involuntary conversion (other than from casualty or theft) of property and capital assets held for business or profit.

● The disposition of noncapital assets other than inventory or property held primarily for sale to customers in the ordinary course of the corporation's trade or business.

● The section 291 adjustment to section 1250 property.

Use Form 4684, Casualties and Thefts, to report involuntary conversions of property due to casualty or theft.

Use Form 6781, Gains and Losses From Section 1256 Contracts and Straddles, to report gains and losses from section 1256 contracts and straddles.

Use Form 8824, Like-Kind Exchanges, if the corporation made one or more "like-kind" exchanges. A like-kind exchange occurs when the corporation exchanges business or investment property for property of a like kind. For exchanges of capital assets, include the gain or (loss) from Form 8824, if any, on line 3 or line 9.

For Privacy Act and Paperwork Reduction Act Notice, see the Instructions for Forms 1120 and 1120-A.      Cat. No. 11460M      **Schedule D (Form 1120) 2005**

¶ **40**

Form 4684 (2005)     Attachment Sequence No. **26**     Page **2**

| Name(s) shown on tax return. Do not enter name and identifying number if shown on other side. | Identifying number |
|---|---|
| **Falcon Machinery Corp.** | **35-08-16830** |

### SECTION B—Business and Income-Producing Property

**Part I**   **Casualty or Theft Gain or Loss** (Use a separate Part I for each casualty or theft.)

**22**   Description of properties (show type, location, and date acquired for each property). Use a separate line for each property lost or damaged from the same casualty or theft.

Property **A**   **Storage shed, 123 O'Leary St., Chicago, IL 01-02-86 ($10,000 cost − $5,236 depreciation= $4,764 adj. basis)**

Property **B** _____

Property **C** _____

Property **D** _____

|  |  |  | Properties | | | |
|---|---|---|---|---|---|---|
|  |  |  | **A** | **B** | **C** | **D** |
| **23** | Cost or adjusted basis of each property. | 23 | 4,764 | | | |
| **24** | Insurance or other reimbursement (whether or not you filed a claim). See the instructions for line 3. | 24 | 0 | | | |
|  | **Note:** *If line 23 is **more** than line 24, skip line 25.* |  |  | | | |
| **25** | Gain from casualty or theft. If line 24 is **more** than line 23, enter the difference here and on line 32 or line 37, column (c), except as provided in the instructions for line 36. Also, skip lines 26 through 30 for that column. See the instructions for line 4 if line 24 includes insurance or other reimbursement you did not claim, or you received payment for your loss in a later tax year. | 25 | 0 | | | |
| **26** | Fair market value **before** casualty or theft | 26 | 3,000 | | | |
| **27** | Fair market value **after** casualty or theft. | 27 | 0 | | | |
| **28** | Subtract line 27 from line 26 | 28 | 3,000 | | | |
| **29** | Enter the **smaller** of line 23 or line 28 | 29 | 4,764 | | | |
|  | **Note:** *If the property was totally destroyed by casualty or lost from theft, enter on line 29 the amount from line 23.* |  |  | | | |
| **30** | Subtract line 24 from line 29. If zero or less, enter -0- | 30 | 4,764 | | | |

**31**   Casualty or theft loss. Add the amounts on line 30. Enter the total here and on line 32 **or** line 37 (see instructions).    | 31 | 4,764 | 00 |

---

**Part II**   **Summary of Gains and Losses** (from separate Parts I)

| (a) Identify casualty or theft | | **(b)** Losses from casualties or thefts | | (c) Gains from casualties or thefts includible in income |
|---|---|---|---|---|
|  |  | (i) Trade, business, rental or royalty property | (ii) Income-producing and employee property |  |

#### Casualty or Theft of Property Held One Year or Less

| **32** | _____ | | (     ) | (     ) | |
|---|---|---|---|---|---|
|  |  | | (     ) | (     ) | |
| **33** | Totals. Add the amounts on line 32 | 33 | (     ) | (     ) | |

**34**   Combine line 33, columns (b)(i) and (c). Enter the net gain or (loss) here and on Form 4797, line 14. If Form 4797 is not otherwise required, see instructions     | 34 | |

**35**   Enter the amount from line 33, column (b)(ii) here. Individuals, enter the amount from income-producing property on Schedule A (Form 1040), line 27, and enter the amount from property used as an employee on Schedule A (Form 1040), line 22. Estates and trusts, partnerships, and S corporations, see instructions     | 35 | |

#### Casualty or Theft of Property Held More Than One Year

| **36** | Casualty or theft gains from Form 4797, line 32 | | | 36 | | |
|---|---|---|---|---|---|---|
| **37** | **Storage shed destroyed by fire (Feb. 2005)** | | (   4,764   00 ) | (     ) | | |
|  |  | | (     ) | (     ) | | |
| **38** | Total losses. Add amounts on line 37, columns (b)(i) and (b)(ii) | 38 | (   4,764   00 ) | (     ) | | |
| **39** | Total gains. Add lines 36 and 37, column (c) | | | | 39 | 0 |
| **40** | Add amounts on line 38, columns (b)(i) and (b)(ii) | | | | 40 | (4,764) |

**41**   If the loss on line 40 is **more** than the gain on line 39:

   **a**   Combine line 38, column (b)(i) and line 39, and enter the net gain or (loss) here. Partnerships (except electing large partnerships) and S corporations, see the note below. All others, enter this amount on Form 4797, line 14. If Form 4797 is not otherwise required, see instructions     | 41a | (4,764) |

   **b**   Enter the amount from line 38, column (b)(ii) here. Individuals, enter the amount from income-producing property on Schedule A (Form 1040), line 27, and enter the amount from property used as an employee on Schedule A (Form 1040), line 22. Estates and trusts, enter on the "Other deductions" line of your tax return. Partnerships (except electing large partnerships) and S corporations, see the note below. Electing large partnerships, enter on Form 1065-B, Part II, line 11.     | 41b | |

**42**   If the loss on line 40 is **less** than or **equal** to the gain on line 39, combine lines 39 and 40 and enter here. Partnerships (except electing large partnerships), see the note below. All others, enter this amount on Form 4797, line 3     | 42 | |

    **Note:** *Partnerships, enter the amount from line 41a, 41b, or line 42 on Form 1065, Schedule K, line 11.*
    *S corporations, enter the amount from line 41a or 41b on Form 1120S, Schedule K, line 10.*

Form **4684** (2005)

¶ **40**

| Form **4562** | **Depreciation and Amortization** | OMB No. 1545-0172 |
|---|---|---|
| Department of the Treasury Internal Revenue Service | **(Including Information on Listed Property)** ▶ See separate instructions. ▶ Attach to your tax return. | **2005** Attachment Sequence No. **67** |

| Name(s) shown on return | Business or activity to which this form relates | Identifying number |
|---|---|---|
| Falcon Machinery Corp. | Manufacturing of Office Supplies | 35-08168830 |

**Part I**   **Election To Expense Certain Property Under Section 179**

Note: *If you have any listed property, complete Part V before you complete Part I.*

| | | | |
|---|---|---|---|
| 1 | Maximum amount. See the instructions for a higher limit for certain businesses | 1 | $105,000 |
| 2 | Total cost of section 179 property placed in service (see instructions) | 2 | |
| 3 | Threshold cost of section 179 property before reduction in limitation | 3 | $420,000 |
| 4 | Reduction in limitation. Subtract line 3 from line 2. If zero or less, enter -0- | 4 | |
| 5 | Dollar limitation for tax year. Subtract line 4 from line 1. If zero or less, enter -0-. If married filing separately, see instructions | 5 | |

| (a) Description of property | (b) Cost (business use only) | (c) Elected cost | |
|---|---|---|---|
| 6 | | | |
| | | | |

| | | | |
|---|---|---|---|
| 7 | Listed property. Enter the amount from line 29 | 7 | |
| 8 | Total elected cost of section 179 property. Add amounts in column (c), lines 6 and 7 | 8 | |
| 9 | Tentative deduction. Enter the **smaller** of line 5 or line 8 | 9 | |
| 10 | Carryover of disallowed deduction from line 13 of your 2004 Form 4562 | 10 | |
| 11 | Business income limitation. Enter the smaller of business income (not less than zero) or line 5 (see instructions) | 11 | |
| 12 | Section 179 expense deduction. Add lines 9 and 10, but do not enter more than line 11 | 12 | |
| 13 | Carryover of disallowed deduction to 2006. Add lines 9 and 10, less line 12 ▶ | 13 | |

Note: *Do not use Part II or Part III below for listed property. Instead, use Part V.*

**Part II**   **Special Depreciation Allowance and Other Depreciation (Do not** include listed property.) (See instructions.)

| | | | |
|---|---|---|---|
| 14 | Special allowance for certain aircraft, certain property with a long production period, and qualified New York Liberty Zone property (other than listed property) placed in service during the tax year | 14 | 150,000 |
| 15 | Property subject to section 168(f)(1) election | 15 | |
| 16 | Other depreciation (including ACRS) | 16 | 9,380 |

**Part III**   **MACRS Depreciation (Do not** include listed property.) (See instructions.)

**Section A**

| | | | |
|---|---|---|---|
| 17 | MACRS deductions for assets placed in service in tax years beginning before 2005 | 17 | 46,924 |
| 18 | If you are electing to group any assets placed in service during the tax year into one or more general asset accounts, check here ▶ ☐ | | |

**Section B—Assets Placed in Service During 2005 Tax Year Using the General Depreciation System**

| (a) Classification of property | (b) Month and year placed in service | (c) Basis for depreciation (business/investment use only—see instructions) | (d) Recovery period | (e) Convention | (f) Method | (g) Depreciation deduction |
|---|---|---|---|---|---|---|
| 19a 3-year property | | | | | | |
| b 5-year property | | | | | | |
| c 7-year property | | 150,000 | 7 yrs | HY | S/L | 10,710 |
| d 10-year property | | | | | | |
| e 15-year property | | | | | | |
| f 20-year property | | | | | | |
| g 25-year property | | | 25 yrs. | | S/L | |
| h Residential rental property | | | 27.5 yrs. | MM | S/L | |
| | | | 27.5 yrs. | MM | S/L | |
| i Nonresidential real property | 06/05 | 250,000 | 39 yrs. | MM | S/L | 3,478 |
| | | | | MM | S/L | |

**Section C—Assets Placed in Service During 2005 Tax Year Using the Alternative Depreciation System**

| | | | | | | |
|---|---|---|---|---|---|---|
| 20a Class life | | | | | S/L | |
| b 12-year | | | 12 yrs. | | S/L | |
| c 40-year | | | 40 yrs. | MM | S/L | |

**Part IV**   **Summary** (see instructions)

| | | | |
|---|---|---|---|
| 21 | Listed property. Enter amount from line 28 | 21 | 0 |
| 22 | **Total.** Add amounts from line 12, lines 14 through 17, lines 19 and 20 in column (g), and line 21. Enter here and on the appropriate lines of your return. Partnerships and S corporations—see instr. | 22 | 220,492 |
| 23 | For assets shown above and placed in service during the current year, enter the portion of the basis attributable to section 263A costs   23   376,000 | | |

For Paperwork Reduction Act Notice, see separate instructions.    Cat. No. 12906N    Form **4562** (2005)

¶ 40

| Form **4626**<br>Department of the Treasury<br>Internal Revenue Service | **Alternative Minimum Tax—Corporations**<br>▶ See separate instructions.<br>▶ Attach to the corporation's tax return. | OMB No. 1545-0175<br>20**05** |
|---|---|---|

| Name<br>XYZ, Inc. | Employer identification number<br>35 : 6417705 |
|---|---|

**Note:** *See the instructions to find out if the corporation is a small corporation exempt from the alternative minimum tax (AMT) under section 55(e).*

| | | | |
|---|---|---|---:|
| **1** | Taxable income or (loss) before net operating loss deduction . . . . . . . . . | **1** | 200,000 |
| **2** | **Adjustments and preferences:** | | |
| **a** | Depreciation of post-1986 property . . . . . . . . . . . | **2a** | 25,000 |
| **b** | Amortization of certified pollution control facilities . . . . . . . . . | **2b** | |
| **c** | Amortization of mining exploration and development costs . . . . . . . . | **2c** | |
| **d** | Amortization of circulation expenditures (personal holding companies only) . . . | **2d** | |
| **e** | Adjusted gain or loss . . . . . . . . . . . . . . | **2e** | 25,000 |
| **f** | Long-term contracts . . . . . . . . . . . . . . | **2f** | |
| **g** | Merchant marine capital construction funds . . . . . . . . . . . | **2g** | |
| **h** | Section 833(b) deduction (Blue Cross, Blue Shield, and similar type organizations only) . . | **2h** | |
| **i** | Tax shelter farm activities (personal service corporations only). . . . . . . | **2i** | |
| **j** | Passive activities (closely held corporations and personal service corporations only) . . . | **2j** | |
| **k** | Loss limitations . . . . . . . . . . . . . . | **2k** | 24,000 |
| **l** | Depletion . . . . . . . . . . . . . . . . | **2l** | |
| **m** | Tax-exempt interest income from specified private activity bonds. . . . . . . | **2m** | 34,000 |
| **n** | Intangible drilling costs . . . . . . . . . . . . . | **2n** | |
| **o** | Other adjustments and preferences . . . . . . . . . . . | **2o** | |
| **△3** | Pre-adjustment alternative minimum taxable income (AMTI). Combine lines 1 through 2o . . | **3** | 308,000 |
| **4** | **Adjusted current earnings (ACE) adjustment:** | | |

| | | | | |
|---|---|---|---:|---:|
| **a** | ACE from line 10 of the ACE worksheet in the instructions . . . . . . | **4a** | 350,000 | |
| **b** | Subtract line 3 from line 4a. If line 3 exceeds line 4a, enter the difference as a negative amount (see instructions) . . . . . . . . . . | **4b** | 42,000 | |
| **c** | Multiply line 4b by 75% (.75). Enter the result as a positive amount . . . | **4c** | 31,500 | |
| **d** | Enter the excess, if any, of the corporation's total increases in AMTI from prior year ACE adjustments over its total reductions in AMTI from prior year ACE adjustments (see instructions). **Note:** *You* **must** *enter an amount on line 4d (even if line 4b is positive)* . . . . . . . . . . | **4d** | 0 | |
| **e** | ACE adjustment.<br>● If line 4b is zero or more, enter the amount from line 4c<br>● If line 4b is less than zero, enter the **smaller** of line 4c or line 4d as a negative amount | | } . . . | **4e** | 31,500 |

| | | | |
|---|---|---|---:|
| **5** | Combine lines 3 and 4e. If zero or less, stop here; the corporation does not owe any AMT . . | **5** | 339,500 |
| **6** | Alternative tax net operating loss deduction (see instructions) *ATNOL < 90% AMTI* . . | **6** | 0 |
| **7** | **Alternative minimum taxable income.** Subtract line 6 from line 5. If the corporation held a residual interest in a REMIC, see instructions . . . . . . . . . . | **7** | 339,500 |
| **8** | **Exemption phase-out** (if line 7 is $310,000 or more, skip lines 8a and 8b and enter -0- on line 8c): | | |

| | | | | |
|---|---|---|---|---:|
| **a** | Subtract $150,000 from line 7 (if completing this line for a member of a controlled group, see instructions). If zero or less, enter -0- . . . . . . . | **8a** | | |
| **b** | Multiply line 8a by 25% (.25) . . . . . . . . . . | **8b** | | |
| **c** | Exemption. Subtract line 8b from $40,000 (if completing this line for a member of a controlled group, see instructions). If zero or less, enter -0-. | | **8c** | 0 |

| | | | |
|---|---|---|---:|
| **9** | Subtract line 8c from line 7. If zero or less, enter -0- . . . . . . . | **9** | 339,500 |
| **10** | Multiply line 9 by 20% (.20) . . . . . . . . . . . | **10** | 67,900 |
| **11** | Alternative minimum tax foreign tax credit (AMTFTC) (see instructions) . . . . . | **11** | 0 |
| **12** | Tentative minimum tax. Subtract line 11 from line 10 . . . . . . . . | **12** | 67,900 |
| **13** | Regular tax liability before applying all credits except the foreign tax credit and possessions tax credit | **13** | 61,250 |
| **14** | **Alternative minimum tax.** Subtract line 13 from line 12. If zero or less, enter -0-. Enter here and on Form 1120, Schedule J, line 4, or the appropriate line of the corporation's income tax return . . | **14** | 6,650 |

**For Paperwork Reduction Act Notice, see the instructions.**          Cat. No. 12955I          Form **4626** (2005)

¶ **40**

## Adjusted Current Earnings (ACE) Worksheet

▶ See ACE Worksheet Instructions (which begin on page 8).

| | | | |
|---|---|---|---|
| △ **1** | Pre-adjustment AMTI. Enter the amount from line 3 of Form 4626 . . . . . . . . | **1** | 308,000 |
| **2** | ACE depreciation adjustment: | | |
| **a** | AMT depreciation . . . . . . . . . **2a** 25,000 | | |
| **b** | ACE depreciation: | | |
| | (1) Post-1993 property . . . . . . **2b(1)** 6,000 | | |
| | (2) Post-1989, pre-1994 property . . . **2b(2)** 6.500 | | |
| | (3) Pre-1990 MACRS property . . . . **2b(3)** 2.500 | | |
| | (4) Pre-1990 original ACRS property . . **2b(4)** | | |
| | (5) Property described in sections 168(f)(1) through (4) . . . . . **2b(5)** | | |
| | (6) Other property . . . . . . . . **2b(6)** | | |
| | (7) Total ACE depreciation. Add lines 2b(1) through 2b(6) . . . . **2b(7)** 15,000 | | |
| **c** | ACE depreciation adjustment. Subtract line 2b(7) from line 2a . . . . . . . . | **2c** *not included in AMTI* | 10,000 |
| **3** | Inclusion in ACE of items included in earnings and profits (E&P): | | |
| **a** | Tax-exempt interest income . . . . . . . . . . **3a** 20,000 | | |
| **b** | Death benefits from life insurance contracts . . . . . . . . **3b** | | |
| **c** | All other distributions from life insurance contracts (including surrenders) . **3c** | | |
| **d** | Inside buildup of undistributed income in life insurance contracts . **3d** | | |
| **e** | Other items (see Regulations sections 1.56(g)-1(c)(6)(iii) through (ix) for a partial list) . . . . . . . . . . . . . . . **3e** | | |
| **f** | Total increase to ACE from inclusion in ACE of items included in E&P. Add lines 3a through 3e | **3f** | 20,000 |
| **4** | Disallowance of items not deductible from E&P: | | |
| **a** | Certain dividends received . . . . . . . . . . **4a** | | |
| **b** | Dividends paid on certain preferred stock of public utilities that are deductible under section 247 . . . . . . . . . . **4b** 9,000 | | |
| **c** | Dividends paid to an ESOP that are deductible under section 404(k). **4c** | | |
| **d** | Nonpatronage dividends that are paid and deductible under section 1382(c) . . . . . . . . . . . . . . . . **4d** | | |
| **e** | Other items (see Regulations sections 1.56(g)-1(d)(3)(i) and (ii) for a partial list) . . . . . . . . . . . . . . . **4e** | | |
| **f** | Total increase to ACE because of disallowance of items not deductible from E&P. Add lines 4a through 4e . . . . . . . . . . | **4f** | 9,000 |
| **5** | Other adjustments based on rules for figuring E&P: | | |
| **a** | Intangible drilling costs . . . . . . . . . . **5a** | | |
| **b** | Circulation expenditures . . . . . . . . . . **5b** | | |
| **c** | Organizational expenditures . . . . . . . . . . **5c** | | |
| **d** | LIFO inventory adjustments . . . . . . . . . . **5d** | | |
| **e** | Installment sales . . . . . . . . . . . . **5e** | | |
| **f** | Total other E&P adjustments. Combine lines 5a through 5e . . . . . . | **5f** | 0 |
| **6** | Disallowance of loss on exchange of debt pools . . . . . . . . | **6** | |
| **7** | Acquisition expenses of life insurance companies for qualified foreign contracts . . . . . . | **7** | |
| **8** | Depletion . . . . . . . . . . . . . . . . | **8** | |
| **9** | Basis adjustments in determining gain or loss from sale or exchange of pre-1994 property . . | **9** | 3,000 |
| **10** | **Adjusted current earnings.** Combine lines 1, 2c, 3f, 4f, and 5f through 9. Enter the result here and on line 4a of Form 4626 . . . . . . . . . . . . . . . | **10** | 350,000 |

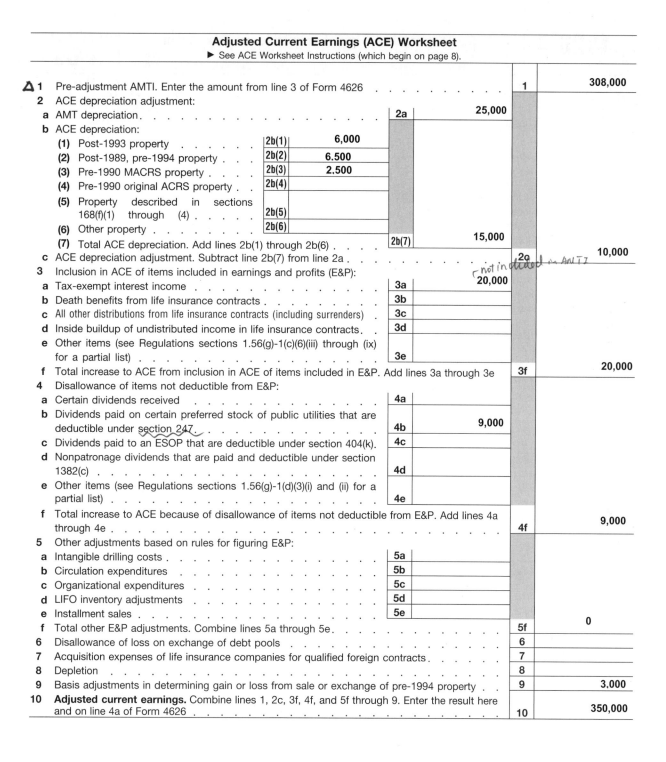

¶ **40**

**Form 1120-A**

Department of the Treasury
Internal Revenue Service

**U.S. Corporation Short-Form Income Tax Return**

For calendar year 2005 or tax year beginning............., 2005, ending............., 20.....

▶ See separate instructions to make sure the corporation qualifies to file Form 1120-A.

OMB No. 1545-0890

**2005**

**A** Check this box if the corporation is a personal service corporation (see instructions). ☐

Use IRS label. Otherwise, print or type.

| Name | **B** Employer identification number |
|---|---|
| Rose Flower Shop | 10 ¦ 2134567 |
| Number, street, and room or suite no. If a P.O. box, see instructions. | **C** Date incorporated |
| 38 Superior Lane | 07/01/83 |
| City or town, state, and ZIP code | **D** Total assets (see instructions) |
| Fair City, MD 21117 | |

**E** Check if:   (1) ☐ Initial return   (2) ☐ Final return   (3) ☐ Name change   (4) ☐ Address change   $ 65,987 | 00

**F** Check accounting method:   (1) ☐ Cash   (2) ☑ Accrual   (3) ☐ Other (specify) ▶

**Income**

| | | | | | | |
|---|---|---|---|---|---|---|
| 1a | Gross receipts or sales | 268,000 00 | **b** Less returns and allowances | 7,500 00 | **c** Balance ▶ | **1c** | 260,500 | 00 |
| 2 | Cost of goods sold (see instructions) . . . . . . . | | | | **2** | 144,000 | 00 |
| 3 | Gross profit. Subtract line 2 from line 1c . . . . . | | | | **3** | 116,500 | 00 |
| 4 | Domestic corporation dividends subject to the 70% deduction. | | | | **4** | | |
| 5 | Interest . . . . . . . . . . . . . . . | | | | **5** | 942 | 00 |
| 6 | Gross rents . . . . . . . . . . . . . | | | | **6** | | |
| 7 | Gross royalties . . . . . . . . . . . . | | | | **7** | | |
| 8 | Capital gain net income (attach Schedule D (Form 1120)) | | | | **8** | | |
| 9 | Net gain or (loss) from Form 4797, Part II, line 17 (attach Form 4797). | | | | **9** | | |
| 10 | Other income (see instructions—attach schedule). . | | | | **10** | | |
| 11 | **Total income.** Add lines 3 through 10 . . . . . ▶ | | | | **11** | 117,442 | 00 |

**Deductions** (See instructions for limitations on deductions.)

| | | | | | | |
|---|---|---|---|---|---|---|
| 12 | Compensation of officers (see instructions). . . . . | | | **12** | 43,000 | 00 |
| 13 | Salaries and wages (less employment credits). . . . | | | **13** | 24,320 | 00 |
| 14 | Repairs and maintenance . . . . . . . . . | | | **14** | | |
| 15 | Bad debts . . . . . . . . . . . . . | | | **15** | | |
| 16 | Rents. . . . . . . . . . . . . . . | | | **16** | 6,000 | 00 |
| 17 | Taxes and licenses . . . . . . . . . . | | | **17** | 3,320 | 00 |
| 18 | Interest . . . . . . . . . . . . . . | | | **18** | 1,340 | 00 |
| 19 | Charitable contributions (see instructions for 10% limitation) | | | **19** | 1,820 | 00 |
| 20a | Depreciation (attach Form 4562) . . . . . . | **20a** | | | | |
| **b** | Less depreciation claimed elsewhere on return . . . | **20b** | | **20c** | | |
| 21 | Domestic production activities deduction (attach Form 8903) . . | | | **21** | | |
| 22 | Other deductions (attach schedule) . . . . . . | | | **22** | 3,000 | 00 |
| 23 | **Total deductions.** Add lines 12 through 22 . . . . ▶ | | | **23** | 82,800 | 00 |
| 24 | Taxable income before net operating loss deduction and special deductions. Subtract line 23 from line 11 . | | | **24** | 34,642 | 00 |
| 25 | **Less:**  **a** Net operating loss deduction (see instructions) . . . . | **25a** | | | | |
| | **b** Special deductions (see instructions) . . . . . . . . . | **25b** | | **25c** | 0 | |

**Tax and Payments**

| | | | | | | |
|---|---|---|---|---|---|---|
| 26 | **Taxable income.** Subtract line 25c from line 24 . . . . . | | | | **26** | 34,642 | 00 |
| 27 | **Total tax** (page 2, Part I, line 5) . . . . . . . . . | | | | **27** | 5,196 | 00 |
| 28 | **Payments:** | | | | | | |
| **a** | 2004 overpayment credited to 2005. . . | **28a** | | | | | |
| **b** | 2005 estimated tax payments . . . . | **28b** | 6,000 00 | | | | |
| **c** | Less 2005 refund applied for on Form 4466 | **28c** ( ) | Bal ▶ | **28d** | 6,000 00 | | |
| **e** | Tax deposited with Form 7004 | | | **28e** | | | |
| **f** | Credits: **(1)** Form 2439 _____ **(2)** Form 4136 _____ | | | **28f** | | | |
| **g** | **Total payments.** Add lines 28d through 28f | | | | **28g** | 6,000 | 00 |
| 29 | Estimated tax penalty (see instructions). Check if Form 2220 is attached. . . . ▶ ☐ | | | | **29** | | |
| 30 | **Tax due.** If line 28g is smaller than the total of lines 27 and 29, enter amount owed . . . | | | | **30** | | |
| 31 | **Overpayment.** If line 28g is larger than the total of lines 27 and 29, enter amount overpaid . | | | | **31** | 804 | 00 |
| 32 | Enter amount of line 31 you want: **Credited to 2006 estimated tax** ▶ _____ Refunded ▶ | | | | **32** | 804 | 00 |

**Sign Here**

Under penalties of perjury, I declare that I have examined this return, including accompanying schedules and statements, and to the best of my knowledge and belief, it is true, correct, and complete. Declaration of preparer (other than taxpayer) is based on all information of which preparer has any knowledge.

| ▶ _____ | _____ | ▶ **President** | May the IRS discuss this return with the preparer shown below (see instructions)? ☑ Yes ☐ No |
|---|---|---|---|
| Signature of officer | Date | Title | |

**Paid Preparer's Use Only**

| Preparer's signature ▶ | | Date | | Check if self-employed ☑ | Preparer's SSN or PTIN 311-62-4121 |
|---|---|---|---|---|---|
| Firm's name (or yours if self-employed), address, and ZIP code | John Sevice 1510 Steward Bldg., Chicago, IL 60672 | | EIN | | |
| | | | Phone no. ( 847 ) 012-0612 | | |

**For Privacy Act and Paperwork Reduction Act Notice, see separate instructions.**          Cat. No. 11456E          Form **1120-A** (2005)

¶40

Form 1120-A (2005)
Page **2**

## Part I — Tax Computation (see instructions)

| | | | | |
|---|---|---|---|---|
| 1 | Income tax. If the corporation is a qualified personal service corporation (see instructions), check here . ▶ ☐ | 1 | 5,196 | 00 |
| 2 | General business credit. Check box(es) and indicate which forms are attached: ☐ Form 3800  ☐ Form(s) (specify) ▶ .......... | 2 | 0 | |
| 3 | Subtract line 2 from line 1 | 3 | 5,196 | 00 |
| 4 | Other taxes. Check if from: ☐ Form 4255 ☐ Form 8611 ☐ Form 8697 ☐ Form 8866 ☐ Form 8902 ☐ Other (attach schedule) | 4 | 0 | |
| 5 | **Total tax.** Add lines 3 and 4. Enter here and on page 1, line 27 . . . . . . . . . . . | 5 | 5,196 | 00 |

## Part II — Other Information (see instructions)

1 See instructions and enter the:
  a Business activity code no. ▶ 453110
  b Business activity ▶ **Florists**
  c Product or service ▶ **Flowers**

2 At the end of the tax year, did any individual, partnership, estate, or trust own, directly or indirectly, 50% or more of the corporation's voting stock? (For rules of attribution, see section 267(c).) . . . . . . . . . . ☐ Yes ☑ No
If "Yes," attach a schedule showing name and identifying number.

3 Enter the amount of tax-exempt interest received or accrued during the tax year . . . . . ▶ |$ 0|

4 Enter total amount of cash distributions and the book value of property distributions (other than cash) made during the tax year . . . . . . . . . . ▶ |$ 0|

5a If an amount is entered on page 1, line 2, enter from worksheet in instructions:

| | | | |
|---|---|---|---|
| (1) | Purchases . . . . . | 134,014 | 00 |
| (2) | Additional 263A costs (attach schedule) | | |
| (3) | Other costs (attach schedule) . | 9,466 | 00 |

b If property is produced or acquired for resale, do the rules of section 263A apply to the corporation?. . . . . ☐ Yes ☑ No

6 At any time during the calendar year, did the corporation have an interest in or a signature or other authority over a financial account (such as a bank account, securities account, or other financial account) in a foreign country? ☐ Yes ☑ No
If "Yes," the corporation may have to file Form TD F 90-22.1.
If "Yes," enter the name of the foreign country ▶ ....................

7 Are the corporation's total receipts (line 1a plus lines 4 through 10 on page 1) for the tax year **and** its total assets at the end of the tax year less than $250,000? . . . . . . . ☐ Yes ☑ No
If "Yes," the corporation is **not** required to complete Parts III and IV below.

## Part III — Balance Sheets per Books

| | | (a) Beginning of tax year | | (b) End of tax year | |
|---|---|---|---|---|---|
| **Assets** | | | | | |
| 1 | Cash . . . . . . . . . . | 20,540 | 00 | 18,498 | 00 |
| 2a | Trade notes and accounts receivable | | | | |
| b | Less allowance for bad debts . . . . . . . | ( | ) | ( | ) |
| 3 | Inventories . . . . . . . . | 2,530 | 00 | 2,010 | 00 |
| 4 | U.S. government obligations . . . . . | 13,807 | 00 | 45,479 | 00 |
| 5 | Tax-exempt securities (see instructions). . . . . | | | | |
| 6 | Other current assets (attach schedule) . . . . . | | | | |
| 7 | Loans to shareholders . . . . . . | | | | |
| 8 | Mortgage and real estate loans . . . . . | | | | |
| 9a | Depreciable, depletable, and intangible assets . | | | | |
| b | Less accumulated depreciation, depletion, and amortization | ( | ) | ( | ) |
| 10 | Land (net of any amortization) . . . . . | | | | |
| 11 | Other assets (attach schedule) . . . . . | | | | |
| 12 | Total assets . . . . . . . . | 36,877 | 00 | 65,987 | 00 |
| **Liabilities and Shareholders' Equity** | | | | | |
| 13 | Accounts payable . . . . . . | 6,415 | 00 | 6,079 | 00 |
| 14 | Other current liabilities (attach schedule). . . . . | | | | |
| 15 | Loans from shareholders . . . . . | | | | |
| 16 | Mortgages, notes, bonds payable. . . . . | | | | |
| 17 | Other liabilities (attach schedule) | | | | |
| 18 | Capital stock (preferred and common stock) . . . . | 20,000 | 00 | 20,000 | 00 |
| 19 | Additional paid-in capital . . . . . . | | | | |
| 20 | Retained earnings . . . . . . | 10,462 | 00 | 39,908 | 00 |
| 21 | Adjustments to shareholders' equity (attach schedule) . | | | | |
| 22 | Less cost of treasury stock . . . . . | ( | ) | ( | ) |
| 23 | Total liabilities and shareholders' equity . . . . | 36,877 | 00 | 65,987 | 00 |

## Part IV — Reconciliation of Income (Loss) per Books With Income per Return

| | | | | | | |
|---|---|---|---|---|---|---|
| 1 | Net income (loss) per books . . . . . | 29,466 | 00 | 6 Income recorded on books this year not included on this return (itemize): ............. | | |
| 2 | Federal income tax per books. . . . . | 5,196 | 00 | | | |
| 3 | Excess of capital losses over capital gains . . | | | 7 Deductions on this return not charged against book income this year (itemize): ............ | | |
| 4 | Income subject to tax not recorded on books this year (itemize): ................ | | | ............................ | | |
| 5 | Expenses recorded on books this year not deducted on this return (itemize): | | | 8 Income (page 1, line 24). Enter the sum of lines 1 through 5 less the sum of lines 6 and 7 | 34,642 | 00 |

Form **1120-A** (2005)

 Printed on recycled paper

¶ **40**

Form **3800**

Department of the Treasury
Internal Revenue Service (99)

**General Business Credit**

▶ See instructions.
▶ Attach to your tax return.

OMB No. 1545–0895

**2005**

Attachment
Sequence No. **22**

| Name(s) shown on return | Identifying number |
|---|---|
| CXX Corporation | 36-06185268 |

**Part I**   **Current Year Credit**

| | | | | |
|---|---|---|---|---|
| 1a | Investment credit (Form 3468) | 1a | | |
| b | Work opportunity credit (Form 5884) | 1b | 3,000 | 00 |
| c | Welfare-to-work credit (Form 8861) | 1c | | |
| d | Credit for increasing research activities (Form 6765) | 1d | 6,350 | 00 |
| e | Low-income housing credit (Form 8586) | 1e | | |
| f | Enhanced oil recovery credit (Form 8830) | 1f | | |
| g | Disabled access credit (Form 8826) | 1g | | |
| h | Renewable electricity production credit (Form 8835, Section A only) | 1h | | |
| i | Indian employment credit (Form 8845) | 1i | | |
| j | Credit for employer social security and Medicare taxes paid on certain employee tips (Form 8846) | 1j | | |
| k | Orphan drug credit (Form 8820) | 1k | | |
| l | New markets credit (Form 8874) | 1l | | |
| m | Credit for small employer pension plan startup costs (Form 8881) | 1m | | |
| n | Credit for employer-provided child care facilities and services (Form 8882) | 1n | | |
| o | Qualified railroad track maintenance credit (Form 8900) | 1o | | |
| p | Biodiesel and renewable diesel fuels credit (Form 8864) | 1p | | |
| q | Low sulfur diesel fuel production credit (Form 8896) | 1q | | |
| r | Distilled spirits credit (Form 8906) | 1r | | |
| s | Nonconventional source fuel credit (Form 8907) | 1s | | |
| t | Energy efficient home credit (Form 8908) | 1t | | |
| u | Alternative motor vehicle credit (Form 8910) | 1u | | |
| v | Alternative fuel vehicle refueling property credit (Form 8911) | 1v | | |
| w | Credit for contributions to selected community development corporations (Form 8847) | 1w | | |
| x | Trans-Alaska pipeline liability fund credit (see instructions) | 1x | | |
| y | General credits from an electing large partnership (Schedule K-1 (Form 1065-B)) | 1y | | |
| z | Credits for employers affected by Hurricane Katrina, Rita, or Wilma (Form 5884-A) | 1z | | |
| 2 | **Current year credit.** Add lines 1a through 1z | 2 | 9,350 | 00 |
| 3 | Passive activity credits included on line 2 (see instructions) | 3 | 0 | |
| 4 | Subtract line 3 from line 2 | 4 | 9,350 | 00 |
| 5 | Passive activity credits allowed for 2005 (see instructions) | 5 | | |
| 6 | Carryforward of general business credit to 2005. See instructions for the schedule to attach | 6 | | |
| 7 | Carryback of general business credit from 2006 (see instructions) | 7 | | |
| 8 | **Current year credit.** Add lines 4 through 7 | 8 | 9,350 | 00 |

**For Paperwork Reduction Act Notice, see instructions.**              Cat. No. 12392F              Form **3800** (2005)

Form 3800 (2005)                                                                        Page **2**

## Part II  Allowable Credit

| | | | | |
|---|---|---|---|---|
| **9** | Regular tax before credits (see instructions) . . . . . . . . . . . . . | **9** | 75,000 | 00 |
| **10** | Alternative minimum tax (see instructions) . . . . . . . . . . . . . . | **10** | 0 | |
| **11** | Add lines 9 and 10 . . . . . . . . . . . . . . . . . . . . . . . . | **11** | 75,000 | 00 |

| | | |
|---|---|---|
| **12a** | Foreign tax credit . . . . . . . . . . . . . . . . . | **12a** |
| **b** | Credits from Form 1040, lines 48 through 54 . . . . . . . | **12b** |
| **c** | Possessions tax credit (Form 5735, line 17 or 27) . . . . . | **12c** |
| **d** | Nonconventional source fuel credit (Form 8907, line 23) . . . | **12d** |
| **e** | Other specified credits (see instructions) . . . . . . . . | **12e** |

| | | | | |
|---|---|---|---|---|
| **f** | Add lines 12a through 12e . . . . . . . . . . . . . . . . | **12f** | 0 | |
| **13** | Net income tax. Subtract line 12f from line 11. If zero, skip lines 14 through 17 and enter -0- on line 18 | **13** | 75,000 | 00 |

| | | |
|---|---|---|
| **14** | Net regular tax. Subtract line 12f from line 9. If zero or less, enter -0- | **14** |
| **15** | Enter 25% (.25) of the excess, if any, of line 14 over $25,000 (see instructions) | **15** |
| **16** | Tentative minimum tax (see instructions) . . . . . . . . . | **16** |

| | | | | |
|---|---|---|---|---|
| **17** | Enter the greater of line 15 or line 16 . . . . . . . . . . . . . . . . | **17** | 12,500 | 00 |
| **18** | Subtract line 17 from line 13. If zero or less, enter -0- . . . . . . . . . | **18** | 62,500 | 00 |
| **19** | **Credit allowed for the current year.** Enter the **smaller** of line 8 or line 18 here and on Form 1040, line 55; Form 1120, Schedule J, line 6d; Form 1120-A, Part I, line 2; Form 1041, Schedule G, line 2c; or the applicable line of your return. If line 19 is smaller than line 8, see instructions. **Individuals, estates, and trusts:** See instructions if claiming the research credit. **C corporations:** See Schedule A if claiming any regular investment credit carryforward and the line 19 instructions if there has been an ownership change, acquisition, or reorganization . . . . . . . . . . | **19** | 9,350 | 00 |

## Schedule A—Additional General Business Credit Allowed by Code Section 38(c)(2) *(Before Repeal by the Revenue Reconciliation Act of 1990)*—Only Applicable to C Corporations

| | | |
|---|---|---|
| **20** | Enter the portion of the credit shown on line 6 that is attributable to the regular investment credit under section 46 (before amendment by the Revenue Reconciliation Act of 1990) . . . . . . | **20** |
| **21** | Tentative minimum tax (from line 16) . . . . . . . . . . . | **21** |
| **22** | Multiply line 21 by 25% (.25) . . . . . . . . . . . . . . | **22** |
| **23** | Enter the amount from line 18 . . . . . . . . . . . . . . | **23** |
| **24** | Enter the portion of the credit shown on line 8 that is not attributable to the regular investment credit under section 46 (before amendment by the Revenue Reconciliation Act of 1990) . . . . . . . . . . | **24** |
| **25** | Subtract line 24 from line 23. If zero or less, enter -0- . . . . . . . . | **25** |
| **26** | Subtract line 25 from line 20. If zero or less, enter -0- . . . . . . . . | **26** |
| **27** | For purposes of this line only, refigure the amount on Form 4626, line 10, by using zero on Form 4626, line 6, and enter the result here . . | **27** |
| **28** | Multiply line 27 by 10% (.10) . . . . . . . . . . . . . . . | **28** |
| **29** | Net income tax (from line 13) . . . . . . . . . . . . . . . | **29** |
| **30** | Enter the amount from line 19 . . . . . . . . . . . . . . | **30** |
| **31** | Subtract line 30 from line 29 . . . . . . . . . . . . . . . | **31** |
| **32** | Subtract line 28 from line 31 . . . . . . . . . . . . . . . | **32** |
| **33** | Enter the smallest of line 22, line 26, or line 32 . . . . . . . . . . . | **33** |
| **34** | Subtract line 33 from line 21 . . . . . . . . . . . . . . . | **34** |
| **35** | Enter the greater of line 15 or line 34 . . . . . . . . . . . . . . . | **35** |
| **36** | Subtract line 35 from line 29. Also enter this amount on line 19 instead of the amount previously figured on that line. Write "Sec. 38(c)(2)" next to your entry on line 19 . . . | **36** |

Form **3800** (2005)

¶ **40**

# Filled-In Form 1120-W • Corporate Estimated Taxes • Explanation

## ¶41

**New This Year:** For tax years beginning after December 31, 2005, new laws may impact a taxpayer's estimated tax calculations as follows:

- **New tax credits.** For new tax credits that are effective for tax years ending after December 31, 2005, see ¶32 for the discussion of Schedule J, Form 1120.

- **New deductions.** New deductions in tax years ending after December 31, 2005 include the deduction for energy efficient commercial building property under Code Sec. 179D for assets placed in service after 2005.

- **Extraterritorial income (ETI) exclusion.** Although the ETI exclusion provisions were generally repealed for transactions after 2004, certain transition rules apply for transactions during 2006. For further discussion, see the Instructions for Form 8873.

- **Who Must Make Estimated Tax Payments**

- Corporations generally must estimated tax payments if they expect their estimated tax (income tax less credits) to be $500 or more.

- S corporations must make estimated tax payments if the total of these taxes is $500 or more:

  (A) The tax on built-in gains,

  (B) The excess net passive income tax, and

  (C) The investment credit recapture tax.

The amount of estimated tax required to be paid annually is the smaller of:

(a) The total of the above taxes shown on the return for the tax year (or if no return if filed, the total of these taxes for the year) or

(b) The sum of

  (i) The investment credit recapture tax and the built-in gains tax shown on the return for the tax year (or if no return is filed, the total of these taxes for the tax year) and

  (ii) Any excess net passive income tax shown on the corporation's return for the preceding tax year. If the preceding tax year was less than 12 months, the estimated tax must be determined under (a).

- Tax-exempt corporations subject to the unrelated business income tax must make estimated tax payments using Form 990-W to compute their estimated tax. This form need not be filed with the IRS. Taxpayers should retain it with their records.

- **When to Make Estimated Tax Payments**

The installments are due by the 15th day of the 4th, 6th, 9th, and 12th months of the tax year. If the due date falls on a Saturday, Sunday, or legal holiday, the installment is due on the next regular business day.

- **Underpayment of Estimated Tax**

A corporation that fails to make estimated tax payments when due may be subject to an underpayment penalty for the period of underpayment.

- **Overpayment of Estimated Tax**

A corporation that has overpaid its estimated tax may apply for a quick refund if the overpayment is at least 10 percent of its expected income tax liability and at least $500. To apply, file Form 4466, Corporation Application for Quick Refund of Overpayment of Estimated tax, after the end of the tax year and before the corporation files it income tax return. Form 4466 may not be filed later than the 15th day of the 3rd month after the end of the tax year. A corporation may also elect to apply any overpayment against the earliest installment of its next year's estimated tax. An extension of time to file Form 1120 does not extent the time to file Form 4466.

- **Depository Methods of Tax Payment**

Some corporations are required to electronically deposit all depository taxes, including estimated tax payments.

**Electronic Deposit Requirement.** The corporation must make electronic deposits of all depository taxes which include employment tax, excise tax, and corporate income tax, using the Electronic Federal Tax Payment System (EFTPS) in 2005 if:

- The total deposits of such taxes in 2004 were more than $200,000, or

- The corporation was required to use EFTPS in 2005.

If the corporation is required to use EFTPS and fails to do so, it may be subject to a 10 percent penalty. If the corporation is not required to use EFTPS, it may participate voluntarily. In order for EFTPS to be made timely, the corporation must initiate the transaction at least one business day before the date that the deposit is due. The corporation must make EFTPS deposits at least 1 business day before the date the deposit is due in order for the deposits to be made on time.

**Depositing on time.** For EFTPS deposits to be made timely, the corporation must initiate the transaction at least 1 business day before the date the deposit is due.

**Deposits with Form 8109.** If the corporation does not use EFTPS, the corporation should deposit corporation income tax payments (and estimated tax payments) with Form 8109, Federal Tax Deposit Coupon. If they do not have preprinted Form 8109, they should use Form 8109-B to make deposits.

Form 8109 should not be sent directly to an IRS office. The corporation should mail or deliver the completed Form 8109 with the payment to an authorized commercial bank or other financial institution authorized to accept Federal tax deposits. The checks or money orders should be made payable to the depositary institution. Alternatively, the corporation could mail the coupon and payment to: Financial Agent, Federal Tax Deposit Processing, P.O. Box 970030, St. Louis, MO 63197 and make the check or money order payable to the "Financial Agent."

**Refiguring Estimated Tax.** If, after the corporation figures and deposits estimated tax, it finds that its tax liability for the year will be more or less than originally estimated, it may have to refigure its required installments. If earlier installments were underpaid, the corporation may owe a penalty. An immediate catch-up payment should be made to reduce the amount of any penalty resulting from the underpayment of any earlier installments, whether caused by a change in estimate, failure to make a deposit, or a mistake.

**Computation of Estimated Tax Payments.** Corporations use Form 1120-W to calculate their estimated tax liability and compute the amount of their estimated tax payments. Note that this form should not be sent to the IRS but should be retained with the taxpayer's records.

Generally, the estimated tax liability is the expected tax (including the alternative minimum tax (Code Sec. 55)) plus any recapture taxes, less tax credits.

**Members of Controlled Group.** Members of a group of controlled corporations must apportion the income tax brackets among the members of the group in computing each corporation's estimated taxes. Such apportionment can be made in accordance with a plan adopted by the members, or, in the absence of such a plan, the brackets must be apportioned equally among the members.

**Qualified personal service Corporations**. Qualified personal service corporations also use Form 1120-W. They are taxed at a 35% rate, and do not complete Lines 2–13 of the form.

- **Amount of Payments**

The amount of any required installment is generally 25% of the required annual payment, which is the lesser of (1) 100% of the estimated tax determined on Line 22 of Form 1120-W or (2) 100% of the tax shown on the preceding year's tax return (for a 12-month tax year) (Line 23a of Form 1120-W) (Code Sec. 6655(d)).

**Annualized Income Installment Method**. A lower required installment may apply if a corporation establishes that an annualized income installment or adjusted seasonal installment is less than the required installment determined above. In determining the payment due under the annualized income installment method, income is annualized over 3 months for the first installment due date, 3 months for the second installment due date, 6 months for the third installment due date, and 9 months for the fourth installment due date. However, a corporation may elect to use different annualization periods (2, 4, 7, and 10 months (option 1) or 3, 5, 8, and 11 months (option 2)) if it files Form 8842, Election to Use Different Annualization Periods for Corporate Estimated Tax, on or before the due date of the first required installment payment. This election is irrevocable for the particular tax year for which it was filed (Code Sec. 6655(e)(2)(C)).

Where there is a reduction in an estimated tax payment from the use of the annualization (or adjusted seasonal installment) exception, 100% of the amount otherwise required to be made up under Code Sec. 6655(e)(1) must be included in the next payment for which the corporation does not use the exception. To use one or both of these methods to figure one or more required installments, use Form 1120-W, Schedule A. Schedule A automatically selects the smallest of the annualized income installment, the adjusted seasonal installment (if applicable) or the regular installment under Code Sec. 6655(d), as increased by any reduction recapture under Code Sec. 6655(e)(1)(B). Although credits may not be annualized, items of income or deduction used to determine the credit are annualized. Enter in each column on Line 25 of Form 1120-W the amounts from the corresponding column of Line 38 of Schedule A.

The only time a large corporation (taxable income of $1 million or more in any of the three tax years before the tax year in issue) may base an estimated tax payment on the amount shown on the preceding year's return is when the corporation is determining the amount of the first installment due in any tax year (Code Sec. 6655(d)(2)(B)). In determining whether a corporation is a large corporation, taxable income is computed without considering net operating losses or capital loss carryforwards and carrybacks. Members of a controlled group of corporations must determine whether they are large corporations by allocating the $1 million amount among the members of the group either equally or in a manner agreed upon by the members.

## ON THE RETURN

The illustrative filled-in Form 1120-W on page 83 is for calendar year 2005. *It has no relation to the Form 1120 on pages 67–75, which is filled in for another taxpayer.* The amount for Line 22 equals $131,750, which is greater than the 2005 tax liability of the corporation ($102,000) entered on Line 23a.

**Form 1120-W**
**(WORKSHEET)**
Department of the Treasury
Internal Revenue Service

## Estimated Tax for Corporations

For calendar year 2006, or tax year beginning .......... , 2006, and ending .......... , 20 .....

**(Keep for the corporation's records—Do *not* send to the Internal Revenue Service.)**

OMB No. 1545-0975

**2006**

| | | | |
|---|---|---|---:|
| 1 | Taxable income expected for the tax year | **1** \| 400,000 | |
| | Qualified personal service corporations (defined in the instructions), skip lines 2 through 13 and go to line 14. Members of a controlled group, see instructions. | | |
| 2 | Enter the **smaller** of line 1 or $50,000 | **2** \| 50,000 | |
| 3 | Multiply line 2 by 15% | **3** | 7,500 |
| 4 | Subtract line 2 from line 1 | **4** \| 350,000 | |
| 5 | Enter the **smaller** of line 4 or $25,000 | **5** \| 25,000 | |
| 6 | Multiply line 5 by 25% | **6** | 6,250 |
| 7 | Subtract line 5 from line 4 | **7** \| 325,000 | |
| 8 | Enter the **smaller** of line 7 or $9,925,000 | **8** \| 325,000 | |
| 9 | Multiply line 8 by 34% | **9** | 110,500 |
| 10 | Subtract line 8 from line 7 | **10** \| 0 | |
| 11 | Multiply line 10 by 35% | **11** | 0 |
| 12 | If line 1 is greater than $100,000, enter the **smaller** of **(a)** 5% of the excess over $100,000 or **(b)** $11,750. Otherwise, enter -0- | **12** | 11,750 |
| 13 | If line 1 is greater than $15 million, enter the **smaller** of **(a)** 3% of the excess over $15 million or **(b)** $100,000. Otherwise, enter -0- | **13** | 0 |
| 14 | Add lines 3, 6, 9, and 11 through 13. (Qualified personal service corporations, multiply line 1 by 35%.) | **14** | 136,000 |
| 15 | Alternative minimum tax (see instructions) | **15** | 0 |
| 16 | **Total.** Add lines 14 and 15 | **16** | 136,000 |
| 17 | Tax credits (see instructions) | **17** | 4,250 |
| 18 | Subtract line 17 from line 16 | **18** | 131,750 |
| 19 | Other taxes (see instructions) | **19** | 0 |
| 20 | **Total tax.** Add lines 18 and 19 | **20** | 131,750 |
| 21 | Credit for Federal tax paid on fuels (see instructions) | **21** | 0 |
| 22 | Subtract line 21 from line 20. **Note:** *If the result is less than $500, the corporation is not required to make estimated tax payments* | **22** | 131,750 |
| 23a | Enter the tax shown on the corporation's 2005 tax return (see instructions). **Caution:** *If the tax is zero or the tax year was for less than 12 months, skip this line and enter the amount from line 22 on line 23b* | **23a** | 102,000 |
| b | Enter the **smaller** of line 22 or line 23a. If the corporation is required to skip line 23a, enter the amount from line 22 | **23b** | 102,000 |

| | | (a) | (b) | (c) | (d) |
|---|---|---|---|---|---|
| 24 | **Installment due dates** (see instructions) ▶ **24** | 04-17-06 | 06-15-06 | 09-15-06 | 12-15-06 |
| 25 | **Required installments.** Enter 25% of line 23b in columns **(a)** through **(d)** unless the corporation uses the annualized income installment method or adjusted seasonal installment method or is a "large corporation" (see instructions) ..... **25** | 25,500 | 25,500 | 25,500 | 25,500 |

**For Paperwork Reduction Act Notice, see instructions.**     Cat. No. 11525G     Form **1120-W** (2006)

# Filled-In Form 1065 •
# Partnerships • Explanation

## ¶42 FORM 1065 IN BRIEF

### • Partnership Income Taxed to Partners

Partnerships are not subject to income tax but are required to file a return on Form 1065 (Code Sec. 6031). The purpose of the return is to provide information about the partnership and to show each individual partner's distributive share of partnership income or loss. Partners are taxed on their distributive shares of partnership income, even though it is not distributed to them and even though, by agreement, the shares cannot be withdrawn but must be retained as partnership capital (Code Sec. 702). For sales or exchanges of partnership interests involving unrealized receivables or inventory items as defined in Code Sec. 751, the partnership is also required to file Form 8308, Report of a Sale or Exchange of Certain Partnership Interests.

### • Which Organizations File Partnership Returns

Every partnership that engages in a trade or business or has gross income derived from sources in the United States must file a partnership return. Entities formed as limited liability companies and treated as partnerships for federal income tax purposes also must file Form 1065.

Partnership classification is determined under the "check-the-box" regulations (Reg. §§301.7701-1 through 301.7701-3). These regulations generally treat any domestic entity with two or more members as a partnership, unless the entity elects to be taxed as a corporation. An entity can also elect to be treated as a partnership by submitting Form 8832, Entity Classification Election. Foreign entities are generally limited to corporate status.

Certain publicly traded partnerships are treated as corporations under Code Sec. 7704 and would file a corporate return on Form 1120, rather than a partnership return. A publicly traded partnership is defined as any partnership in which partnership interests are traded on an established securities market or are readily tradable on a secondary market (or its substantial equivalent). However, a publicly traded partnership is not treated as a corporation for any tax year if at least 90% of its gross income

consists of interest, dividends, rents and other passive-type income.

Except for the 3.5% tax, an electing 1987 partnership will not be treated as a corporation for federal tax purposes. However, like other grandfathered partnerships under the Code Sec. 7704 provisions, an electing 1987 partnership will lose its partnership status as of the first day after December 31, 1997, on which it adds a substantial new line of business (Code Sec. 7704(g)).

**Foreign Partnership.** A foreign partnership generally must file a partnership return if it has gross income that is either U.S.-source or effectively connected with a U.S. trade or business. An exception exists for foreign partnerships with de minimis U.S.-source income and de minimis U.S. partners (Code Sec. 6031(e); Reg. §1.6031(a)-1(b)).

**Nonservice Partnerships.** Nonservice partnerships with 100 or more partners during the preceding tax year may elect a simplified reporting system by filing Form 1065-B, U.S. Return of Income for Electing Large Partnerships, instead of Form 1065. Such partnerships may be eligible to significantly reduce the number of items that must be separately reported to their numerous partners. A qualified partnership must make an election in order for the large partnership reporting rules to apply. Service partnerships and commodity pools are generally ineligible to elect large partnership status. An electing large partnership combines most items of partnership income, deductions, credits and loss at the partnership level and passes through net amounts to the partners. Special rules apply to partnerships engaging in oil and gas activities. See Code Secs. 771–777 and Form 1065-B and its instructions for more information.

### • Who Must Sign the Return

A partnership return must be signed by one general partner (or limited liability company member). A general partner is a member of the organization who is personally liable for partnership obligations. If a receiver, trustee in bankruptcy, or assignee controls the partnership's property or business, that person must sign the return. A person who is paid to prepare the return must also sign the return as preparer, and the "Paid Preparer's Use Only" section must be completed.

- **Due Dates**

A domestic, calendar-year partnership must file its 2005 return on or before April 15, 2006. A fiscal-year partnership should file its return on or before the 15th day of the 4th month following the close of the fiscal year (Code Sec. 6072(a)). A partnership whose partners are all nonresident aliens must file its return by the 15th day of the 6th month following the date its tax year ended (Code Sec. 6072(c)). The return should be filed with the designated service center for the state in which the partnership has its principal place of business or principal office or agency. A partnership may apply for an automatic three-month extension of the time for filing its return by filing Form 8736 by the regular due date. An application for an additional extension of up to three months may be filed on Form 8800, if reasonable cause for the additional time to file can be shown. However, an extension does not extend the time for filing a partner's income tax return or the time for payment of a partner's tax.

- **Failure-to-File Penalty**

A partnership that fails to file a timely and complete Form 1065 is subject to a penalty if this failure is not due to reasonable cause (Code Sec. 6698). This penalty is equal to $50 times the total number of partners in the partnership at any time during the tax year times the number of months or fraction of a month that the failure continues, but not to exceed five months.

A penalty may also be imposed on the partnership for (1) failure to furnish copies of Schedule K-1 to its partners or (2) failure to include all of the required information or inclusion of incorrect information (Code Sec. 6722). This penalty is equal to $50 for each statement with respect to which a failure occurs, up to a maximum of $100,000 for any calendar year. If failures are due to intentional disregard, penalties are increased to $100 per statement, or, if greater, 10% of the aggregate amount of items required to be reported, and the $100,000 maximum does not apply.

- **Accounting Period**

The tax year of a partnership is determined by reference to its partners (Code Sec. 706(b)). In general, a partnership must adopt or retain the same tax year as that of one or more of its partners who own a combined interest in partnership profits and capital of more than 50%. If there is no common tax year for partners owning a majority interest, then the partnership must adopt the same tax year as that of all of its principal partners. A principal partner is a partner with an interest of 5% or more in partnership profits or capital. If a tax year cannot be determined under either of the above rules, then the partnership must use a tax year that results in the least aggregate amount of deferred income (Reg. §1.706-1).

A partnership may have a tax year other than that determined under the above rules if it establishes a business purpose for that tax year. A partnership may also elect to use a tax year other than the tax year determined above, if the deferral period of the tax year elected is not longer than three months (Code Sec. 444). A partnership that makes such an election by filing Form 8716, Election to Have a Tax Year Other Than a Required Tax Year, must also complete Form 8752, Required Payment or Refund Under Section 7519, to compute the payments required when a Code Sec. 444 election is in effect.

Generally, a partnership return should cover a full tax year even though there may have been a change of membership during the year. The disposition by a partner of less than his entire interest or the addition of a new partner will not necessarily result in the closing of the partnership's tax year. But the partnership year *will* close as to a partner who dies or sells, exchanges, or otherwise liquidates his entire interest (Code Sec. 706(c)).

- **Tax Elections**

As a general rule, the partnership must make the elections affecting the computation of taxable income from its operations (Code Sec. 703(b)). Thus, elections as to the accounting method employed, the method of computing depreciation and cost recovery, nonrecognition of gain on an involuntary conversion, adjustments to basis under Code Sec. 754, and the election to expense the cost of certain depreciable property under Code Sec. 179 are made by the partnership and are binding on all partners. However, an individual partner, rather than the partnership, makes certain elections for purposes of filing his own tax return. These elections include use of the foreign tax credit under Code Sec. 901, the deduction and recapture of certain mining exploration expenditures under Code Sec. 617, the optional 10-year write-off of certain tax

¶ 42

preferences under Code Sec. 59(e), and basis reduction related to discharge of indebtedness under Code Sec. 108(b)(5) or (c)(3).

- **Attachments**

If a partnership needs more space than is provided on the forms or schedules to complete its return, it may attach separate sheets to provide the required information. Any attached sheet should be the same size and format as the printed forms or schedules. The totals from the attachments must be reported on the applicable form or schedule. The partnership's name and employer identification number should appear on each separate sheet.

## ON THE RETURN

For the purpose of illustrating the preparation of a partnership return, it is assumed that the partnership of Bilco Products is a toy manufacturer, reporting on an accrual and calendar-year basis. Under the articles of the partnership, the two partners share equally in the income or loss of the business. Warden's capital contribution is $40,000 more than that of his partner, Williams, to adjust for the fact that he devotes only part of his time to this business—25% as compared with 100% on the part of Williams. Both partners are involved in the operation of the business on a regular, continuous, and substantial basis. Both partners are jointly liable for partnership liabilities. Other facts are indicated by the entries on the return and the related explanations on these pages.

The items on the filled-in return and general rules for these and other situations most likely to be encountered are explained herein. For details and special rules, always consult the 2006 CCH Federal Tax Reporters.

- **Designation of Tax Matters Partner**

Partnership administrative proceedings (such as deficiency proceedings) are conducted at the partnership level. All notices sent by the IRS to a partnership are sent to the tax matters partner. A partnership may designate a tax matters partner and an alternate tax matters partner when filing its return (Reg. §301.6231(a)(7)-1). If no such designation has been made, the tax matters partner is the general partner having the largest interest in partnership profits at the close of the tax year (Code Sec. 6231(a)(7)). If there are two or more such partners, the tax matters partner will be the one whose name would come first alphabetically. In certain cases, the IRS may designate the tax matters partner or the Tax Court may appoint a tax matters partner for litigation purposes.

## ON THE RETURN

Bilco Products is not required to be governed by the consolidated partnership audit and litigation procedures of Code Secs. 6221 through 6234 because it has 10 or fewer partners and qualifies for the small partnership exception under Code Sec. 6231(a)(1)(B). However, Bilco has elected (by a statement attached to a prior year's return) to be subject to the unified procedures and has named Warden as its tax matters partner (Form 1065, Schedule B, Question 4).

- **Schedule K-1**

The partnership uses Schedule K-1 of Form 1065 to report each partner's share of the partnership's gross income, deductions, credits, etc. In general, the partnership will enter an asterisk (*) after any code that appears in the column to the left of the dollar amount entry space for each item for which it has attached a statement providing additional information. For those informational items that cannot be reported as a single dollar amount, the partnership will enter an asterisk in the left column and write "STMT" in the dollar amount entry space to indicate the information is provided on an attached statement.

## ¶43 MISCELLANEOUS INFORMATION—ITEMS A–I AND SCHEDULE B

The principal business activity and the principal product or service are reported in Items A and B, respectively, on page 1, Form 1065. The chief product or service should be stated as a general term such as "food," "toys," etc. A partnership's six-digit business code number is determined from the official instructions and is listed at Item C. The partnership's total assets at the end of the year are reported at Item F (but see below for an exception to completion of Item F).

A partnership must also indicate on page 1 of Form 1065 whether the form is being filed as an initial, final or amended return or to reflect a change of name or address (Item G). Also to be answered are questions concerning the partnership's accounting method (Item H) and the number of Schedules K-1 filed with the return (Item I).

Other miscellaneous information is reported on page 2, Schedule B. The partnership must indicate what type of entity it is (Question 1), whether any partners are also partnerships (Question 2), whether the partnership itself is a partner in another partnership (Question 3), and whether the partnership elected to be subject to the consolidated audit procedures of Code Secs. 6221 through 6234 (Question 4).

Partnerships that meet all of the following conditions must answer "yes" to Question 5 and are not required to complete Schedules L, M-1, and M-2 on page 4 of Form 1065, Item F on page 1 of Form 1065, or Item N on Schedule K-1: the partnership's total receipts for the tax year must be less than $250,000, the partnership's total assets at the end of the tax year must be less than $600,000, and Schedules K-1 must be filed with the return and furnished to the partners on or before the due date (including extensions) of the partnership return.

The partnership must indicate whether it has any foreign partners (Question 6). If so, it may have to file Forms 8804, 8805, and 8813, relating to the Code Sec. 1446 withholding tax based on effectively connected taxable income allocable to foreign partners. The partnership also must indicate whether it is a publicly traded partnership as defined in Code Sec. 469(k)(2) (Question 7). In addition, the partnership must indicate whether Form 8264, Application for Registration of a Tax Shelter, has been filed or is required to be filed (Question 8). If the partnership falls within the reporting requirements of Code Sec. 6111, it must file Form 8264 and the partners must file Form 8271, Investor Reporting of Tax Shelter Registration Number. If the partnership is a registration-required tax shelter or if it has invested in such a tax shelter, the partnership must supply the tax shelter registration number at Item E of Schedule K-1. The partnership must file a disclosure statement for each reportable tax shelter transaction in which it participated. Form 8886 is to be used for reporting such transactions.

The partnership must indicate whether the partnership had an interest in or a signature or other authority over any foreign financial accounts, such as bank or securities accounts (Question 9), and whether it received a distribution from, was a grantor of, or transferor to, a foreign trust (Question 10). If the answer is "yes," the partnership may be required to file Form 3520, Annual Return to Report Transactions With Foreign Trusts and Receipt of Certain Foreign Gifts.

The partnership must indicate whether there was a distribution of property or a transfer of a partnership interest during the tax year (Question 11). If so, the partnership may elect to adjust the basis of partnership assets by attaching a statement that includes the name and address of the partnership, a declaration that it elects under Code Sec. 754 to apply the provisions of Code Secs. 734(b) and 743(b), and the signature of the general partner authorized to sign the return. Finally, the partnership must indicate the number of Forms 8865, Return of U.S. Persons With Respect to Certain Foreign Partnerships, attached to the Form 1065 (Question 12).

## ¶44 GROSS PROFIT OR LOSS • COST OF GOODS

The amount entered at Line 1c, page 1, of Form 1065 represents the gross receipts from all trade or business activities of the partnership after separate deduction of allowances and returns. If the production, manufacture, purchase or sale of merchandise is an income-producing factor, the gross profit (Line 3) is the balance of gross receipts from such operations (Line 1c) after deduction of the cost of goods sold (Line 2) from Schedule A, Line 8. When computing the cost of goods sold in Schedule A, page 2, of Form 1065, it is necessary to deduct from purchases the cost of items withdrawn for personal use (Line 2).

### ON THE RETURN

Bilco reported $7,900 of "other costs" on Line 5 of Schedule A, which consisted of $874 of depreciation from Form 4562, Depreciation and Amortization (see ¶51-¶52), $2,470 in insurance costs attributable to its manufacturing operations, $2,126 for materials and supplies, and $2,430 in utility costs. Bilco would attach a schedule in support of Line 5 that lists these costs.

Partnerships must apply the uniform capitalization rules of Code Sec. 263A to determine which expenses must be capitalized. These rules apply to real and tangible personal property produced by the partnership for use in its trade or business, real and tangible personal property produced by the partnership to be held in inventory or for sale in the ordinary course of business, and to certain property acquired for resale. See Reg. §1.263A-1. Some costs that previously were not treated as inventory costs must now be included in inventory costs. These "additional Code Sec. 263A costs" are separately entered on Line 4 of Schedule

A by taxpayers who elect a simplified method of accounting under the regulations.

## ON THE RETURN

For 2005, it is assumed that the Bilco partnership had no additional Code Sec. 263A costs.

Where income is derived from a service business or a business not involving inventories, the appropriate lines of Schedule A are used to determine the cost of operations that is carried to Line 2, page 1, Form 1065.

## ¶45  SALARIES AND WAGES PAID

Salaries and wages should be reported on Line 9, page 1, of Form 1065, unless they were paid to partners, were allocable to an activity other than a trade or business activity, or were required to be reported elsewhere (such as a cost of labor on Schedule A or other capitalizable expense). Partnerships must reduce their salary and wage payments prior to reporting them on Line 9 by the amount of any:

- undistributed capital gains credit (Form 2439),

- credit for alcohol used as fuel (Form 6478),

- credit for increasing research activities (Form 6765),

- credit for employer social security and medicare taxes (Form 8846),

- backup withholding credit,

- work opportunity credit (Form 5884),

- welfare-to-work credit (Form 8861),

- disabled access credit (Form 8826),

- empowerment zone and renewal community employment credit (Form 8844),

- new market credit (Form 8874),

- see ¶65 as to treatment of the credits by the partners.

## ¶46  PAYMENTS TO PARTNERS

Guaranteed payments to partners are reported and deducted on Line 10, page 1, of Form 1065. Guaranteed payments include payments to a partner for services or interest for the use of capital if the pay-

ments are determined without regard to partnership income, are allocable to a trade or business activity, and are not capitalizable. Amounts paid for medical care insurance for a partner, spouse, or dependents during the tax year are also included on Line 10. However, the partners' distributive shares of partnership profits are not reported on Line 10. Deductible guaranteed payments to partners are further reported on Line 4 of Schedule K and in Box 4 of Schedule K-1 (see ¶65) and on Line 4a of the worksheet for computing net earnings from self-employment located in the Form 1065 instructions (see ¶68).

## ON THE RETURN

In the illustrative filled-in form it is assumed that the partner (Williams) who devoted all his time to the business receives a salary of $16,800, and the other partner (Warden) receives $6,000 in salary and $2,400 in interest on the $40,000 excess of his capital contribution over that of the other partner at the beginning of the year.

Partners receiving guaranteed payments are not employees. Thus, guaranteed payments are not subject to withholding, and the partners are ineligible for certain deferred compensation plans (Reg. §1.707-1(c)). Although payments to a partner for services rendered in organizing or syndicating a partnership can be treated as guaranteed payments, they are not deductible on Line 10 of Form 1065 because they are capital expenditures. See ¶52 for the amortization or deduction election concerning organizational expenditures. Guaranteed payments to partners for organizational or syndication services should be reported on Line 4 of Schedule K and in Box 4 of Schedule K-1 (see ¶65) and also included on Line 4a of the worksheet in the instructions (see ¶68) for purposes of computing net earnings from self-employment.

Guaranteed payments made in liquidation of the interest of a retiring or deceased partner are also reported on Line 10. In the case of partners who retire or die after January 4, 1993, a liquidation payment attributable to unrealized receivables and unstated goodwill may not qualify as a guaranteed payment unless made to a retiring or deceased general partner of a partnership in which capital is not a material income-producing factor (Code Sec. 736(b)(3)). A payment made to a retiring partner pursuant to a written contract that was binding on January 4, 1993, and thereafter, however, may continue to qualify as a guaranteed payment (P.L. 103-66, Act Sec. 13262(c)(2)). **The rules are highly technical, and the 2006 CCH Federal Tax Reporters should be consulted for details.**

## ¶47 REPAIRS

On Line 11, page 1, of Form 1065, a partnership enters the cost of incidental repairs related to a trade or business activity (including labor, supplies, and other items) that do not add to the value of or appreciably prolong the life of the property and that are not claimed elsewhere on the return. Expenditures for restoring, permanently improving, or replacing property are not currently deductible. Rather, they may be either depreciated or amortized.

## ¶48 BAD DEBTS

In general, partnerships must use the specific charge-off method of accounting for bad debts and deduct business bad debts as they become worthless in whole or in part during the tax year (Code Sec. 166). Cash-method partnerships cannot take a bad-debt deduction unless the amount was previously included in income.

### ON THE RETURN

In the illustrative return, the deduction on Line 12, page 1, of Form 1065 reflects a business debt that became wholly worthless during 2005.

## ¶49 RENT EXPENSE

The deduction at Line 13, page 1, of Form 1065 is for rent on property that a partnership uses in a trade or business activity but does not own. A partnership that leased a vehicle should complete Part V of Form 4562, Depreciation and Amortization, to determine if its deduction for rent is reduced by an "inclusion amount."

## ¶50 DEDUCTIBLE TAXES AND LICENSES

The general income tax provisions covering the deductibility of taxes apply to partnerships (Code Sec. 164). The Code provides for proration of real estate taxes between buyer and seller for the year of sale and specifically authorizes month-by-month accruals of real property taxes.

A partnership deducts taxes paid or incurred on business property used in a trade or business (and not included elsewhere on the return or on Schedules K and K-1) on Line 14, page 1, Form 1065. Taxes that must be capitalized under the uniform capitalization rules are not deducted on Line 14 but may be recovered as part of the cost of goods sold (see ¶43) or otherwise. Taxes paid or incurred for the production or collection of income, or for the management, conservation, or maintenance of property held to produce income, are reported on Line 13e of Schedule K and in Box 13 of Schedule K-1 (Code T), not on Line 14. Taxes allocable to portfolio income are not reported on Line 14 but are reported on Line 13b of Schedule K and in Box 13 of Schedule K-1 (Code G). Taxes allocable to rental real estate activities are reported on Form 8825, Rental Real Estate Income and Expenses of a Partnership or an S Corporation, and taxes allocable to other rental activities are reported on Line 3b of Schedule K. Foreign taxes are reported separately on Line 16l of Schedule K and in Box 16 of Schedule K-1 (Codes L and M), and not on Line 14.

### ON THE RETURN

On the filled-in form, the $10,610 of taxes and licenses that did not have to be capitalized under the uniform capitalization rules includes $188 in unincorporated business tax, $200 for a business license and inspection fees, and $10,222 in social security and employment taxes.

## ¶51 INTEREST EXPENSE

Only interest that is paid on debts incurred by the partnership for the operation of its trade or business and that is not claimed elsewhere on the return is entered on Line 15. Both cash-method and accrual-method partnerships deduct prepaid interest over the period of the loan instead of when the interest is paid. The $1,050 interest on the filled-in form is interest on business loans that is not required to be capitalized and does not represent a prepayment.

Investment interest incurred by a partnership on funds borrowed to purchase or carry property held for investment is subject to investment interest limitation rules that are applied at the partner level. Such interest and applicable items of investment income and expenses are allocated to the partners and are reported on Line 13c of Schedule K and in Box 13 of Schedule K-1 (Code I) (see ¶65) instead of on Line 15, page 1, Form 1065.

Pursuant to the passive activity rules of Code Sec. 469, the following items are not included on Line 15 of page 1: (1) interest allocable to portfolio income, (2) interest required to be capitalized because it is allocated to certain designated property produced by the partnership for its own use or sale, (3) interest on debt used to purchase rental property or debt used in a rental activity, or (4) interest on debt proceeds allocable to partner distributions. Interest allocable to a rental real estate activity is reported on Form 8825 and is used to compute net income or loss from rental real estate activities on Line 2 of Schedule K and in Box 2 of Schedule K-1. Interest allocable to other rental activities is included on Line 3b of Schedule K and is used to compute net income or loss from a rental activity on Line 3c of Schedule K and in Box 3 of Schedule K-1. See ¶62.

Interest paid to a partner for the use of capital is deductible in determining partnership ordinary income, but it is reported on Line 10 of Form 1065, along with salaries paid to partners, instead of on Line 15. See ¶45. Interest on debt proceeds allocated to distributions made to partners is reported on Line 13e of Schedule K and in Box 13 of Schedule K-1 (Code T). Interest is allocated among a partnership's various activities in the same manner as debt, and debt generally is allocated by tracing disbursements of the debt proceeds to specific expenditures. See Temp. Reg. §1.163-8T.

## ¶52 DEPRECIATION

Generally, for assets placed in service after 1986, the Modified Accelerated Cost Recovery System (MACRS) must be used. For assets placed in service after 1980 but before 1987, the Accelerated Cost Recovery System (ACRS) must be used. For tangible personal property placed in service before 1981, the straight-line method, declining-balance method, sum of the years-digits method or any other acceptable depreciation method may be used. An additional first-year depreciation allowance of 50 percent (30 percent in some cases) may be claimed for qualifying MACRS property. See ¶23. The amount of depreciation for depreciable property used in a trade or business activity is computed on Form 4562, and the total amount on Line 22 is carried to Line 16a of Form 1065; depreciation claimed elsewhere on Form 1065 is subtracted on Line 16b, and the difference is entered on Line 16c.

## ON THE RETURN

In 2005, Bilco Products acquired office furniture for $10,000, which it chose to depreciate under the general depreciation system under MACRS. It elects out of bonus depreciation. The deduction for the furniture (seven-year property) is $1,429, which is entered on Line 19c of Form 4562 (not reproduced here). The MACRS deduction for depreciable property placed in service before 2005 is entered on Line 17. The $3,658 that would be entered on Bilco Products' Form 4562, Line 17, represents the partnership's MACRS depreciation, computed using IRS tables for the 200% declining-balance method for (1) a truck with a five-year recovery period acquired on March 2, 2002, for $20,000, (2) machinery for manufacturing plastic toys with a seven-year recovery period acquired on June 14, 2002, for $7,000, and (3) a photocopier with a five-year recovery period acquired on April 8, 2003, for $2,500. The deduction for ACRS and other depreciation is entered on Line 16 of Form 4562. The $200 Bilco Products would enter on Line 16 represents the partnership's depreciation computed under the straight-line method on a patent acquired for $4,000 on August 2, 1989, with a 20-year useful life. The depreciation on the patent is reported on Line 13b of Schedule K and in Box 13 of Schedule K-1 (Code G), as a deduction related to portfolio income, and it is included on Line 16b of Form 1065. The $874 depreciation on the machinery (Form 4562, Line 17) is reflected as part of the cost of goods sold on Line 5, Schedule A (see ¶43). If a depreciation deduction for automobiles and other "listed property" is claimed, detailed information must be provided for the listed property regardless of when such property was placed in service. It is assumed that Bilco has no listed property.

The amount of depreciable property expensed under Code Sec. 179 on Line 12, Part I of Form 4562 should not be included in the amount on Line 16a of Form 1065, because it is not deductible by the partnership. Instead, this amount is passed through to the partners on Line 12 of Schedule K and in Box 12 of Schedule K-1. The expense deduction is subject to a maximum dollar limitation of $105,000 for 2005 and a limitation based on taxable income. These limitations apply at both the partner and partnership levels.

## ¶53 AMORTIZATION

The types of expenditures that may be amortized on Part VI of Form 4562 and deducted on Line 20, page

1, Form 1065, include (1) research and experimental costs under Code Sec. 174, (2) certified pollution control facility costs under Code Sec. 169, (3) business start-up expenditures under Code Sec. 195 (see below), (4) partnership organizational costs under Code Sec. 709 (see below), (5) certain bond premiums under Code Sec. 171, (6) costs of acquiring a lease under Code Sec. 178, (7) Code Sec. 197 intangibles, and (8) qualified revitalization expenditures under Code Sec. 1400I.

A partnership may elect to amortize start-up and organizational costs over a period of 60 or more months. The amortization period starts with the month in which the partnership begins business. If the partnership is liquidated before the end of the amortization period, the balance of the deferred organizational expenditures can be written off as a loss. An expenditure is eligible for amortization if it is incident to the creation of the partnership, is chargeable to the capital account, and is of a character which, if expended incident to the creation of a partnership with an ascertainable life, would be amortized over that life. This amortization election is not available for syndication fees.

A partnership can elect to deduct, under Code Sec. 709, up to $5,000 of organizational costs for the year the partnership begins business operations. The $5,000 deduction is reduced (but not below zero) by the amount the total costs exceed $50,000. If the total costs are $55,000 or more, the deduction is reduced to zero. If the election is made, any costs that are not deductible must be amortized ratably over a 180-month period beginning with the month the partnership begins business. Similar rules under Code Sec. 195 apply separately to business start-up costs. The deductible amount of these costs and any amortization are reported on Line 20, page 1, Form 1065.

The partnership must separately state the amortizable basis of reforestation expenditures, and the reforestation expense deduction. The amortization of reforestation expenditures is reported on Line 20c of Schedule K and in Box 20 of Schedule K-1 (Code O), but is not included on Line 20, page 1, Form 1065. The portion of reforestation expenditures in excess of the expense deduction can be amortized. The reforestation expense deduction is reported on Line 13e of Schedule K and in Box 13 of Schedule K-1 (Code S). Only the amortization of the excess amount is deducted on Line 20, page 1, Form 1065.

The optional write-off of certain tax preferences under Code Sec. 59(e) is reported on Line 13d of Schedule K and in Box 13 of Schedule K-1 (Code K), but is not included in Line 20, page 1, Form 1065.

## ¶54 DEPLETION

A partnership that takes a deduction for timber depletion on Line 17, Form 1065, should also attach Form T, Forest Activities Schedule, to the return. Depletion on oil and gas properties is not deductible by the partnership and is not reported on Line 17. Information needed to figure each partner's depletion deduction for oil and gas properties is reported on an attached statement for Line 20c of Schedule K and in Box 20 of Schedule K-1 (Code N).

## ¶55 RETIREMENT PLANS AND EMPLOYEE BENEFIT PROGRAMS

Deductible contributions made by a partnership for its common-law employees under a qualified pension, profit-sharing, annuity, SIMPLE, or simplified employee pension (SEP) plan, and under any other deferred compensation plan, are entered at Line 18, Form 1065. It is assumed that the Bilco partnership did not have such a plan. If a partnership contributes to individual retirement arrangements (IRAs) for employees, the amount of the contributions is entered as compensation on Line 9 on page 1 of Form 1065 or on Line 3 of Schedule A, and not on Line 18. Payments to qualified plans, SEPs, SIMPLE plans, or IRAs on behalf of partners are reported in Box 13 of Schedule K-1 (Code R).

Payments for health insurance for a partner, spouse, or dependents should be included on Line 10, page 1, Form 1065, as guaranteed payments and reported on Lines 4 and 13e of Schedule K and in Boxes 4 and 13 (Code L) of Schedule K-1. A partnership's contributions to other employee benefit programs for common-law employees are deducted on Line 19, page 1, Form 1065.

An employer that has adopted a pension, profit-sharing, or other funded deferred compensation plan (other than a SEP or SIMPLE IRA), regardless of whether or not the plan is qualified or a deduction is claimed for the current tax year, must file annual returns, which are due on or before the last day of the seventh month following the close of a plan year. See ¶27 for more information on such returns.

## ¶56 MISCELLANEOUS DEDUCTIONS

The total of the deductions related to a trade or business activity for which no specific line is provided on page 1 of form 1065 is entered on Line 20. A schedule should be attached to Form 1065.

### ON THE RETURN

Bilco Products in the filled-in form had the following deductions:

| | |
|---|---:|
| Light | $340 |
| Postage | 550 |
| Stationery | 40 |
| Insurance (other than shop) | 500 |
| Customer entertainment ($400 of expenses × 50% limit on deductibility) | 200 |
| Miscellaneous | 50 |
| Total | $1,680 |

Those items of expense that require separate computation should be excluded from Line 20, page 1, of Form 1065 and reported on Schedules K and K-1 instead. The $200 of nondeductible entertainment expenses is included on Form 1065, Schedule K, Line 18c, and on Schedule M-1, Line 4b (see ¶67). Each partner's share is entered on Schedule K-1, Box 18 (Code C).

## ¶57 ORDINARY INCOME OR LOSS

Line 22 on page 1 of Form 1065 shows all the partnership's ordinary income (or loss) from trade or business activities. The total income or loss is included on Line 1, Schedule K. Each partner's share of the income or loss is included in Box 1 of a separate Schedule K-1 (see ¶65). Specially allocated ordinary income or loss is reported on Line 11 of Schedule K and in Box 11 of Schedule K-1 (Code F). For more on losses, see ¶61.

Long-term and short-term capital gains and losses, portfolio income, rental income, and other items separately treated in Schedule K-1 are not shown on page 1 of Form 1065. They are included on the appropriate lines of Schedules K and boxes of Schedule K-1.

## ¶58 NET FARM PROFIT OR LOSS

Net farm profit or loss is entered on Line 5, page 1, of Form 1065. Details of the computation of farm income must be shown in a separate Schedule F (Form 1040),

Profit or Loss from Farming. However, farm income or losses from other partnerships are reported on Line 4, Form 1065.

## ¶59 INCOME OR LOSS FROM OTHER PARTNERSHIPS, ESTATES, AND TRUSTS

On Line 4, page 1 of Form 1065, enter the partnership's share of the ordinary income (whether or not received) or loss of another partnership and from estates and trusts. Losses are limited to the partnership's adjusted basis in the other partnership at the end of the other partnership's tax year that falls within the tax year of the partnership, and losses can also be limited by the "at risk" rules discussed at ¶60. Other items should be treated according to the character of each item in the other partnership's hands. Thus, the distributive share of another partnership's capital gains or losses should be reported on Lines 4 and 9 of Schedule D, Form 1065. Income from an estate or trust is reported in the same manner. Portfolio income or rental activity income or loss from another partnership or an estate or trust is reported on the applicable lines of Schedules K and K-1 or on Line 20a of Form 8825, not on Line 4, page 1.

## ¶60 SALE OR EXCHANGE OF PROPERTY

- **Capital Gains and Losses**

Partnership capital gains and losses are reported on Schedule D of Form 1065. Such amounts are generally included in portfolio income. (See passive activity loss rules at ¶62.) Every sale or exchange of a capital asset is to be reported on this schedule even though there is no gain or loss. However, those gains and losses that are specially allocated to partners should not be reported on Schedule D. Specially allocated short-term capital gains and losses must be entered in Box 8 of the applicable partner's Schedule K-1 and the total amount on Line 8 of Schedule K, while such long-term gains and losses are similarly entered on Line 9a of Schedule K and in Box 9a of Schedule K-1.

Short-term and long-term capital gains and losses are reported separately on Schedule D and carried over to the appropriate lines of Schedules K and K-1. The net short-term capital gain or loss from Line 5, Part I of Schedule D, is entered on Line 8 of Schedule K and in Box 8 of Schedule K-1. The net long-term capital gain or loss from Line 11 of Schedule D is entered on Line 9a of Schedule K and in Box 9a of Schedule K-1.

Gain from the sale of collectibles (28% rate gain or loss) included on Line 11 of Schedule D is reported on Line 9b of Schedule K and each partner's share is reported in Box 9b of Schedule K-1. Collectibles include works of art, rugs, antiques, metals (such as gold, silver, and platinum bullion), gems, stamps, coins, alcoholic beverages, and certain other tangible property.

Gains or losses from like-kind exchanges of capital assets are reported on Form 8824, Like-Kind Exchanges, and entered on Schedule D, Line 3 for short-term transactions and Line 8 for long-term transactions.

## ON THE RETURN

In the illustrative filled-in form, it is assumed that the partnership had a net long-term capital gain of $600 and that this amount was retained as partnership capital.

Gains and losses from sales or exchanges between partner and partnership are treated generally in the same manner as sales or exchanges between the partnership and nonpartners. However, loss is disallowed if the sale or exchange is between a partnership and a partner whose direct or indirect interest in capital or profits is more than 50%, or between partnerships in which the same persons own more than 50% of the capital or profits interests (Code Sec. 707(b)(1)).

- **Installment Sales**

In general, nondealer dispositions of property where a payment is to be received in a year after the year of sale must be reported under the installment method, unless the taxpayer elects to report the entire gain in the year of sale. Form 6252, Installment Sale Income, is used to compute the gain from such installment sales and is also used if the partnership received a payment in 2005 from a sale made in an earlier year that was reported under the installment method. As computed, short-term gains from installment sales are carried to Form 1065, Schedule D, Line 2, and long-term gains are carried to Schedule D, Line 7.

A partnership may elect out of the installment method in the year of sale for an installment gain that is not specially allocated among the partners by reporting the full amount of the gain on Schedule D of Form 1065. If the installment gain is specially allocated, the partnership may elect out of the installment method in the year of sale (1) by reporting the full

amount of the gain on Schedule K, Line 8 or 11, for a short-term capital gain, or on Schedule K, Line 9a or 11, for a long-term capital gain and (2) by entering each partner's share of the full amount of the gain in Box 8, 9a, or 11 of Schedule K-1, whichever applies. The election must be made on a timely filed return (including extensions) or on an amended return filed within six months of the due date (excluding extensions) under the rules of Reg. §301.9100-2.

Dealer dispositions of (1) personal property by a person who regularly sells such property on the installment plan or (2) real property held for sale to customers in the ordinary course of business may not be reported under the installment method (Code Sec. 453(l)). Income from dealer dispositions before March 1, 1986, dispositions of farm property, and certain dispositions of timeshares and residential lots may be reported under the installment method by including the gross profit on collections during the year from such sales on Line 1a of Form 1065. A schedule must be attached that shows the following for the current tax year and the three preceding years: (1) gross sales, (2) cost of goods sold, (3) gross profits, (4) percentage of gross profits to gross sales, (5) amount collected, and (6) gross profit on amount collected.

- **Gain from Recapture Property**

Gain from the disposition of Sec. 1245, 1250, 1254, and 1255 property is computed in Part III, Form 4797, Sales of Business Property. Partnerships (other than electing large partnerships) do not complete Line 27 of Part III, on which the recapture under Code Sec. 1252 is computed. The total amount of the ordinary income recapture is entered on Line 31, Part III, and then is carried to Line 13, Part II, Form 4797. This gain is added to other ordinary gains and losses on Line 17, Form 4797, and this total is carried to the partnership's Form 1065, Line 6. The balance of the gain, as computed on Line 32, Part III, Form 4797, qualifies for capital gain treatment under Code Sec. 1231. The portion of this gain that is attributable to a casualty or theft is carried to Line 33, Section B, Form 4684, Casualties and Thefts (see below), and any gain from other dispositions is carried to Line 6, Part I, Form 4797.

Amounts recaptured when the business use of Sec. 179 or 280F property drops to 50% or less are computed on Lines 33–35, columns (a) and (b), of Part IV of Form 4797. Recapture under Sec. 280F is reported on Line 7 of Form 1065. For the recapture of

Code Sec. 179 expense deductions, the partnership should attach a statement to Line 20c of Schedule K and Box 20 of Schedule K-1 (Code G) indicating the partner's distributive share of the original basis, depreciation allowed or allowable, and any Code Sec. 179 deduction passed through for the property and the partnership's tax year in which the amount was passed through.

## ON THE RETURN

Bilco Products has no transactions to report on Form 4797. Form 4797, for an S corporation, appears in ¶111.

### • Casualty and Theft Losses

Gains and losses arising from casualties and thefts of partnership property are reported on Form 4797 and/or on Form 4684 and are reflected on Schedules K and K-1. Such gains and losses are reported in the following manner on these forms: First, gains from dispositions of recapture property (see above) are reported in Part III of Form 4797, and the excess of the gain over the ordinary income portion (from Line 32, Part III, Form 4797) is carried over to Form 4684, where it is entered on Line 33 in Section B. Second, gains and losses from short-term property, gains and losses from long-term property that are not subject to ordinary income recapture, and losses sustained on recapture property are all reported first on Form 4684.

In Part II of Section B, Form 4684, gains and losses are separated into casualties and thefts for short-term and long-term property. For short-term gains and losses, losses from trade, business, rental, or royalty property other than property used in performing services (column b(i)) are offset against gains from all sources (column c), and the net gain or loss is entered on Line 31. The net gain or loss on Line 31 is entered on Form 4797, Part II, Line 14, or, if Form 4797 does not have to be otherwise filed, on Line 6, page 1, Form 1065, with the notation "Form 4684." Losses from other property (column b(ii)) are entered on Line 32 in Section B, Form 4684 and on Line 13e of Schedule K and each partner's share of the amount is entered in Box 13 of Schedule K-1 (Code T). Partners should be notified of gains or losses from casualties or thefts involving property not used in a trade or business or for income-producing purposes, and each partner will have to complete his own Form 4684.

For long-term gains and losses from casualties and thefts, total gains (Line 36, Section B, Form 4684)

are netted against total losses (Line 37). If a loss results, losses from trade, business, rental, or royalty property are offset against gains from all sources. A resulting net loss (Line 38a) is entered on Line 11 of Schedule K and is not entered on the partnership's Form 4797. Long-term losses from other property are entered on Line 38b, Form 4684, and are also entered on Line 11 of Schedule K. A net gain resulting from the above offset is reported on Line 39 of Form 4684 and is entered on Line 11 of Schedule K, and each partner's share is entered in Box 11 of Schedule K-1 (Code B). The partnership must give each partner a schedule for Box 11 of Schedule K-1 that shows the amounts to be entered on the partner's Form 4684, Section B, Line 34.

### • Code Sec. 1231 Transactions

Long-term gains and losses from sales, exchanges, and involuntary conversions, other than thefts and casualties, are reported in Part I, Form 4797. The amount of the gain that qualifies for capital gain treatment on dispositions of recapture property, other than thefts and casualties, from Line 32, Part III, Form 4797, is also reported on Line 6 in Part I of Form 4797. Total gains and losses from Part I (Line 7), Form 4797, are entered on Line 10, Schedule K, of Form 1065, and each partner's share is entered in Box 10, Schedule K-1. If the partnership has more than one activity, a statement must be attached to Schedule K-1 identifying the amount of Code Sec. 1231 gain or loss from each separate activity.

Sec. 1231 gain or loss from like-kind exchanges of business property is reported on Form 8824 and entered on Line 5, Part I of Form 4797. Each partner must combine his share of the partnership casualty gains and losses and Sec. 1231 gains and losses with his individual casualty gains and losses and Sec. 1231 gains and losses (if any) on Schedule D, Form 1040, and his Form 4797 to determine whether or not the capital gain or loss provisions apply and if there is any recapture of current net Sec. 1231 gains for non-recaptured net Sec. 1231 losses from prior years.

### • Rental and Other Property

On Line 10, Part II, of Form 4797, the partnership reports any gains and losses from sales or exchanges of properties that are not capital assets or Sec. 1231 assets. Gain or loss on property held one year or less and losses from the sale of Sec. 1244 stock are also reported on Line 10. Gains on the sale of Sec. 1244 stock are reported on Schedule D. Other items reported in

Part II and included in the total on Line 18, Part II, of Form 4797 are: Code Secs. 1245, 1250, 1254, and 1255 ordinary income (from Line 31, Part III, Form 4797); the net gain or loss from a casualty or theft of property held one year or less (from Line 31, Section B, Form 4684); and ordinary gain from installment sales (from Line 25 or 36 of Form 6252).

Partnerships that sell or otherwise dispose of property for which the Code Sec. 179 expense deduction was previously claimed and passed through to the partners must report all details of the sale or other disposition on Line 20c of Schedule K and in Box 20 of Schedule K-1 (Code F). Partners who receive a Schedule K-1 reporting such a transaction must report their distributive share on Form 4797 (sale), Form 4684 (casualty or theft), Form 6252 (installment sale), or Form 8824 (like-kind exchange), whether or not they were partners at the time the expense deduction was claimed. A worksheet is provided in the instructions to Form 4797 to figure the amount of gain or loss to report on the appropriate form.

Ordinary gains or losses from like-kind exchanges of property that are not capital assets are reported on Form 8824 and entered on Line 16, Part II of Form 4797. The net ordinary gain or loss on Line 17, Form 4797, is entered on Line 6, page 1, of Form 1065. Only gains and losses relating to assets used in a trade or business are generally included on Line 6, page 1. Gains and losses relating to rental activity assets are reported on Line 3 of Schedule K and in Box 3 of Schedule K-1, generally as part of the net income or loss from the rental activity, and on Line 19, Form 8825, Rental Real Estate Income and Expenses of a Partnership or an S Corporation, for rental real estate activities.

## ¶61 OTHER INCOME

At Line 7, page 1, Form 1065, any taxable trade or business income or loss for which no provision is made in Lines 1a–6 should be entered, including taxable income from insurance proceeds, interest income derived in the ordinary course of business, recoveries of bad debts, the credit for alcohol used as fuel reported on Form 6478 and (beginning in 2005) the credit for biodiesel fuels reported on Form 8864, all Code Sec. 481 income adjustments due to changes in accounting methods, any recapture of the Code Sec. 179A deduction for clean fuel vehicles, and any Code Sec. 280F recapture amount from Part IV of Form 4797. However, those items requiring separate computations that must be reported on Schedules K and K-1, including portfolio or rental activity income, are not included on Line 7 (see ¶65).

## ¶62 PARTNERSHIP LOSSES

At Line 22, page 1, Form 1065, the partnership ordinary income or loss should be entered. If there is a loss, the loss may be deducted by the partners on their individual returns as a business loss, subject to the passive activity rules discussed at ¶62. Although a partnership may not carry the loss back or forward to other years as a net operating loss, the partners' shares of the loss may result in net operating loss carrybacks or carryovers on their individual returns.

Under Code Sec. 704(d), a partner's share of the partnership loss (including capital loss) is allowed only to the extent of the adjusted basis of his partnership interest at the end of the partnership's tax year in which the loss occurred (but before reduction by the current year's loss). This is *not* necessarily the same as the balance in his capital account. Any excess is allowed as a deduction in later years to the extent that the partner's basis is increased above zero.

• **"At-Risk" Limitation on Deductible Losses**

The "at-risk" rules of Code Sec. 465 may also limit the amount of partnership losses that a partner can deduct. The at-risk rules apply to all activities conducted by a partnership as a trade or business or for the production of income. In addition, the at-risk rules apply to losses attributable to (1) the holding of real property that was placed in service after 1986 and (2) all real property held by the partnership if the partnership interest was acquired after 1986. Partners must consider the at-risk rules before the passive activity rules in preparing their returns.

Generally, a partner is considered at risk for an activity to the extent of the cash and the adjusted basis of other property that the partner has contributed to the activity, plus any amounts borrowed for use in the activity for which the partner is personally liable. Normally, nonrecourse loans are not treated as amounts at risk. A partnership must indicate the balances of any nonrecourse loans at the beginning and end of the year on Line 18 of Schedule L. However, if a nonrecourse loan is secured by a partner's personal assets (other than property used in the activity) and the loan proceeds are used in the activity, the lesser of the amount borrowed or the net fair market value of the assets is generally treated as an amount at risk by the partner. If a partnership is engaged in any activity, loans that are made to a partner from any person who has an interest in the activity (other than as a creditor) or who is related to a person having such an interest are not treated as amounts at risk. Invested amounts are also treated as not at risk to the extent that the partner is protected against loss by means of a guarantee, stop-loss order or other similar arrangement. Partners engaged in the activity of holding real property are considered at risk for their share of qualified nonrecourse financing determined on the basis of the partner's share of partnership liabilities incurred in connection with the financing (Code Sec. 465(b)(6)(c)). The partners' shares of all partnership nonrecourse liabilities, including qualified nonrecourse financing, are reported on their Schedules K-1, Item M. See ¶65.

If a partner has amounts not at risk for an activity and the partner shares in a loss for the activity, he is required to use Form 6198, At-Risk Limitations, to compute the amount of his allowable loss or deduction. In determining whether there is a loss from an activity, the profit and loss from the activity must be combined with any gain or loss realized by the partnership from the sale or disposition of an asset used in the activity, or with any gain or loss realized by the partner upon the sale or disposition of an interest (either total or partial) in such an activity.

The at-risk rules apply separately to each activity of the taxpayer, although activities may be aggregated in many instances. See the instructions for Form 6198. Any loss from an activity that is not allowed because of the at-risk limitation may be treated as a deduction allocable to such activity in the first succeeding tax year. Partners should be furnished a separate statement of income, expenses, deductions, and credits for each activity at risk or not at risk.

## ¶63 PASSIVE ACTIVITIES

Code Sec. 469 limits the amount of losses, deductions, and credits that partners may claim from "passive activities." Losses and credits from passive activities can only be used to offset income and tax from other passive activities. Passive activity losses cannot be used to offset nonpassive income, such as salaries, self-employment income from a trade or business in which the taxpayer materially participates, or "portfolio income" (see **Portfolio Income,** below).

A passive activity is one that involves the conduct of a trade or business (including any activity with respect to which expenses are deductible under Code Sec. 212) in which the taxpayer does not materially participate or a rental activity.

The passive activity rules apply to each partner's share of any income, loss or credit from the partnership. In order for the partner to comply with these rules, the partnership must report separately the income or loss and credits from each of the following: (1) trade or business activity (reported on page 1 of Form 1065); (2) rental real estate activity (reported on Form 8825 and Schedules K and K-1); (3) rental activity other than rental real estate activity (reported on Schedules K and K-1); and (4) portfolio income (reported on Schedules K and K-1).

The partnership must also identify certain items from passive activities that may be subject to recharacterization as nonpassive income. Activities subject to recharacterization are: (1) significant participation passive activities; (2) renting of substantially nondepreciable property; (3) passive equity-financed lending activities; (4) rental activities incidental to a development activity; (5) renting of property to a nonpassive activity; and (6) acquisition of an interest in a passthrough entity that licenses intangible property (Temp. Reg. §1.469-2T(f) and Reg. §1.469-2(f)).

- **Special Reporting Requirements for Passive Activities**

If the partnership has more than one activity, it must attach a statement to Schedules K and K-1 for each activity that is conducted through the partnership. The attachment for each activity must include the following information:

(1) a schedule, using the same box numbers as shown on Schedule K-1, showing the net income or loss, credits, and items required to be separately stated under Code Sec. 702(a) from each activity;

(2) the net income or loss and credits from each oil and gas well drilled or operated pursuant to a working interest that any general partner holds through the partnership, and other specified information for general partners who held their partnership interests during less than the entire year;

(3) the net income or loss and partner's share of partnership interest expense from each activity of renting a dwelling unit that the partner uses for personal purposes;

(4) the net income or loss and partner's share of partnership interest expense from each activity of trading personal property through the partnership;

(5) for any gain or loss from the disposition of an interest in an activity, the identity of the activity, the amount of nonpassive gain, if any, and whether the gain is investment income;

(6) for any gain or loss from the disposition of property used in a partnership activity, the identity of the activity or activities in which the property was used, any allocation of basis between activities, the amount of nonpassive gain, if any, and whether the gain is investment income;

(7) gross portfolio income and related expense;

(8) payments to partners for services, guaranteed payments, and payments to a retiring or deceased partner in liquidation of his interest;

(9) the ratable portion of any Code Sec. 481 adjustment;

(10) any gross income from sources that were specifically excluded from passive activity gross income;

(11) deductions that are not passive activity deductions;

(12) gain or loss allocable to each activity conducted through another entity, if the partnership makes a full or partial disposition of its interest in that entity;

(13) various items with respect to activities that may be subject to recharacterization as nonpassive income under Temp. Reg. §1.469-2T(f) and Reg. §1.469-2(f);

(14) credits associated with each activity conducted by or through the partnership;

(15) the partner's distributive share of the partnership's self-charged interest income or expense; and

(16) gross income from each oil or gas property of the partnership.

- **Portfolio Income**

Portfolio income includes gross income, other than income derived in the ordinary course of a trade or business, that is attributable to interest, dividends, royalties, income from a real estate investment trust, regulated investment company, real estate mortgage investment conduit, common trust fund, controlled foreign corporation, or qualified electing fund or cooperative. Interest earned on working capital is treated as portfolio income. Portfolio income also includes any gain or loss on the disposition of property producing portfolio income or of property held for investment. Portfolio income or loss is reported on Lines 5-9 of Schedule K and in Boxes 5-9 of Schedule K-1, not on page 1 of Form 1065. Expenses relating to portfolio income generally are reported on Line 13b of Schedule K and in Box 13 of Schedule K-1 (Codes G, H, and J); however, interest expense allocable to portfolio income is generally reported on Line 13c of Schedule K and in Box 13 of Schedule K-1 (Code I).

Reduced tax rates apply to dividends received during the tax year from a domestic corporation or a qualified foreign corporation (Code Sec. 1(h)(11)). Corporate stock dividends passed through to investors by a mutual fund or other regulated investment company, partnership, real estate investment trust, or held by a common trust fund are also eligible for the reduced rate assuming the distribution would otherwise be classified as qualified dividend income. In general, qualified dividends are excluded from investment income. But an election may be made on Form 4952, Investment Interest Expense Deduction, to include part or all of qualified dividends in investment income (Code Sec. 163(d)(4)(B)).

## ON THE RETURN

In the illustrative return, the partnership has $200 of qualified dividends, which it elects to include in investment income. The dividends are reported on Line 6b on Schedule K and $100 is allocated to each partner in Box 6b of Schedule K-1. It is assumed that the dividends were distributed during 2005, and this fact is indicated on Line 6a of Schedule M-2 of the filled-in form. Interest on bonds of $520 is reported on Line 5 of Schedule K and allocated to each partner in Box 5 of Schedule K-1. Royalty income is reported on Line 7 of Schedule K and in Box 7 of Schedule K-1. In this case, the partnership's royalties of $886 were received for use of a patent that was granted in 1988.

Net short-term capital gain or loss from Line 5 of Schedule D is entered on Line 8 of Schedule K and in Box 8 of Schedule K-1. Net long-term capital gain or loss from Line 11 of Schedule D is entered on Line 9a of Schedule K and in Box 9a of Schedule K-1.

Generally, amounts reported on Schedule D represent gain or loss from the disposition of property held for investment, that is, property that produced portfolio income. Any other portfolio income is reported on

Line 11 of Schedule K and and in Box 11 of Schedule K-1 (Code A) and is identified on an attached statement. Code Sec. 212 expenses from a partnership's residual interest in a REMIC are reported on the attached statement for Line 11 of Schedule K. Any gain or loss from Line 5 or 11 of Schedule D that is from the disposition of nondepreciable personal property used in a trade or business may not be treated as portfolio income, and is reported on Line 11 of Schedule K and in Box 11 of Schedule K-1 (Code F).

- **Rental Real Estate Activities**

If a partnership receives income from rental real estate activities, Form 8825 is completed and the net income or loss is entered on Line 2 of Schedule K and and in Box 2 of Schedule K-1. Generally, income or loss from rental real estate activities is a passive activity amount to all partners. However, partners who are individuals (or certain estates) and who actively participate in a rental real estate activity may be able to deduct up to $25,000 of losses from the activity (and the deduction equivalent of the tax credits) against income from nonpassive activities. The $25,000 amount is gradually phased out for high-income taxpayers (Code Sec. 469(i)). Also, the passive activity limitations do not apply to any rental real estate activity in which a partner materially participates if, during the tax year, more than half of the partner's personal services were performed in real property trades or businesses in which he materially participated and the personal services in such trades or businesses exceeded 750 hours (Code Sec. 469(c)(7)).

Low-income housing credits related to rental real estate activities are reported on Lines 15a and 15b of Schedule K and in Box 15 of Schedule K-1 (Codes A and B). Qualified rehabilitation expenditures are reported on Line 15c of Schedule K and in Box 15 of Schedule K-1 (Code C) and entered on Form 3468, Investment Credit, to figure the partner's allowable investment credit. Other credits related to rental real estate activities are reported on Line 15d of Schedule K and in Box 15 of Schedule K-1 (Code G). If there are losses or credits from a qualified low-income housing project, the passive activity loss and credit limitations may not apply. Any loss from such a project should be identified on a statement attached to the Schedule K-1 of any partner who is a qualified investor in the project.

- **Other Rental Activities**

Rental income, other than from rental real estate activities, is reported on Line 3a of Schedule K. The gain (loss) from Line 17 of Form 4797 that is attributable to the sale, exchange, or involuntary conversion of an asset used in such a rental activity is included on Line 3a. The deductible expenses related to the rental activity are reported on Line 3b, with a schedule of the expenses attached to Form 1065. The net income or loss is entered on Line 3c of Schedule K and each partner's share is entered in Box 3 of Schedule K-1. If the partnership has more than one rental activity, the amount from each activity must be identified on an attachment to Schedule K-1. Credits related to other rental activities are reported on Line 15e of Schedule K and in Box 15 of Schedule K-1 (Code H).

## ¶64 CHARITABLE CONTRIBUTIONS

Charitable contributions are not deductible by the partnership in determining ordinary partnership income or loss. Instead, each partner reports his share of the partnership contribution, along with his own contributions, on his individual return. The 50%, 30%, and 20% of adjusted gross income limitations on the partner's deduction apply to the total amount of contributions—his own contributions and his share of the partnership's contributions. However, the partnership must enter its total charitable contributions on Line 13a of Schedule K and each partner's share in Box 13 of Schedule K-1 (Codes A-F). In an attached schedule for Line 13a, the partnership must indicate by amount those contributions that are subject to the 50% and 30% limitations on cash and noncash contributions, and the 20% and 30% limitations on contributions of capital gain property.

### ON THE RETURN

On the filled-in form, Bilco Products reported a $200 contribution on Line 13a of Schedule K and Warden's $100 share of the contribution in Box 13 of his Schedule K-1 (Code A).

For contributions of property other than cash, the partnership must complete Form 8283, Noncash Charitable Contributions, if the deduction claimed exceeds $500. For contributions of $250 or more, no deduction is allowed unless the partnership obtains a written acknowledgement from the donee organization.

## ¶65 PARTNERS' SHARES OF INCOME AND CREDITS

The members of the partnership are liable for income tax in their individual capacities. Partners are taxable upon their distributive shares of the income of the partnership, whether or not the income is actually distributed. Schedule K is a summary of all of the partners' shares of partnership items and is required to be filed as part of Form 1065. Schedule K-1 is similar to Schedule K, except that Schedule K-1 shows one partner's distributive share of partnership items.

A Schedule K-1 must be prepared for each partner and must include the names, addresses, and identifying numbers of the partner and the partnership. All the questions on the schedule must be answered, and the analysis of the partner's capital account in Item N must also be completed. See ¶42 for an exception. See Schedule M-2, page 4, Form 1065, for the analysis totals. The partnership is responsible for filing one copy of each Schedule K-1 with Form 1065, keeping one copy for the partnership's records, and furnishing one copy, along with instructions, to the partner. The partner's distributive share of each partnership item is reported on the partner's tax return.

• **Distributions**

Distributions, whether cash or property, are ordinarily not taxable events. However, capital gain is recognized to the extent that cash distributions (and most distributions of marketable securities) exceed the partner's adjusted basis for his partnership interest (Code Sec. 731(a)(1)). Moreover, a partner contributing appreciated property may have to recognize built-in gain, termed "precontribution gain," if, within a seven-year period, either (1) the appreciated property is distributed to another partner (Code Sec. 704(c)(1)(B)) or (2) other property is distributed to the partner who contributed the appreciated property (Code Sec. 737). Such gain is not reported anywhere on Form 1065, but rather is reflected by the partner on Form 1040, Schedule D. The partnership does report the amount of cash and property distributions on Form 1065, Schedule M-2, Lines 6a and 6b, as reflected in the partners' capital accounts.

• **Allocation of Income, Deductions, and Credits to Partners**

Partnership income, gains and losses, deductions, and credits are allocated among the members in accordance with the partnership agreement concerning the sharing of income and losses generally. If the partners agree, partnership items may be specially allocated among the partners in a different ratio, provided the allocations have substantial economic effect (Code Sec. 704(b)). Specially allocated ordinary

gain or loss is reported on Line 11 of Schedule K and in Box 11 of Schedule K-1. Other specially allocated items are reported in the appropriate box of the applicable partner's Schedule K-1 and the total on the appropriate line of Schedule K. As to specially allocated items, see ¶59.

Income or losses are allocated to a partner only for that portion of the year in which he or she is a member of the partnership. It may be necessary to divide the partnership year into daily or other segments in order to satisfy this rule. Special allocation rules apply to cash-method partnerships and tiered partnership arrangements for allocating distributive share items where the partner's interest changed during the tax year (Code Sec. 706(d)). In addition, a partner's share of income, gains and losses, deductions, and credits is to be determined in accordance with the partner's interest in the partnership in cases (1) where the partnership agreement does not provide for an allocation of the above items or (2) where allocations under the partnership agreement lack substantial economic effect. Generally, a partner who treats partnership items in a manner different from the way the partnership treated the item must file Form 8082, Notice of Inconsistent Treatment or Administrative Adjustment Request (AAR).

• **"At Risk," Passive Activities and Allocation Rules**

Schedule K-1 contains a series of questions in Part II of the schedule that must be answered so that the "at risk" rules (see ¶61), the passive activity rules (see ¶62), and the allocation rules discussed above can be enforced and properly followed by each partner.

The partnership must indicate whether the partner for whom the Schedule K-1 is prepared is (1) a general partner or limited liability company (LLC) member-manager or a limited partner or other LLC member (Item I), (2) a domestic partner or a foreign partner (Item J), or (3) an individual, partnership or other entity (Item K).

Item L pertains to a partner's profit, loss, and capital sharing percentages. If there is a termination or decrease in a partner's profit- or loss-sharing percentage, the partnership should provide the partner with the necessary information so that gain or loss on the disposition of the interest can be computed. The information should include the partner's share of partnership liabilities, the partner's adjusted basis of any property distributed, and data that are necessary to apply the unrealized receivables and inventory items rule of Code Sec. 751.

The "Ending" column of Item L is completed for the percentages that existed at the end of the year. If a partner's interest terminated during the year, the "Beginning" column is completed, showing the percentages that existed immediately before the termination occurred. When the profit or loss percentage has changed during the year, the pre-change percentage should be shown in the "Beginning" column and the end-of-year percentages in the "Ending" column. If there are multiple changes in the profit- or loss-sharing percentage during the year, a statement must be attached that lists the date and percentage before each change. A partner's ownership of capital percentage is the percentage interest in partnership assets and liabilities that would be distributed to the partner if the partnership were liquidated at the end of the tax year.

- **Item M Schedule K-1 (Partner's Share of Liabilities)**

The partnership will enter the amount of the partner's share of partnership nonrecourse liabilities, partnership-level qualified nonrecourse financing secured by real property, and other recourse liabilities as of the end of the partnership's tax year on the corresponding Item M line. The amounts entered on the lines for recourse and nonrecourse liabilities are determined by reference to the rules contained in Reg. §1.752-1 through Reg. §1.752-3. Qualified nonrecourse financing is determined by reference to the at-risk rule definitions (Code Sec. 465(b)(6); Reg. §1.465-27). The total of the three Item M amounts are used to help compute the adjusted basis of the partner's partnership interest.

Partnership liabilities are shown in the "Liabilities and Capital" section of Schedule L. Total partnership liabilities for the Bilco Partnership are $23,764. This is the sum of Lines 15(d) ($6,337), 16(d) ($7,277), and 19(d) ($10,150) on Schedule L. It is assumed that George Warden is considered personally liable for one-half of this amount or $11,882. Accordingly, $11,882 is entered on the "Recourse" line for Item M of his Schedule K-1.

The amounts entered next to "Qualified nonrecourse financing" and "Recourse" for Item M are generally considered at risk-amounts for purposes of the at-risk rules (Code Sec. 465) described immediately below. However, it is possible that amounts entered by the partnership on these lines may not be considered at-risk. In this case, the Form K-1

instructions advise that those amounts should not be treated as at-risk. Note that both the partnership and the partner must meet the qualified nonrecourse rules before the amount shown next on the qualified nonrecourse financing line can be considered at-risk by the partner under Code Sec. 465. A partnership must enter on an attached statement any information the partner needs to determine if the qualified nonrecourse rules are also met at the partner level.

A partnership must give each partner a separate statement of income, expenses, and deductions for each at-risk and not-at-risk activity (Form 6198 instructions). The Schedule K-1 instructions for Item M indicate that if a partnership is engaged in two or more at-risk activities or in an at-risk activity and an activity not subject to the at-risk rules, a statement for each activity should be provided showing the partner's share of nonrecourse liabilities, partnership-level qualified nonrecourse financing, and recourse liabilities.

- **Distributive Share of Income**

A partner's distributive share of the ordinary income or loss from the partnership's trade or business activities, as reported on Line 22 of Form 1065 (see ¶**61**), is entered in Box 1 of Schedule K-1. If the partnership reports a loss on Line 22, the full amount of the partner's distributive share of the loss—determined without regard to the adjusted basis of the partner's interest in the partnership, the at risk amount (see ¶**61**) or passive activity limitations (see ¶**62**)—is to be entered in Box 1 of Schedule K-1. These limitations on losses apply at the partner level. A partner's distributive share of income or loss from rental real estate activities, as reported on Form 8825, is entered in Box 2 of Schedule K-1. A partner's share of income or loss from other rental activities is entered in Box 3 of Schedule K-1. Portfolio income or loss is entered in Boxes 5-9. A partnership that has more than one trade or business activity (or more than one rental real estate or other rental activity) must identify on an attachment to Schedule K-1 the amount from each activity.

- **Credits**

A credit for backup withholding on dividends, interest, and other types of partnership income is reported on Line 15f of Schedule K and in Box 15 of Schedule K-1 (Code Q). The amount reported on Schedule K-1 must be included in the total on Line 63, page 2, Form

1040. Any unused credits from cooperatives are apportioned among persons who were partners in the partnership on the last day of the partnership's tax year and are reported on Line 15f of Schedule K and in Box 15 of Schedule K-1 (Code U). If a partnership is required to recapture the low-income housing credit, each partner's share of the credit recapture is entered in Box 15 of Schedule K-1 (Code R or S). The partnership must also attach Form 8611, Recapture of Low-Income Housing Credit, to Form 1065.

Any investment credit allowed on partnership property is claimed by the individual partners rather than the partnership. The partnership reports the following investment credit information in Box 15 of Schedule K-1:

(1) qualified rehabilitation expenditures (Code C for rental real estate activities and Code D for other activities);

(2) the basis of energy property placed in service during the year (Code E); and

(3) the amortizable basis of qualified timber property (Code F). These items are also reported on the appropriate lines of Form 3468. The partnership indicates in a statement attached to Schedule K-1 the Form 3468 line number for reporting qualified rehabilitation expenditures for pre-1936 buildings (Line 1b) or for certified historic structures (Line 1c).

When partnership investment credit property is disposed of or ceases to qualify, or when there is a decrease in the percentage of business use before the expiration of the recapture period or useful life, any investment credit claimed may be subject to recapture, and any information that is needed to figure the recapture tax on Form 4255, Recapture of Investment Credit, must be reported on Line 15f of Schedule K and in Box 15 of Schedule K-1 (Code T).

The undistributed capital gains tax credit is also reported on Line 15f of Schedule K and in Box 15 of Schedule K-1 (Code I). This credit represents taxes paid on undistributed capital gains by a regulated investment company (RIC) or a real estate investment trust (REIT). As a shareholder of a RIC or REIT, the partnership will receive notice of the amount of taxes paid on undistributed capital gains on Form 2439.

The work opportunity credit is computed by the partnership on Form 5884, which must be attached to the partnership's return. The total credit is reported on Line 15f of Schedule K. The credit is then apportioned among the partners in accordance with each partner's interest in the partnership at the time the wages on which the credit is computed were paid or incurred and is entered in Box 15 of Schedule K-1 (Code J). The welfare-to-work credit, computed by the partnership on Form 8861, is apportioned in the same manner as the work opportunity credit and also is reported on Line 15f of Schedule K and in Box 15 of Schedule K-1 (Code K).

A credit is allowed for the sale of alcohol fuel or the use of alcohol as a fuel by a partnership. The credit is computed at the partnership level using Form 6478 and included on Line 7 of Form 1065 and on Line 15f of Schedule K. The credit is then apportioned to persons who are partners on the last day of the partnership's tax year. The apportioned credit is entered in Box 15 of each partner's Schedule K-1 (Code U). Each partner must also submit a Form 6478 with his tax return. Similar treatment now applies to the credit for low sulfur diesel fuel production (Form 8896) and will apply to the credit for biodiesel fuels (Form 8864) beginning in 2005.

A credit is allowed for the sale of qualified fuels produced from nonconventional sources. The credit is computed at the partnership level and then is apportioned to the partners based on their distributive shares of partnership income attributable to sales of qualified fuels. The apportioned amount is entered on Line 15f of Schedule K and in Box 15 of Schedule K-1 (Code U). The partnership must also attach a schedule showing the computation of the credit.

The amount of credit for increasing research activities is computed on Form 6765 and entered on Line 15f of Schedule K and in Box 15 of Schedule K-1 (Code U).

Form 8826 is used by an eligible small business to claim the disabled access credit and is attached to Form 1065. Part I of the form is completed by a partnership to figure the credit that is passed through to its partners. This credit is reported on Line 15f of Schedule K and in Box 15 of Schedule K-1 (Code L). Each partner must also complete Form 8826 and attach it to his return.

A credit is allowed for certain costs paid or incurred in connection with qualified oil recovery projects located in the United States. The credit is computed at the partnership level on Form 8830, which must be attached to the partnership's return. The credit is entered on Line 15f of Schedule K and in Box 15 of Schedule K-1 (Code U) of Form 1065.

On an attached statement to Box 15 of Schedule K-1 (Code V), the partnership provides any information the partners will need to report the recapture of credits, including the qualified electric vehicle credit, the new markets credit, the Indian employment credit, and the credit for employer-provided childcare facilities and services.

- **Tax Preference Items**

Income and deduction items affecting the computation of the alternative minimum tax (AMT) by partners are reported on Lines 17a-17f of Schedule K and in Box 17 of Schedule K-1. Each partner combines his distributive shares of these items with his individual amounts to determine whether Form 6251, Alternative Minimum Tax—Individuals, Form 4626, Alternative Minimum Tax—Corporations, or Form 1041, Schedule I, Alternative Minimum Tax (for estates and trusts) should be filed. If a partner's election under Code Sec. 59(e) may apply to any qualified expenditure, it is not included as a tax preference item; rather, such expenditures are reported on Line 13 of Schedule K and in Box 13 of Schedule K-1 (Code K). A schedule must be attached for Line 17f of Schedule K that shows each partner's share of other tax preference items or items needed to complete Form 4626, Form 6251 or Form 1041, Schedule I, not shown on Lines 17a-17e.

- **Other Items**

Income or profits taxes of a foreign country or U.S. possession paid or accrued by the partnership are entered on Lines 16a-16m of Schedule K. Each partner's share of these taxes and additional information needed to compute each partner's foreign tax credit are reflected in Box 16 of Schedule K-1 using the appropriate code.

The information and codes to be provided in Box 16 of Schedule K-1 include:

- name of country or U.S. possession (Code A),

- gross income from all sources (Code B),

- and gross income sourced at the partner level (Code C). Information relating to foreign gross income sourced at the partnership level includes:

- passive income (Code D),

- listed categories of income (Code E),

- and general limitation (all other) foreign source income (Code F).

Information on deductions allocated and apportioned at the partner level includes interest expense (Code G) and other deductions or losses (Code H); information on deductions allocated and apportioned at the partnership level includes passive income (Code I), listed categories of income (Code J) and general limitation (all other) foreign source income (Code K). Other information listed in Box 16 includes: total foreign taxes paid (Code L), total foreign taxes accrued (Code M), reduction in taxes available for credit (Code N), foreign trading gross receipts (Code O), the extraterritorial income exclusion (Code P), and other foreign transactions (Code Q).

Codes A-N for Box 16 of Schedule K-1 correspond with Lines 16a-16m of Schedule K. Codes O, P, and Q for Box 16 are reported on Line 20c of Schedule K. On Schedule K-1 for the items coded C, E, J, L, M and N, the code is followed by an asterisk and the partner's distributive share of the dollar amount and a statement is attached providing additional required information.

Other items for which no line is provided are reported on Schedules K and K-1 on Line 11 and in Box 11 (income or loss), Line 13e and Box 13 (deductions), Line 15f and Box 15 (credits), or Line 20c and Box 20 (other items). For each of these lines, the partnership must identify the amount and the activity to which the amount relates (if the partnership has more than one activity) on an attachment and use the appropriate code in the Schedule K-1 box.

The "Other income (loss)" items reported on Line 11 of Schedule K and in Box 11 of Schedule K-1 include:

- portfolio income not included on Lines 5-10 (Code A);

- net gain or loss from involuntary conversions due to casualty or theft (Code B);

- net gain or loss from Code Sec. 1256 contracts from Form 6781 (Code C);

- information needed to recapture certain mining exploration expenditures (Code D);

- cancellation of debt (Code E);

- and other income or loss (Code F), including recoveries of tax benefit items; gambling gains and losses; net gain or loss from gains from the disposition of farm recapture property and other items to which Code Sec. 1252 applies;

¶ 65

- gains from the disposition of an interest in oil, gas, geothermal or other mineral properties under Code Sec. 1254;

- any eligible gain from the sale or exchange of qualified small business stock under Code Sec. 1202(c);

- any income, gain, or loss to the partnership from distribution of unrealized receivables or inventory under Code Sec. 751;

- especially allocated ordinary gain or loss;

- gain eligible for Code Sec. 1045 rollover; and any gain or loss from Lines 5 or 11 of Schedule D that is not portfolio income. A statement that separately identifies the type and amount of income for each of the coded categories should be attached to Form 1065.

The "Other deductions" reported on Line 13e of Schedule K and in Box 13 of Schedule K-1 include deductions not included on Lines 12, 13a, 13b, 13c, 13d(2), 16l(1) and 16l(2) of Schedule K.

On Line 13d of Schedule K and in Box 13 of Schedule K-1 (Code K), the partnership reports the total qualified expenditures to which a Code Sec. 59(e) election (for deduction of certain expenses over a 10-year period rather than currently) may apply. A list is attached to Schedules K and K-1 showing the amount of each type of expense included in the total. The statement should also identify the property for which the expenditures were paid or incurred.

Tax-exempt interest income is reported on Line 18a of Schedule K and in Box 18 of Schedule K-1 (Code A) and includes any exempt-interest dividends received from a mutual fund or other regulated investment company. Line 18b and Box 18 (Code B) include all other tax-exempt income, such as life insurance proceeds. The amounts on Lines 18a and 18b are used to increase the adjusted basis in the partner's interest under Code Sec. 705(a)(1)(B). Nondeductible expenses paid or incurred by the partnership are reflected at Line 18c of Schedule K and in Box 18 of Schedule K-1 (Code C), and this amount decreases the adjusted basis of the partner's interest under Code Sec. 705(a)(2)(B). In the illustrative return, the $200 of nondeductible customer entertainment expense has been reflected at Line 18c of Schedule K and at Line 4b of Schedule M-1. Each partner's share is entered on Schedule K-1, Box 18 (Code C).

Items attributable to Line 20c of Schedule K are listed on a statement attached to Form 1065. The appropriate code is listed in Box 20 of Schedule K-1, followed by an asterisk in the left-hand column of the entry space. "STMT" is entered in the right-hand column of the box. Line 20c and Box 20 items include: the number of gallons of each fuel sold or used for a nontaxable use qualifying for the credit for taxes paid on fuel type of use and the applicable credit per gallon (Code C); information needed to compute interest due or to be refunded under Code Sec. 460(b)(2), relating to the look-back method for long-term contracts (Code D); information needed to figure the interest due or to be refunded under the look-back method of Code Sec. 167(g)(2) for certain property placed in service after September 13, 1995, and depreciated under the income forecast method (Code E); gain or loss and other information on the sale, exchange, or other disposition of property for which a Code Sec. 179 expense deduction was passed through to partners (Code F); the recapture of the expense deduction and other information for Sec. 179 property if business use dropped to 50% or less (Code G); the computation of any Code Sec. 743(b) basis adjustment relating to an acquired interest in an oil and gas partnership and the allocation of the basis adjustment to specific properties (Code H); information needed to compute the interest due under Code Sec. 453(l)(3) with respect to the disposition of certain timeshares and residential lots on the installment method (Code I); information needed to compute the interest due under Code Sec. 453A(c) with respect to certain installment sales (Code J); information needed to figure the interest due under Code Sec. 1260(b) (Code K); information relating to interest expense the partner is required to capitalize under Code Sec. 263A for production expenditures (Code L); nonqualified withdrawals by the partnership from a capital construction fund (CCF) (Code M); information necessary to compute a partner's depletion deduction for oil and gas wells (Code N); the amortizable basis of reforestation expenditures paid or incurred before October 23, 2004 (Code O); and information needed to figure unrelated business taxable income under Code Sec. 512(a)(1) for partners that are tax-exempt organizations (Code P).

Other information reported on the statement for Line 20c of Schedule K and Box 20 of Schedule K-1 (Code Q) includes: information needed by a partner that is a publicly traded partnership to determine if it meets the 90% qualifying income test of Code Sec. 7704(c)(2); any information needed by the partners to comply with Code Sec. 6662(d)(2)(B)(ii), regarding adequate disclosure of items that may cause an understatement of tax liability, and Code Sec. 6111, regarding tax shelter reporting requirements; information needed to file Form 8886, Reportable Transaction Disclosure Statement, if required; any income or gains reported on Lines 1-11 of Schedule K that qualify as inversion gain and related information, if the partnership is an expatriated entity or is a partner in an expatriated entity; and any other information the partners need to prepare their tax returns.

Investment interest expense is reported on Line 13c of Schedule K and in Box 13 of Schedule K-1 (Code I). This is interest that is properly allocable to debt on property held for investment. Property held for investment includes property that produces income (unless derived in the ordinary course of a trade or business) from interest, dividends, annuities, or royalties; and gains from the disposition of property that produces those types of income or is held for investment. Investment interest expense does not include interest expense allocable to a passive activity. This information is to be used by each partner in computing the allowable investment interest deduction on Form 4952. Investment income and expenses other than interest are reported on Lines 20a and 20b, respectively, of Schedule K and in Box 20 (Codes A and B) of Schedule K-1.

On Line 19a of Schedule K and and in Box 19 of Schedule K-1 (Code A), the partnership enters the total amount of distributions to each partner of cash and marketable securities that are treated as money under Code Sec. 731(c)(1). Marketable securities are valued at fair market value on the date of distribution. The value of marketable securities does not include the distributee partner's share of the gain on the securities distributed to that partner. For marketable securities treated as money, the partnership should attach a separate statement showing the partnership's adjusted basis in the securities immediately before distribution and their fair market value on the date of distribution.

Line 19b of Schedule K and and Box 19 of Schedule K-1 (Code B) show the total distributions to each partner of property other than money or marketable securities included in Line 19a. The property is valued at its adjusted basis to the partnership immediately before the distribution.

On Line 1 of the Analysis of Net Income (Loss) section at the top of page 4, Form 1065, the partnership enters the total amount of distributive income and payment

items from Lines 1 through 11 of Schedule K, less the sum of Lines 12 through 13e, 16l(1), and 16l(2) of Schedule K. Then, the total from Line 1 is allocated to general and limited partners and by type of partner (corporate, active or passive individual, partnership, exempt organization, or nominee), on Line 2.

## ¶66 BALANCE SHEETS

The partnership balance sheets at the beginning and end of the tax year are shown in Schedule L, page 4, of Form 1065. Generally, the balance sheets should agree with the books. Accordingly, the items shown in these balance sheets should tie in with the inventories, capital asset transactions, and reserves shown in the return. Where the amounts listed in Schedule L are not the same as the book amounts, the difference should be explained in a statement attached to the return. Schedule L need not be completed if the partnership's total receipts are less than $250,000, the partnership's total assets at the end of the tax year are less than $600,000, and if Schedules K-1 are filed with the return and furnished to partners by the due date (including extensions).

## ¶67 RECONCILIATION SCHEDULES

- **Reconciliation of Income Per Books with Income Per Return**

Schedule M-1, page 4, Form 1065, reconciles partnership book and taxable income. Neither this Schedule nor Schedule M-2 needs to be completed, however, if the partnership's total receipts are less than $250,000, the partnership's total assets at the end of the tax year are less than $600,000, and if Schedules K-1 are filed with the return and furnished to partners by the due date (including extensions).

On Line 1, the partnership reports the partnership net income per books as of the end of the tax year. Amounts that must be included for tax purposes are added on Lines 2 and 3. On Line 2, the partnership reports income included on Lines 1, 2, 3c, 5, 6a, 7, 8, 9a, 10 and 11 of Schedule K that was not recorded on partnership books. Guaranteed payments, other than health insurance, made to partners and recorded on Line 4, Schedule K are reflected at Line 3, Schedule M-1. On Line 4a, the partnership reports any expenses, including depreciation, recorded on partnership books that is not included on Schedule K, Lines 1-13e, 16l(1) and 16l(2). The $874 depreciation deduction that Bilco reported on Schedule A is not reported on Line 4a because partnership income reported on Line 1, Schedule K, takes this amount into account. Any disallowed travel and entertainment expenses are reported on Line 4b. This amount includes: the 50% of meals and entertainment disallowed under Code Sec. 274(n); any expenses for the use of an entertainment facility; business gifts in excess of $25; cruise ship convention expenses in excess of $2,000; employee achievement awards in excess of $400; the cost of entertainment tickets in excess of the face value; the cost of skyboxes in excess of the face value of nonluxury box seats; the disallowed portion of luxury water travel; educational travel expenses; nondeductible club dues; and any other disallowed travel and entertainment expenses. The total amount of Lines 1–4 is reported on Line 5.

On Line 6, the partnership reports any tax-exempt income and tax-exempt interest. Any deductions that were not charged against book income for the tax year are reported on Line 7. The total of Lines 6 and 7 is entered on Line 8 and then subtracted from the amount on Line 5. The remainder, which is entered on Line 9, should match the amount reported on Line 1 of the Analysis of Net Income (Loss) section at the top of page 4, Form 1065.

• **Analysis of Partners' Capital Accounts**

Schedule M-2 analyzes the partners' capital accounts by showing the changes during the year. The rules for determining the basis of a partner's interest in his capital account that are contained in Reg. §1.704-1(b)(2)(iv) may be used, but are not required. The beginning and ending capital accounts should agree with the partnership's books and with the balance sheet amounts reported on Line 21 of Schedule L, Balance Sheets per Books. Any difference should be explained in an attached statement. The analysis of each partner's capital account is located on Schedule K-1 at Item N. See ¶**42** for an exception.

Contributions to the partnership capital during the tax year are reported on Line 2 of Schedule M-2. In 2005, partner Williams contributed land with a basis of $7,000 and a fair market value of $12,000. The partners have agreed that Williams will be taxed on the first $5,000 of gain if the land is sold to take account of the variation between the adjusted tax basis and the fair market value. Williams' capital account for book (and Schedule M-2) purposes includes the $12,000 fair market value of the land contributed, which is

reflected on Line 2b. Partner Warden contributed $12,000 in cash, which is reported on Line 2a, to equal the $12,000 value of the land contributed. Thus, the capital contributed to the partnership during the year is $24,000. On Line 3, the partnership reports the net income shown on partnership books from Schedule M-1, Line 1. On Line 4, the partnership enters other increases to the capital accounts. On Line 6, the partnership reports the total distributions of cash and property to partners. Bilco Products reports the $200 cash distribution to the partners on Line 6a. On Line 7, the partnership reports any other decreases that are not included in Line 6. The total from Lines 6 and 7 is deducted from the amount on Line 5 and reported on Line 9. The amount on Line 9 should equal the total of all the amounts reported on the "Ending capital account" line in Item N on Schedule K-1.

## ¶68 NET EARNINGS FROM SELF-EMPLOYMENT

To calculate the self-employment tax on individuals, partnership net earnings from self-employment are computed on a worksheet provided in the instructions for Form 1065, page 28. The resulting amount, here $38,706, is entered on Line 14a, Schedule K. The partnership ordinary income portion of the net earnings from self-employment is allocated in the same proportion as the partners' percentage shares of the general profits of the partnership. The salary payments to the partners are allocated on the basis of the amounts actually paid or accrued to the partners. The total amount allocated to each partner is entered in Box 14 of his Schedule K-1 (Code A) ($15,153 for Warden and $23,553 for Williams). These amounts are also entered as nonfarm income (Code C) in Box 14 (see below).

A limited partner's share of partnership ordinary income (loss) shown on Line 1 of Schedules K and K-1 is not self-employment income. Limited partners may treat as self-employment income only guaranteed payments for services. Such amounts treated as self-employment income, including guaranteed payments for services, are reported in Box 14 of Schedule K-1.

The partnership's gross farming or fishing income from self-employment is entered on Line 14b of Schedule K. Each partner's distributive share is entered in Box 14 of Schedule K-1 (Code B). Individual partners need this amount to figure net earnings from self-employment under the farm optional method in Section B, Part II of Schedule SE, Form 1040. The partnership's gross nonfarm income from self-employment is entered on Line 14c of Schedule K. Each partner's distributive share is entered in Box 14 of Schedule K-1 (Code C). Individual partners need this amount to figure net earnings from self-employment under the nonfarm optional method in Section B, Part II of Schedule SE, Form 1040.

| Form **1065** | **U.S. Return of Partnership Income** | OMB No. 1545-0099 |
|---|---|---|

Department of the Treasury
Internal Revenue Service

For calendar year 2005, or tax year beginning .........., 2005, ending .........., 20...... .
► See separate instructions.

**2005**

**A** Principal business activity
Manufacturing

**B** Principal product or service
Toys

**C** Business code number
339900

Use the IRS label. Otherwise, print or type.

Name of partnership
Bilco Products

Number, street, and room or suite no. If a P.O. box, see the instructions.
131 Mill Street

City or town, state, and ZIP code
Chicago, IL 60600

**D** Employer identification number
21 8253431

**E** Date business started
01-02-78

**F** Total assets (see the instructions)
$ 150,024

**G** Check applicable boxes: (1) ☐ Initial return  (2) ☐ Final return  (3) ☐ Name change  (4) ☐ Address change  (5) ☐ Amended return

**H** Check accounting method: (1) ☐ Cash  (2) ☑ Accrual  (3) ☐ Other (specify) ►.............

**I** Number of Schedules K-1. Attach one for each person who was a partner at any time during the tax year ►.............

**Caution.** Include **only** trade or business income and expenses on lines 1a through 22 below. See the instructions for more information.

**Income**

| | | | |
|---|---|---|---|
| **1a** Gross receipts or sales | 1a | 250,446 | |
| **b** Less returns and allowances | 1b | 5,400 | 1c 245,066 |
| **2** Cost of goods sold (Schedule A, line 8) | | | 2 146,200 |
| **3** Gross profit. Subtract line 2 from line 1c | | | 3 98,866 |
| **4** Ordinary income (loss) from other partnerships, estates, and trusts (attach statement) | | | 4 |
| **5** Net farm profit (loss) (attach Schedule F (Form 1040)) | | | 5 |
| **6** Net gain (loss) from Form 4797, Part II, line 17 (attach Form 4797) | | | 6 |
| **7** Other income (loss) (attach statement) | | | 7 |
| **8** **Total income (loss).** Combine lines 3 through 7 | | | 8 98,866 |

**Deductions** (see the instructions for limitations)

| | | |
|---|---|---|
| **9** Salaries and wages (other than to partners) (less employment credits) | 9 | 26,000 |
| **10** Guaranteed payments to partners | 10 | 25,200 |
| **11** Repairs and maintenance | 11 | 4,836 |
| **12** Bad debts | 12 | 2,000 |
| **13** Rent | 13 | 9,771 |
| **14** Taxes and licenses | 14 | 10,610 |
| **15** Interest | 15 | 1,050 |
| **16a** Depreciation (if required, attach Form 4562) | 16a 5,287 | |
| **b** Less depreciation reported on Schedule A and elsewhere on return | 16b 1,074 | 16c 4,213 |
| **17** Depletion (**Do not deduct oil and gas depletion.**) | 17 | |
| **18** Retirement plans, etc. | 18 | |
| **19** Employee benefit programs | 19 | |
| **20** Other deductions (attach statement) | 20 | 1,680 |
| **21** **Total deductions.** Add the amounts shown in the far right column for lines 9 through 20 | 21 | 85,360 |
| **22** **Ordinary business income (loss).** Subtract line 21 from line 8 | 22 | 13,506 |

**Sign Here**

Under penalties of perjury, I declare that I have examined this return, including accompanying schedules and statements, and to the best of my knowledge and belief, it is true, correct, and complete. Declaration of preparer (other than general partner or limited liability company member) is based on all information of which preparer has any knowledge.

► Signature of general partner or limited liability company member manager        Date

May the IRS discuss this return with the preparer shown below (see instructions)? ☑ Yes ☐ No

**Paid Preparer's Use Only**

| Preparer's signature | Date | Check if self-employed ► ☑ | Preparer's SSN or PTIN 330-24-1049 |
|---|---|---|---|
| Firm's name (or yours if self-employed), address, and ZIP code | Robert Landers 1212 Lomax Rd., Chicago, IL 60641 | EIN ► | Phone no. ( 773 ) 555-1255 |

**For Privacy Act and Paperwork Reduction Act Notice, see separate instructions.**        Cat. No. 11390Z        Form **1065** (2005)

Form 1065 (2005)                                                                                    Page **2**

## Schedule A    Cost of Goods Sold (see the instructions)

| | | | |
|---|---|---|---:|
| 1 | Inventory at beginning of year. | 1 | 50,000 |
| 2 | Purchases less cost of items withdrawn for personal use | 2 | 46,300 |
| 3 | Cost of labor | 3 | 103,000 |
| 4 | Additional section 263A costs *(attach statement)* | 4 | |
| 5 | Other costs *(attach statement)*. | 5 | 7,900 |
| 6 | **Total.** Add lines 1 through 5 | 6 | 207,200 |
| 7 | Inventory at end of year | 7 | 61,000 |
| 8 | **Cost of goods sold.** Subtract line 7 from line 6. Enter here and on page 1, line 2 | 8 | 146,200 |

9a  Check all methods used for valuing closing inventory:

   (i)  ☐ Cost as described in Regulations section 1.471-3

   (ii) ☑ Lower of cost or market as described in Regulations section 1.471-4

   (iii) ☐ Other (specify method used and attach explanation) ▶ ................................................................

   b  Check this box if there was a writedown of "subnormal" goods as described in Regulations section 1.471-2(c) . . . ▶ ☐

   c  Check this box if the LIFO inventory method was adopted this tax year for any goods *(if checked, attach Form 970)*. . ▶ ☐

   d  Do the rules of section 263A (for property produced or acquired for resale) apply to the partnership?. . ☑ **Yes** ☐ **No**

   e  Was there any change in determining quantities, cost, or valuations between opening and closing inventory? ☐ **Yes** ☑ **No**
   If "Yes," attach explanation.

## Schedule B    Other Information

| | | Yes | No |
|---|---|:---:|:---:|
| 1 | What type of entity is filing this return? Check the applicable box: | | |

   a ☑ Domestic general partnership          b ☐ Domestic limited partnership

   c ☐ Domestic limited liability company     d ☐ Domestic limited liability partnership

   e ☐ Foreign partnership                    f ☐ Other ▶ ................................................................

| | | Yes | No |
|---|---|:---:|:---:|
| 2 | Are any partners in this partnership also partnerships? | | ✔ |
| 3 | During the partnership's tax year, did the partnership own any interest in another partnership or in any foreign entity that was disregarded as an entity separate from its owner under Regulations sections 301.7701-2 and 301.7701-3? If yes, see instructions for required attachment | | ✔ |
| 4 | Did the partnership file Form 8893, Election of Partnership Level Tax Treatment, or an election statement under section 6231(a)(1)(B)(ii) for partnership-level tax treatment, that is in effect for this tax year? See Form 8893 for more details | ✔ | |
| 5 | Does this partnership meet all three of the following requirements? | | |
| a | The partnership's total receipts for the tax year were less than $250,000; | | |
| b | The partnership's total assets at the end of the tax year were less than $600,000; and | | |
| c | Schedules K-1 are filed with the return and furnished to the partners on or before the due date (including extensions) for the partnership return. | | |
| | If "Yes," the partnership is not required to complete Schedules L, M-1, and M-2; Item F on page 1 of Form 1065; or Item N on Schedule K-1. | | ✔ |
| 6 | Does this partnership have any foreign partners? If "Yes," the partnership may have to file Forms 8804, 8805 and 8813. See the instructions | | ✔ |
| 7 | Is this partnership a publicly traded partnership as defined in section 469(k)(2)? | | ✔ |
| 8 | Has this partnership filed, or is it required to file, a return under section 6111 to provide information on any reportable transaction? | | ✔ |
| 9 | At any time during calendar year 2005, did the partnership have an interest in or a signature or other authority over a financial account in a foreign country (such as a bank account, securities account, or other financial account)? See the instructions for exceptions and filing requirements for Form TD F 90-22.1. If "Yes," enter the name of the foreign country. ▶ ................................ | | ✔ |
| 10 | During the tax year, did the partnership receive a distribution from, or was it the grantor of, or transferor to, a foreign trust? If "Yes," the partnership may have to file Form 3520. See the instructions | | ✔ |
| 11 | Was there a distribution of property or a transfer (for example, by sale or death) of a partnership interest during the tax year? If "Yes," you may elect to adjust the basis of the partnership's assets under section 754 by attaching the statement described under *Elections Made By the Partnership* in the instructions | | ✔ |
| 12 | Enter the number of Forms 8865, Return of U.S. Persons With Respect to Certain Foreign Partnerships, attached to this return ▶ | | |

### Designation of Tax Matters Partner (see the instructions)

Enter below the general partner designated as the tax matters partner (TMP) for the tax year of this return:

| | | | |
|---|---|---|---|
| Name of designated TMP ▶ | **George A. Warden** | Identifying number of TMP ▶ | **330-24-1049** |
| Address of designated TMP ▶ | **789 Code Drive**<br>**Chicago, IL 60600** | | |

Form **1065** (2005)

¶ **68**

Form 1065 (2005) — Page **3**

## Schedule K — Partners' Distributive Share Items

| | | Total amount |
|---|---|---|
| **Income (Loss)** | **1** Ordinary business income (loss) (page 1, line 22) | **1** 13,506 |
| | **2** Net rental real estate income (loss) *(attach Form 8825)* | **2** |
| | **3a** Other gross rental income (loss) — **3a** | |
| | **b** Expenses from other rental activities *(attach statement)* — **3b** | |
| | **c** Other net rental income (loss). Subtract line 3b from line 3a | **3c** |
| | **4** Guaranteed payments | **4** 25,200 |
| | **5** Interest income | **5** 520 |
| | **6** Dividends: **a** Ordinary dividends | **6a** |
| | **b** Qualified dividends — **6b** | |
| | **7** Royalties | **7** 886 |
| | **8** Net short-term capital gain (loss) *(attach Schedule D (Form 1065))* | **8** |
| | **9a** Net long-term capital gain (loss) *(attach Schedule D (Form 1065))* | **9a** 600 |
| | **b** Collectibles (28%) gain (loss) — **9b** | |
| | **c** Unrecaptured section 1250 gain *(attach statement)* — **9c** | |
| | **10** Net section 1231 gain (loss) *(attach Form 4797)* | **10** |
| | **11** Other income (loss) *(see instructions)* Type ▶ | **11** |
| **Deductions** | **12** Section 179 deduction *(attach Form 4562)* | **12** |
| | **13a** Contributions | **13a** 200 |
| | **b** Investment interest expense | **13b** 200 |
| | **c** Section 59(e)(2) expenditures: **(1)** Type ▶ **(2)** Amount ▶ | **13c(2)** |
| | **d** Other deductions *(see instructions)* Type ▶ | **13d** |
| **Self-Employment** | **14a** Net earnings (loss) from self-employment | **14a** 38,706 |
| | **b** Gross farming or fishing income | **14b** |
| | **c** Gross nonfarm income | **14c** 38,706 |
| **Credits & Credit Recapture** | **15a** Low-income housing credit (section 42(j)(5)) | **15a** |
| | **b** Low-income housing credit (other) | **15b** |
| | **c** Qualified rehabilitation expenditures (rental real estate) *(attach Form 3468)* | **15c** |
| | **d** Other rental real estate credits *(see instructions)* Type ▶ | **15d** |
| | **e** Other rental credits *(see instructions)* Type ▶ | **15e** |
| | **f** Other credits and credit recapture *(see instructions)* Type ▶ | **15f** |
| **Foreign Transactions** | **16a** Name of country or U.S. possession ▶ | |
| | **b** Gross income from all sources | **16b** |
| | **c** Gross income sourced at partner level | **16c** |
| | *Foreign gross income sourced at partnership level* | |
| | **d** Passive ▶ **e** Listed categories *(attach statement)* ▶ **f** General limitation ▶ | **16f** |
| | *Deductions allocated and apportioned at partner level* | |
| | **g** Interest expense ▶ **h** Other | **16h** |
| | *Deductions allocated and apportioned at partnership level to foreign source income* | |
| | **i** Passive ▶ **j** Listed categories *(attach statement)* ▶ **k** General limitation ▶ | **16k** |
| | **l** Total foreign taxes (check one): ▶ Paid ☐ Accrued ☐ | **16l** |
| | **m** Reduction in taxes available for credit *(attach statement)* | **16m** |
| | **n** Other foreign tax information *(attach statement)* | |
| **Alternative Minimum Tax (AMT) Items** | **17a** Post-1986 depreciation adjustment | **17a** |
| | **b** Adjusted gain or loss | **17b** |
| | **c** Depletion (other than oil and gas) | **17c** |
| | **d** Oil, gas, and geothermal properties—gross income | **17d** |
| | **e** Oil, gas, and geothermal properties—deductions | **17e** |
| | **f** Other AMT items *(attach statement)* | **17f** |
| **Other Information** | **18a** Tax-exempt interest income | **18a** |
| | **b** Other tax-exempt income | **18b** |
| | **c** Nondeductible expenses | **18c** 200 |
| | **19a** Distributions of cash and marketable securities | **19a** 200 |
| | **b** Distributions of other property | **19b** |
| | **20a** Investment income | **20a** |
| | **b** Investment expenses | **20b** |
| | **c** Other items and amounts *(attach statement)* | |

Form **1065** (2005)

¶ **68**

Form 1065 (2005)                                                                                      Page **4**

## Analysis of Net Income (Loss)

**1**   Net income (loss). Combine Schedule K, lines 1 through 11. From the result, subtract the sum of
       Schedule K, lines 12 through 13d, and 16l . . . . . . . . . . . . . . . . . . . **1**

| **2** Analysis by partner type: | **(i)** Corporate | **(ii)** Individual (active) | **(iii)** Individual (passive) | **(iv)** Partnership | **(v)** Exempt organization | **(vi)** Nominee/Other |
|---|---|---|---|---|---|---|
| **a** General partners | | 40,512 | | | | |
| **b** Limited partners | | | | | | |

**Note:** Schedules L, M-1, and M-2 are not required if Question 5 of Schedule B is answered "Yes."

| Schedule L          Balance Sheets per Books | Beginning of tax year | | End of tax year | |
|---|---|---|---|---|
| **Assets** | **(a)** | **(b)** | **(c)** | **(d)** |
| **1** Cash . . . . . . . . . . . . . . . | | 7,274 | | 32,390 |
| **2a** Trade notes and accounts receivable . . . . | 21,000 | | 23,500 | |
| **b** Less allowance for bad debts . . . . . . . | 0 | 21,000 | 0 | 23,500 |
| **3** Inventories . . . . . . . . . . . . | | 50,000 | | 61,000 |
| **4** U.S. government obligations . . . . . . | | 5,000 | | 5,000 |
| **5** Tax-exempt securities . . . . . . . . | | | | |
| **6** Other current assets (attach statement) . . | | | | |
| **7** Mortgage and real estate loans . . . . . | | | | |
| **8** Other investments (attach statement) . . . . | | 9,000 | | |
| **9a** Buildings and other depreciable assets. . . . | 33,500 | | 43,500 | |
| **b** Less accumulated depreciation . . . . . . | 22,079 | 11,421 | 27,366 | 16,134 |
| **10a** Depletable assets . . . . . . . . . | | | | |
| **b** Less accumulated depletion . . . . . . | | | | |
| **11** Land (net of any amortization). . . . . . | | | | 12,000 |
| **12a** Intangible assets (amortizable only) . . . . | | | | |
| **b** Less accumulated amortization . . . . . | | | | |
| **13** Other assets (attach statement) . . . . . | | | | |
| **14** Total assets . . . . . . . . . | | 103,695 | | 150,024 |
| **Liabilities and Capital** | | | | |
| **15** Accounts payable . . . . . . . . . | | 6,231 | | 6,337 |
| **16** Mortgages, notes, bonds payable in less than 1 year . | | 5,116 | | 7,277 |
| **17** Other current liabilities (attach statement) . . . | | | | |
| **18** All nonrecourse loans . . . . . . . . | | | | |
| **19** Mortgages, notes, bonds payable in 1 year or more . | | 5,000 | | 10,150 |
| **20** Other liabilities (attach statement) . . . . | | | | |
| **21** Partners' capital accounts . . . . . . . | | 87,348 | | 126,260 |
| **22** Total liabilities and capital . . . . . . . . | | 103,695 | | 150,024 |

| Schedule M-1      Reconciliation of Income (Loss) per Books With Income (Loss) per Return | | | |
|---|---|---|---|
| **1** Net income (loss) per books . . . . | 15,112 | **6** Income recorded on books this year not included on Schedule K, lines 1 through 11 (itemize): | |
| **2** Income included on Schedule K, lines 1, 2, 3c, 5, 6a, 7, 8, 9a, 10, and 11, not recorded on books this year (itemize): | 0 | **a** Tax-exempt interest $ .............. | 0 |
| **3** Guaranteed payments (other than health insurance) . . . . . . . . . | 25,200 | **7** Deductions included on Schedule K, lines 1 through 13d, and 16l, not charged against book income this year (itemize): | |
| **4** Expenses recorded on books this year not included on Schedule K, lines 1 through 13d, and 16l (itemize): | | **a** Depreciation $ .............. | |
| **a** Depreciation $ .............. | | | 0 |
| **b** Travel and entertainment $ .............. | | **8** Add lines 6 and 7 . . . . . . | 0 |
| | 200 | **9** Income (loss) (Analysis of Net Income (Loss), line 1). Subtract line 8 from line 5 . . . . | 40,512 |
| **5** Add lines 1 through 4 . . . . . | 40,512 | | |

| Schedule M-2      Analysis of Partners' Capital Accounts | | | |
|---|---|---|---|
| **1** Balance at beginning of year . . . . | 87,348 | **6** Distributions: **a** Cash . . . . . . . | 200 |
| **2** Capital contributed: **a** Cash . . . . | 12,000 | **b** Property . . . . . | 0 |
| **b** Property . . . | 12,000 | **7** Other decreases (itemize): .............. | |
| **3** Net income (loss) per books . . . . | 15,112 | | |
| **4** Other increases (itemize): .............. | | | 0 |
| | 0 | **8** Add lines 6 and 7 . . . . . . . . . | 200 |
| **5** Add lines 1 through 4 . . . . . . | 126,460 | **9** Balance at end of year. Subtract line 8 from line 5 | 126,260 |

Form **1065** (2005)

¶ **68**

| SCHEDULE D (Form 1065)<br>Department of the Treasury<br>Internal Revenue Service | **Capital Gains and Losses**<br><br>▶ Attach to Form 1065. | OMB No. 1545-0099<br><br>**2005** |

| Name of partnership | Employer identification number |
| --- | --- |
| **Bilco Products** | 21 ¦ 8253431 |

### Part I — Short-Term Capital Gains and Losses—Assets Held 1 Year or Less

| (a) Description of property (e.g., 100 shares of "Z" Co.) | (b) Date acquired (month, day, year) | (c) Date sold (month, day, year) | (d) Sales price (see instructions) | (e) Cost or other basis (see instructions) | (f) Gain or (loss) Subtract (e) from (d) |
| --- | --- | --- | --- | --- | --- |
| **1** | | | | | |
| | | | | | |
| | | | | | |
| | | | | | |

| | | |
| --- | --- | --- |
| **2** Short-term capital gain from installment sales from Form 6252, line 26 or 37 . . . . . . | **2** | |
| **3** Short-term capital gain (loss) from like-kind exchanges from Form 8824 . . . . . . . | **3** | |
| **4** Partnership's share of net short-term capital gain (loss), including specially allocated short-term capital gains (losses), from other partnerships, estates, and trusts . . . . . . . . . | **4** | |
| **5** **Net short-term capital gain or (loss).** Combine lines 1 through 4 in column (f). Enter here and on Form 1065, Schedule K, line 8 or 11 . . . . . . . . . . . . . . . . | **5** | |

### Part II — Long-Term Capital Gains and Losses—Assets Held More Than 1 Year

| (a) Description of property (e.g., 100 shares of "Z" Co.) | (b) Date acquired (month, day, year) | (c) Date sold (month, day, year) | (d) Sales price (see instructions) | (e) Cost or other basis (see instructions) | (f) Gain or (loss) Subtract (e) from (d) |
| --- | --- | --- | --- | --- | --- |
| **6** M. Specialty Bonds | 06-05-2002 | 01-09-2005 | 4,900 | 4,900 | 900 |
| Harper Lumber Co. | 09-09-2002 | 01-24-2005 | 4,700 | 5,000 | (300) |
| 50 shares | | | | | |
| | | | | | |

| | | |
| --- | --- | --- |
| **7** Long-term capital gain from installment sales from Form 6252, line 26 or 37 . . . . . . | **7** | |
| **8** Long-term capital gain (loss) from like-kind exchanges from Form 8824 . . . . . . . | **8** | |
| **9** Partnership's share of net long-term capital gain (loss), including specially allocated long-term capital gains (losses), from other partnerships, estates, and trusts . . . . | **9** | |
| **10** Capital gain distributions . . . . . . . . . . . . . . . . . . . . . | **10** | |
| **11** **Net long-term capital gain or (loss).** Combine lines 6 through 10 in column (f). Enter here and on Form 1065, Schedule K, line 9a or 11 . . . . . . . . . . . . . . | **11** | 600 |

**For Privacy Act and Paperwork Reduction Act Notice, see the Instructions for Form 1065.**     Cat. No. 11393G     **Schedule D (Form 1065) 2005**

☐ Final K-1    ☐ Amended K-1    OMB No. 1545-0099

## Schedule K-1
### (Form 1065)

**20**05

Department of the Treasury
Internal Revenue Service

For calendar year 2005, or tax

year beginning _____, 2005

ending _____, 20____

## Partner's Share of Income, Deductions, Credits, etc.
▶ **See back of form and separate instructions.**

| Part III | Partner's Share of Current Year Income, Deductions, Credits, and Other Items |
|---|---|

| **Part I** | **Information About the Partnership** |
|---|---|

**A**   Partnership's employer identification number
21-8253431

**B**   Partnership's name, address, city, state, and ZIP code

**Bilco Products**
**131 Mill Street**
**Chicago, IL 60600**

**C**   IRS Center where partnership filed return
**Cincinnati**

**D** ☐   Check if this is a publicly traded partnership (PTP)
**E** ☐   Tax shelter registration number, if any _____
**F** ☐   Check if Form 8271 is attached

| **Part II** | **Information About the Partner** |
|---|---|

**G**   Partner's identifying number
330-24-1049

**H**   Partner's name, address, city, state, and ZIP code

**George A. Warden**
**789 Code Drive**
**Chicago, IL 60600**

**I** ☑   General partner or LLC member-manager      ☐ Limited partner or other LLC member

**J** ☑   Domestic partner      ☐ Foreign partner

**K**   What type of entity is this partner?   **Individual**

**L**   Partner's share of profit, loss, and capital:

|  | Beginning | Ending |
|---|---|---|
| Profit | % | 50.000 % |
| Loss | % | 50.000 % |
| Capital | % | 50.000 % |

**M**   Partner's share of liabilities at year end:

| Nonrecourse | . . . . . | $ |  |
| Qualified nonrecourse financing | . . | $ |  |
| Recourse | . . . . . . . | $ | 11,882 |

**N**   Partner's capital account analysis:

| Beginning capital account | . . . . | $ | 63,674 |
| Capital contributed during the year | . | $ | 12,000 |
| Current year increase (decrease) | . . | $ | 7,556 |
| Withdrawals & distributions | . . | $ ( | 100 ) |
| Ending capital account | . . . . | $ | 83,180 |

☑ Tax basis   ☐ GAAP   ☐ Section 704(b) book
☐ Other (explain)

| # | Item | | | # | Item |
|---|---|---|---|---|---|
| 1 | Ordinary business income (loss) | | 6,753 | 15 | Credits & credit recapture |
| 2 | Net rental real estate income (loss) | | | | |
| 3 | Other net rental income (loss) | | | 16 | Foreign transactions |
| 4 | Guaranteed payments | | 8,400 | | |
| 5 | Interest income | | 260 | | |
| 6a | Ordinary dividends | | | | |
| 6b | Qualified dividends | | 100 | | |
| 7 | Royalties | | 443 | | |
| 8 | Net short-term capital gain (loss) | | | | |
| 9a | Net long-term capital gain (loss) | | 300 | 17 | Alternative minimum tax (AMT) items |
| 9b | Collectibles (28%) gain (loss) | | | | |
| 9c | Unrecaptured section 1250 gain | | | | |
| 10 | Net section 1231 gain (loss) | | | 18 | Tax-exempt income and nondeductible expenses |
| 11 | Other income (loss) | | | C | 100 |
| 12 | Section 179 deduction | | | 19 | Distributions |
| | | | | A | 100 |
| 13 | Other deductions | | | | |
| A | | 100 | | 20 | Other information |
| G | | 100 | | | |
| 14 | Self-employment earnings (loss) | | | | |
| A | | 15,153 | | | |
| C | | 15,153 | | | |

*See attached statement for additional information.

*For IRS Use Only*

For Privacy Act and Paperwork Reduction Act Notice, see Instructions for Form 1065.      Cat. No. 11394R      **Schedule K-1 (Form 1065) 2005**

# FILLED-IN FORM 1065 • PARTNERSHIPS • EXPLANATION

**This list identifies the codes used on Schedule K-1 for all partners and provides summarized reporting information for partners who file Form 1040. For detailed reporting and filing information, see the separate Partner's Instructions for Schedule K-1 and the instructions for your income tax return.**

1. **Ordinary business income (loss).** You must first determine whether the income (loss) is passive or nonpassive. Then enter on your return as follows:

| | *Enter on* |
|---|---|
| Passive loss | See the Partner's Instructions |
| Passive income | Schedule E, line 28, column (g) |
| Nonpassive loss | Schedule E, line 28, column (h) |
| Nonpassive income | Schedule E, line 28, column (j) |

2. **Net rental real estate income (loss)** — See the Partner's Instructions
3. **Other net rental income (loss)**
   - Net income — Schedule E, line 28, column (g)
   - Net loss — See the Partner's Instructions
4. **Guaranteed payments** — Schedule E, line 28, column (j)
5. **Interest income** — Form 1040, line 8a
6a. **Ordinary dividends** — Form 1040, line 9a
6b. **Qualified dividends** — Form 1040, line 9b
7. **Royalties** — Schedule E, line 4
8. **Net short-term capital gain (loss)** — Schedule D, line 5, column (f)
9a. **Net long-term capital gain (loss)** — Schedule D, line 12, column (f)
9b. **Collectibles (28%) gain (loss)** — 28% Rate Gain Worksheet, line 4 (Schedule D Instructions)
9c. **Unrecaptured section 1250 gain** — See the Partner's Instructions
10. **Net section 1231 gain (loss)** — See the Partner's Instructions
11. **Other income (loss)**

    *Code*
    - A Other portfolio income (loss) — See the Partner's Instructions
    - B Involuntary conversions — See the Partner's Instructions
    - C Sec. 1256 contracts & straddles — Form 6781, line 1
    - D Mining exploration costs recapture — See Pub. 535
    - E Cancellation of debt — Form 1040, line 21 or Form 982
    - F Other income (loss) — See the Partner's Instructions
12. **Section 179 deduction** — See the Partner's Instructions
13. **Other deductions**
    - A Cash contributions (50%)
    - B Cash contributions (30%)
    - C Noncash contributions (50%)
    - D Noncash contributions (30%)
    - E Capital gain property to a 50% organization (30%)
    - F Capital gain property (20%)
    - G Cash contributions (100%)

      } See the Partner's Instructions
    - H Investment interest expense — Form 4952, line 1
    - I Deductions—royalty income — Schedule E, line 18
    - J Section 59(e)(2) expenditures — See the Partner's Instructions
    - K Deductions—portfolio (2% floor) — Schedule A, line 22
    - L Deductions—portfolio (other) — Schedule A, line 27
    - M Amounts paid for medical insurance — Schedule A, line 1 or Form 1040, line 29
    - N Educational assistance benefits — See the Partner's Instructions
    - O Dependent care benefits — Form 2441, line 12
    - P Preproductive period expenses — See the Partner's Instructions
    - Q Commercial revitalization deduction from rental real estate activities — See Form 8582 Instructions
    - R Pensions and IRAs — See the Partner's Instructions
    - S Reforestation expense deduction — See the Partner's Instructions
    - T Domestic production activities information — See Form 8903 instructions
    - U Qualified production activities income — Form 8903, line 7
    - V Employer's W-2 wages — Form 8903, line 13
    - W Other deductions — See the Partner's Instructions
14. **Self-employment earnings (loss)**
    **Note.** *If you have a section 179 deduction or any partner-level deductions, see the Partner's Instructions before completing Schedule SE.*
    - A Net earnings (loss) from self-employment — Schedule SE, Section A or B
    - B Gross farming or fishing income — See the Partner's Instructions
    - C Gross non-farm income — See the Partner's Instructions
15. **Credits & credit recapture**
    - A Low-income housing credit (section 42(j)(5)) — Form 8586, line 4
    - B Low-income housing credit (other) — Form 8586, line 4
    - C Qualified rehabilitation expenditures (rental real estate) — Form 3468, line 1
    - D Qualified rehabilitation expenditures (other than rental real estate) — Form 3468, line 1
    - E Basis of energy property — See the Partner's Instructions
    - F Other rental real estate credits — See the Partner's Instructions
    - G Other rental credits — See the Partner's Instructions
    - H Undistributed capital gains credit — Form 1040, line 70; check box a
    - I Credit for alcohol used as fuel — See the Partner's Instructions

| *Code* | | *Enter on* |
|---|---|---|
| J | Work opportunity credit | Form 5884, line 3 |
| K | Welfare-to-work credit | Form 8861, line 3 |
| L | Disabled access credit | Form 8826, line 7 |
| M | Empowerment zone and renewal community employment credit | Form 8844, line 3 |
| N | Credit for increasing research activities | Form 6765, line 42 |
| O | New markets credit | Form 8874, line 2 |
| P | Credit for employer social security and Medicare taxes | Form 8846, line 5 |
| Q | Backup withholding | Form 1040, line 64 |
| R | Recapture of low-income housing credit (section 42(j)(5)) | Form 8611, line 8 |
| S | Recapture of low-income housing credit (other) | Form 8611, line 8 |
| T | Recapture of investment credit | See Form 4255 |
| U | Other credits | See the Partner's Instructions |
| V | Recapture of other credits | See the Partner's Instructions |

16. **Foreign transactions**
    - A Name of country or U.S. possession — Form 1116, Part I
    - B Gross income from all sources — Form 1116, Part I
    - C Gross income sourced at partner level — Form 1116, Part I

    *Foreign gross income sourced at partnership level*
    - D Passive — Form 1116, Part I
    - E Listed categories — Form 1116, Part I
    - F General limitation — Form 1116, Part I

    *Deductions allocated and apportioned at partner level*
    - G Interest expense — Form 1116, Part I
    - H Other — Form 1116, Part I

    *Deductions allocated and apportioned at partnership level to foreign source income*
    - I Passive — Form 1116, Part I
    - J Listed categories — Form 1116, Part I
    - K General limitation — Form 1116, Part I

    *Other information*
    - L Total foreign taxes paid — Form 1116, Part II
    - M Total foreign taxes accrued — Form 1116, Part II
    - N Reduction in taxes available for credit — Form 1116, line 12
    - O Foreign trading gross receipts — Form 8873
    - P Extraterritorial income exclusion — Form 8873
    - Q Other foreign transactions — See the Partner's Instructions

17. **Alternative minimum tax (AMT) items**
    - A Post-1986 depreciation adjustment
    - B Adjusted gain or loss
    - C Depletion (other than oil & gas)
    - D Oil, gas, & geothermal—gross income
    - E Oil, gas, & geothermal—deductions
    - F Other AMT items

      } See the Partner's Instructions and the Instructions for Form 6251

18. **Tax-exempt income and nondeductible expenses**
    - A Tax-exempt interest income — Form 1040, line 8b
    - B Other tax-exempt income — See the Partner's Instructions
    - C Nondeductible expenses — See the Partner's Instructions
19. **Distributions**
    - A Cash and marketable securities — See the Partner's Instructions
    - B Other property — See the Partner's Instructions
20. **Other information**
    - A Investment income — Form 4952, line 4a
    - B Investment expenses — Form 4952, line 5
    - C Fuel tax credit information — Form 4136
    - D Look-back interest—completed long-term contracts — Form 8697
    - E Look-back interest—income forecast method — Form 8866
    - F Dispositions of property with section 179 deductions
    - G Recapture of section 179 deduction
    - H Special basis adjustments
    - I Section 453(l)(3) information
    - J Section 453A(c) information
    - K Section 1260(b) information
    - L Interest allocable to production expenditures
    - M CCF nonqualified withdrawals
    - N Information needed to figure depletion—oil and gas
    - O Amortization of reforestation costs
    - P Unrelated business taxable income
    - Q Other information

      } See the Partner's Instructions

**♲ Printed on recycled paper**

# Filled-In Form 1041 • Estates, Trusts • Explanation

## ¶71 FILING REQUIREMENTS

Most fiduciaries of estates and trusts are required to use Form 1041. However, a fiduciary of a nonresident alien estate or foreign trust must file Form 1040NR, U.S. Nonresident Alien Income Tax Return.

A trustee of a taxable domestic trust must file Form 1041 if (1) the trust has $600 or more in gross income, (2) the trust has taxable income in any amount, or (3) the trust has a beneficiary who is a nonresident alien. Most trusts are required to file on the basis of a calendar year. Thus, a trustee must file the 2005 Form 1041 by April 17, 2006. Fiscal years may be used by: (1) trusts that are tax exempt under Code Sec. 501(a); (2) charitable trusts under Code Sec. 4947(a)(1); and (3) trusts that are treated as wholly owned by a grantor under Code Secs. 671–679.

As an alternative to filing Form 1041, trustees of certain grantor trusts are provided with three optional filing methods. These methods are described in the Form 1041 instructions.

An administrator or executor for a decedent's estate is required to file a return if either (1) the estate has gross income of $600 or more during the year or (2) the estate has a beneficiary who is a nonresident alien. Decedents' estates may elect to use either a calendar year or a fiscal tax year beginning on the date that the decedent died. If the latter option is chosen, the due date for the return is generally the 15th day of the 4th month following the close of the tax year. Thus, if an estate has a tax year that ends on May 31, 2006, the return must be filed by September 15, 2006.

- **Election to treat trust as part of estate.**

For the estates of decedents dying after August 5, 1997, the executor of the estate and the trustee of a qualified revocable trust can elect to treat the trust as part of the estate instead of filing a separate Form 1041 (Code Sec. 645). A qualified revocable trust is one that, because of a power held by the grantor, is treated as owned by the decedent whose estate is making the election. The election to treat the trust as part of the estate must be made by the due date

(including extensions) of the estate's Form 1041 for its first tax year and is irrevocable.

A fiduciary for an estate of an individual that is involved in a bankruptcy proceeding under chapter 7 or 11 of the Bankruptcy Code should file a Form 1041 as a transmittal document with the related Form 1040. A return for 2005 is due if the bankrupt's estate has gross income of $8,200 or more.

- **Other Forms that may be required**

Fiduciaries, including bankruptcy trustees, may be required to file various additional documents, such as Form 56 (notice concerning fiduciary relationship),

- Form 2758 (extension of time to file fiduciary return for an estate),
- Form 8736 (extension of time to file fiduciary return for a trust),
- Form 8800 (fiduciary's application for additional extension of time to file trust return),
- Form 706 or Form 706-NA (estate tax returns),
- Form 706-GS(D) (return for generation-skipping transfer tax for distributions),
- Form 706-GS(D-1) (notification of distribution from generation-skipping trust),
- Form 706-GS(T) (return for trust terminations subject to generation-skipping transfer tax),
- Form 720 (quarterly excise tax return, Form 940 or Form 940-EZ (employer's FUTA tax return),
- Form 945 (withheld federal income tax),
- Form 1041-ES (estimated tax payments),
- Form 1041-A (trust accumulations of charitable amounts),
- Form 1041-T (allocation of estimated tax payments to beneficiaries),
- Forms 1042 and 1042-S (U.S. source income of foreign persons),
- and Forms 1099-A, -B, -INT, -LTC, -MISC, -MSA, -OID, -R, and -S (various beneficiary information

returns). The use of the 1099 forms, however, is not necessary where they would merely duplicate income information that is otherwise required to be reported on Schedule K-1. Forms 8275 and 8275-R are disclosure statements, filed to avoid parts of the accuracy-related penalty and preparer penalties. Forms 8288 and 8288-A are used with regard to dispositions by foreign persons of U.S. real property interests. Form 8300 is used to disclose a trade or business' receipt of cash payments of more than $10,000. Unless requested to do so by the IRS, fiduciaries are not required to attach copies of trust instruments or wills to Form 1041.

Fiduciaries are required to indicate the number of Schedules K-1 attached to Form 1041 in Item B on page 1 of Form 1041.

Fiduciaries that would like to take part in the electronic/magnetic media filing program should file Form 9041, Application for Electronic/Magnetic Media Filing of Business and Employee Benefit Plan Returns, unless they participated in the program last year and there have been no changes in the firm's name, employer identification number, mailing address, and contact person's phone and FAX number. Form 8453-F, U.S. Estate or Trust Income Tax Declaration and Signature for Electronic and Magnetic Media Filing, is the signature document that completes the filing of Form 1041 on electronic or magnetic media.

## ¶72 TAX PAYMENTS

A trust is required to make estimated tax payments starting with its first tax year. However, an estate (or a grantor trust receiving the residue of a decedent's estate) is required to make estimated tax payments starting with any tax year that ends two or more years after the date of a decedent's death. Generally, an estate or trust will have to pay the estimated tax for 2006 if it expects to owe, after subtracting withholding and credits, at least $1,000 in tax for the current tax year and it expects the withholding and credits to be less than the smaller of: (1) 90% of the tax shown on the 2006 (current) year's tax return, or (2) 100% of the tax shown on the tax return for the 2005 (preceding) tax year (110% if adjusted gross income on the 2005 return is more than $150,000 and less than $^2/_3$ of gross income for 2005 or 2006 is from farming or fishing (Code Sec. 6654).

If the estate or trust does not file a 2005 return or that return does not cover a full 12 months, item (2) does not apply. Form 1041-ES may be used to compute the required estimated tax payments. In determining whether an estate or trust should pay estimated tax in 2006, household employment taxes should be included in the tax shown on the tax return if (1) the estate or trust will have federal income tax withheld for 2006 or (2) the estate or trust would be required to make estimated tax payments for 2006, even if it did not include household employment taxes when figuring estimated tax. If there has been an underpayment of estimated taxes, the fiduciary should file a Form 2210 and report any penalty for underpayment of estimated taxes on Line 26, Form 1041.

- **Allocation of Estimated Taxes to Beneficiaries**

A trustee or executor may elect to allocate any portion of the estimated tax payments to any beneficiary. The allocation election is available for an estate only for its final tax year. The fiduciary makes the election by (1) completing and filing Form 1041-T and (2) completing Line 14a of Schedule K-1 for each beneficiary to whom the estimated tax payments are allocated. A trust's or estate's election must be filed on or before the 65th day after the close of its tax year otherwise it will be considered invalid (Code Sec. 643(g)). For calendar tax year 2005, Form 1041-T must be filed on or before March 7, 2006. Form 1041-T should be attached to Form 1041 only if the election is made before Form 1041 is filed. Otherwise, Form 1041-T is signed and filed separately.

## ¶73 TRUST EXAMPLES

The amounts and computations appearing in the filled-in Form 1041 (**¶96**) are based on an assumed factual situation, designed to illustrate the preparation of a return for a complex testamentary trust. For purposes of this return, it is assumed that John Tyler, who died in 1987, created by his will a trust that provided that:

(1) An amount equal to two-thirds of the income is to be currently distributed to a niece, Mrs. Mary S. Warden, and a nephew, Mr. Harold Draper, in equal parts, for the duration of their respective lives.

(2) The balance of the annual income is to be accumulated and added to the corpus, which upon the death of both beneficiaries goes to designated remaindermen. (None of the remaindermen is a charitable organization.)

(3) The income is to be distributed as above after deduction for any expenses, including depreciation,

of the trust. The trustee is required to otherwise keep the trust corpus intact.

## ¶74 INCOME WHICH IS TAXED TO AN ESTATE OR COMPLEX TRUST

• **Accumulations and Other Special Types of Income**

The gross income of an estate or trust includes:

(1) Income accumulated in trust for the benefit of unborn or unascertained persons or persons with contingent interests, and income accumulated or held for future distribution under the terms of the will or trust;

(2) Income that is to be distributed currently by the fiduciary to the beneficiaries, and income collected by a guardian of an infant that is to be held or distributed as the court may direct;

(3) Income received by estates of deceased persons during the period of administration or settlement of the estate; and

(4) Income that, in the discretion of the fiduciary, may either be distributed to the beneficiaries or be accumulated (Code Sec. 641(a)).

Income in category (1) is taxed to the estate or trust; income in category (2) that is currently distributable (not in excess of distributable net income) is deductible by the fiduciary and taxed to the beneficiary; income in categories (3) and (4) may be eventually taxed to the fiduciary or to the beneficiary, depending upon the amounts that are properly paid or credited to the beneficiary. However, all taxable income that passes through the hands of an estate or trust is includible in its gross income.

• **Page 1 Income and Deductions**

The income shown on page 1 of Form 1041 on Lines 1–8 and the deductions on Lines 10–15b are entered as if the entire net income were taxable to the trust. From the net income of the trust are deducted the amount distributed or required to be distributed to the beneficiaries (Line 18), certain estate or generation-skipping taxes (Line 19), and the appropriate exemption (Line 20). The remainder (Line 22) is the taxable income on which the fiduciary pays the tax.

In order to deduct administrative expenses or selling expenses incurred when disposing of property from a decedent's estate or casualty and theft losses incurred during the settlement of the estate, a statement must be filed indicating an election to waive the right to deduct those items on Form 706 for estate tax purposes.

• **Income and Expenses in Respect of a Decedent**

Items of income to which a decedent was entitled, but that were not includible in computing the decedent's taxable income for the tax year ending with the date of death, or for a previous tax year under the decedent's method of accounting, are includible in the gross income of the estate, trust or person receiving them as "income in respect of a decedent." Similarly, deductions for business expenses, interest, taxes, investment expenses, and percentage depletion and foreign tax credits that were not allowable on the decedent's final return are allowed to the estate generally in the tax year in which the underlying expense is paid (Code Sec. 691(a) and (b)).

## ¶75 INTEREST INCOME

The $5,000 reported on Line 1, page 1, of the filled-in Form 1041 represents taxable interest that was received by the trust from bank deposits, mortgage notes, corporation bonds, and government obligations, and as a regular interest holder in a real estate mortgage investment conduit (REMIC).

## ¶76 INTEREST ON GOVERNMENT OBLIGATIONS

Many obligations of a state or political subdivision are exempt from tax. But interest on such securities (as adjusted) must be excluded from the distributions deduction on Line 18, page 1 (as computed on Schedule B, page 2, of Form 1041). Taxable interest on U.S. government obligations is included on Line 1, page 1, Form 1041.

## ¶77 DIVIDENDS

The total amount of taxable dividends is entered on Line 2a, page 1. The beneficiary's allocable share of qualified dividends is entered on line 2b(1), and the trust's or estate's share is entered on line 2b(2). Qualified dividends are eligible for a lower tax rate than other ordinary income, and are generally dividends reported to the estate or trust in box 1b of Form 1099-DIV. For exceptions, see the 1041 instructions.

Dividends in the Tyler Trust are not allocable to corpus. They are, therefore, apportionable between the trustee and beneficiaries. Each beneficiary's share is shown on Line 2 of a separate Schedule K-1.

## ¶78 BUSINESS PROFIT OR LOSS

If an estate or a trust was engaged in a trade or business or in farming during the tax year, the net profit (or loss) from the business is entered on Line 3, page 1, Form 1041, and the net profit (or loss) from the farming is entered on Line 6, page 1, Form 1041. The net income from such enterprises is computed on either Schedule C or C-EZ (business income) or Schedule F (farming income) of Form 1040. However, only the estate's or trust's share of the depreciation is deducted on the schedules.

## ¶79 INCOME FROM RENTS, ROYALTIES, AND FLOW-THROUGH ENTITIES

The estate's or trust's share of income or losses from rentals of real estate, royalties, partnerships, S corporations, other estates and trusts, and REMICs (attributable to a residual interest in the REMIC) is reported on Schedule E (Form 1040), and the net profit or loss is entered on Line 5, page 1, of Form 1041.

Items for which a determination must be made at the individual partner or shareholder level (interest, dividends, capital gains or losses) that are contained in a Schedule K-1 received from a flow-through entity are reported on the corresponding line of Form 1041. Losses attributable to passive activities may be disallowed (see ¶81 and the related Form 8582 in the 2005 edition of *Individuals' Filled-In Tax Return Forms*).

The Tyler Trust on Schedule E, Form 1040 (not included), reported receiving $45,000 in total rents from an apartment building and depreciation of $2,000. The trust's "other" expenses amounted to $17,529, including: repairs, $950; heating costs, $10,000; insurance premiums, $2,050; janitor costs, $1,300; and real estate taxes, $3,229. Net rental income of $25,471 from Line 26, Schedule E, is reported on Line 5, page 1, of Form 1041.

## ¶80 DEPRECIATION

The estate's or trust's share of depreciation, amortization, or depletion expenses attributable to certain activities is reported on Schedule C, C-EZ, E, or F of Form 1040. The net profit or loss amounts from the schedules are reported on Line 3, 5, or 6 of Form 1041. Line 15a of Form 1041 is used to report depreciation, amortization, and depletion expenses unrelated to a specific business or activity. In the case of a trust, these deductions are apportioned between the fiduciary and the beneficiaries as specified in the trust instrument. If the trust instrument is silent on this point, the deductions are apportioned between the fiduciary and the beneficiaries in the same manner that income is divided between them. In the case of an estate, the deductions for amortization, depreciation, and depletion are apportioned between the estate and the beneficiaries in the same way.

Form 4562 is filed only if depreciable property is placed in service in the 2005 tax year, depreciation is claimed on listed property, or amortization of costs begins in the 2005 tax year.

## ON THE RETURN

The trust instrument forming the basis of the illustrative return provides that the trust is to keep the corpus intact, thereby requiring it to maintain a reserve for depreciation. Accordingly, because the income set aside by the trustee for the depreciation reserve is equal to the allowable depreciation deduction, no depreciation is allocated to the beneficiaries on Line 5b of each Schedule K-1 of Form 1041.

If the $2,000 depreciation deduction for the Tyler Trust had been allocated equally among the beneficiaries and the trustee, under the terms of the trust or because of state law, the trust's depreciation deduction would amount to one-third of $2,000, or $667. In addition, each beneficiary's share of the depreciation ($667) would have appeared on Line 5b of the beneficiary's Schedule K-1.

An estate or trust may not elect to expense recovery property under Code Sec. 179. A trust is also not allowed to deduct or amortize reforestation expenditures under Code Sec. 194. Depreciation or amortization deductions are not allowed for any term interest in property held directly or indirectly by a related person (as defined in Code Sec. 267(b) or (e)) (Code Sec. 167(e)). In tax years beginning after August 5, 1997, the executor and beneficiary of an estate are considered related persons, except in the case of a sale or exchange in satisfaction of a pecuniary bequest (Code Sec. 267(b)(13)).

Generally, the basis of property must be reduced by the disallowed depreciation or amortization deduction, and the basis of the remainder interest must be increased by such amount. The disallowance does not apply to holders of life estates or terminable interests (as described in Code Sec. 273).

## ¶81 AT-RISK AND PASSIVE ACTIVITY LOSS LIMITATIONS

An estate or trust may be subject to the at-risk and the passive activity loss limitations. If an estate or trust is subject to both loss limitation rules, the at-risk rules apply before the passive activity rules.

### • At-Risk Limitations on Losses

The at-risk rules of Code Sec. 465 apply to estates and trusts engaged in any activity carried on as a trade or business or for the production of income. The deductible loss is limited to the amount at risk in the activity. See ¶29 and ¶61 for further details.

When applying the at-risk rules, each of the following items is treated as a separate activity:

(1) motion picture and video tape holding, producing, and distribution;

(2) personal property leasing;

(3) farming;

(4) exploring for, or exploiting, oil and gas properties; and

(5) exploring for, or exploiting, geothermal properties. All other activities can be treated as a single activity if the fiduciary is an active participant in the enterprise. The at-risk adjustment of a loss is made on Schedules C, E, or F of Form 1040 and will be reflected in the net income or loss entered on Line 3, 5, or 6 of Form 1041. If an estate or trust has a loss from a business, rental of real estate, or a farm and is not at risk with regard to some related amounts, the fiduciary must attach Form 6198.

### • Passive Activity Loss and Credit Limitations

Losses derived from passive activities are limited to the amount of income derived from all passive activities conducted by the estate or the trust (Code Sec. 469). Similarly, tax credits from passive activities are limited to the tax liability generated by the passive activities. These limitations are first applied at the estate or trust level.

Generally, a passive activity is one that involves the conduct of a trade or business in which the taxpayer does not materially participate. While rental activities are generally considered passive activities, rental real estate activities are not subject to passive loss limitations for certain taxpayers who materially participate in real property trades and businesses (Code Sec. 469(c)(7)). In the case of a grantor trust, material participation is determined by reference to the activities conducted by the grantor. The IRS has not released guidelines for determining what constitutes material participation for an estate or nongrantor trust (Temp. Reg. §1.469-5T(g)).

Portfolio income received by an estate or trust (interest, dividends, royalties, annuity income (Code Sec. 469(e)) is not treated as income derived from a passive activity. Similarly, income derived from a working interest in oil and gas property is not income from a passive activity (Code Sec. 469(c)(3)).

An estate can deduct up to $25,000 in rental real estate activity expenses incurred in tax years ending within two years after the decedent's death, provided that the decedent actively participated in the activity (Code Sec. 469(i)(4)). Any unused losses or credits are suspended and are carried forward indefinitely. Also, if an estate or trust distributes an interest in a passive activity, the basis of the property immediately before the distribution is increased by passive losses allocable to the interest. The amount of such losses is not deductible by the distributing estate or trust (Code Sec. 469(j)(12)).

The amount of an allowable passive activity loss is computed on Form 8582, Passive Activity Loss Limitations. The amount of an allowable credit is computed on Form 8582-CR, Passive Activity Credit Limitations. Form 8582 should be completed first so that the deductible amount of net loss from real estate can be determined on Schedule E of Form 1040, the amount of a loss reported on Schedule C or F of Form 1040 can be determined, and the amount of a loss from a partnership or other fiduciary can be determined on Schedule E.

## ¶82 CAPITAL GAINS AND LOSSES

Gains and losses from the sale or exchange of capital assets are computed on Parts I and II of Schedule D, Form 1041 and allocated between the fiduciary and the beneficiaries on Part III of Schedule D, Form 1041. Capital assets are defined in Instructions for Form 1041 (2005).

The maximum capital gain rate is generally 10% for estates and trusts that would be taxed at the 15% rate on ordinary income. A 15% maximum tax rate replaces the 20% rate and a 5% maximum rate replaces the 10% rate that existed under prior law.

A 25% rate applies to unrecaptured section 1250 gain (i.e., unrecaptured depreciation) from the sale, exchange, etc., of depreciable real estate if the property was held for more than one year. Unrecaptured section 1250 gain is computed on a worksheet provided in the Form 1041 instructions.

A 28% rate applies to long-term collectibles gain and the amount of gain equal to the exclusion claimed for qualified small business stock under Code Sec. 1202. (Fifty percent of qualified small business stock gain is exempt from tax; the remaining gain is treated as 28% rate gain.)

Property acquired by a decedent's estate from a decedent is considered held for more than 12 months (Code Sec. 1223(11)).

The short and long-term carryover amounts entered on Lines 4 and 11 are determined using the capital loss carryover worksheet contained in the Form 1041 instructions.

Part III of Schedule D is used to show the allocation of the net short term capital gain or loss reported on Line 5 and the net long-term capital gain or loss reported on Line 12 between the estate or trust and the beneficiaries as a group. The amount allocated to each beneficiary is shown on each beneficiary's Schedule K-1.

The beneficiaries' share of net short-term capital gain or loss is reported on Line 13, column 1, Part III. The estate or trust's share is reported in column 2. Net long-term capital gain is allocated between the beneficiaries and estate or trust on Line 14a, columns 1 and 2, respectively. Twenty-eight percent rate gain or loss and unrecaptured section 1250 gain are identified separately on Lines 14(b) and 14(c), respectively. Each beneficiary's share of net capital gain is reported on Schedule K-1 as follows: net short-term capital gains, Line 3; total net long-term capital gains, Line 4a; unrecaptured section 1250 gain, Line 4b; and long-term capital gain subject to the 28% rate, Line 4c.

Capital gain may only be allocated to beneficiaries to the extent that it is considered as paid, credited, or required to be distributed to any beneficiary during the tax year (Reg. §1.643(a)-3(a)). Similarly, capital losses are taken into account only to the extent that they enter into the determination of any capital gains that are paid, credited, or required to be distributed to any beneficiary during the tax year (Reg. §1.643(a)(3)-3(b)).

Generally, capital gain is considered paid, credited, or required to be distributed to a beneficiary only if it is:

(1) allocated to income under the terms of the governing instrument or local law;

(2) allocated to corpus and actually distributed to beneficiaries; or

(3) utilized (pursuant to the terms of the governing instrument or the practice followed by the fiduciary) in determining the amount distributed or required to be distributed to the beneficiaries (Reg. §1.643(a)(3)-3(b)).

Any capital gain paid or permanently set aside for a charitable purpose specified in Code Sec. 642(c) must be allocated to the estate or trust in column 2 (Reg. §1.643(a)-3).

Except for the year in which an estate or trust terminates, if there is a net short-term capital loss from the sale or exchange of capital assets on Line 5, the entire net loss must be allocated to the estate or trust (Reg. §1.642(h)-1). Similarly, a net long-term capital loss on Line 13 of schedule D must be allocated entirely to the estate or trust.

Part IV is completed to determine the capital loss limitation (the smaller of the loss reported on Line 15, column (3) or $3,000) if a total net loss is reported on Line 15, column 3. If the Line 15, column (3) loss is greater than $3,000 (or a negative taxable income (net operating loss) is reported on Line 22 of Form 1041) the capital loss carryover worksheet contained in the instructions should be completed.

In the final year of a trust or decedent's estate, short-term and long-term capital loss carryovers may be claimed by the beneficiaries on Schedule K-1, Lines 13b and 13c, respectively.

Part V of Schedule D applies the appropriate tax rates to net long-term gain reported elsewhere on the schedule.

A short-term or long-term capital loss carryover is reported on Line 4 or 11 of Schedule D, respectively.

## ON THE RETURN

For the illustrative Form 1041, the sale of stock that produced long-term capital gain took place on May 1, 2005. The governing trust instrument is silent on the treatment of gains from the sales of corpus. Under most state laws, such gains are not distributable to the life beneficiaries, but are added to, and become a part of, the corpus held for the remaindermen unless the trust instrument directs otherwise. Accordingly, no part of this gain in the filled-in form is included in Lines 3 and 4a–4c of separate Schedule K-1. It remains as capital gain income, taxable to the trust. The trust's gain of $16,200 on Line 15a, column (3), Schedule D, is entered on Line 4, page 1, Form 1041.

An estate or trust that incurs a net capital loss must complete Part IV of Schedule D to compute its capital loss limitation. A worksheet is provided in the 2005 Form 1041 instructions to determine any capital loss carryover.

Gain from the disposition or involuntary conversion of property subject to recapture under Sec. 1245, 1250, 1252, 1254, or 1255 is entered in Part III, Form 4797 Sales of Business Property. Any ordinary income from the recapture is carried to Part II, Form 4797. Code Sec. 1231 transactions are reported in Part I of Form 4797, including gains from installment sales and casualties. If the Sec. 1231 items result in a net gain on Part I, the net gain is carried to Line 10, Part II, Schedule D of Form 1041 and is treated as a long-term capital gain. If a net Sec. 1231 loss results, it is entered in Part II, Form 4797, and combined with other ordinary gain or loss items. The net ordinary gain or loss on Line 18, Part II, Form 4797, is transferred to Line 7, page 1, of Form 1041. A Sec. 1231 gain from a casualty or theft of recapture property is transferred from Line 32, Part III, Form 4797, to Line 33, Part II, Section B, Form 4684.

- **Casualty or Theft Gain or Loss**

Gains and losses from casualties and thefts of property are reported item-by-item on Form 4684, Casualties and Thefts, in either Section A (for property not used in a trade or business or for income-producing purposes) or Section B (for property used in a trade or business or for income-producing purposes). Nonbusiness losses are deductible only to the extent that the total amount of such losses, after a $100 reduction for each casualty or theft, exceeds 10% of a taxpayer's adjusted gross income.

Casualty and theft losses are allowable to an estate only if the loss has not been claimed as a deduction from the gross estate of the decedent in a federal estate tax return. See ¶88 for the method of determining adjusted gross income.

Section B, Part II, of Form 4684, which deals with property used in a trade or business or for income-producing purposes, separates casualty and theft gains and losses into two general types. The first involves such gains and losses on short-term property. Net gains of this type are taxed as ordinary income, and net losses are treated as ordinary losses. The second type involves such gains and losses on long-term property. Net gains from this type of property qualify for Sec. 1231 (capital gain) treatment, and net losses are treated as ordinary losses. The gains and losses reported on Form 4684 may be reported directly on page 1 of Form 1041 and on Schedule D of Form 1041, or on Form 4797 in accordance with the following rules:

1. *Casualty or theft of property held short term (Form 4684, Section B, Part II, Lines 29–32).*—Short-term casualty and theft gains and losses are separated into (1) losses involving trade, business, rental or royalty property (column (b)(i)), (2) losses involving income-producing property (column (b)(ii)), and (3) gains from casualties and thefts includible in income (column (c)). The net gain or loss from combining columns (b)(i) and (c) of Line 30 is an ordinary gain or loss and is transferred to Line 14, Part II, Form 4797. However, if Form 4797 does not otherwise have to be filed, the net gain or loss is reported on Line 7, page 1, Form 1041, with the notation "Form 4684." Total losses from other property (column (b)(ii), Line 30) are entered on Line 32 of Form 4684 and are then deducted as "other deductions" on Line 15a, page 1, Form 1041.

2. *Casualty or theft of property held long term (Form 4684, Section B, Part II, Lines 33–39).*—In Part II, long-term casualty and theft gains and losses are also categorized into losses involving trade or business, etc., property, losses from income-producing property, and gains from casualties or thefts includible in income. The gain from recapture property from Form 4797 is reflected in the computation. A net loss from Line 38a is transferred to Line 14, Part II, Form 4797, where it becomes part of the ordinary gain and loss computation. If Form 4797 does not otherwise have to be filed, the net loss from Line 38a is reported on

Line 7, page 1, Form 1041, with the notation "Form 4684." In addition, total losses from income-producing property (Line 35, Form 4684, column (b)(ii)) are entered on Line 38b and then are deducted on Line 15a, page 1, Form 1041. However, if the netting of total gains on Line 36 against the total losses on Line 37 produces a net gain, the net gain is reported on Line 39 and is treated as a capital gain. The net gain, as reported on Line 39, is carried to Line 3, Part I, Form 4797, where it becomes part of the capital gain-ordinary loss computation.

## ON THE RETURN

The Tyler trust did not have any dispositions of assets that required the filing of Form 4684 or 4797. A filled-in Form 4797 for an S corporation appears at pages 163–164.

## ¶83 OTHER INCOME

If an estate or trust has other income not provided for on Lines 1 through 7 on page 1 of Form 1041, the type and amount of such income should be entered on Line 8, page 1. This includes (1) wages received as income in respect of a decedent, and (2) any portion of a lump-sum distribution from a qualified employee benefit plan that is taxable as ordinary income (see Form 1099-R and Form 4972).

## ¶84 DEDUCTIONS

An estate or trust can claim two general classes of deductions. The first class includes deductions from total income reported on Line 9 to arrive at the adjusted total income amount reported on Line 17, Form 1041. These deductions include: interest expenses (Line 10) (see ¶85), taxes (Line 11) (see ¶85), fiduciary fees (Line 12) (see ¶86), charitable contributions (Line 13) (see ¶87), fees paid to attorneys, accountants, and return preparers (Line 14) (see ¶86), other deductions that are not subject to the 2% floor (Line 15a), and those that are subject to the 2% floor (Line 15b). The sum of Lines 10 through 15b is entered on Line 16 (see ¶88).

If an estate or trust has tax-exempt income, the deduction amounts claimed on Lines 10 through 15b must be reduced by an allocable portion attributable to tax-exempt income. This is done by multiplying the amount of each deduction by a percentage factor that is derived by dividing the total tax-exempt income by gross income (including tax-exempt income) included in distributable net income.

The second general class of deductions is reported on Lines 18 through 20. It includes the income distribution deduction (Line 18) (see ¶89), the estate tax deduction (Line 19) (see ¶93), and the exemption (Line 20) (see ¶94).

## ¶85 INTEREST AND TAXES

All interest paid or accrued during the tax year, except interest deducted elsewhere on the return, is entered on Line 10. The types of interest that are deductible on Line 10 (subject to limitations) include: (1) investment interest; (2) "qualified residence interest"; and (3) interest on the estate tax that is deferred or paid in installments under Code Sec. 6601. Interest on a debt that was incurred or continued in order to buy or carry tax-exempt obligations is not deductible. Interest on debts incurred in connection with business activities (including rental activities) is deducted on Schedule C, C-EZ, E or F of Form 1040 rather than on Line 10 of Form 1041.

Qualified residence interest includes interest incurred by an estate or trust on debt secured by the qualified residence of a beneficiary. A deduction may be claimed only if the beneficiary has a present or residuary interest in the estate or trust.

The deduction for investment interest is limited to net investment income for the tax year and is computed on Form 4952. The box on Line 10 must be checked.

- **Taxes**

On Line 11, the fiduciary deducts all deductible taxes that have not been deducted elsewhere on Form 1041. Deductible taxes include state and local income or real property taxes and the generation-skipping tax imposed on income distributions.

## ¶86 FIDUCIARY, ACCOUNTANT, ATTORNEY, AND RETURN PREPARER FEES

The total amount of deductible fees paid to the fiduciary for administering the estate or trust should be entered on Line 12, Form 1041. Other deductible fees paid to the attorneys, accountants, and/or return preparers of the estate or trust should be entered on Line 14. Some deductions of an estate or trust are subject to a 2% floor on adjusted gross income. See ¶88.

ON THE RETURN

For purposes of the John Tyler trust, it is assumed that the expenses are costs paid or incurred in the administration of an estate or trust that would not have been so paid had the property not been held in trust.

## ¶87 CHARITABLE DEDUCTION

Estates and complex trusts may claim a charitable deduction, which is first computed on Schedule A, Line 7, and then entered on Line 13, page 1, of Form 1041. A charitable deduction may be claimed only if the contribution is provided for in the governing instrument and the contribution is made from the gross income of the estate or trust. In the case of an estate, the deduction is available for actual payments made during a year and for amounts permanently set aside for a charity. However, trusts (other than certain pre-1969 trusts) may claim a deduction only for cash payments to a charity. An election is available whereby a fiduciary can treat payouts made up to the end of the following tax year as having been paid in the prior year for deduction purposes. This election is made by attaching a statement to the return (or to an amended return) for the tax year in which the fiduciary chooses to claim the contribution deduction. Complex trusts claiming a charitable contribution deduction must also file Form 1041-A, U.S. Information Return—Trust Accumulation of Charitable Amounts.

## ¶88 OTHER DEDUCTIONS

Expenses that are not deductible elsewhere are deducted on either Line 15a or Line 15b of Form 1041. Schedules itemizing these deductions must also be submitted.

- **Deductions Not Subject to Two Percent of AGI Floor**

On Line 15a, the fiduciary deducts miscellaneous expenses that are *not* subject to the 2%-of-adjusted-gross-income (AGI) floor and that are not deducted elsewhere. These expenses include: (1) bond premiums that the fiduciary has elected to amortize; (2) nonbusiness casualty and theft losses from Form 4684, provided that an estate tax deduction has not been claimed and the necessary waiver has been filed (see ¶82); (3) the deduction for clean-fuel vehicles and certain refueling property; (4) net operating loss, supported by a statement showing its computation;

(5) the estate's or trust's share of amortization, depreciation, and depletion not claimed elsewhere; and (6) commercial revitalization deductions described in Code Sec. 1400I.

- **Deductions Subject to Two Percent of AGI Floor**

The estate or trust deducts on Line 15b miscellaneous itemized deductions that *are* subject to the 2% of AGI floor. This deduction is the excess of the total amount of miscellaneous itemized expenses over 2% of the estate's or trust's AGI for the year. The most common types of deductions subject to the 2% floor are expenses for the production or collection of income such as investment advisory fees, safe deposit box rentals, and subscriptions to investment advisory publications.

An estate or trust has to make a special AGI computation to apply the above rules. This special AGI amount is computed by subtracting from total income (Line 9): (1) the total administration costs as reported on Lines 12, 14, and 15a (see ¶86); (2) the income distribution deduction reported on Line 18 (see ¶89); (3) the estate's or trust's exemption reported on Line 20 (see ¶94); (4) the deduction for clean-fuel vehicles claimed on Line 15a; and (5) the net operating loss deduction claimed on Line 15a.

The income distribution deduction (see ¶89) is computed in different ways depending on whether distributions are less than or more than distributable net income (DNI). If the amount of such distributions is less than DNI, the amount of the actual distributions is used. If the amount of the distributions is more than DNI, the DNI must be computed by taking into account the miscellaneous itemized deductions after applying the 2% floor. An algebraic formula for this computation is provided in the Form 1041 instructions.

## ¶89 DISTRIBUTIONS DEDUCTION

An estate or trust claims a deduction from income for distributions to beneficiaries, and the amount so allowed is included in the income of the beneficiaries (Code Sec. 661(a)). The distributions deduction claimed on Line 18, page 1, of Form 1041 is computed on Schedule B, Line 15. (Instead of completing Schedule B, a pooled income fund attaches a statement showing how the income distribution deduction was determined.)

Schedules K-1 must be attached for the beneficiaries of an estate or trust that claims the income distribution deduction. Also, the distribution deduction must be recomputed on a minimum tax basis on Schedule I (see ¶95). The deduction is the total of the amounts paid, credited or required to be distributed to the beneficiaries, or the distributable net income, whichever is less. In either case, the amount must be adjusted to exclude any tax-exempt income (it is assumed that there is none in the filled-in return).

- **Cemetery Perpetual Care Fund**

On Line 18, page 1, of Form 1041, the amount paid for the maintenance of cemetery property (limited to $5 per gravesite) may be deducted. The number of gravesites should be entered to the right of the entry space for Line 18. Also, "(Section 642(i) Trust)" should be written after the trust's name at the top of Form 1041. It is not necessary to complete Schedules B and K-1 for a cemetery perpetual care fund.

- **65-Day Election**

A trustee of a complex trust can make a yearly irrevocable election to treat a distribution, or any part of it, made within the first 65 days of the trust's tax year as having been distributed to the beneficiary on the last day of the trust's preceding tax year. This 65-day election is also available to decedents' estates. The election is made by checking the box at Item 6 under "Other Information" on the bottom of page 2 of Form 1041.

The amount of income required to be distributed currently in the filled-in Form 1041, $19,514 (see ¶91, below), is less than the distributable net income of $29,271 (see ¶90, below). Therefore, the income distribution deduction is $19,514. This amount is carried from Line 15, Schedule B, page 2, Form 1041, to Line 18, page 1.

## ¶90 DISTRIBUTABLE NET INCOME

Before the amount of the deduction for distributions to beneficiaries, to be entered on Line 18, page 1, of Form 1041 may be determined, it is necessary to compute distributable net income. DNI must also be determined before the separate Schedules K-1 for each beneficiary's share of income, deductions, and credits can be completed.

The distributable net income, which is computed in Schedule B, page 2, of Form 1041, is the income of the trust for the current year that is available for distribution. It includes all tax-exempt interest and all dividends. (Instead of using Schedule B to compute the income distribution deduction, pooled income funds attach a statement showing how the deduction was computed.)

If a single trust has more than one beneficiary with separate and independent shares of the trust, their shares are treated as separate trusts in determining distributable net income allocable to each beneficiary. A similar rule applies to treat beneficiaries' substantially separate and independent shares of the estate of a decedent dying after August 5, 1997, as separate estates. When the separate share rule applies, distributable net income allocable to each beneficiary should be computed on a separate sheet attached to the return.

In determining distributable net income, if capital gains are required to be distributed to beneficiaries or if the trust takes a deduction for a charitable contribution that is made up in whole or in part of capital gains, the net capital gain distributable to beneficiaries and the long-term capital gain and short-term capital gain that are paid or permanently set aside for charitable, etc., purposes are to be included. Otherwise, capital gains are excluded.

## ON THE RETURN

In the illustrative return, the amount of $45,471 entered on Line 1 of Schedule B is the trust's adjusted total income from Line 17, page 1, of Form 1041. This amount is computed by taking the trust's total income on Line 9 of page 1 and subtracting the trust's total deductions reported on Line 16 on page 1. Thus, the distributions deduction and the deduction for estate taxes attributable to income in respect of a decedent are disregarded. Adjustments for items of tax-exempt interest, etc., described above are to be accounted for on Lines 2 through 6 of Schedule B. In this illustrative return, since the capital gains are assumed not to be distributable to the beneficiaries, they are to be excluded from distributable net income and, accordingly, are deducted on Line 6 of Schedule B. The deduction of $16,200 of capital gains leaves a distributable net income of $29,271, as noted on Line 7, Schedule B. This amount also is the trust's accounting (or Code Sec. 643(b)) income, which is determined under the terms of the governing instruments and the applicable local law, as reported on Line 8, Schedule B.

## ¶91 REQUIRED DISTRIBUTIONS • OTHER DISTRIBUTIONS

The amounts of income of the estate or trust required to be distributed currently to each beneficiary, whether distributed or not, and any other amounts paid, credited, or required to be distributed during the tax year, are to be entered on Lines 9 and 10 of Schedule B, page 2, Form 1041. In the illustrative return, no amounts are entered on Line 10 because the only distribution made by the trust for 2005 was the required two-thirds of current income less expenses.

## ON THE RETURN

The $19,514 in the illustrative return, which appears on Line 9 of Schedule B and constitutes the amount of income currently distributable to the beneficiaries, is computed from the amounts appearing on page 1 as follows:

failing to include the identification number on a Schedule K-1, unless such failure is due to reasonable cause.

- **Income Shares Shown in Schedule K-1**

Each beneficiary must include in gross income the smaller of (1) the amounts paid, credited or required to be distributed, or (2) the proportionate share of distributable net income. Either is reduced by the share of distributable tax-exempt income (decreased by the share of expenses incurred in earning that income). The character of the income reported on each separate Schedule K-1 by the fiduciary should be the same as the items that enter into the computation of distributable net income.

Income:

| | | | |
|---|---|---|---|
| Line 1: | Interest on bank deposits, notes, and corporation bonds | $ 5,000 |
| Line 2: | Dividends | 1,200 |
| Line 5: | Net rents | 25,471 |
| Total | | $31,671 |

Expense:

| | | |
|---|---|---|
| Line 11: | Taxes | $ 1,575 |
| Line 12: | Fiduciary fees | 675 |
| Line 14: | Return preparer fees | 150 |
| Total | | $ 2,400 |

Current income less expenses ... $29,271
Distributable to beneficiaries (2/3 of $29,271) ... $19,514

Since the trust instrument specifies that the beneficiaries are to share equally in two-thirds of the trust income after deduction of expenses, one-half of the $19,514, or $9,757, is assigned to Mary S. Warden, and $9,757 is assigned to Harold Draper.

## ¶92 BENEFICIARIES' INCOME AND CREDITS

- **Separate Schedule K-1**

Schedule K-1 is used to report a beneficiary's share of the income, deductions, and credits from the estate or trust. Three copies of Schedule K-1 must be prepared for each beneficiary. One copy of each Schedule K-1 is filed with Form 1041, another copy is given to the beneficiary, and the third copy is retained by the fiduciary. The fiduciary must request an identification number from each beneficiary. Further, the fiduciary is subject to a $50 penalty under Code Sec. 6723 for

If the total of the amounts paid, credited or required to be distributed is more than the amount of distributable net income shown in Schedul;e B, then the amounts that go into the computation of distributable net income are reported on each Schedule K-1 in proportion to each beneficiary's share of income.

If the total payments, credits, and required distributions are less than the distributable net income, only a proportionate part of each item entering into the computation of distributable net income is reported on Schedule K-1, according to the ratio of each particular item of income to the distributable net income. This is the situation in the case of the illustrative filled-in form as explained below.

If capital gains and losses are involved (see below) or a charitable deduction is claimed (see ¶87), special computations are required to determine the beneficiaries' shares of income.

## • Allocation of Deductions

Deductible items that enter into the computation of distributable net income are allocated among income items in a manner that is not inconsistent with the passive activity loss limitations under Code Sec. 469. In determining the amount of each item of distributable net income, deductions directly related to a particular class of income are deducted from that class. Deductions not directly related to any particular class of income may be deducted from any class, as long as a reasonable proportion is deducted from tax-exempt income. If the deductions allocable to one class of income exceed that income, the excess may be allocated to other classes of income. However, excess deductions allocable to tax-exempt income may not be allocated to other classes of income. Additionally, excess deductions from passive activities may not be allocated against nonpassive activities or portfolio income earned by an estate or trust. Deductions that enter into the computation of distributable net income may not be allocated to corpus items or to income not included in distributable net income.

Trust or estate deductions cannot generally be claimed by the beneficiary. Therefore, no negative amounts may be shown for any class of income except in the final year or for amortization, depreciation or depletion.

## • Capital Gains and Losses

Generally, capital gains are not included in distributable net income unless they are (1) allocated to income under the governing instrument or local law, (2) allocated to corpus and actually distributed to beneficiaries during the taxable year, (3) used, under the governing instrument or the practice followed by the fiduciary, in determining the amount which

is distributed or required to be distributed, or (4) paid or to be used for charitable purposes so that a contributions deduction is allowed. See ¶82.

Capital losses are excluded from the computation of distributable net income. But if capital gains are distributed, the capital losses are offset against the gains to determine the net capital gains distributed.

## • Credits

Income tax credits are generally allocated between an estate or a trust and its beneficiaries, based on the division of income.

The general business credit limitation based on tax liability generally may not exceed "net income tax" minus the greater of the tentative minimum tax or 25% of the "net regular tax liability" over $25,000. For estates and trusts, the $25,000 limitation amount must be reduced to an amount that bears the same ratio to $25,000 as the portion of the income of the estate or trust that is not allocated to beneficiaries bears to the total income of the estate or trust (Code Sec. 38(c)(3)(D)).

## • Filling in Schedule K-1

In the filled-in form, there is no interest or other income exempt from tax, and no capital gains are distributable. This leaves only dividends and other taxable income to be reported on each separate Schedule K-1 (Form 1041).

Total income, exclusive of capital gains, includes dividends of $1,200, interest of $5,000, and net rental income of $25,471. Assuming they are not directly related to any income item, the following expenses are to be allocated in the fiduciary's discretion:

| | |
|---|---|
| Personal property tax | $ 1,575 |
| Trustee fees | 675 |
| Fee for preparing income tax return | 150 |
| Total | $ 2,400 |

## ON THE RETURN

In this filled-in return, the fiduciary elects to reduce the rental income by these deductions. This leaves taxable dividends of $1,200, interest of $5,000, and rental income of $23,071 (net rents of $25,471 minus $2,400).

Because the total amount distributed, $19,514 (see ¶91), is less than the distributable net income, $29,271 (see ¶90), only proportionate parts of the dividends and the other taxable income are reported on each separate Schedule K-1.

The dividends allocable to the beneficiaries are determined by multiplying the gross dividends of $1,200 by a fraction with the actual amount distributed ($19,514) as the numerator and the distributable net income ($29,271) as the denominator. The result is $800 allocable to the beneficiaries, $400 to each.

Similarly, this fraction is applied to the interest and rental income to arrive at interest of $3,333 applicable to the beneficiaries, $1,667 to each, and rental income of $15,380, $7,690 to each.

On Schedule K-1 (Form 1041) for Mary S. Warden, interest of $1,667 is reported on Line 1 and qualified dividends of $400 are reported on Lines 2a and 2b. A similar Schedule K-1 would be prepared for Harold Draper (not reproduced).

Net short-term capital gains and net long-term capital gains are reported on Lines 3 and 4a–d, respectively, of Schedule K-1. Total net long-term capital gain for the year is reported on Line 4a, unrecaptured section 1250 gain is reported on Line 4b, and net long-term capital gain subject to the 28% capital gains rate (collectible gains and the nonexcludible gain from the sale of qualified small business stock) is reported on Line 4c. For a beneficiary other than a corporation, the beneficiary's allocable share of a capital loss carryover upon termination of the estate or trust is entered as a loss in parentheses on Line 11b or 11c, depending on whether the loss is short-term or long-term. See ¶82.

On Line 5, the beneficiary's share of annuities, royalties or any other income that is not subject to any of the passive activity loss limitations (see ¶81) is reported. Line 7 is used to report income items that could be subject to the passive activity rules at the beneficiary's level, such as rental and rental real estate income. Rental income from real estate activities of $7,690 is reported on Line 7 of the filled-in return. To assist the beneficiary in computing any applicable passive activity loss limitations, a separate schedule should be attached showing the beneficiary's share of income derived from rental real estate, other rental, trade or business activities. On Line 9, with appropriate code, the beneficiary's shares of depreciation, depletion, and amortization are reported. There are no allocations of depreciation (see ¶80), depletion, or amortization on the filled-in Schedule K-1. Any adjustments or tax preferences attributable to these three items are reported on Line 12.

The adjustment for minimum tax purposes are reported on Line 12, Schedule K-1, Form 1041, and also reported by each beneficiary on, Form 6251, Alternative Minimum Tax—Individuals.

The allocable portion of an estate tax deduction is reported on Line 10, Schedule K-1, Form 1041. Allocable portions of unused loss carryovers or excess deductions upon termination are reported on Lines 13a through 13d, and allocable portions of foreign taxes are reported on Line 11, Schedule K-1. A computation for each should be prepared on a separate sheet.

A number of miscellaneous items, not reported elsewhere on Schedule K-1, are reported on Line 14 or on an attached statement. These include the beneficiary's share of: (1) estimated taxes (¶72); (2) tax-exempt interest; (3) gross farming and fishing income; (4) investment income under Code Sec. 163(d); (5) foreign trading gross income as defined in Code Sec. 942(a); and (6) various tax credits.

## ON THE RETURN

The John Tyler Trust must complete Schedule I, even though it has no alternative minimum tax liability, because it has made an income distribution to its beneficiaries in 2005 (see ¶95).

The John Tyler Trust has an adjusted total income of $45,471 (Line 17, Form 1041) to which taxes of $1,575 (Line 11, Form 1041) are added to obtain an adjusted alternative minimum taxable income of $47,046 (Line 25, Schedule I) (the trust does not have any alternative minimum tax adjustments, tax preference items or net operating losses).

The trust is entitled to a distribution deduction on a minimum tax basis of $19,514 (Line 44, Schedule I), and the trust's allocable share of the alternative minimum taxable income (Line 29, Part I, Schedule I) is $27,532 ($47,046 - $19,514).

¶ 92

The portion of income for minimum tax purposes allocable to Mary S. Warden (reported on Line 7, Schedule K-1, Form 1041) is her share of the income distribution deduction computed on a minimum tax basis from Line 44 of Schedule I. The income distribution deduction computed on a minimum tax basis is allocated among the beneficiaries in the same manner as the income was allocated for regular tax purposes. Thus, one half of $19,514, or $9,757, is reported (see ¶91).

On her individual return, Mary S. Warden will report $1,667 in interest on Line 1, Part I, Schedule B, and $400 in total dividends on Line 5, Part II, Schedule B, Form 1040. The $7,690 in rental income is reported on Part III, Schedule E, Form 1040.

## ¶93  ESTATE TAX DEDUCTION

If an estate or trust includes in gross income an item of income that had accrued as of the date of death so that the item was included in the decedent's estate for estate tax purposes, the estate or trust may claim a corresponding deduction based on the estate tax attributable to the item's net value. A deduction is also allowed for the generation skipping transfer tax that is imposed because of a taxable termination or a direct skip that results from the death of a transferor (Code Sec. 691(c)).

The above deductions are claimed on Line 19, page 1 of Form 1041. They are computed on a separate sheet that must be attached to Form 1041.

## ¶94  EXEMPTIONS

An estate is entitled to an exemption of $600. The exemption of a simple trust is $300. Complex trusts, such as the one used in the example, are entitled to a $100 exemption. A $100 exemption is therefore entered on Line 20, page 1, Form 1041. No exemption is allowed on a final return.

A qualified disability trust established solely for the benefit of a disabled person under age 65 is allowed a $3,200 exemption if the trust's modified AGI does not exceed $145,950.

## ¶95  COMPUTATION OF TAX

The tax computation is made on Schedule G, page 2, Form 1041. The taxable income of the trust or estate on Line 22, page 1, Form 1041, is either multiplied by the rates appearing in the 2005 tax table on page 6 of this publication or, if eligible, the trust or estate may use the applicable rate for net capital gains. The total tax liability (Line 7, Schedule G) is reported on Line 23, page 1, Form 1041.

## ON THE RETURN

The John Tyler Trust has taxable income of $25,857, which is subject to the top marginal rate of 35%. Using the 2005 Tax Rate Schedule, the regular tax on that amount would be $8,156. However, the trust has net capital gains of $16,200 and may compute its tax liability using the appropriate capital gains tax rate (Part V, Schedule D, Form 1041). The maximum tax taking into account the capital gains tax rate, as shown on Line 35, Schedule D, is $4,846. Because this amount is smaller than the regular tax on Line 37, it is entered on Line 1a, Schedule G, Form 1041, and the box for Schedule D is checked.

Tax credits are offset against the tax liability in two different places on Form 1041. The nonrefundable tax credits are reported on Line 2, Schedule G, page 2, Form 1041, and the refundable credits are reflected on Line 24, page 1, Form 1041. As to the nonrefundable credits, the trust's or estate's share of the foreign tax credit is reported on Schedule G, Line 2a (attach Form 1116); other nonbusiness credits, such as the nonconventional source fuel tax credit and the qualified electric vehicle credit are reported on Line 2b; the trust's or estate's share of business credits is reported on Line 2c (attach the appropriate form (see ¶5)); and the credits for prior years' minimum tax (attach Form 8801) are reported on Line 2d.

Recapture taxes from Line 5, Schedule G, are reported either on Form 4255, Recapture of Investment Credit, or on Form 8611, Recapture of Low-Income Housing Credit. The alternative minimum tax is reported on Line 1c (from Schedule I). An estate or trust that incurs household employment taxes lists the amount of these taxes on Schedule G, Line 6 (attach Schedule H, Form 1040).

- **Alternative Minimum Tax**

Schedule I, Form 1041, Alternative Minimum Tax, consists of four parts. The estate or trust computes its share of alternative minimum taxable income in Part I, its income distribution deduction on a minimum tax basis in Part II, its alternative minimum tax liability in Part III, and the Part III Line 52 capital gain amount in Part IV.

The alternative minimum tax liability from Part III is reported on Line 1c, Schedule G, page 2, Form 1041. Part I and Part II of Schedule I have to be completed for any year for which an income distribution deduction (see ¶89) has been claimed, regardless of whether or not there is an alternative minimum tax liability. Part III must be completed if the estate's or trust's share of alternative minimum taxable income (Line 29, Part I) exceeds $22,500. The computation in Part IV is required for estates and trusts that have qualified dividends or complete Schedule D, Form 1041, and have a gain on Lines 14a and 15 of column (2) of Schedule D (Form 1041), as refigured for the AMT. The reduced rates that apply to net long-term capital gain also apply when figuring the alternative minimum tax.

*Adjusted Alternative Minimum Taxable Income.*—In determining adjusted alternative minimum taxable income (AAMTI) on Line 25, Schedule I, a fiduciary for an estate or a trust must combine Lines 1 through 24. Lines 1 through 24 represent the estate's or trust's adjusted total income or loss (Line 17, Form 1041 as entered on Line 1 of Schedule I) increased by its tax preferences and adjustments (Lines 2 through 23 of Schedule I) and reduced by its alternative minimum tax net operating loss deduction (Line 24 of Schedule I).

The alternative tax net operating loss deduction (AT-NOLD) entered on Line 24 of Schedule I is the sum of the alternative tax net operating loss (ATNOL) carryovers and carrybacks to the 2004 tax year.

The deduction for an ATNOLD carried forward to a tax year ending in 2004 or 2005, or arising in a tax year ending in 2004 or 2005 and carried back to a prior tax year is not subject to the usual 90 percent of alternative minimum taxable income limitation.

An election to forego the carryback period for regular tax purposes also applies for minimum tax purposes.

The alternative tax net operating loss deduction (ATNOLD) is computed by (1) adding adjustments (or subtracting if the adjustments were negative) made under Code Secs. 56 and 58 to the NOL under Code Sec. 172 and (2) reducing the NOL by any item of tax preference under Code Sec. 57 (except for the appreciated charitable contribution preference item). When computing an NOL from a loss year prior to 1987, the net operating loss must be reduced by both the tax preference items and the itemized deductions that were not allowed in computing the AMT to the extent that the items were included in the NOL for that year.

*Estate's or Trust's Share of Alternative Minimum Taxable Income.*—The income distribution deduction from Part II and the estate tax deduction are subtracted from AAMTI (Lines 26 and 27, Schedule I) to obtain the estate's or trust's share of alternative minimum taxable income on Line 29, Schedule I.

*Credits.*—Nonrefundable credits (other than the foreign tax credit) may not be claimed against alternative minimum tax liability. The foreign tax credit cannot offset more than 90% of the AMT liability computed without regard to foreign tax credits and net operating losses. When a trust or estate seeks to offset its alternative minimum tax liability with foreign tax credits, it must complete and attach a separate Form 1116 for each type of income specified at the top of Form 1116. Then, at the top of that form, the trust or estate should also add the phrase "Alt Min Tax."

## ON THE RETURN

The John Tyler Trust must complete all four parts of Schedule I. The John Tyler Trust is not subject to the tax because its regular tax of $4,846 exceeded its tentative alternative minimum tax (AMT) liability of $755.

The zero AMT tax liability was determined by first reducing the trust's alternative minimum taxable income ($27,532 on Line 29) by the $22,500 exemption amount. The $5,032 difference (Line 51) is the amount subject to the applicable AMT tax rate. Although the applicable tax rate is generally 26% on the first $175,000 of AMTI as reduced by the exemption amount, long-term capital gain of the trust which is subject to the 15% rate for regular tax purposes is also subject to a 15% rate for AMT purposes. Since the Trust had $16,200 in long-term capital gain and $400 in dividends subject to a 15% rate for regular tax purposes, the entire $5,032 of AMTI is deemed attributable to long-term capital gain and its tentative alternative minimum tax is $755 ($5,032 × 15%) (Lines 72 and 73). No AMT is due because the $755 tentative alternative minimum tax is less than the $4,846 regular income tax liability entered on Line 55.

- **Payments and Refundable Tax Credits**

Any payments for 2005 estimated taxes (including amounts applied from the previous year) are reported on Line 24a of Form 1041. If the fiduciary has elected to allocate estimated taxes to beneficiaries (see ¶72), the amount so allocated from Form 1041-T is entered on Line 24b, the amount on Line 24b is subtracted from Line 24a, and the result is entered on Line 24c. Taxes paid with extensions of time to file are reported on Line 24d (attach Form 2758, 8736, or 8800). Any erroneously withheld (and not repaid) income taxes on wages and salaries of a decedent that were received by the decedent's estate and any credit for back up withholding is reported on Line 24e (attach Form W-2). Any credit for backup withholding for income distributed should be reported on Line 14, Schedule K-1.

The refundable tax credits for regulated investment companies (attach Copy B of Form 2439) and the credit for federal tax on special fuels (attach Form 4136) are reported on Line 24f–g and totaled on Line 24h.

## ON THE RETURN

In the example for the John Tyler Trust, a total of $7,000 was paid for estimated taxes. This figure is entered on Line 24a. Since there are no applicable tax credits, the $7,000 figure is carried to Line 25 before being subtracted from the amount on Line 23.

## ¶96 COMPLETION OF RETURN

The declaration at the bottom of page 1 calls for the signature of the fiduciary, without a requirement of notarization. Financial institutions that act as trustees and submit estimated tax payments must provide their employee identification number (EIN). A person who received compensation for preparing the return must also sign. The additional information required at the bottom of page 2 must be supplied.

Form **1041**
Department of the Treasury—Internal Revenue Service
**U.S. Income Tax Return for Estates and Trusts**    20**05**    OMB No. 1545-0092

For calendar year 2005 or fiscal year beginning , 2005, and ending , 20

**A** Type of entity (see instr.):

- [ ] Decedent's estate
- [ ] Simple trust
- [✔] Complex trust
- [ ] Qualified disability trust
- [ ] ESBT (S portion only)
- [ ] Grantor type trust
- [ ] Bankruptcy estate–Ch. 7
- [ ] Bankruptcy estate–Ch. 11
- [ ] Pooled income fund

Name of estate or trust (If a grantor type trust, see page 12 of the instructions.)
**John Tyler Trust**

Name and title of fiduciary
**South End Trust Co.**

Number, street, and room or suite no. (If a P.O. box, see page 12 of the instructions.)
**28 Beach St.**

City or town, state, and ZIP code
**Detroit, MI 48226**

**C** Employer identification number
21 : 1234567

**D** Date entity created
**01-01-87**

**E** Nonexempt charitable and split-interest trusts, check applicable boxes (see page 13 of the instr.):

- [ ] Described in section 4947(a)(1)
- [ ] Not a private foundation
- [ ] Described in section 4947(a)(2)

**B** Number of Schedules K-1 attached (see instructions) ▶ **2**

**F** Check applicable boxes:
- [ ] Initial return
- [ ] Final return
- [ ] Amended return
- [ ] Change in fiduciary
- [ ] Change in fiduciary's name

- [ ] Change in trust's name
- [ ] Change in fiduciary's address

**G** Pooled mortgage account (see page 14 of the instructions): [ ] Bought [ ] Sold Date:

**Income**

| | | | |
|---|---|---|---|
| 1 | Interest income | 1 | 5,000 |
| 2a | Total ordinary dividends | 2a | 1,200 |
| b | Qualified dividends allocable to: (1) Beneficiaries 800 (2) Estate or trust 400 | | |
| 3 | Business income or (loss) (attach Schedule C or C-EZ (Form 1040)) | 3 | |
| 4 | Capital gain or (loss) (attach Schedule D (Form 1041)) | 4 | 16,200 |
| 5 | Rents, royalties, partnerships, other estates and trusts, etc. (attach Schedule E (Form 1040)) | 5 | 25,471 |
| 6 | Farm income or (loss) (attach Schedule F (Form 1040)) | 6 | |
| 7 | Ordinary gain or (loss) (attach Form 4797) | 7 | |
| 8 | Other income. List type and amount | 8 | |
| 9 | **Total income.** Combine lines 1, 2a, and 3 through 8 ▶ | 9 | 47,871 |

**Deductions**

| | | | |
|---|---|---|---|
| 10 | Interest. Check if Form 4952 is attached ▶ [ ] | 10 | |
| 11 | Taxes | 11 | 1,575 |
| 12 | Fiduciary fees | 12 | 675 |
| 13 | Charitable deduction (from Schedule A, line 7) | 13 | |
| 14 | Attorney, accountant, and return preparer fees | 14 | 150 |
| 15a | Other deductions **not** subject to the 2% floor (attach schedule) | 15a | |
| b | Allowable miscellaneous itemized deductions subject to the 2% floor | 15b | |
| 16 | Add lines 10 through 15b ▶ | 16 | 2,400 |
| 17 | Adjusted total income or (loss). Subtract line 16 from line 9 . | 17 | 45,471 | | |
| 18 | Income distribution deduction (from Schedule B, line 15) (attach Schedules K-1 (Form 1041)) | 18 | 19,514 |
| 19 | Estate tax deduction (including certain generation-skipping taxes) (attach computation) | 19 | |
| 20 | Exemption | 20 | 100 |
| 21 | Add lines 18 through 20 ▶ | 21 | 19,614 |

**Tax and Payments**

| | | | |
|---|---|---|---|
| 22 | Taxable income. Subtract line 21 from line 17. If a loss, see page 20 of the instructions | 22 | 25,857 |
| 23 | **Total tax** (from Schedule G, line 7) | 23 | 4,846 |
| 24 | **Payments: a** 2005 estimated tax payments and amount applied from 2004 return | 24a | 7,000 |
| b | Estimated tax payments allocated to beneficiaries (from Form 1041-T) | 24b | 0 |
| c | Subtract line 24b from line 24a | 24c | 7,000 |
| d | Tax paid with Form 7004 (see page 20 of the instructions) | 24d | |
| e | Federal income tax withheld. If any is from Form(s) 1099, check ▶ [ ] | 24e | |
| | Other payments: **f** Form 2439 ; **g** Form 4136 ; Total ▶ | 24h | |
| 25 | **Total payments.** Add lines 24c through 24e, and 24h ▶ | 25 | 7,000 |
| 26 | Estimated tax penalty (see page 20 of the instructions) | 26 | |
| 27 | **Tax due.** If line 25 is smaller than the total of lines 23 and 26, enter amount owed | 27 | 0 |
| 28 | **Overpayment.** If line 25 is larger than the total of lines 23 and 26, enter amount overpaid | 28 | 2,154 |
| 29 | Amount of line 28 to be: **a** Credited to 2006 estimated tax ▶ ; **b** Refunded ▶ | 29 | 2,154 |

**Sign Here**

Under penalties of perjury, I declare that I have examined this return, including accompanying schedules and statements, and to the best of my knowledge and belief, it is true, correct, and complete. Declaration of preparer (other than taxpayer) is based on all information of which preparer has any knowledge.

▶ Signature of fiduciary or officer representing fiduciary    Date    ▶ 76 : 5432101 EIN of fiduciary if a financial institution

May the IRS discuss this return with the preparer shown below (see instr.)? [✔] Yes [ ] No

**Paid Preparer's Use Only**

| | |
|---|---|
| Preparer's signature ▶ | Date |
| Firm's name (or yours if self-employed), address, and ZIP code ▶ **Riley P. Burns** **51 N. Oak St. Detroit, MI 48216** | |

Check if self-employed [✔]

Preparer's SSN or PTIN **456-08-6347**

EIN 66 : 10713
Phone no. ( 317 ) 578-3261

**For Privacy Act and Paperwork Reduction Act Notice, see the separate instructions.**    Cat. No. 11370H    Form **1041** (2005)

Form 1041 (2005)                                                                                                      Page **2**

## Schedule A Charitable Deduction. Do not complete for a simple trust or a pooled income fund.

| | | | |
|---|---|---|---|
| 1 | Amounts paid or permanently set aside for charitable purposes from gross income (see page 21) | 1 | |
| 2 | Tax-exempt income allocable to charitable contributions (see page 21 of the instructions) . . | 2 | |
| 3 | Subtract line 2 from line 1 . . . . . . . . . | 3 | |
| 4 | Capital gains for the tax year allocated to corpus and paid or permanently set aside for charitable purposes | 4 | |
| 5 | Add lines 3 and 4 . . . . . . . . . | 5 | |
| 6 | Section 1202 exclusion allocable to capital gains paid or permanently set aside for charitable purposes (see page 21 of the instructions) . . . . . . . . . . | 6 | |
| 7 | **Charitable deduction.** Subtract line 6 from line 5. Enter here and on page 1, line 13 . . . . | 7 | |

## Schedule B Income Distribution Deduction

| | | | |
|---|---|---|---|
| 1 | Adjusted total income (see page 22 of the instructions) . . . . . . . . | 1 | 45,471 |
| 2 | Adjusted tax-exempt interest . . . . . . . . . | 2 | 0 |
| 3 | Total net gain from Schedule D (Form 1041), line 15, column (1) (see page 22 of the instructions) | 3 | |
| 4 | Enter amount from Schedule A, line 4 (reduced by any allocable section 1202 exclusion) . . | 4 | |
| 5 | Capital gains for the tax year included on Schedule A, line 1 (see page 22 of the instructions) | 5 | |
| 6 | Enter any gain from page 1, line 4, as a negative number. If page 1, line 4, is a loss, enter the loss as a positive number . . . . . . . . . | 6 | (16,200) |
| 7 | **Distributable net income (DNI).** Combine lines 1 through 6. If zero or less, enter -0- . . . | 7 | 29,271 |
| 8 | If a complex trust, enter accounting income for the tax year as determined under the governing instrument and applicable local law [8  29,271] | | |
| 9 | Income required to be distributed currently . . . . . . . . . | 9 | 19,514 |
| 10 | Other amounts paid, credited, or otherwise required to be distributed . . . . . . | 10 | 0 |
| 11 | Total distributions. Add lines 9 and 10. If greater than line 8, see page 22 of the instructions | 11 | 19,514 |
| 12 | Enter the amount of tax-exempt income included on line 11 . . . . . . . | 12 | 0 |
| 13 | Tentative income distribution deduction. Subtract line 12 from line 11 . . . . . . | 13 | 19,514 |
| 14 | Tentative income distribution deduction. Subtract line 2 from line 7. If zero or less, enter -0- | 14 | 29,271 |
| 15 | **Income distribution deduction.** Enter the smaller of line 13 or line 14 here and on page 1, line 18 | 15 | 19,514 |

## Schedule G Tax Computation (see page 23 of the instructions)

| | | | |
|---|---|---|---|
| **1 Tax: a** Tax on taxable income (see page 23 of the instructions) . . | 1a | 4,846 | |
| **b** Tax on lump-sum distributions (attach Form 4972) . . . . | 1b | | |
| **c** Alternative minimum tax (from Schedule I, line 56) . . . . | 1c | 0 | |
| **d Total.** Add lines 1a through 1c . . . . . . . . ▶ | 1d | | 4,846 |
| **2a** Foreign tax credit (attach Form 1116) . . . . . . . | 2a | | |
| **b** Other nonbusiness credits (attach schedule) . . . . . . | 2b | | |
| **c** General business credit. Enter here and check which forms are attached: ☐ Form 3800 ☐ Forms (specify) ▶ _____ | 2c | | |
| **d** Credit for prior year minimum tax (attach Form 8801) . . . . | 2d | | |
| **3** **Total credits.** Add lines 2a through 2d . . . . . . . ▶ | 3 | | |
| **4** Subtract line 3 from line 1d. If zero or less, enter -0- . . . . . . | 4 | | 4,846 |
| **5** Recapture taxes. Check if from: ☐ Form 4255 ☐ Form 8611 . . . | 5 | | |
| **6** Household employment taxes. Attach Schedule H (Form 1040) . . . | 6 | | |
| **7** **Total tax.** Add lines 4 through 6. Enter here and on page 1, line 23 . . . . ▶ | 7 | | 4,846 |

| | Other Information | Yes | No |
|---|---|---|---|
| 1 | Did the estate or trust receive tax-exempt income? If "Yes," attach a computation of the allocation of expenses Enter the amount of tax-exempt interest income and exempt-interest dividends ▶ $ _____ | | ✔ |
| 2 | Did the estate or trust receive all or any part of the earnings (salary, wages, and other compensation) of any individual by reason of a contract assignment or similar arrangement? . . . . . . . . . | | ✔ |
| 3 | At any time during calendar year 2005, did the estate or trust have an interest in or a signature or other authority over a bank, securities, or other financial account in a foreign country? . . . . . . . . . | | ✔ |
| | See page 25 of the instructions for exceptions and filing requirements for Form TD F 90-22.1. If "Yes," enter the name of the foreign country ▶ _____ | | |
| 4 | During the tax year, did the estate or trust receive a distribution from, or was it the grantor of, or transferor to, a foreign trust? If "Yes," the estate or trust may have to file Form 3520. See page 25 of the instructions | | ✔ |
| 5 | Did the estate or trust receive, or pay, any qualified residence interest on seller-provided financing? If "Yes," see page 25 for required attachment . . . . . . . . . | | ✔ |
| 6 | If this is an estate or a complex trust making the section 663(b) election, check here (see page 25) . ▶ ☐ | | |
| 7 | To make a section 643(e)(3) election, attach Schedule D (Form 1041), and check here (see page 25) . ▶ ☐ | | |
| 8 | If the decedent's estate has been open for more than 2 years, attach an explanation for the delay in closing the estate, and check here ▶ ☐ | | |
| 9 | Are any present or future trust beneficiaries skip persons? See page 26 of the instructions . . . . . | | ✔ |

Form **1041** (2005)

¶**96**

Form 1041 (2005)                                                                                         Page **3**

| **Schedule I** | **Alternative Minimum Tax** (see pages 26 through 32 of the instructions) | | |
|---|---|---|---|

**Part I—Estate's or Trust's Share of Alternative Minimum Taxable Income**

| | | | |
|---|---|---|---:|
| 1 | Adjusted total income or (loss) (from page 1, line 17) . . . . . . . . . . . . . | **1** | 45,471 |
| 2 | Interest . . . . . . . . . . . . . . . . . . . . . . . . . . . | **2** | |
| 3 | Taxes . . . . . . . . . . . . . . . . . . . . . . . . . . . | **3** | 1,575 |
| 4 | Miscellaneous itemized deductions (from page 1, line 15b) . . . . . . . | **4** | |
| 5 | Refund of taxes . . . . . . . . . . . . . . . . . . . . . . | **5** | ( ) |
| 6 | Depletion (difference between regular tax and AMT) . . . . . . . . . . | **6** | |
| 7 | Net operating loss deduction. Enter as a positive amount . . . . . . . | **7** | |
| 8 | Interest from specified private activity bonds exempt from the regular tax . . . . | **8** | |
| 9 | Qualified small business stock (see page 27 of the instructions) . . . . . . . | **9** | |
| 10 | Exercise of incentive stock options (excess of AMT income over regular tax income) . . . . | **10** | |
| 11 | Other estates and trusts (amount from Schedule K-1 (Form 1041), box 12, code A) . . . . | **11** | |
| 12 | Electing large partnerships (amount from Schedule K-1 (Form 1065-B), box 6) . . . . | **12** | |
| 13 | Disposition of property (difference between AMT and regular tax gain or loss) . . . . . | **13** | |
| 14 | Depreciation on assets placed in service after 1986 (difference between regular tax and AMT) | **14** | |
| 15 | Passive activities (difference between AMT and regular tax income or loss) . . . . | **15** | |
| 16 | Loss limitations (difference between AMT and regular tax income or loss) . . . . | **16** | |
| 17 | Circulation costs (difference between regular tax and AMT) . . . . . . . | **17** | |
| 18 | Long-term contracts (difference between AMT and regular tax income) . . . . . | **18** | |
| 19 | Mining costs (difference between regular tax and AMT) . . . . . . . . . | **19** | |
| 20 | Research and experimental costs (difference between regular tax and AMT) . . . . | **20** | |
| 21 | Income from certain installment sales before January 1, 1987 . . . . . . . | **21** | ( ) |
| 22 | Intangible drilling costs preference . . . . . . . . . . . . . . . | **22** | |
| 23 | Other adjustments, including income-based related adjustments . . . . . . | **23** | |
| 24 | Alternative tax net operating loss deduction (See the instructions for the limitation that applies.) | **24** | ( ) |
| 25 | Adjusted alternative minimum taxable income. Combine lines 1 through 24 . . . . . | **25** | 47,046 |

**Note:** *Complete Part II below before going to line 26.*

| | | | | | |
|---|---|---|---:|---|---:|
| 26 | Income distribution deduction from Part II, line 44 . . . . . . | **26** | 19,514 | | |
| 27 | Estate tax deduction (from page 1, line 19) . . . . . . . . . | **27** | 0 | | |
| 28 | Add lines 26 and 27 . . . . . . . . . . . . . . . . . . | | | **28** | 19,514 |
| 29 | Estate's or trust's share of alternative minimum taxable income. Subtract line 28 from line 25 | | | **29** | 27,532 |

If line 29 is:

- $22,500 or less, stop here and enter -0- on Schedule G, line 1c. The estate or trust is not liable for the alternative minimum tax.
- Over $22,500, but less than $165,000, go to line 45.
- $165,000 or more, enter the amount from line 29 on line 51 and go to line 52.

**Part II—Income Distribution Deduction on a Minimum Tax Basis**

| | | | |
|---|---|---|---:|
| 30 | Adjusted alternative minimum taxable income (see page 30 of the instructions) . . . . . | **30** | 47,046 |
| 31 | Adjusted tax-exempt interest (other than amounts included on line 8) . . . . . . | **31** | |
| 32 | Total net gain from Schedule D (Form 1041), line 15, column (1). If a loss, enter -0- . . . . | **32** | |
| 33 | Capital gains for the tax year allocated to corpus and paid or permanently set aside for charitable purposes (from Schedule A, line 4) | **33** | |
| 34 | Capital gains paid or permanently set aside for charitable purposes from gross income (see page 30 of the instructions) . . . . | **34** | |
| 35 | Capital gains computed on a minimum tax basis included on line 25 . . . . . . | **35** | ( 16,200 ) |
| 36 | Capital losses computed on a minimum tax basis included on line 25. Enter as a positive amount | **36** | |
| 37 | Distributable net alternative minimum taxable income (DNAMTI). Combine lines 30 through 36. If zero or less, enter -0- | **37** | 30,846 |
| 38 | Income required to be distributed currently (from Schedule B, line 9) . . . . . . | **38** | 19,154 |
| 39 | Other amounts paid, credited, or otherwise required to be distributed (from Schedule B, line 10) | **39** | 0 |
| 40 | Total distributions. Add lines 38 and 39 . . . . . . . . . . . . | **40** | 19,154 |
| 41 | Tax-exempt income included on line 40 (other than amounts included on line 8) . . . . | **41** | 0 |
| 42 | Tentative income distribution deduction on a minimum tax basis. Subtract line 41 from line 40 | **42** | 19,154 |
| 43 | Tentative income distribution deduction on a minimum tax basis. Subtract line 31 from line 37. If zero or less, enter -0- | **43** | 30,846 |
| 44 | **Income distribution deduction on a minimum tax basis.** Enter the smaller of line 42 or line 43. Enter here and on line 26 . . . . . . | **44** | 19,514 |

Form **1041** (2005)

¶ **96**

Form 1041 (2005)                                                                                                    Page **4**

## Part III—Alternative Minimum Tax

| | | | | |
|---|---|---|---|---|
| 45 | Exemption amount . . . . . . . . . . . . . . . . . . . . . | **45** | $22,500 | 00 |
| 46 | Enter the amount from line 29 . . . . . . . . . . . | **46** 27,532 | | |
| 47 | Phase-out of exemption amount . . . . . . . . . | **47** $75,000 00 | | |
| 48 | Subtract line 47 from line 46. If zero or less, enter -0- | **48** 0 | | |
| 49 | Multiply line 48 by 25% (.25) . . . . . . . . . . . | | **49** | 0 |
| 50 | Subtract line 49 from line 45. If zero or less, enter -0- | | **50** | 22,500 |
| 51 | Subtract line 50 from line 46 . . . . . . . . . . . | | **51** | 5,032 |
| 52 | Go to Part IV of Schedule I to figure line 52 if the estate or trust has qualified dividends or has a gain on lines 14a and 15 of column (2) of Schedule D (Form 1041) (as refigured for the AMT, if necessary). Otherwise, if line 51 is— <br>• $175,000 or less, multiply line 51 by 26% (.26). <br>• Over $175,000, multiply line 51 by 28% (.28) and subtract $3,500 from the result . . . . . | | **52** | 755 |
| 53 | Alternative minimum foreign tax credit (see page 30 of the instructions) . . . . . . . . . | | **53** | 0 |
| 54 | Tentative minimum tax. Subtract line 53 from line 52 . . . . . . . . . . . . . . . . . | | **54** | 755 |
| 55 | Enter the tax from Schedule G, line 1a (minus any foreign tax credit from Schedule G, line 2a) | | **55** | 4,846 |
| 56 | **Alternative minimum tax.** Subtract line 55 from line 54. If zero or less, enter -0-. Enter here and on Schedule G, line 1c . . . . . . . . . . . . . . . . . . . . . | | **56** | 0 |

## Part IV—Line 52 Computation Using Maximum Capital Gains Rates

| | | | | |
|---|---|---|---|---|
| | **Caution:** *If you did not complete Part V of Schedule D (Form 1041), the Schedule D Tax Worksheet, or the Qualified Dividends Tax Worksheet, see page 32 of the instructions before completing this part.* | | | |
| 57 | Enter the amount from line 51 . . . . . . . . | | **57** | 5,032 |
| 58 | Enter the amount from Schedule D (Form 1041), line 22, line 13 of the Schedule D Tax Worksheet, or line 4 of the Qualified Dividends Tax Worksheet, whichever applies (as refigured for the AMT, if necessary) | **58** 16,600 | | |
| 59 | Enter the amount from Schedule D (Form 1041), line 14b, column (2) (as refigured for the AMT, if necessary). If you did not complete Schedule D for the regular tax or the AMT, enter -0- . . . . . | **59** 0 | | |
| 60 | If you did not complete a Schedule D Tax Worksheet for the regular tax or the AMT, enter the amount from line 58. Otherwise, add lines 58 and 59 and enter the **smaller** of that result or the amount from line 10 of the Schedule D Tax Worksheet (as refigured for the AMT, if necessary) | **60** 16,600 | | |
| 61 | Enter the **smaller** of line 57 or line 60 . . . . . . . . . . . | | **61** | 5,032 |
| 62 | Subtract line 61 from line 57 . . . . . . . . . . . | | **62** | 0 |
| 63 | If line 62 is $175,000 or less, multiply line 62 by 26% (.26). Otherwise, multiply line 62 by 28% (.28) and subtract $3,500 from the result . . . . . . . . . ▶ | | **63** | 0 |
| 64 | Maximum amount subject to the 5% rate . . . . . . . . | **64** $2,000 00 | | |
| 65 | Enter the amount from line 23 of Schedule D (Form 1041), line 14 of the Schedule D Tax Worksheet, or line 5 of the Qualified Dividends Tax Worksheet, whichever applies (as figured for the regular tax). If you did not complete Schedule D or either worksheet for the regular tax, enter -0- | **65** 9,257 | | |
| 66 | Subtract line 65 from line 64. If zero or less, enter -0- . . . . . | **66** 0 | | |
| 67 | Enter the **smaller** of line 57 or line 58 . . . . . . . . . | **67** 5,032 | | |
| 68 | Enter the **smaller** of line 66 or line 67 . . . . . . . . . | **68** 0 | | |
| 69 | Multiply line 68 by 5% (.05) . . . . . . . . . . . . . ▶ | | **69** | 0 |
| 70 | Subtract line 68 from line 67 . . . . . . . . . . . | **70** 5,032 | | |
| 71 | Multiply line 70 by 15% (.15) . . . . . . . . . . . ▶ | | **71** | 755 |
| | **If line 59 is zero or blank, skip lines 72 and 73 and go to line 74. Otherwise, go to line 72.** | | | |
| 72 | Subtract line 67 from line 61 . . . . . . . . . . . | **72** | | |
| 73 | Multiply line 72 by 25% (.25) . . . . . . . . . . . ▶ | | **73** | |
| 74 | Add lines 63, 69, 71, and 73 . . . . . . . . . . . | | **74** | 755 |
| 75 | If line 57 is $175,000 or less, multiply line 57 by 26% (.26). Otherwise, multiply line 57 by 28% (.28) and subtract $3,500 from the result . . . . . . . . . | | **75** | 1,308 |
| 76 | Enter the **smaller** of line 74 or line 75 here and on line 52 . . . . . . . . . | | **76** | 755 |

Form **1041** (2005)

¶ **96**

| SCHEDULE D<br>(Form 1041)<br><br>Department of the Treasury<br>Internal Revenue Service | **Capital Gains and Losses**<br><br>▶ Attach to Form 1041, Form 5227, or Form 990-T. See the separate<br>instructions for Form 1041 (also for Form 5227 or Form 990-T, if applicable). | OMB No. 1545-0092<br><br>20**05** |
|---|---|---|

| Name of estate or trust<br>John Tyler Trust | Employer identification number<br>22 : 1234567 |
|---|---|

**Note:** *Form 5227 filers need to complete **only** Parts I and II.*

### Part I — Short-Term Capital Gains and Losses—Assets Held One Year or Less

| (a) Description of property<br>(Example, 100 shares 7%<br>preferred of "Z" Co.) | (b) Date<br>acquired<br>(mo., day, yr.) | (c) Date sold<br>(mo., day, yr.) | (d) Sales price | (e) Cost or other basis<br>(see page 34) | (f) Gain or (Loss)<br>for the entire year<br>(col. (d) less col. (e)) |
|---|---|---|---|---|---|
| 1 Co-Work Corp.<br>7,000 shares common | 2-6-2005 | 4-22-2005 | 44,000 | 50,000 | (6,000) |
| | | | | | |
| | | | | | |
| | | | | | |
| | | | | | |

| | | | |
|---|---|---|---|
| 2 | Short-term capital gain or (loss) from Forms 4684, 6252, 6781, and 8824 . . . . . . . . . | 2 | |
| 3 | Net short-term gain or (loss) from partnerships, S corporations, and other estates or trusts . | 3 | |
| 4 | Short-term capital loss carryover. Enter the amount, if any, from line 9 of the 2004 Capital Loss Carryover Worksheet . . . . . . . . . . . . . . | 4 ( | ) |
| 5 | **Net short-term gain or (loss).** Combine lines 1 through 4 in column (f). Enter here and on line 13, column (3) below . . . . . . . . . . . . . . . . . . . . . . ▶ | 5 | (6,000) |

### Part II — Long-Term Capital Gains and Losses—Assets Held More Than One Year

| (a) Description of property<br>(Example, 100 shares 7%<br>preferred of "Z" Co.) | (b) Date<br>acquired<br>(mo., day, yr.) | (c) Date sold<br>(mo., day, yr.) | (d) Sales price | (e) Cost or other basis<br>(see page 34) | (f) Gain or (Loss)<br>for the entire year<br>(col. (d) less col. (e)) |
|---|---|---|---|---|---|
| 6 Mixture Corp.<br>5,000 shares common | 2-6-2000 | 5-1-2005 | 47,200 | 25,000 | 22,200 |
| | | | | | |
| | | | | | |
| | | | | | |

| | | | |
|---|---|---|---|
| 7 | Long-term capital gain or (loss) from Forms 2439, 4684, 6252, 6781, and 8824 . . . . . . . . | 7 | |
| 8 | Net long-term gain or (loss) from partnerships, S corporations, and other estates or trusts . | 8 | |
| 9 | Capital gain distributions . . . . . . . . . . . . . | 9 | |
| 10 | Gain from Form 4797, Part I . . . . . . . . . . . . . . | 10 | |
| 11 | Long-term capital loss carryover. Enter the amount, if any, from line 14 of the 2004 Capital Loss Carryover Worksheet . . . . . . . . . . . . . | 11 ( | ) |
| 12 | **Net long-term gain or (loss).** Combine lines 6 through 11 in column (f). Enter here and on line 14a, column (3) below . . . . . . . . . . . . . . . . . . . . . . ▶ | 12 | 22,200 |

### Part III — Summary of Parts I and II

*Caution: Read the instructions **before** completing this part.*

| | | (1) Beneficiaries'<br>(see page 36) | (2) Estate's<br>or trust's | (3) Total |
|---|---|---|---|---|
| 13 | **Net short-term gain or (loss)** . . . . . . . . . | 13 | | (6,000) | (6,000) |
| 14 | **Net long-term gain or (loss):** | | | | |
| a | Total for year . . . . . . . . . . . . | 14a | | 22,200 | 22,200 |
| b | Unrecaptured section 1250 gain (see line 18 of the worksheet on page 35) . . . . . . . . . . . | 14b | | | |
| c | 28% rate gain or (loss) . . . . . . . . . . | 14c | | | |
| 15 | **Total net gain or (loss).** Combine lines 13 and 14a . ▶ | 15 | | 16,200 | 16,200 |

**Note:** *If line 15, column (3), is a net gain, enter the gain on Form 1041, line 4. If lines 14a and 15, column (2), are net gains, go to Part V, and **do not** complete Part IV. If line 15, column (3), is a net loss, complete Part IV and the **Capital Loss Carryover Worksheet,** as necessary.*

For Paperwork Reduction Act Notice, see the Instructions for Form 1041.   Cat. No. 11376V   Schedule D (Form 1041) 2005

| **Part IV** | **Capital Loss Limitation** |
|---|---|

**16**    Enter here and enter as a (loss) on Form 1041, line 4, the **smaller** of:

   **a**   The loss on line 15, column (3) **or**

   **b**   $3,000 . . . . . . . . . . . . . . . . . . . . . . . . . . . . . . . . **16** (      )

*If the loss on line 15, column (3), is more than $3,000, **or** if Form 1041, page 1, line 22, is a loss, complete the **Capital Loss Carryover Worksheet** on page 37 of the instructions to determine your capital loss carryover.*

| **Part V** | **Tax Computation Using Maximum Capital Gains Rates** (Complete this part **only** if both lines 14a and 15 in column (2) are gains, or an amount is entered in Part I or Part II and there is an entry on Form 1041, line 2b(2), **and** Form 1041, line 22 is more than zero.) |
|---|---|

   **Note:** *If line 14b, column (2) or line 14c, column (2) is more than zero, complete the worksheet on page 38 of the instructions and skip Part V. Otherwise, go to line 17.*

| | | | |
|---|---|---|---|
| **17** Enter taxable income from Form 1041, line 22 . . . . . . . . . | **17** | | 25,857 |
| **18** Enter the **smaller** of line 14a or 15 in column (2) but not less than zero . . . . . . . . **18** 16,200 | | | |
| **19** Enter the estate's or trust's qualified dividends from Form 1041, line 2b(2) . . . . . . **19** 400 | | | |
| **20** Add lines 18 and 19 . . . . . . . . . . **20** 16,600 | | | |
| **21** If the estate or trust is filing Form 4952, enter the amount from line 4g; otherwise, enter -0- ▶ **21** 0 | | | |
| **22** Subtract line 21 from line 20. If zero or less, enter -0- . . . . . | **22** | | 16,600 |
| **23** Subtract line 22 from line 17. If zero or less, enter -0- . . . . . | **23** | | 9,257 |
| **24** Enter the **smaller** of the amount on line 17 or $2,000 . . . . | **24** | | 1,950 |
| **25** Is the amount on line 23 equal to or more than the amount on line 24? ☐ **Yes.** Skip lines 25 through 27; go to line 28 and check the "No" box. ☐ **No.** Enter the amount from line 23 . . . . . . . . . . . . | **25** | | |
| **26** Subtract line 25 from line 24 . . . . . . . . . . . . . . | **26** | | |
| **27** Multiply line 26 by 5% (.05) . . . . . . . . . . . . . . . | **27** | | |
| **28** Are the amounts on lines 22 and 26 the same? ☐ **Yes.** Skip lines 28 through 31; go to line 32. ☐ **No.** Enter the **smaller** of line 17 or line 22 . . . . . . . . | **28** | | 16,600 |
| **29** Enter the amount from line 26 (If line 26 is blank, enter -0-). . . . . | **29** | | 0 |
| **30** Subtract line 29 from line 28 . . . . . . . . . . . . . . | **30** | | 16,600 |
| **31** Multiply line 30 by 15% (.15) . . . . . . . . . . . . . . . | **31** | | 2,490 |
| **32** Figure the tax on the amount on line 23. Use the 2005 Tax Rate Schedule on page 23 of the instructions . . . . . . . . . . . . . . . . . . . . . . . . . . | **32** | | 2,356 |
| **33** Add lines 27, 31, and 32 . . . . . . . . . . . . . . . . . | **33** | | 4,846 |
| **34** Figure the tax on the amount on line 17. Use the 2005 Tax Rate Schedule on page 23 of the instructions . . . . . . . . . . . . . . . . . . . . . . . . . . | **34** | | 8,156 |
| **35** **Tax on all taxable income.** Enter the **smaller** of line 33 or line 34 here and on line 1a of Schedule G, Form 1041 . . . . . . . . . . . . . . . . . . . . . . | **35** | | 4,846 |

                                   **Schedule D (Form 1041) 2005**

☐ Final K-1    ☐ Amended K-1    OMB No. 1545-0092

**Schedule K-1**
**(Form 1041)**
20**05**

Department of the Treasury
Internal Revenue Service

For calendar year 2005,
or tax year beginning _____ , 2005
and ending _____ , 20 _____

**Beneficiary's Share of Income, Deductions, Credits, etc.**   ► See back of form and instructions

| **Part I** | **Information About the Estate or Trust** |
|---|---|

**A** Estate's or trust's employer identification number

21-1234567

**B** Estate's or trust's name

John Tyler Trust

**C** Fiduciary's name, address, city, state, and ZIP code

South End Trust
25 South Beach St.
Detroit, MI 48226

**D** ☐ Check if Form 1041-T was filed and enter the date it was filed
_____ / _____ / _____

**E** ☐ Check if this is the final Form 1041 for the estate or trust

**F** ☐ Tax shelter registration number, if any _____

**G** ☐ Check if Form 8271 is attached

| **Part II** | **Information About the Beneficiary** |
|---|---|

**H** Beneficiary's identifying number
311-62-4070

**I** Beneficiary's name, address, city, state, and ZIP code

Mary S. Warden
7891 Code Drive
Chicago, IL 60600

**J** ☐ Domestic beneficiary    ☐ Foreign beneficiary

| **Part III** | **Beneficiary's Share of Current Year Income, Deductions, Credits, and Other Items** |
|---|---|

| | | | |
|---|---|---|---|
| 1 | Interest income 1,667 | 11 | Final year deductions |
| 2a | Ordinary dividends 267 | | |
| 2b | Qualified dividends 133 | | |
| 3 | Net short-term capital gain | | |
| 4a | Net long-term capital gain | | |
| 4b | 28% rate gain | 12 | Alternative minimum tax adjustment |
| 4c | Unrecaptured section 1250 gain | | |
| 5 | Other portfolio and nonbusiness income | | |
| 6 | Ordinary business income | | |
| 7 | Net rental real estate income 7,690 | 13 | Credits and credit recapture |
| 8 | Other rental income | | |
| 9 | Directly apportioned deductions | | |
| | | 14 | Other information |
| 10 | Estate tax deduction | | |

*See attached statement for additional information.

**Note:** A statement must be attached showing the beneficiary's share of income and directly apportioned deductions from each business, rental real estate, and other rental activity.

For IRS Use Only

For Paperwork Reduction Act Notice, see the Instructions for Form 1041.    Cat. No. 11380D    **Schedule K-1 (Form 1041) 2005**

¶ **96**

# Filled-In Form 1120S • S Corporations • Explanation

## ¶101

An S corporation is generally not a tax paying entity. Instead, the taxable income of an S corporation is generally passed through to its shareholders and taxed at their individual tax rates. The items of income and expense retain their character and are reported as if the shareholders had engaged in the transaction that caused the item of income, loss, etc.

## ON THE RETURN

Even though the S corporation is usually not a tax-paying entity, it must file the required tax form, Form 1120S, U.S. Income Tax Return for an S Corporation. The purpose of this form is to report the corporation's income, deductions, gains, losses, and credits of a domestic corporation or other entity for any tax year covered by an election to be an S corporation. An S corporation must show the date the S corporation election was made at Item A on page 1 of Form 1120S.

- **Eligible S Corporations:**

Only certain corporations can become S corporations. There are five basic requirements that must be met for a corporation to achieve S corporation status. It must:

- Be a domestic corporation organized under the laws of any state or U.S. territory

- Have no more than one class of stock

- Have no more than 100 shareholders. A husband and wife are treated as a single shareholder under both limits, without regard to how they hold their shares. Family members may elect to be treated as one shareholder, effective for tax years beginning after December 31, 2004. A family is defined as a common ancestor, the lineal descendants of the common ancestor, and the spouse (or former spouse) of the ancestor and the descendants. The common ancestor can be no more than six generations removed from the youngest shareholder who is treated as a member of the family.

- Have as shareholders only individuals, estates (including estates of individuals in bankruptcy), and certain trusts (including grantor trusts, voting trusts, certain testamentary trusts, and qualified subchapter S trusts). No partnerships or corporations qualify as S corporation shareholders.

- Have shareholders who are citizens or U.S. residents

**How the election is made:** Satisfying all the requirements of the Internal Revenue Code does not automatically confer S corporation status. To become an S corporation, the corporation must file Form 2553, Election by a Small Business Corporation, along with consents signed by all the shareholders of record when the election is made. An election for a given tax year can be made:

(1) any time during the previous tax year, or

(2) by the 15th day of the third month of the tax year to which the election is to apply.

**For calendar year corporations, the 2005 election must be made by March 15, 2006.** If the due date falls on a Saturday, Sunday or legal holiday, the corporation may file on the next business day.

**Late Election.** An election made after March 15, 2006 will be effective for 2006.

- **Who must file Form 1120S.**

A corporation must file Form 1120S for each year that the S corporation election is in effect if:

- The corporation elected to be an S corporation by filing Form 2553,

- The IRS accepted the election, and

- The election remains in effect.

Taxpayers should not file Form 1120S for any tax year before the year the election takes effect. A taxpayer cannot file Form 1120S unless he has filed a properly completed Form 2553. After filing Form 2553, the taxpayer should receive confirmation that Form 2553 was accepted. If the taxpayer did not receive notification of acceptance or nonacceptance of the election with 2 months of filing Form 2553 (5 months if taxpayer checked box Q-1 to request a letter ruling), the taxpayer should contact the service center where the form was filed to make sure that the IRS received the election. If the taxpayer has not filed Form 2553, or did not file Form 2553 on time, he may be entitled to relief for a late filed election to be an S corporation.

**Termination of Election.** An S corporation election applies to all succeeding tax year unless it is terminated. If the S corporation election was terminated during the tax year and the corporation reverts to a Corporation, the taxpayer should file Form 1120S for the S corporation's short year by the due date (including extensions) of the C corporation's short year return.

## ON THE RETURN

Douglas Plastics Company, which has a calendar tax year, was incorporated in North Dakota on January 1, 1978, and has one class of common stock (2,500 shares) equally divided between two U.S. shareholders, Doug Pratt and Rickie L. Jones. It qualified for, and elected, S corporation status on March 12, 1978.

An S corporation that terminates its election must have IRS consent to re-elect subchapter S status during the five-year waiting period specified in Code Sec. 1362(g). IRS consent is not required during the waiting period if, on the first day of the first tax year for which the election is to be effective, the corporation revokes its election or does not qualify as a small business corporation (Reg. §1.1362-5(c)).

### • How Shareholders Report Income

Income of an S corporation is generally treated as if it is directly received by S corporation shareholders. Thus, the S corporation is a conduit through which the income, losses, expenses, credits, and other tax items are passed to the shareholders pro rata on a per share, daily basis. Items distributed to shareholders retain their same character as when received or incurred by the S corporation. The items are reported in the shareholder's tax year that ends with the corporation's tax year, or in the shareholder's tax year that includes the end of the corporation's tax year. The ordinary income of the corporation is passed through as one amount and is reported on Schedule E of Form 1040. Some items, however, are passed through separately if their separate treatment affects the tax liability of the shareholder.

### • Pass-through items.

Items that are passed through to shareholders include (but are not limited to) the following:

- Gains and losses from the sale or exchange of capital assets from the S corporation's Schedule D;

- Gains and losses from the sale or exchange of Section 1231 business property computed on the S corporation's Form 4797;

- Excess net passive income if the corporation is subject to the tax on excess net passive income

- Charitable contributions;

- Tax-exempt interest;

- Recoveries of bad debts, prior taxes or delinquency amounts;

- Foreign taxes paid by the S corporation pass-through to the shareholders who claim them either as a deduction or a credit on their personal returns;

- Depletion of oil and gas properties;

- Soil and water conservation costs that the corporation elects to expense;

- Intangible drilling and development costs that are expensed;

- Exploration cost of new mineral deposits;

- Investment interest expense;

- Expensing deduction;

- Items involved in calculating all credits, except the credit on gas and special fuels, are passed through to the shareholder. Credits are calculated at the shareholder level;

- Net income from a rental real estate activity or other rental activity;

- Portfolio income and loss including interest, dividends, royalties, and gain or loss from disposition;

- Tax preference and adjustment items needed to calculate the shareholder's alternative minimum tax.

**Note:** Income items that are passed through to a shareholder increase the shareholder's basis in the S corporation stock. Subsequent distribution of the income to shareholders will not be taxable, but will reduce the shareholder's basis in the S corporation stock.

- **Tax Years of S Corporations**

An S corporation selects its tax year on Form 2553 (the same form on which it makes its S corporation election). Generally, an S corporation must use a calendar tax year unless it can establish a business purpose for having a different tax year (Code Sec. 1378). Form 8716 is filed to elect a tax year other than the required tax year (Code Sec. 444). Generally, such an election must be made by the earlier of: (1) the 15th day of the fifth month following the month that includes the first day of the tax year for which the election is first effective or (2) the due date (without extensions) of the return for the tax year that results from the election (Temp. Reg. §1.444-3T(b)(1)).

An election remains in effect until the S corporation changes its tax year or otherwise terminates the election. If an election is terminated, no further election may be made and the S corporation must use a calendar year.

To neutralize tax benefits resulting from a tax year other than a required tax year, an electing S corporation must compute and make any required payments (the amount of tax that would otherwise be due from stockholders had such entity used the required tax year) exceeding $500 (Code Sec. 7519). The required payment is due on or before May 15 of the calendar year following the calendar year in which the election year begins (Temp. Reg. §1.7519-2T(a)(4)(ii)). The payment is reported on Form 8752.

For new S corporations electing a tax year for the first time, there is a three-month limit on the number of months that may fall between the end of an elected tax year and the end of the required tax year (i.e., the calendar year). For S corporations that want to change an existing tax year, the deferral period between the end of the elected and required tax years may not exceed the shorter of three months or the deferral period of the existing tax year (Temp. Reg. §1.444-1T(b)(2)).

- **Schedule K-1**

The total amount of each item of income, loss, deduction, or credit that is passed through to the shareholders is reported on Schedule K, Form 1120S. A separate Schedule K-1 must be prepared for each shareholder showing that shareholder's pro rata share of the amounts reported on Schedule K. Shareholders are liable for tax on their shares of the corporation's income (reduced by any taxes paid by the corporation on income). Shareholders must include their share of the income on their tax return whether or not it is distributed to them.

> **Practice Pointer:** Unlike most partnership income, S corporation income is not self-employment income and is not subject to self-employment tax.

**Schedule K.** This schedule is a summary schedule of all shareholders' shares of the corporation's income, deductions, credits, etc. All corporations must complete Schedule K.

**Schedule K-1.** This schedule reports each shareholder's share of an S corporation's income, deductions, credits, etc. The total amounts entered on the separate Schedule K-1's must equal the total reported on Schedule K. A copy of each shareholder's K-1 must be attached to the Form 1120S that is filed with the IRS. The corporation must furnish each shareholder with a copy of his or her own Schedule K-1, along with a copy of the instructions.

- **Computing Shareholder's Pro Rata Share:**

Items of income, loss, deduction, etc., are allocated to a shareholder on a daily basis according to the number of shares of stock held by the shareholder each day during the corporation's tax year. These items are reported by the shareholder on his or her tax return for the year within which the corporation's tax year-ends. If there was a change in stock ownership, each shareholder's ownership percentage must be weighted for the number of days in the tax year that stock was owned.

## ON THE SCHEDULE K-1

The shareholder's percentage of stock ownership is entered in Item H, Schedule K-1.

## ¶102 DETAILS OF CORPORATION INCOME

In completing Form 1120S, it should be noted that only ordinary income or loss from business operations is reflected on Lines 1–6 on page 1. Capital gains or losses and separately stated income, such as rents, interest, and dividend income, are reported directly on Schedules K and K-1.

## ON THE RETURN

To calculate its total ordinary income, Douglas Plastics Company must complete Lines 1–6 of Form 1120S. During 2005, Douglas had gross receipts of $612,759 and returns totaling $7,360, leaving a balance of $605,399 to be reported on Line 1c of Form 1120S. From this amount Douglas must subtract the cost of goods sold during the year ($331,795) on Line 2 to derive its gross profit ($273,604) on Line 3. On Line 4, Douglas reports $4,857 of net ordinary gain from the sale of depreciable business property, which, when added to gross profit, gives Douglas total ordinary income of $278,461 on Line 6. More details on net ordinary gain calculations, which are made on Form 4797, are provided at ¶**103**.

Other income reported on Line 5 would include:

- Interest income derived in the ordinary course of the corporation's trade or business, such as interest charged on receivable balances

- Recoveries of bad debts deducted in prior years under the specific charge-off method

- Taxable income from insurance proceeds

- The amount included in income from Form 8864, Credit for Alcohol Used as Fuel

- The recapture amount if the business used of listed property drops to 50 percent or less.

- Any recapture amount under Code Sec. 179A for certain clean-fuel vehicle property (or clean-fuel vehicle refueling property) that ceases to qualify.

- All Code Sec. 481 income adjustments resulting from changes in accounting methods. Show the computation of the Code Sec. 481 adjustments on an attached schedule.

## ON THE RETURN

Calculations of the cost of goods sold are made on Schedule A, Lines 1–8, where Douglas reports an opening inventory of $118,765 (Line 1), purchases of $100,650 (Line 2), and labor costs of $180,235 (Line 3). A supporting schedule is required for costs shown on Line 5, where Douglas reports costs totaling $57,475. These costs include freight expenses of $950, insurance of $4,200, water charges of $1,150, and heat, light, and power expenses of $10,850. They also include depreciation and taxes that are allocable

to manufacturing operations. The depreciation so allocated amounts to $19,215 (see ¶**105**), and the taxes so allocated amount to $21,110 ($16,790 in employment taxes and $4,320 in property taxes). After the amounts on Lines 1–5 are added and reported on Line 6 ($457,125), Douglas must subtract its ending inventory of $125,330 on Line 7 to arrive at its cost of goods figure of $331,795 as reported on Line 8. This cost of goods amount is then reflected on Line 2 of Form 1120S. On Line 9a of Schedule A, Douglas indicates that it uses the lower of cost or market value to value inventories.

## ¶103 REPORTING GAINS AND LOSSES FROM PROPERTY

Net long- and short-term capital gains and losses, the tax on certain capital gains, and the built-in gains tax (see ¶**106**) are computed on Schedule D of Form 1120S. Gains or losses from casualties and thefts are initially reported on Form 4684, except for the recapture of ordinary gain, which is initially reported on Form 4797.

## ON THE RETURN

No Form 4684 is required of Douglas because no casualty or theft loss occurred in 2005.

Douglas sustained a long-term capital loss of $1,914 from the sale of the Nicole Co. stock in January 2005. This transaction is initially reported in Part II of Form 1120S, Schedule D (not reproduced).

- **Form 4797- Sales of Business Property**
- **Purpose of Form 4797**

Form 4797 should be used by taxpayers to report:

- The sale or exchange of:

  1. Property used in a taxpayer's trade or business;

  2. Depreciable and amortizable property;

  3. Oil, gas, geothermal, or other mineral properties; and

  4. Code Sec. 126 property.

- The involuntary conversion (from other than casualty or theft) of property used in your trade or business and capital assets held in connection with a trade or business or a transaction entered into for profit.

- The disposition of noncapital assets (other than inventory or property held primarily for sale to customers in the ordinary course of a taxpayer's trade or business).

- The disposition of capital assets not reported on Schedule D

- The gain or loss (including any related recapture) for partners and S corporation shareholders from certain Code Sec. 179 property dispositions by partnerships (other than electing large partnerships) and S corporation.

- The computation of recapture amounts under Code Secs 179 and 280F(b)(2) when the business use of Code Sec. 179 or listed property decreases to 50 percent or less.

- **Part I**

Part I is used to report section 1231 transactions. In general, these are sales or exchanges of real or depreciable property used in a trade or business and held for more than one year and involuntary conversions of trade or business property or capital assets held more than one year in connection with a trade or business or a transaction entered into for profit.

- **Part III**

Part III is used to compute ordinary income recapture (generally, depreciation recapture from real and personal property).

- **Part II**

Part II is used to report ordinary income transactions that are not reportable in Part I or Part III.

In the case of section 1250 property for which depreciation was claimed, an S corporation must compute the amount of gain which constitutes "unrecaptured section 1250 gain." Unrecaptured section 1250 gain is the lesser of the depreciation which is not recaptured as ordinary income or the long-term capital gain from the sale of the property. Unrecaptured section 1250 gain is eligible for a 25% capital gains tax rate (Code Sec. 1(h)). The unrecaptured section 1250 gain is reported on Line 8c of Schedule K and in Box 8c of Schedule K-1. Reg. §1.453-12 provides special rules for the allocation of unrecaptured section 1250 gain reported on the installment method.

## ON THE RETURN

Douglas Plastics does not have unrecaptured section 1250 gain.

The net section 1231 gain or loss reported on Form 4797, Part I, Line 7, is entered on Line 9 of Schedule K, Form 1120S. However, net gain or loss from involuntary conversions due to casualty or theft is included on Line 10 of Schedule K, not on Line 9. Each shareholder will report its distributive shares, as shown on Schedule K-1 (Code B), on its own Form 4797.

In Part II of Form 4797, ordinary gains and losses are determined, and transactions of noncapital assets not involving Sec. 1231 property (such as property held for one year or less) are reported. The ordinary income recapture from Part III of Form 4797 and the ordinary income or loss from Form 4684 are reflected in the Part II computations. A net gain or loss from Part II of Form 4797 (Line 17) is entered on Line 4, page 1, Form 1120S. In Part III of Form 4797, gains from dispositions of recapture property are reported, and the portions of the total gains that are taxed as ordinary income or as Sec. 1231 gains are determined.

Any Sec. 1231 gain from installment sales from Form 6252 is reported on Line 4 of Form 4797, and any ordinary gain from installment sales is reported on Line 15 of Form 4797. In addition, any Sec. 1231 gain or loss from like-kind exchanges from Form 8824 is reported on Line 5 of Form 4797, and any ordinary gain or loss from like-kind exchanges is reported on Line 16 of Form 4797.

## ON THE RETURN

In the filled-in Form 4797, the sale of a building during 2005 results in both Sec. 1231 gain and Sec. 1250 ordinary income recapture. The building was purchased on January 10, 1981, at a cost of $90,000, and was sold on January 18, 2004, for $49,223. It had been depreciated by using the 150% declining-balance method over a 40-year life. Assume depreciation claimed on the building from 1981 through 2005 amounted to $57,564 and Douglas realized a gain of $16,787 from the sale. This gain is reported on Line 24 of Part III. The total ordinary income recapture (Line 26g) amounts to $3,564. This amount represents the excess depreciation recapture of $3,564, as computed on Lines 26a and 26b. The depreciation recapture is the difference between the accelerated depreciation claimed ($57,564) and straight-line depreciation ($54,000). Douglas does not have to report any Code Sec. 291 depreciation recapture on Line 26f because it has always been an S corporation.

In addition, a sale of a seven-year MACRS machine acquired in 2002 resulted in a Code Sec. 1245 recapture as reported on Lines 19–25b, Part III, Form 4797. The $1,293 gain is fully recaptured as ordinary income.

On Line 30, the total gain on the machinery and building ($18,080) is reflected. The ordinary income portion of the gain ($4,857) is reported on Line 31. The remaining gain ($13,223 from the sale of the building) is reflected on Line 32 and is carried over on Line 6 of Part I.

In Part I of Form 4797, Douglas also reports a gain of $3,000 from the sale of land, which is combined with the $13,223 gain from Part III. The total Sec. 1231 gain of $16,223 is reported on Line 9 of Schedule K. Douglas would report the $1,914 long-term capital loss from the stock sale initially reported on Line 13 of Form 1120S, Schedule D, on Line 8a of Schedule K. One half of that amount, or $957, is reported on Line 8a of Douglas Pratt's Schedule K-1.

The $4,857 of ordinary income from Line 31, Part III, Form 4797, is carried to Line 13, Part II. Because there are no other transactions reportable in Part II, the $4,857 from Line 17 is reported on page 1 of Form 1120S (Line 4) and is thus included in the computation of Douglas's overall ordinary income.

Gross proceeds from sales or exchanges of real estate that are reported to the S corporation on Form 1099-S (or a substitute statement) and included on Line 2, 10, or 20 of Form 4797 are entered on Line 1 of Form 4797. Douglas reports $62,223 on this line from the sale of the land ($13,000) and building ($49,223). Line 1 should also include certain amounts from the sale of securities or commodities by traders who make a mark-to-market election.

An election not to use the installment method can be made by reporting the full amount of the gain on Form 4797. Form 6252 is used to report a sale on the installment method.

See ¶106 for the built-in gains tax that is computed on Schedule D of Form 1120S.

## ¶104 DETAILS ABOUT DEDUCTIONS

ON THE RETURN

To calculate its net ordinary income, Douglas Plastics Company must complete Lines 7–20 of Form 1120S to determine the total amount of deductions that may offset the total amount of ordinary income reported on Line 6. The difference between the two amounts is reported on Line 21. This amount must then be allocated pro rata among shareholders, being reported in lump-sum form on Line 1 of Schedule K and pro rata in Box 1 of each Schedule K-1 prepared for shareholders.

**Line 7. Compensation of offices and Line 8. Salaries and Wages.** In 2005, Douglas paid compensation of $36,000 to both its president and vice-president and $24,000 to its secretary-treasurer. The total ($96,000) is claimed as a deduction from ordinary income on Line 7 of Form 1120S. Wages of $39,446 paid to a salesperson and office personnel are deducted on Line 8. Wages of manufacturing workers are included in the cost of goods sold at Line 3 of Schedule A. Reduce the amounts on Lines 7 and 8 by the amount claimed on:

- Form 5884, Work Opportunity Credit, line 2,
- Form 5884-A, Hurricane Katrina Employee Retention Credit
- Form 8844, Empowerment Zone and Renewal Community Employment Credit
- Form 8845, Indian Employment Credit, and
- Form 8861, Welfare-to-Work Credit

Do not include salaries and wages deductible elsewhere on the return such as amounts included in cost of goods sold, elective contributions to a Code Sec. 401(k) cash or deferred arrangement, or amounts contributed under a salary reduction SEP agreement or a SIMPLE IRA plan.

Include fringe benefit expenditures made on behalf of officers and employees owning more than 2 percent of the corporation's stock. Do not include amounts paid or incurred for fringe benefits of officers and employees owning 2 percent or less of the corporation's stock.

Report amounts paid for health insurance coverage for a more than 2 percent shareholder (including that shareholder's spouse and dependents) as an information item in box 14 of that shareholder's Form W-2.

**Line 9. Repairs and Maintenance.** On Line 9, a deduction of $3,694 is claimed for incidental repairs. **Line 10. Bad Debts. Line 11. Rents**. On Lines 10–11, deductions are claimed for bad debts ($4,500) and rent payments ($1,200).

**Line 12. Taxes and Licenses**. On Line 12, a total deduction of $13,237 is claimed for employment taxes ($11,157), a motor vehicle tax ($100), a franchise tax ($300), and a real property tax ($1,680). The employment and real estate taxes as reported on Line 12 are the balances of these taxes after allocation to manufacturing operations (see ¶**102**). The deduction is allowed only for taxes paid or incurred on business property or in carrying on a trade or business.

**Schedule K. Line 12.** Charitable contributions of $1,500 are reported on Schedule K, Line 12a. Other deductions, such as penalties for early withdrawal of corporate savings and expenses for removal of architectural barriers to the handicapped, are reported on Schedule K, Line 12e (see also ¶**108**).

**Line 13. Interest.** Interest expenses of $3,620 are listed on Line 13 of Form 1120S. This figure does not include interest that must be separately stated on Schedule K, Line 12c, where Douglas must report interest expenses on investment indebtedness.

**Line 14. Depreciation**. Depreciation deductions of $1,150 ($400 for furniture and fixtures + $750 for brick building) are claimed on Line 14c, the rest being allocated to the cost of goods sold on Line 5 of Schedule A (see ¶**105**). If there were any amortization expenses, they would be deducted on Line 19.

**Line 16. Advertising**. A deduction for advertising expenses of $3,500 is claimed on Line 16. The entire amount represents the fixed contract price paid to an advertising firm for current advertising in magazines.

**Line 17. Pension, Profit-Sharing, etc. Plans**. Douglas's contributions of $8,805 to a pension plan for its employees are deducted on Line 17. Contributions to other employee benefit programs, such as insurance and health and welfare programs that are not an incidental part of a plan that is represented on Line 17, are deducted on Line 18, where a $4,000 deduction is claimed for contributions to an employee hospital plan. However, employee benefits that are paid on behalf of shareholder-employees who own on any day of the tax year more than 2% of the outstanding shares are not deductible and are excluded from the amounts claimed on Line 18. Instead, they are reported on Line 7 or 8 of Form 1120S, whichever applies. Douglas Plastics did not provide these benefits.

**Line 19. Other Deductions.** On Line 19, a total deduction of $16,373 is claimed for postage ($4,683), office supplies ($3,760), telephones ($4,630), and entertainment ($3,300). Douglas actually incurred entertainment expenses totaling $6,600 but is able to claim a deduction for only 50% of the amount ($3,300) under the ceiling imposed on deductions for entertainment expenses (Code Sec. 274(n)). The difference ($3,300) is reported on Line 3b of Schedule M-1 and included in the total on Line 5 of the accumulated adjustments account of Schedule M-2. See ¶**110** and ¶**111**.

**Line 20. Total Deductions.** Douglas's total deductions amount to $195,525 (Line 20). These deductions are applied against total ordinary income ($278,461 (Line 6)), resulting in net ordinary income of $82,936 (Line 21). This amount is also reflected on Line 1 of Schedule K for pro rata allocation among shareholders.

# ¶105 DEPRECIATION

**Line 14. Depreciation.** An S corporation reports its total depreciation deduction, excluding any Sec. 179 expense deduction, on Line 14a of Form 1120S. The Sec. 179 expense deduction is not deductible by the corporation. Instead, it is passed through to the shareholders on Line 11 of Schedule K and in Box 11 of Schedule K-1. The depreciation allocable to the Schedule A cost of goods sold computation is entered on Line 14b.

An S corporation must file and attach Form 4562 to its Form 1120S only if it is claiming (1) depreciation or amortization on property placed in service during the current tax year; (2) a Code Sec. 179 expense deduction (including carryovers); or (3) depreciation on a vehicle or other listed property.

## ON THE RETURN

The following four general categories of assets were depreciated by Douglas in 2005 and reported on Form 4562 (not reproduced):

1. Douglas claimed MACRS depreciation of $4,000 for used molds and patterns acquired on January 3, 2005, at a cost of $12,000. The molds and patterns are 3-year recovery property and were depreciated by using the MACRS 200% declining-balance method and a half-year convention. Depreciation on these assets is allocable to Schedule A, Line 5.

2. MACRS depreciation is claimed for factory equipment acquired on June 18, 2004, at a cost of $138,500 and for office furniture and fixtures acquired on February 11, 2004 at a cost of $4,000. Douglas elected

for both groups of assets to use the MACRS alternative (straight-line) depreciation system (ADS) with a half-year convention. Under ADS, depreciation is computed using the 10-year class life of the furniture and 11-year class life of the factory equipment as the recovery periods. Thus, depreciation on the factory equipment amounts to $12,590 ($138,500 × .0909), and depreciation on the furniture and fixtures amounts to $400 ($4,000 × 10%). The depreciation on the factory equipment is allocable to Schedule A, Line 5.

3. MACRS depreciation of $625 on a 7-year machine that was acquired on January 14, 2002, at a cost of $10,000 and that was sold during the year. The depreciation is calculated using the 200% declining-balance method and a half-year convention. It is also allocable to Schedule A, Line 5.

4. Douglas claimed depreciation of $2,750 for a brick building acquired on January 2, 1981, at a cost of $110,000. The building was depreciated by using the straight-line method over a 40-year life. $2,000 of the depreciation claimed on the building is attributable to manufacturing and is allocable to Schedule A, Line 5.

No depreciation was allowed during 2005 on another building which was acquired in January 1981 and sold in January 2005. See ¶103.

## ¶106  TAXES PAYABLE BY S CORPORATIONS

Although an S corporation does not have to pay income taxes, it may be subject to certain special taxes that are payable with the return. These special taxes are:

(1) the excess net passive investment income tax;

(2) the built-in gains tax;

(3) the investment credit recapture tax on an investment credit claimed before an S corporation election became effective; and

(4) the LIFO recapture tax. These taxes do not apply to Douglas Plastics Company.

- **Estimated Tax**

S corporations are required to make estimated tax payments for tax liability attributable to the taxes described in categories (1) through (3), above, if the estimated tax liability is $500 or more (Code

Sec. 6655(f) and (g)(4)). For the corporate estimated tax rules generally applicable to S corporations, see ¶39.

The required annual estimated tax payment is the lesser of: (1) 100% of the tax shown on the return for the tax year (i.e., category (1)–(3) taxes), or (2) the sum of 100% of the tax liability incurred in the current year by virtue of the built-in gains tax, and the tax due because of investment credit recapture, plus 100% of the tax on the net excess passive investment income reported by the S corporation in the preceding year (Code Sec. 6655(d) and (g)(4)(C)). If the preceding tax year was less than 12 months, the amount of the required annual estimated tax must be determined under the first method.

The rule that allows estimated tax payments to be based on a corporation's prior year's tax cannot be used by an S corporation when it is computing estimated tax payments attributable to built-in gains and investment credit recapture (Code Sec. 6655(g)(4)(C)). However, the rule for making required payments under an annualized income method or adjusted seasonal installment method (Code Sec. 6655(e)) can be applied by all S corporations.

- **Tax on Excess Net Passive Investment Income**

If the corporation has always been an S corporation, the excess net passive income tax does not apply. An S corporation will be subject to the excess net passive income tax if: (1) it has accumulated earnings and profits at the close of the tax year; (2) more than 25 percent of its gross receipts is passive investment income; and (3) has taxable income at year-end. Passive investment income generally means gross receipts from interest, dividends, rents, royalties, annuities and gains from sales or exchanges of stock or securities. If the corporation has "excess net passive income" for the year, it must pay a tax on this amount or its taxable income, if lower, at the 35 percent corporate tax rate for the year.

Complete Lines 1 through 3 and Line 9 of the worksheet on page 17 of the Instructions to Form 1120S (reproduced below) to determine if the S corporation must pay a tax on the excess net passive income. If Line 2 if greater than Line 3 and the corporation has taxable income, it must pay the tax. Complete a separate schedule using the format of Lines 1 through 11 of the worksheet to figure the tax. Enter the tax on Line 22a, page 1, Form 1120S, and attach the computation schedule to Form 1120S.

To illustrate the computation of this tax, assume that an S corporation's passive investment income for the year is $70,000, consisting of $25,000 of dividends, $25,000 of interest, and $20,000 of long-term capital gain from the sale of stock. Expenses directly related to the production of this income are $7,000. In addition, the corporation has gross receipts of $90,000 and taxable income of $55,000. The worksheet that is provided in the instructions for Form 1120S must be completed as shown below.

• **Tax on Built-In Gains**

A built-in gains tax under Code Sec. 1374 affects corporations that make an S election and that are C corporations at the time of the election. The tax is imposed on net recognized built-in gains from the disposition of an asset in any of a corporation's first 10 years as an S corporation. No tax is imposed if the asset was not held by the corporation at the start of its first tax year as an S corporation, or if gains exceed the excess of the fair market value of the asset at the start of the first tax year over the adjusted basis of the asset at that time (i.e., the gain is attributable to appreciation). The tax is computed by applying the highest rate of corporate taxation (35%) against the lower of either (1) net recognized built-in gains for the tax year or (2) the amount of income that would be subject to corporate taxation if the corporation were not an S corporation. The amount of gain subject to taxation may be no higher than the excess of net unrealized built-in gain over net recognized built-in gain for prior tax years in the 10-year spread. Net unrealized built-in gain is the amount by which the fair market value of an S corporation's assets at the start of the 10-year period exceeds the aggregate adjusted bases of the assets.

## ON THE RETURN

Douglas Plastics Company is unaffected by the built-in gains tax since it has always been an S corporation and elected S status in 1977. However, if it had to pay the tax, Part III of Schedule D, Form 1120S, would be used to make computations (Blank copy of Form 1120S attached). The tax would be recorded on Line 21 of Schedule D and Line 22b of page 1 of Form 1120S. Shareholders may treat a pro rata portion of a tax payment as a loss and allocate it proportionately among the recognized built-in gains that resulted in the tax (Code Sec. 1366(f)(2)).

• **Investment Credit and LIFO Recapture Taxes**

The investment credit recapture tax applies if an S corporation makes an early disposition of investment credit property that was acquired before the corporation became an S corporation. It is computed on Form 4255, which must be attached to Form 1120S and included in the total amount to be entered on Line 22c, page 1, Form 1120S.

C corporations that used the LIFO inventory method before converting to S status may have to pay a tax that recaptures the benefits of using the LIFO method in lieu of the FIFO method. The LIFO recapture tax may also apply where a C corporation transfers LIFO inventory to the corporation in a nonrecognition transaction in which the assets were transferred basis property. C corporations must increase the amount of their gross income at the close of their last tax year as a C corporation (or year of transfer) by the excess of (1) inventory valued under the FIFO method over (2) inventory valued under the LIFO method. The increase in tax attributable to the increase in gross income must be paid in four equal annual installments, the first being payable when the corporate income tax return is due (not including extensions) for the last C year (or year of transfer). The remaining three installments are paid by the S corporation over the next three years when returns are due (not including extensions) and are included in the total amount to be entered on Line 22c of Form 1120S.

• **Interest Due Under the Look-Back Method**

Interest calculated on Form 8697, Interest Computation Under the Look-Back Method for Completed Long-Term Contracts, is also included on Line 22c. Form 8697 must be attached to Form 1120S. Interest calculated on Form 8866, Interest Computation Under the Look-Back Method for Property Depreciated Under the Income Forecast Method, is also included on Line 22c of Form 1120S. Form 8866 must be attached.

## ¶107 DISTRIBUTIONS

Distributions of cash or property to shareholders are taxed under a priority system that depends upon whether the S corporation has accumulated earnings and profits (Code Sec. 1368). An S corporation can have accumulated earnings and profits only from tax years when it was not an S corporation or from S corporation tax years beginning before 1983.

However, for an S corporation's first tax year beginning after 1996, it must reduce its accumulated earnings and profits (as of the first day of that tax year) by the earnings and profits accumulated from any tax year beginning before 1983 when the corporation was a subchapter S corporation. Thus, an S corporation's post-1996 earnings and profits are solely attributable to tax years when the corporation did not have an S corporation election in effect.

If an S corporation does not have accumulated earnings and profits, distributions are treated first as a nontaxable return of capital to the extent of the shareholder's basis in his stock and second as gain from the sale or exchange of property. This is determined by reference to the "accumulated adjustments account" (AAA) and the "other items" account (see ¶111).

If an S corporation has accumulated earnings and profits, distributions are treated as:

(1) a nontaxable return of capital to the extent of the corporation's "accumulated adjustments account" (AAA) (see Schedule M-2, Line 1, and ¶111);

(2) a dividend to the extent of the corporation's accumulated earnings and profits;

(3) a nontaxable return of capital to the extent of the shareholder's remaining basis in his stock after (1), above; and

(4) gain from the sale or exchange of property. Actual dividend distributions paid out of accumulated earnings and profits are reported on Line 17c of Schedule K and are reported to the shareholder on Form 1099-DIV, and not on Schedule K-1. Actual dividend distributions do not increase or decrease a shareholder's basis in stock. The shareholder reports actual dividend distributions on Schedule B (Form 1040). Other distributions are reported on Line 16d of Schedule K.

• **Repayments of Loans**

An S corporation that has borrowed funds from a stockholder must indicate the amounts of any repayments on the indebtedness on Line 16e of Schedule K and in Box 16 of the stockholder-creditor's Schedule K-1 (Code E). If the loan repayments are made on indebtedness with a reduced basis, the repayments result in income to the shareholder to the extent that the repayments exceed the adjusted basis of the loan.

# ¶108 APPORTIONMENT TO SHAREHOLDERS

• **Schedule K, Shareholders' Shares Of Income, Credits, Deductions, Etc.**

Schedule K is a summary schedule of all shareholders' shares of the corporation's income, deductions, credits, etc. All corporations must complete Schedule K.

• **Schedule K-1 (Form 1120s), Shareholder's Share of Income, Credits, Deductions, Etc.**

A separate Schedule K-1 (Form 1120S) must be completed by the S corporation for each shareholder and given to them on or before the day on which Form 1120S is filed with the IRS. The corporation uses Schedule K-1 to report each S corporation shareholder's pro rata share of the corporation's income (reduced by any tax the corporation paid on the income), credits, deductions, etc. The Schedule K-1 should be kept with the shareholder's records and not filed with the tax return. Note that Schedule K on page 2 of Form 1120S is a summary schedule of all the shareholders' shares of the corporation's income, deductions, credits, etc. Contrast this with Schedule K-1(Form 1120S) which shows each individual shareholder's pro rata share of each item based on his or her ownership interest.

Although the corporation may have to pay a built-in gains tax and an excess net passive income tax, the shareholder is liable for income tax on his share of the corporation's income, whether or not distributed, and the shareholder's pro rata share must be included on his tax return if a return is required. The shareholder's pro rata share of S corporation income is not self-employment income and is not subject to self-employment tax.

Schedule K-1 does not show the amount of actual dividend distributions the corporation made to the shareholder. The corporation must report such amounts totaling $10 or more for the calendar year on Form 1099-DIV, "Dividends and Distributions."

## SHAREHOLDER ALERT

Generally, shareholders must treat the items on their returns consistent with the way the S corporation reported them on its return. A shareholder who reports the items differently from the way the S corporation reported them on Schedule K-1 should complete Form 8082, "Notice of Inconsistent Treatment or

Amended Return (Administrative Adjustment Request (AAR))."

he amounts shown in boxes 1 through 17 of Schedule K-1 reflect the taxpayer's share of income, loss, deductions, credits, and other information from all corporate activities without reference to limitations on losses, credits, or other items that may have to be adjusted because of:

1. the adjusted basis of the taxpayer's stock and debt in the corporation.

2. the at-risk limitations

3. the passive activity limitations, or

4. any other limitations that must be taken into account at the shareholder level in figuring taxable income (e.g., the Code Sec. 179 expense deduction).

If the taxpayer is an individual and his pro rata share of items is not affected by any of the limitations, he should take the amounts shown and enter them on the lines of his tax return as indicated in the summarized reporting information shown on the back of the Schedule K-1. If any of the limitations apply, adjust the amounts for the limitations before entering them on the return. When applicable, the passive activity limitations on losses are applied after the limitations on losses for a shareholder's basis in stock and debt and the shareholder's at-risk amount.

**Codes.** In box 10 and boxes 12 through 17, the corporation will identify each item by entering a code in the column to the left of the dollar amount entry space. These codes are identified on page 2 of the instructions to Schedule K-1 and are reproduced here.

The amount in Box 1 of Schedule K-1 reflects the shareholder's share of ordinary income or loss from all corporate business operations, including at-risk activities, without reference to the shareholder's adjusted basis in stock and debt of the corporation, the amount for which the shareholder is at risk (see below), or the shareholder's passive activity limitations. These limitations, if applicable, are determined at the shareholder level. A shareholder's share of losses is generally limited to the basis of his stock in the corporation, plus any adjustments that increase the basis for the tax year, plus the amount of any debt owed by the corporation to him. Losses are applied first against the basis of the stock and then against the debt. If the loss exceeds the stock basis and debt, it can be carried over indefinitely. Basis adjustments for distributions made by an S corpora-

tion during the tax year are taken into account before applying the loss limitation for the year.

- **Passive Activities Reported on Schedule K-1**

Schedule K-1 shows Mr. Pratt's share of rental and portfolio income as follows: $2,000 of rental income in Box 2, $1,731 of interest income in Box 4, $394 of ordinary dividend income in Box 5a, a net long-term capital loss of $957 in Box 8a, and a net Sec. 1231 gain of $8,116.50 in Box 9. Rental income and portfolio income are stated separately to assist Mr. Pratt in the calculation of his passive activity loss and credit limitations for the tax year. Losses from passive activities may be deducted only from passive income, while tax credits for passive activities may offset only a shareholder's tax liability for passive income. However, shareholders who are individuals (including their estates) may claim up to $25,000 of losses or credits from rental activities in which they actively participate against nonpassive income. Mr. Pratt must aggregate his passive losses and passive income from all passive activities (such as his participation in Douglas Plastics Company) on Form 8582 and attach the form to his individual return.

A tax deduction for Douglas's charitable contributions in 2005 may not be included in the deductions applied against ordinary income on Form 1120S. Instead, Mr. Pratt's share of the contributions is separately stated in Box 12 of Schedule K-1 (Code A) in the amount of $750.

- **At-Risk Limitation on Losses**

The amount of S corporation losses that a shareholder can deduct may be limited by the "at-risk" rules of Code Sec. 465 that are applied only at the shareholder level. These rules apply where a shareholder has a loss from a corporate activity carried on as a trade or business or for the production of income and has amounts in the activity for which he is personally liable. In such cases, a shareholder completes Form 6198, At-Risk Limitations, to figure the allowable loss reportable on his return. At-risk losses may be carried forward to the S corporation's post-termination period, for tax years beginning after 1996.

- **Specific Instructions for Schedule K.**

On Schedule K, Douglas Plastics Company must report the lump-sum amount of each item of income, loss, deduction, or credit that is passed on to shareholders. A separate Schedule K-1 must be prepared for each shareholder to show his pro rata share of the amounts reported on Schedule K. These items are then reported by the shareholder on his or her tax return for the year within which the corporation's tax year-ends. If there was a change in stock ownership, each shareholder's ownership percentage must be weighted for the number of days in the tax year that stock was owned.

**Line 1, Ordinary business income (loss) :** Enter the amount from Line 21, page 1. Enter the income or loss without reference to: the shareholders' basis in the stock of the corporation and in any indebtedness of the corporation to the shareholders; shareholders' at-risk limitations; and shareholders' passive activity limitations.

## ON THE RETURN

On Line 1, Douglas enters the ordinary income of $82,936 as a lump sum as reported on Line 21, page 1. On Schedule K-1, enter each shareholder's pro rata share of ordinary business income and loss in box 1 of Schedule K-1. Since Douglas has two shareholders, this amount is split in half on the Schedule K-1 prepared for each shareholder. Thus, Doug Pratt, a shareholder, will receive a Schedule K-1 that shows a pro rata share of $41,468 of ordinary income on Line 1.

**Line 2, Net rental real estate income (loss):** Enter the net income or loss of the corporation from rental real estate activities from Form 8825.

## ON THE RETURN

**Line 3a-3b, Other gross rental income (loss): :** Enter on Lines 3a and 3b, the income and expenses of rental activities other than those reported on Form 8825. Enter in Box 3 of Schedule K-1 each shareholder's pro rata share of other net rental income or loss reported on Line 3c of Schedule K.

**Line 4, Interest income:** Enter on Line 4 only portfolio interest. Interest income derived in the ordinary course of the corporation's trade or business, such as interest charged on receivable balances, is reported on Line 5, page 1 of Form 1120A. Be sure to enter each shareholder's pro rata share of interest income in Box 4 of Schedule K-1.

**Line 5a, Ordinary Dividends.** Enter only taxable ordinary dividends on Line 5a. Enter each shareholder's pro rata share of ordinary dividends in Box 5a of Schedule K-1.

**Line 5b, Qualified Dividends.** Enter qualified dividends on Line 5b. In general, qualified dividends are ordinary dividends received from domestic corporations and qualified foreign corporations. Enter each shareholder's pro rata share of qualified dividends in Box 5a of Schedule K-1. .

**Line 6, Royalties.** Enter the royalties received by the corporation. Enter each shareholder's pro rata share of royalties in Box 6 of Schedule K-1.

**Line 7, Net short-term capital gain (loss):** Enter the gain or loss from Line 6 of Schedule D (Form 1120S). Enter each shareholder's pro rata share of net short-term capital gain or loss in Box 7 of Schedule K-1.

**Line 8a, Net long-term capital gain (loss):** Enter the gain or loss that is portfolio income (loss) from Schedule D (Form 1120S), line 13. Enter each shareholder's pro rata share of net long-term capital gain or loss in Box 8a of Schedule K-1.

**Line 8b, Collectibles (28%) gain (loss):** Enter the amount attributable to collectibles from the amount reported on Schedule D (Form 1120S). A collectibles gain (loss) is any long-term gain or deductible long-term loss from the sale or exchange of a collectible that is a capital asset. Collectibles include works of art, rugs, antiques, metal (such as gold, silver, platinum bullion), gems, stamps, coins, alcoholic beverages, and certain other tangible property. Also include gain (but not loss) from the sale or exchange of an interest in a partnership or trust held for more than 1 year and attributable to unrealized appreciation of collectibles. Enter each shareholder's pro rata share of collectibles (28%) gain or loss in Box 8b of Schedule K-1.

**Line 8c, Unrecaptured Section 1250 gain:** The following three types of unrecaptured IRC Section 1250 gain must be reported separately on an attached statement to Form 1120S:

- From the sale or exchange of the corporation's business assets.
- From the sale or exchange of an interest in a partnership
- From an estate, trust, RIC, or REIT

Report each shareholder's pro rata share of unrecaptured IRC Sec. 1250 gain from the sale or exchange of the corporation's business assets in Box 8c of Schedule K-1. If the corporation is reporting unrecaptured

IRC Sec. 1250 gain from an estate, trust, REIT, or RIC or from the corporation's sale or exchange of an interest in a partnership, enter "STMT" in box 8c and an asterisk (*) in the left column of the box and attach a statement that separately identifies the amount of unrecaptured IRC Sec. 1250 gain from:

- From the sale or exchange of the corporation's business assets.

- From the sale or exchange of an interest in a partnership

- From an estate, trust, RIC, or REIT.

**Line 9, Net section 1231 gain (loss) (other than due to casualty or theft):** Enter the net section 1231 gain (loss) (excluding net gain from involuntary conversions due to casualty or theft) from Form 4797, line 7, column (g). Report net gain or loss from involuntary conversions due to casualty or theft on Line 10 of Schedule K. Enter each shareholder's pro rata share of net section 1231 gain or loss in Box 9 of Schedule K-1.

**Line 10, Other income (loss):** Enter any other item of income or loss not included on lines 1 through 9. Attach a statement to Form 1120S that separately identifies each type and amount of income for each of the following five categories. The codes needed for Schedule K-1 reporting are provided for each category:

- other portfolio income (loss) - code A

- involuntary conversions - code B

- 1256 contracts and straddles - code C

- Mining exploration costs recapture - code D

- Other income (loss) - code E including: recoveries of tax benefit items; gambling gains and losses; gains from the disposition of an interest in oil, gas, geothermal, or other mineral properties; gain from the sale or exchange of qualified small business stock that is eligible for the partial Code Sec. 1202 exclusion; and gain eligible for IRC Sec. 1045 rollover (replacement stock purchased by the corporation).

Enter each shareholder's pro rata share of the five other income categories listed above in Box 10 of Schedule K-1.

## DEDUCTIONS

**Line 11, Section 179 expense deduction:** A shareholder of an S corporation may elect to expense part of the cost of certain property that the corporation purchased during the tax year for use in its trade or business or certain rental activities. Complete Part 1 of Form 4562 to compute the amount of the Section 179 deduction. The corporation itself does not claim the deduction, but passes it through to the shareholders. Attach Form 4562 to Form 1120S and show the total Section 179 expense deduction on Schedule K, Line 11. Enter each shareholder's pro rata share of section 179 expense deduction in Box 11 of Schedule K-1. .

**Line 12a, Contributions:** Enter on Line 12a, the amount of charitable contributions paid during the tax year. Generally, no deduction is allowed for any contribution of $250 or more unless the corporation obtains a written acknowledgment from the charitable organization that shows the amount of cash contributed, describes any property contributed, and gives an estimate of the value of any goods or services provided in return for the contribution. The acknowledgment must be obtained by the due date (including extensions) of the corporation's return, or if earlier, the date the corporation files its return. Do not attach the acknowledgment to the tax return, but keep it with the corporation's records. These rules apply in addition to the filing requirements for Form 8283.

On Line 12a enter the amount of charitable contributions made during the tax year. Attach a statement to Form 1120S that separately identifies the corporation's contributions for each of the following six categories. The codes needed for Schedule K-1 reporting are provided for each category.

- Cash contributions (50%) (code A)

- Cash contributions (30%) (code B)

- Noncash contributions (50%) (code C)

- Noncash contributions (30%) (code D)

- Capital gain property to a 50% organization (30%) (code E)

- Capital gain property (20%) (code F)

- Cash contributions (100%) (code G). Enter the cash contributions paid during the period from August 28, 2005, through December 31, 2005, to a charitable organization.

**Line12b, Investment interest expense:** Enter on Line 12b the interest properly allocable to debt on property held for investment purposes. Property held for investment includes property that produces income (unless derived in the ordinary course of a trade or business) from interest, dividends, annuities, or royalties; and gains from the disposition of property that produces those types of income or is held for investment. Investment interest expense does not include interest expense allocable to a passive activity.

Enter each shareholder's pro rata share of investment interest expense in Box 12 of Schedule K-1.

**Line 12c, Section 59(e)(2) expenditures:** Each shareholder is allowed to make an election to deduct their pro rata share of the corporation's otherwise deductible *qualified expenditures* ratably over 10 years (3 years for circulation expenditures), beginning with the tax year in which the expenditures were made (or for intangible drilling and development costs, over the 60-month period beginning with the month in which such costs were paid or incurred). The term *qualified expenditures* includes only the following types of expenditures paid or incurred during the tax year:

- circulation expenditures

- research and experimental expenditures

- intangible drilling development costs

- mining exploration and development costs

On Line 12c(1) enter the type of expenditures claimed on Line 12c(2). Enter on Line 12c(2) the qualified expenditures paid or incurred during the tax year to which an election under Code Sec. 59(e) may apply. Enter this amount for all shareholders whether or not any shareholder makes an election under Code Sec. 59(e). On an attached statement, identify the property for which the expenditures were paid or incurred. If the expenditures were for intangible drilling costs for oil and gas properties, identify the month(s) in which the expenditures were paid or incurred. If there is more than one type of expenditure, or more than one property, provide the amounts (and the months paid or incurred if required) for each type of expenditure separately for each property.

**Schedule K-1.** Enter each shareholder's pro rata share of the five deduction categories listed above in Box 12 of Schedule K-1.

**Line 12d, Other Deductions:** Enter deductions not included on Lines 11, 12a, 12b, 12c(2), 14l. Attach a statement to Form 1120S that separately identifies the type and amount of each deduction for the following five categories. The codes needed for Schedule K-1 reporting are provided for each category:

- Deductions-royalty income (code I). Enter the deductions related to royalty income.

- Deductions-portfolio (2% floor) (code K). Enter the deductions related to portfolio income that are subject to the 2% of AGI floor.

- Deductions-portfolio (other) (code L). Enter the amount of any other deductions related to portfolio income. No deduction is allowed for expenses allocable to a convention, seminar, or similar meeting. Because these expenses are not deductible by shareholders, the corporation does not report these expenses on line 12d of Schedule K. The expenses are nondeductible and are reported as such on line 16c of Schedule K.

- Reforestation expense deduction (code M). The corporation may elect to deduct a limited amount of its reforestation expenditures. The amount the corporation may elect to deduct is limited to $10,000 for each qualified timber property. Provide a description of the qualified timber property on an attached statement to Form 1120S and Schedule K-1. If the corporation is electing to deduct amounts for more than one qualified timber property, provide a description and the amount on the statement for each property. The corporation must amortize over 84 months any amount not deducted.

- Preproductive period expenses (code N). If the corporation is required to use an accrual method of accounting, it must capitalize these expenses. If the corporation is permitted to use the cash method, enter the amount of preproductive period expenses. An election not to capitalize these expenses must be made at the shareholder level.

- Commercial revitalization deduction from rental real estate activities (code O). Enter the commercial revitalization deduction on Line 12d only if it is for a rental real estate activity.

- Domestic production activities information (code P). If the corporation is not using the small business simplified overall method to allocate and apportion cost of goods sold and apportion cost of goods sold and deductions between domestic production gross receipts and other receipts, attach a statement with the following information to enable each shareholder to figure the domestic production activities deduction.

- Domestic production gross receipts (DPGR)

- Gross receipts from all sources

- Cost of goods sold allocable to DPGR

- Total deductions, expenses, and losses directly allocation to DPGR

- Total deductions, expenses, and losses not directly allocable to DPGR or another class of income

- Form W-1 wages.

- Domestic production activity information (small business simplified overall method) If the corporation elected to use the small business simplified method to allocate and apportion cost of goods sold and deductions between domestic production gross receipts and other receipts, report the following information in box 12 of Schedule K-1 using codes Q and R.

  - Qualified production activities income (code Q)

  - Employer's W-2 wages (code R)

- Other deductions (code S). Include any other deductions such as:

  - Amounts paid by the corporation that would be allowed as itemized deduction on any of the shareholders' income tax returns if they were paid directly by a shareholder for the same purpose. These amounts include, but are not limited to, expenses for the production of income other than from the corporation's trade or business. However, do not enter expenses related to portfolio income or investment income expense reported on Line 12b of Schedule K on this line.

  - Soil and water conservation expenditures.

  - Expenditures paid or incurred for the removal of architectural and transportation barriers to the elderly and disabled that the corporation has elected to treat as a current expense.

  - Interest expense allocated to debt-financed distributions.

  - Contributions to a capital construction fund.

  - Any penalty on early withdrawal of savings because the corporation withdrew funds from its time savings deposit before its maturity

  - Film and television production expenses.

Enter each shareholder's pro rata share of the deduction categories listed above in Box 12 of Schedule K-1.

## CREDITS & CREDIT RECAPTURE

**Lines 13a & 13b, Low-income housing credit:** On Line 13a enter the credit that is available to owners of low-income residential rental buildings. If shareholders are eligible to claim the low-income housing credit, complete the applicable parts of Form 8586, "Low-Income Housing Credit," and attach it to Form 1120S. Enter on Line 13b any low-income housing credit not reported on Line 13a. Enter each shareholder's pro rata share of the low-income housing credit in Box 13 of Schedule K-1 using code A if reported on Line 13a and code B if reported on Line 13b.

**Line 13c, Qualified rehabilitation expenditures (rental real estate):** Enter total qualified rehabilitation expenditures related to rental real estate activities of the corporation. Enter each shareholder's pro rata share of the qualified rehabilitation expenditures in Box 13 of Schedule K-1 using code C.

**Line 13d, Other rental real estate credits:** Enter on Line 13d any other credit (other than credits reported above) related to rental real estate activities. On the dotted line to the left of the entry space for Line 13d, identify the type of credit. If there is more than one type of credit, attach a statement to Form 1120S that identifies the type and amount for each credit. Enter each shareholder's pro rata share of other rental real estate credits reported on Line 13d of Schedule K in Box 13 of Schedule K-1 using code G.

**Line 13e, Other rental credits:** Enter on Line 13e any other credit (other than credits reported above) related to rental activities. On the dotted line to the left of the entry space for Line 13e, identify the type of credit. If there is more than one type of credit attach a statement to Form 1120S that identifies the type and amount for each credit. Enter each shareholder's pro rata share of other rental credits reported on Line 13e of Schedule K in Box 13 of Schedule K-1 using code H.

**Line 13f, Credit for alcohol used as fuel:** Enter on Line 13f of Schedule K the credit for alcohol used as fuel attributable to trade or business activities. Figure the credit on Form 6478, "Credit for Alcohol Used as Fuel," and attach it to Form 1120S. Enter each shareholder's pro rata share of credits for alcohol used as fuel reported on Line 13f of Schedule K in Box 13 of Schedule K-1 using code R.

**Line 13g, Other credits and credit recapture:** Enter on Line 13g any other credits and credit recapture. On the dotted line to the left of the entry space for Line 13, identify the type of credit. If there is more than one type of credit or if there are any credits subject to recapture, attach a statement to Form 1120A that separately identifies each type and amount of credit and credit recapture information for the following categories. The codes needed for Schedule K-1 reporting are provided for each category:

- Qualified rehabilitation expenditures (other than rental real estate) (code D). Enter each shareholder's pro rata share of qualified rehabilitation expenditures related to other than rental real estate activities in Box 13 of Schedule K-1 using code D.

- Basis of energy property (code E)

- Qualified timber property (code F)

- Undistributed capital gains credit (code H)

- Work opportunity credit (code J)

- Welfare-to-work credit (code K)

- Disabled access credit (code L)

- Empowerment zone and renewal community employment credit (code M)

- Credit for increasing research activities (code N)

- New markets credit (code O)

- Credit for employer social security and Medicare taxes (code P)

- Backup withholding (code Q)

- Recapture of low-income housing credit (codes R and S)

- Recapture of investment credit (code T)

- Other credits (code U). Attach a statement to Form 1120S that identifies the type and amount of any other credits no reported elsewhere, such as:
  - Nonconventional Source Fuel Credit.
  - Qualified Electric Vehicle Credit.
  - Unused Investment Credit From Cooperatives
  - Enhanced Oil Recovery Credit
  - Renewable Electricity, Refined Coal and Indian Coal Production Credit
  - Indian Employment Credit

- Orphan Drug Credit
- Credit for Contributions To Selected Community Development Corporations
- Credit for Small Employer Pension Plan Start-Up Cost
- Credit for Employer-Provided Childcare Facilities And Services
- Qualified Railroad Track Maintenance
- Biodiesel And Renewable Diesel Fuels Credit
- Low Sulfur Diesel Fuel Production Credit
- General credits from Electing Large Partnership
- Qualified Zone Academy Bond Credit
- Distilled Spirits Credit
- Energy Efficient Home Credit
- Alternative Fuel Vehicle Refueling Property Credit
- Clean Renewable Energy Bond Credit
- Basis in qualifying advanced coal project property
- Basis in qualifying gasification project property.
- Hurricane Katrina Employee Retention Credit.

- Recapture of other credits (code V). On an attached statement to Schedule K-1, provide any information shareholders will need to report recapture of credits (other than recapture of low-income housing credit and investment credit reported on Schedule K-1 using codes R, S, and T). Examples of credit recapture information reported using code V include:
  - Any information needed by a shareholder to compute recapture of the qualified electric vehicle credit
  - Any information needed by a shareholder to compute recapture of the new markets credit
  - Any information needed by a shareholder to compute recapture of the Indian employment credit.
  - Any information needed by a shareholder to compute recapture of the credit for employer-provided child care facilities and services.

Enter each shareholder's pro rata share of the credit and credit recapture categories listed above in Box 13 of Schedule K-1. Enter the applicable code, D through V, in the column to the left of the dollar amount of the entry space.

## ON THE RETURN

In December 2005, Douglas Plastics Company incurred $5,250 of eligible expenditures for removing architectural barriers to make its business accessible to disabled individuals. It claims a disabled access credit of $2,500 (($5,250 minus $250) times 50%) that is reported on Form 8826 and on Form 1120S, Schedule K, Line 13g. One-half of the credit is passed through to each of Douglas's shareholders on Schedule K-1, Box 13 (Code L).

## FOREIGN TRANSACTIONS

**Lines 14a-14n.** Lines 14a through 14n must be completed if the corporation has foreign income, deductions, or losses, or has paid or accrued foreign taxes.

**Line 14a, Name of country of U.S. possession.** Enter the name of the foreign country or U.S. possession from which the corporation had income or to which the corporation paid or accrued taxes.

**Line 14b, Gross income from all sources.** Enter the corporation's gross income from all sources (both U.S. and foreign).

**Line 14c, Gross income sourced at shareholder level.** Enter the total gross income of the corporation that is required to be sourced at the shareholder level. This includes income from the sale of most personal property, other than inventory, depreciable property and certain intangible property.

**Lines 14d-14f, Foreign gross income sourced at corporation level.** Separately report gross income from sources outside the United States by category of income as identified under Lines 14d, 14e, and 14f.

**Line 14d**: Passive foreign source income.

**Line 14e:** Attach a schedule showing the amount of foreign source income included in each of the following listed categories:

- Financial services income
- High withholding tax interest
- Shipping income

- Dividends from a domestic international sales corporation (DISC) or form DISC
- Distributions from a foreign sales corporation (FSC) or a former FSC
- Section 901(j) income; and
- Certain income resourced by treaty.

**Line 14f:** General limitation foreign source income (all other foreign source income).

**Lines 14g-14h, Deductions allocated and apportioned at shareholder level.** Enter the corporation's total interest expense (including interest equivalents). Do not include interest directly allocable to income from a specific property. This type of interest is allocated and apportioned at the corporate level and is included on Lines 14i through 14k. On Line 14h, enter the total of all other deductions or losses that are required to be allocated at the shareholder level.

**Lines 14i-14k, Deductions allocated and apportioned at corporate level to foreign source income.** Separately report corporate deductions that are apportioned at the corporate level to (a) passive foreign source income, (b) each of the listed foreign categories of income under Lines 14c and 14e. Attach a schedule showing the amount of deductions allocated and apportioned at the corporate level to each of the listed categories from Line 14e.

**Lines 14l, Total foreign taxes paid or accrued.** Enter in U.S. dollars the total foreign taxes that were paid or accrued according to the corporation's method of accounting for such taxes. In Box 14 of Schedule K-1 enter each shareholder's pro rata share of total foreign taxes paid or accrued using code L for the Line 14l taxes and code M for the Line 14m taxes. Check the box on Line 14l to indicate if the foreign taxes were paid or accrued.

**Line 14m, Reduction in taxes available for credit.** Enter the total reductions in taxes available for credit. Attach a schedule showing the reductions for:

- taxes on foreign mineral income
- taxes on foreign oil and gas extraction income
- taxes attributable to boycott operations
- failure to timely file or furnish all of the information required on Forms 5471 and 8865
- any other items as specified.

**Line 14n. Other foreign transactions.** Report any other foreign transactions not accounted for under Line 14a -14m such as

- Foreign trading gross receipts (code O)

- Extraterritorial income exclusion (code P)

- Other foreign transactions (code Q)

## ALTERNATIVE MINIMUM TAX

**LINES 15a - 15f:** Although S corporation are not liable for the alternative minimum tax, their shareholders are subject to a minimum tax on their separate incomes from all source, including income from an S corporation. There, an S corporation must, on Lines 15a -15f of Schedule K, break down the aggregate amount of adjustments and tax preference items that are used to determine minimum tax. On Schedule K-1, report each shareholder's pro rata share of amounts reported on Line 15a through 15f in Box 15 of Schedule K-1 using codes A through F respectively. AMT items include the following:

- Accelerated depreciation of real property under pre-1987 rules

- Accelerated depreciation of leased personal property under pre-1987 rules

- Long-term contracts entered into after February 28, 1986. Except for certain home construction contracts, the taxable income from these contracts must be figured using the percentage of completion method of accounting for the AMT

- Losses from tax shelter farm activities. No loss from any tax shelter farm activity is allowed for the AMT.

See Form 6251, "Alternative Minimum Tax-Individuals," or Schedule 1 of Form 1041, U.S. Income Tax Return for Estates and Trusts, to determine the amounts to enter and for other information.

## ON THE RETURN

Douglas Plastics must report the excess depreciation claimed on the molds and patterns placed in service in 2005 and the machine sold in 2005. The excess depreciation is the difference between the amount actually claimed for the year and the amount allowable for the year using the 150% declining-balance method over the regular recovery period in the case of the molds and patterns and the class life of the

machine (3 years for the molds and patterns and 11 years for the machine). The excess depreciation on the molds and patterns is $1,000 ($4,000 - $3,000). The excess depreciation on the machinery is $151 ($625 - $474). The combined excess depreciation ($1,151) is reported on Line 15a of Schedule K. Mr. Pratt's share ($575.50) is reported in Box 15 of his Schedule K-1 (Code A).

In addition, the company must enter the adjusted gain or loss from the sale of the machine in 2005 on Line 15b of Schedule K. The adjustment is the difference between the gain or loss figured for regular tax purposes and the gain or loss figured using the AMT adjusted basis (i.e., cost reduced by AMT depreciation). The adjustment for the machine is ($2,728). This is the difference between the $1,293 regular gain and the $1,435 AMT loss ($5,041 sales price - ($10,000 cost - $3,524 AMT depreciation)). The adjustment is treated as a negative figure since Douglas Plastics had a regular tax gain on the machine and an AMT loss. Douglas Pratt's share of the adjustment is ($1,364) and is reported in Box 15 of Schedule K-1 (Code B). No adjustment is required on the $90,000 building sold in 2005 since it was placed in service before 1987.

## ITEMS AFFECTING SHAREHOLDER BASIS

**Line 16a, Tax-exempt interest income:** Enter tax-exempt interest income, including any exempt-interest dividends received from a mutual fund or other regulated investment company.

## ON THE RETURN

On Line 16a, Douglas reports its tax-exempt interest income for the year of $1,635.

**Line 16b, Other tax-exempt income:** Enter all income of the corporation exempt from tax other than tax-exempt interest (e.g., life insurance proceeds). Generally, the basis of the shareholder's stock is increased by the amount shown on this line.

**Line 16c, Nondeductible expenses:** Enter nondeductible expenses paid or incurred by the corporation. Do not include separately stated deductions shown elsewhere on Schedules K and K-1, capital expenditures, or items for which the deduction is deferred to a later tax year. Generally, the basis of the shareholder's stock is decreased by the amount shown on this line.

## ON THE RETURN

On Line 16c, Douglas reports nondeductible expenses for the year of $3,390, which consists of $90 of nondeductible expenses related to the tax-exempt interest income and $3,300 of entertainment expense that could not be deducted on Line 19 of Form 1120A because of the 50 percent deduction limitation. These items are also reflected on Schedule K-1, Box 16 (Codes A–C, respectively). Mr. Pratt's share of the tax-exempt interest income amounts to $817.50 and his share of nondeductible expenses amounts to $1,695.

On Line 16d, Douglas reports the total distributions made to its two shareholders ($90,000) during the year. Mr. Pratt's share is $45,000 and is reported in Box 16 of his Schedule K-1 (Code D).

**Line 16d, Property distributions :** Enter the total property distributions (including cash) made to each shareholder other than dividends reported on Line 17c of Schedule K. Distributions of appreciated property are valued at fair market value.

**Line 16e, Repayment of loans from shareholders:** Enter any repayments made to shareholders during the current tax year. Enter each shareholder's pro rata share of amounts entered on Lines 16a, 16b, and 16c in Box 16 of Schedule K-1 using codes A through C respectively. Report property distributions from Line 16d and repayment of loans from shareholders (Line 16e) on the Schedule K-1 of the shareholders that received the distributions or repayments (using codes D and E).

## OTHER INFORMATION

**Lines 17a and 17b, Investment income and expenses:** Enter on Line 17a the investment income included on Lines 4, 5a, 6 and 10 of Schedule K. Do not include other portfolio gains or losses on this line. Enter on Line 17b the investment expense included on Line 12b of Schedule K.

**Line 17c, Dividend distributions paid from accumulated earnings and profits (Schedule K only):** Enter total dividends paid to shareholders from accumulated earnings and profits. Do not report them on Schedule K-1.

**Line 17d, Other items and amounts.** Report the following information on a statement attached to Form 1120S. In Box 17 of Schedule K-1 enter the appropriate code for each information items followed by an asterisk in the left-hand column of the entry space.

In the right-hand column, enter "STMT." The codes are provided below:

- Lookback interest-completed long-term contracts (code C)

- Lookback interest - income forecast method (code D)

- Dispositions of property with section 179 deductions (code E)

- Recapture of section 179 deduction (code F)

- Section 453(l)(3) information (code G)

- Section 453A(c) information (code H)

- Section 1260(b) information (code I)

- Interest allocable to production expenditures (code J)

- CCF nonqualified withdrawal (code K)

- Information needed to figure depletion - oil and gain (code L)

- Amortization of reforestation costs (code M)

- Other information (code N). Report to each shareholder:

  - Any information or statements the shareholders need to allow them to comply with the tax shelter registration, disclosure and list keeping requirements.

  - If the corporation participates in a transaction that must be disclosed on From 8886, "Reportable Transaction Disclosure Statement" both the corporation and its shareholders may be required to file Form 8886.

  - If the corporation is involved in farming or fishing activities, report the gross income from these activities.

  - Any income or gain reported on Lines 1 through 10 of Schedule K that qualify as inversion gain, if the corporation is an expatriated entity or is a partner in an expatriated entity.

  - The shareholder's pro rata share of any amount included in income with respect to qualified zone academy bonds

  - The shareholder's pro rata share of any amount included in income with respect to clean renewable energy bonds

- Any other information the shareholders need to prepare their tax returns.

**Line 17e, Income (loss) reconciliation:** If the corporation has an amount on Line 12d for code P, Q, or R, exclude the amounts from Line 17e.

Douglas Plastics Company did not pay any interest on investment indebtedness in 2005, but nevertheless it must report on Line 17a of Schedule K the amount of investment income ($4,250) disclosed on Lines 4 and 5a. A shareholder's investment interest expense deductions from all sources, including an S corporation, may be calculated on Form 4952.

## ¶109  BALANCE SHEETS

The balance sheet (Schedule L) of an S corporation looks very much like that of any other corporation. Comparative balance sheets for the beginning and end of the tax year are shown on Schedule L. The balance sheets should agree with the S corporation's books and records. Entries should also agree with amounts shown elsewhere on the return. For example, beginning and ending inventory figures must be identical to the figures shown in Schedule A, Lines 1 and 7. Normally, the figures on Schedule L for the "beginning of tax year" will be the same as the "end of tax year" figures shown on Schedule L for the preceding tax year.

If an S corporation's total receipts for the tax year and its total assets at the end of the year are less than $250,000, it is not required to complete Schedule L, Balance Sheets per Books.

To derive the figure of $352,500 on Line 10a of Schedule L for buildings and other depreciable assets that it held at the beginning of 2005, Douglas includes the following items: factory equipment of $138,500, furniture and fixtures of $4,000, a $110,000 brick building, a $90,000 building, and $10,000 of machinery. On Line 10b, column (a), it subtracts $135,693 of depreciation deductions that it has claimed in previous years on these items, including $6,302 for the factory equipment in 2004, $200 for the furniture and fixtures in 2004, $66,000 for the $110,000 brick building during the years 1981–2004, $57,564 for the $90,000 building during the years 1981–2004, and $5,627 for the machinery during the years 2002-2004.

By the end of 2005, Douglas has sold the $90,000 building and the $10,000 of machinery but acquired

depreciable molds and patterns for $12,000, leaving it with depreciable assets totaling $264,500, which are reported on Line 10a, column (c). Its year-end accumulated depreciation is $92,242 (Line 10b, column (c)), which consists of $4,000 of depreciation deductions for the molds and patterns in 2005, $6,302 for the factory equipment in 2004 and $12,590 in 2005, $200 for the furniture and fixtures in 2004 and $400 in 2005, and $66,000 for the brick building during the years 1981–2004 and $2,750 in 2005. Year-end 2005 depreciation does not include any depreciation claimed on the assets sold during the year. For more details on these items, see the discussion on depreciation at ¶105, and on gains and losses from property at ¶103.

## ¶110  RECONCILIATION OF INCOME PER BOOKS WITH INCOME PER RETURN

If an S corporation's total receipts for the tax year and its total assets at the end of the year are $250,000 or more, it must complete Schedule M-1, Reconciliation of Income (Loss) per Books with Income (Loss) per Return.

### ON THE RETURN

On Schedule M-1, Line 1, Douglas reports net income per books of $102,240 (consisting of the following income items: $82,936 of ordinary income (Form 1120S, Line 21); $4,000 of rental income, $3,462 of interest income, $788 of ordinary dividend income, $16,223 of Sec. 1231 gain, and tax-exempt interest of $1,635 (from Schedule K); and the following reduction items: $1,500 of charitable contributions; $1,914 of capital loss; $90 of expenses related to tax-exempt income; and the nondeductible (50%) portion of entertainment expenses, $3,300).

On Schedule M-1, Line 3b, the nondeductible portion of entertainment expenses ($3,300) is entered and included in the total on Line 4. On Line 5, net tax-exempt interest of $1,545 ($1,635 of tax-exempt interest minus $90 of related expenses) is entered and included in the total on Line 7. The Line 7 result is subtracted from the total on Line 4 in arriving at the net income total on Line 8. Net income of $103,995 represents the income reported to shareholders on Schedule K, Line 17e.

## ¶111 RECONCILIATION OF PTI, AAA, AND OTHER ADJUSTMENTS ACCOUNT

Schedule M-2 reconciles the three special equity accounts of S corporations as follows: (1) the accumulated adjustments account (AAA), (2) the other adjustments account, and (3) the previously taxed income account (PTI). The information contained in Schedule M-2 delineates the accounts that affect the shareholders' bases in their stock and the taxability of distributions from the S corporation. In compiling the reconciliations of these accounts, the distribution rules discussed at **¶107** and **¶108** should be followed.

- **Accumulated Adjustments Account**

An S corporation's accumulated adjustments account (AAA) is entered in the first column of Schedule M-2. The AAA generally reflects the corporation's accumulated undistributed net income for the corporation's post-1982 years. The account is used to determine the tax effect of distributions. This account must be maintained by S corporations with accumulated earnings and profits. For those corporations that elect S corporation status in 2005, the beginning balance of the AAA is zero.

An S corporation without accumulated earnings does not need to maintain an accumulated adjustments account (in this situation, the account is not necessary to determine the tax effect of distributions). Nevertheless, the IRS recommends that the account be maintained because an S corporation that engages in certain transactions (e.g., a merger into an S corporation with accumulated earnings) must be able to calculate its AAA at the time of the transaction.

The AAA is computed at the end of the year by taking into account only taxable income and deductible and nondeductible losses and expenses (excluding expenses related to tax-exempt income) for the tax year. Adjustments for nontaxable income and related expenses are made to the other adjustments account (see below). After the year-end income and expense adjustments are made, the account is reduced by the distributions made during the year. An AAA account may have a negative balance at the end of the year (Code Sec. 1368(e)).

In tax years beginning after 1996, the excess of the reductions in the AAA for the tax year (other than reductions for distributions) over the increases in the AAA for the tax year losses and deductions over income ("net negative adjustments") for the tax year are disregarded when computing the amount in the AAA for purposes of determining the taxability of the distributions for the tax year.

Also, for purposes of computing the taxability of distributions, an S corporation's accumulated earnings and profits are reduced as of the first day of its first tax year beginning after 1996 by the earnings and profits accumulated from any tax year beginning before 1983 when the corporation was a subchapter S corporation.

### ON THE RETURN

In this filled-in form, the Douglas Plastics Company had $177,906 as its beginning AAA balance for 2005. Its ordinary income of $82,936 from Line 21 on page 1 of Form 1120S (and Line 1 of Schedule K) is entered on Line 2 of Schedule M-2. The corporation's other additions on Line 3 (all from Schedule K) are made up of rental income totaling $4,000, Sec. 1231 gain of $16,223, $788 in ordinary dividends, and $3,462 in interest income; they total $24,473. Its other reductions on Line 5 are made up of net long-term capital loss of $1,914, $1,500 for charitable contributions, and $3,300 for the portion of entertainment expenses that, because of the 50% limitation on the deductibility of entertainment expenses, could not be deducted on Line 19 of Form 1120S (see **¶104**). The net total of Lines 1–5, $278,601, is entered on Line 6. The corporation then enters its $90,000 in cash distributions on Line 7. The Douglas Plastics Company's balance in its AAA at the end of the tax year is $188,601 ($278,601 - $90,000).

- **Other Adjustments Account**

The other adjustments account is reflected in the second column of Schedule M-2. This account is increased by tax-exempt income and decreased by expenses related to tax-exempt income as well as federal taxes attributable to a C corporation tax year. After the adjustments for these items are made, the account is reduced for distributions made during the tax year.

### ON THE RETURN

For the beginning of the tax year, the Douglas Plastics Company, which had retained earnings at year-end, had a balance of $1,640 in its other adjustments account. The Douglas Plastics Company had $1,635 of tax-free interest income from state bonds, entered on Line 3. It also had a $90 expense related to those tax-exempt bonds, which it entered on Line 5. Thus, the corporation's balance in its other adjustments account at the end of the tax year is $3,185, entered on Lines 6 and 8.

### • Previously taxed income

Schedule M-2 also provides a column for "shareholders' undistributed taxable income previously taxed." Douglas does not have to complete this column. This column pertains to income that was included in the shareholders' income for years that began before 1983. For corporations that still retain a PTI account, a nontaxable PTI distribution reduces a shareholder's basis in S stock and comes after a nontaxable distribution out of AAA and before a dividend distribution out of accumulated earnings and profits.

| Form **1120S** | **U.S. Income Tax Return for an S Corporation** | OMB No. 1545-0130 |
|---|---|---|

Department of the Treasury
Internal Revenue Service

▶ Do not file this form unless the corporation has filed Form 2553
to elect to be an S corporation.
▶ See separate instructions.

**20**05

For calendar year 2005, or tax year beginning _____ , 2005, ending _____ , 20 _____

| **A** Effective date of S election | Use the IRS label. Otherwise, print or type. | Name **Douglas Plastics Company** | **C** Employer identification number |
|---|---|---|---|
| 03-12-1978 | | | 31:0099009 |
| **B** Business code number (see instructions) | | Number, street, and room or suite no. If a P.O. box, see instructions. **244 Lakeview Street** | **D** Date incorporated **01-01-1978** |
| 326100 | | City or town, state, and ZIP code **Fargo, North Dakota 58103** | **E** Total assets (see instructions) $ 562,174 00 |

**F** Check applicable boxes: **(1)** ☐ Initial return  **(2)** ☐ Final return  **(3)** ☐ Name change  **(4)** ☐ Address change  **(5)** ☐ Amended return
**G** Enter number of shareholders in the corporation at end of the tax year . . . . . . . . . . . . . . ▶

**Caution.** *Include **only** trade or business income and expenses on lines 1a through 21. See the instructions for more information.*

### Income

| | | | |
|---|---|---|---|
| **1a** Gross receipts or sales | 612,759 00 | **b** Less returns and allowances  7,360 00  **c** Bal ▶ **1c** | 605,399 00 |
| **2** Cost of goods sold (Schedule A, line 8) . . . . . . . . . . . | | **2** | 331,795 00 |
| **3** Gross profit. Subtract line 2 from line 1c . . . . . . . . . | | **3** | 273,604 00 |
| **4** Net gain (loss) from Form 4797, Part II, line 17 *(attach Form 4797)* | | **4** | 4,857 00 |
| **5** Other income (loss) *(attach statement)* . . . . . . . . . | | **5** | |
| **6** **Total income (loss).** Add lines 3 through 5. . . . . . . . ▶ | | **6** | 278,461 00 |

### Deductions (see the instructions for limitations)

| | | | |
|---|---|---|---|
| **7** Compensation of officers . . . . . . . . . . . . . | | **7** | 96,000 00 |
| **8** Salaries and wages (less employment credits) . . . . . . . | | **8** | 39,446 00 |
| **9** Repairs and maintenance . . . . . . . . . . . . . | | **9** | 3,694 00 |
| **10** Bad debts . . . . . . . . . . . . . . . . . . | | **10** | 4,500 00 |
| **11** Rents . . . . . . . . . . . . . . . . . . . | | **11** | 1,200 00 |
| **12** Taxes and licenses . . . . . . . . . . . . . . . | | **12** | 13,237 00 |
| **13** Interest . . . . . . . . . . . . . . . . . . . | | **13** | 3,620 00 |
| **14a** Depreciation *(attach Form 4562)* | **14a** 20,365 00 | | |
| **b** Depreciation claimed on Schedule A and elsewhere on return . | **14b** 19,215 00 | | |
| **c** Subtract line 14b from line 14a . . . . . . . . . . . | | **14c** | 1,150 00 |
| **15** Depletion **(Do not deduct oil and gas depletion.)** . . . . . | | **15** | |
| **16** Advertising . . . . . . . . . . . . . . . . . | | **16** | 3,500 00 |
| **17** Pension, profit-sharing, etc., plans . . . . . . . . . . | | **17** | 8,805 00 |
| **18** Employee benefit programs . . . . . . . . . . . . | | **18** | 4,000 00 |
| **19** Other deductions *(attach statement)* . . . . . . . . . | | **19** | 16,373 00 |
| **20** **Total deductions.** Add the amounts shown in the far right column for lines 7 through 19 ▶ | | **20** | 195,525 00 |
| **21** **Ordinary business income (loss).** Subtract line 20 from line 6 . . . . . . . | | **21** | 82,936 00 |

### Tax and Payments

| | | |
|---|---|---|
| **22 Tax: a** Excess net passive income tax *(attach statement)* . . . | **22a** | |
| **b** Tax from Schedule D (Form 1120S) . . . . . . . . . . | **22b** | |
| **c** Add lines 22a and 22b (see the instructions for additional taxes) . | **22c** | |
| **23 Payments: a** 2005 estimated tax payments and amount applied from 2004 return | **23a** | |
| **b** Tax deposited with Form 7004 . . . . . . . . . . . | **23b** | |
| **c** Credit for Federal tax paid on fuels *(attach Form 4136)* . . . | **23c** | |
| **d** Add lines 23a through 23c . . . . . . . . . . . . | **23d** | |
| **24** Estimated tax penalty (see instructions). Check if Form 2220 is attached . . . . . ▶ ☐ | **24** | |
| **25** **Tax due.** If line 23d is smaller than the total of lines 22c and 24, enter amount owed. . . . | **25** | |
| **26** **Overpayment.** If line 23d is larger than the total of lines 22c and 24, enter amount overpaid . | **26** | |
| **27** Enter amount of line 26 you want: **Credited to 2006 estimated tax** ▶ _____ Refunded ▶ | **27** | |

**Sign Here**

Under penalties of perjury, I declare that I have examined this return, including accompanying schedules and statements, and to the best of my knowledge and belief, it is true, correct, and complete. Declaration of preparer (other than taxpayer) is based on all information of which preparer has any knowledge.

▶ _____     _____  ▶ President _____
Signature of officer          Date              Title

May the IRS discuss this return with the preparer shown below (see instructions)? ☑ Yes ☐ No

**Paid Preparer's Use Only**

| Preparer's signature ▶ | Date | Check if self-employed ☑ | Preparer's SSN or PTIN  456-78-1010 |
|---|---|---|---|
| Firm's name (or yours if self-employed), address, and ZIP code | **Steven Brand** **24 Center St., Fargo, ND 58103** | EIN 12:9876543 | Phone no. ( 701 ) 555-0334 |

**For Privacy Act and Paperwork Reduction Act Notice, see the separate instructions.**    Cat. No. 11510H    Form **1120S** (2005)

¶ **111**

Form 1120S (2005)                                                                                                          Page **2**

| **Schedule A** | **Cost of Goods Sold** (see instructions) | | | |
|---|---|---|---|---|
| 1 | Inventory at beginning of year | 1 | 118,765 | 00 |
| 2 | Purchases | 2 | 100,650 | 00 |
| 3 | Cost of labor | 3 | 180,235 | 00 |
| 4 | Additional section 263A costs (attach statement) | 4 | | |
| 5 | Other costs (attach statement) | 5 | 57,475 | 00 |
| 6 | **Total.** Add lines 1 through 5 | 6 | 457,125 | 00 |
| 7 | Inventory at end of year | 7 | 125,330 | 00 |
| 8 | **Cost of goods sold.** Subtract line 7 from line 6. Enter here and on page 1, line 2 | 8 | 331,795 | 00 |

**9a** Check all methods used for valuing closing inventory:   *(i)* ☐ Cost as described in Regulations section 1.471-3

    *(ii)* ☑ Lower of cost or market as described in Regulations section 1.471-4

    *(iii)* ☐ Other (specify method used and attach explanation) ▶ --------------------------------------------------

**b** Check if there was a writedown of subnormal goods as described in Regulations section 1.471-2(c) . . . . . . . . ▶ ☐

**c** Check if the LIFO inventory method was adopted this tax year for any goods (if checked, attach Form 970) . . . . . ▶ ☐

**d** If the LIFO inventory method was used for this tax year, enter percentage (or amounts) of closing inventory computed under LIFO . . . . | 9d | |

**e** If property is produced or acquired for resale, do the rules of Section 263A apply to the corporation? . . . . ☑ Yes ☐ No

**f** Was there any change in determining quantities, cost, or valuations between opening and closing inventory? . . ☐ Yes ☑ No
If "Yes," attach explanation.

| **Schedule B** | **Other Information** (see instructions) | Yes | No |
|---|---|---|---|
| 1 | Check method of accounting: **(a)** ☐ Cash   **(b)** ☐ Accrual   **(c)** ☐ Other (specify) ▶ --------------------------- | | |
| 2 | See the instructions and enter the: | | |
| | **(a)** Business activity ▶ ----------------------------   **(b)** Product or service ▶ ------------------------- | | |
| 3 | At the end of the tax year, did the corporation own, directly or indirectly, 50% or more of the voting stock of a domestic corporation? (For rules of attribution, see section 267(c).) If "Yes," attach a statement showing: **(a)** name, address, and employer identification number and **(b)** percentage owned. | | ✔ |
| 4 | Was the corporation a member of a controlled group subject to the provisions of section 1561? . . . . . . | | ✔ |
| 5 | Has this corporation filed, or is it required to file, a return under section 6111 to provide information on any reportable transaction? . . . . . . . . . . . . . . . . . . . | | ✔ |
| 6 | Check this box if the corporation issued publicly offered debt instruments with original issue discount . . ▶ ☐ | | |
| | If checked, the corporation may have to file **Form 8281,** Information Return for Publicly Offered Original Issue Discount Instruments. | | |
| 7 | If the corporation: **(a)** was a C corporation before it elected to be an S corporation **or** the corporation acquired an asset with a basis determined by reference to its basis (or the basis of any other property) in the hands of a C corporation **and (b)** has net unrealized built-in gain (defined in section 1374(d)(1)) in excess of the net recognized built-in gain from prior years, enter the net unrealized built-in gain reduced by net recognized built-in gain from prior years . . . . . . . . . . . . . ▶ $ ---------------- | | |
| 8 | Check this box if the corporation had accumulated earnings and profits at the close of the tax year . . ▶ ☐ | | |
| 9 | Are the corporation's total receipts (see instructions) for the tax year **and** its total assets at the end of the tax year less than $250,000? If "Yes," the corporation is not required to complete Schedules L and M-1. | | ✔ |

**Note:** *If the corporation had assets or operated a business in a foreign country or U.S. possession, it may be required to attach* **Schedule N (Form 1120),** *Foreign Operations of U.S. Corporations, to this return. See Schedule N for details.*

| **Schedule K** | **Shareholders' Shares of Income, Deductions, Credits, etc.** | | | |
|---|---|---|---|---|

| | Shareholders' Pro Rata Share Items | | Total amount | |
|---|---|---|---|---|
| Income (Loss) | 1  Ordinary business income (loss) (page 1, line 21) | 1 | 82,936 | 00 |
| | 2  Net rental real estate income (loss) (attach Form 8825) | 2 | 4,000 | 00 |
| | 3a  Other gross rental income (loss)    3a | | | |
| |   b  Expenses from other rental activities (attach statement)    3b | | | |
| |   c  Other net rental income (loss). Subtract line 3b from line 3a | 3c | | |
| | 4  Interest income | 4 | 3,462 | 00 |
| | 5  Dividends: a Ordinary dividends | 5a | 788 | 00 |
| |         b Qualified dividends    5b | | | |
| | 6  Royalties | 6 | | |
| | 7  Net short-term capital gain (loss) (attach Schedule D (Form 1120S)) | 7 | | |
| | 8a  Net long-term capital gain (loss) (attach Schedule D (Form 1120S)) | 8a | (1,914) | |
| |   b  Collectibles (28%) gain (loss)    8b | | | |
| |   c  Unrecaptured section 1250 gain (attach statement)    8c | | | |
| | 9  Net section 1231 gain (loss) (attach Form 4797) | 9 | 16,223 | 00 |
| | 10  Other income (loss) (see instructions) . . Type ▶ ---------------- | 10 | | |

Form **1120S** (2005)

Form 1120S (2005)                                                                              Page **3**

| | Shareholders' Pro Rata Share Items (continued) | | Total amount | |
|---|---|---|---|---|
| **Deductions** | **11** Section 179 deduction (attach Form 4562). | **11** | | |
| | **12a** Contributions | **12a** | 1,500 | 00 |
| | **b** Investment interest expense | **12b** | | |
| | **c** Section 59(e)(2) expenditures  **(1)** Type ▶_____ **(2)** Amount ▶ | **12c(2)** | | |
| | **d** Other deductions (see instructions)    Type ▶_____ | **12d** | | |
| **Credits & Credit Recapture** | **13a** Low-income housing credit (section 42(j)(5)) | **13a** | | |
| | **b** Low-income housing credit (other) | **13b** | | |
| | **c** Qualified rehabilitation expenditures (rental real estate) (attach Form 3468) | **13c** | | |
| | **d** Other rental real estate credits (see instructions). Type ▶ _____ | **13d** | | |
| | **e** Other rental credits (see instructions)    Type ▶ _____ | **13e** | | |
| | **f** Credit for alcohol used as fuel (attach Form 6478) | **13f** | | |
| | **g** Other credits and credit recapture (see instructions) Type ▶ _____ | **13g** | 2,500 | 00 |
| **Foreign Transactions** | **14a** Name of country or U.S. possession ▶_____ | | | |
| | **b** Gross income from all sources | **14b** | | |
| | **c** Gross income sourced at shareholder level | **14c** | | |
| | *Foreign gross income sourced at corporate level:* | | | |
| | **d** Passive | **14d** | | |
| | **e** Listed categories (attach statement) | **14e** | | |
| | **f** General limitation | **14f** | | |
| | *Deductions allocated and apportioned at shareholder level:* | | | |
| | **g** Interest expense | **14g** | | |
| | **h** Other | **14h** | | |
| | *Deductions allocated and apportioned at corporate level to foreign source income:* | | | |
| | **i** Passive | **14i** | | |
| | **j** Listed categories (attach statement). | **14j** | | |
| | **k** General limitation | **14k** | | |
| | *Other information:* | | | |
| | **l** Total foreign taxes (check one): ▶ ☐ Paid ☐ Accrued | **14l** | | |
| | **m** Reduction in taxes available for credit (attach statement) | **14m** | | |
| | **n** Other foreign tax information (attach statement) | | | |
| **Alternative Minimum Tax (AMT) Items** | **15a** Post-1986 depreciation adjustment | **15a** | 1,151 | 00 |
| | **b** Adjusted gain or loss | **15b** | (2,728) | |
| | **c** Depletion (other than oil and gas) | **15c** | | |
| | **d** Oil, gas, and geothermal properties—gross income | **15d** | | |
| | **e** Oil, gas, and geothermal properties—deductions. | **15e** | | |
| | **f** Other AMT items (attach statement) | **15f** | | |
| **Items Affecting Shareholder Basis** | **16a** Tax-exempt interest income | **16a** | 1,635 | 00 |
| | **b** Other tax-exempt income | **16b** | | |
| | **c** Nondeductible expenses | **16c** | 3,390 | 00 |
| | **d** Property distributions | **16d** | 90,000 | 00 |
| | **e** Repayment of loans from shareholders. | **16e** | | |
| **Other Information** | **17a** Investment income | **17a** | 4,250 | 00 |
| | **b** Investment expenses | **17b** | | |
| | **c** Dividend distributions paid from accumulated earnings and profits | **17c** | | |
| | **d** Other items and amounts (attach statement) | | | |
| | **e** **Income/loss reconciliation.** (Required only if Schedule M-1 must be completed.) Combine the amounts on lines 1 through 10 in the far right column. From the result, subtract the sum of the amounts on lines 11 through 12d and 14l | **17e** | 103,995 | 00 |

Form **1120S** (2005)

Form 1120S (2005)                                                                 Page **4**

**Note:** The corporation is not required to complete Schedules L and M-1 if question 9 of Schedule B is answered "Yes."

### Schedule L — Balance Sheets per Books

| | | Beginning of tax year | | End of tax year | |
|---|---|---|---|---|---|
| | Assets | (a) | (b) | (c) | (d) |
| 1 | Cash | | 97,095 | | 87,943 |
| 2a | Trade notes and accounts receivable | 94,210 | | 92,193 | |
| b | Less allowance for bad debts | | 94,210 | | 92,193 |
| 3 | Inventories | | 118,765 | | 125,330 |
| 4 | U.S. government obligations | | 10,368 | | 24,500 |
| 5 | Tax-exempt securities | | | | 30,000 |
| 6 | Other current assets (attach statement) | | 530 | | 300 |
| 7 | Loans to shareholders | | 2,000 | | |
| 8 | Mortgage and real estate loans | | | | |
| 9 | Other investments (attach statement) | | 3,000 | | 9,700 |
| 10a | Buildings and other depreciable assets | 352,500 | | 264,500 | |
| b | Less accumulated depreciation | 135,693 | 216,807 | 92,242 | 172,258 |
| 11a | Depletable assets | | | | |
| b | Less accumulated depletion | | | | |
| 12 | Land (net of any amortization) | | 30,000 | | 20,000 |
| 13a | Intangible assets (amortizable only) | | | | |
| b | Less accumulated amortization | | | | |
| 14 | Other assets (attach statement) | | | | |
| 15 | Total assets | | 572,775 | | 562,174 |
| | **Liabilities and Shareholders' Equity** | | | | |
| 16 | Accounts payable | | 55,905 | | 50,749 |
| 17 | Mortgages, notes, bonds payable in less than 1 year | | 20,000 | | 10,000 |
| 18 | Other current liabilities (attach statement) | | 2,095 | | 4,410 |
| 19 | Loans from shareholders | | | | |
| 20 | Mortgages, notes, bonds payable in 1 year or more | | 10,000 | | |
| 21 | Other liabilities (attach statement) | | | | |
| 22 | Capital stock | | 255,000 | | 255,000 |
| 23 | Additional paid-in capital | | | | |
| 24 | Retained earnings | | 229,775 | | 242,015 |
| 25 | Adjustments to shareholders' equity (attach statement) | | | | |
| 26 | Less cost of treasury stock | | ( ) | | ( ) |
| 27 | Total liabilities and shareholders' equity | | 572,775 | | 562,174 |

### Schedule M-1 — Reconciliation of Income (Loss) per Books With Income (Loss) per Return

| | | | | | |
|---|---|---|---|---|---|
| 1 | Net income (loss) per books | 102,240 | 5 | Income recorded on books this year not included on Schedule K, lines 1 through 10 (itemize): | |
| 2 | Income included on Schedule K, lines 1, 2, 3c, 4, 5a, 6, 7, 8a, 9, and 10, not recorded on books this year (itemize): | | | a Tax-exempt interest $ _____ | 1,545 |
| 3 | Expenses recorded on books this year not included on Schedule K, lines 1 through 12 and 14l (itemize): | | 6 | Deductions included on Schedule K, lines 1 through 12 and 14l, not charged against book income this year (itemize): | |
| a | Depreciation $ _____ | | | a Depreciation $ _____ | |
| b | Travel and entertainment $ _____ 3,300 | | | | |
| | | 3,300 | 7 | Add lines 5 and 6 | 1,545 |
| 4 | Add lines 1 through 3 | 105,540 | 8 | Income (loss) (Schedule K, line 17e). Line 4 less line 7 | 103,995 |

### Schedule M-2 — Analysis of Accumulated Adjustments Account, Other Adjustments Account, and Shareholders' Undistributed Taxable Income Previously Taxed (see instructions)

| | | (a) Accumulated adjustments account | (b) Other adjustments account | (c) Shareholders' undistributed taxable income previously taxed |
|---|---|---|---|---|
| 1 | Balance at beginning of tax year | 177,906 | 1,640 | 82,936 |
| 2 | Ordinary income from page 1, line 21 | 82,936 | | |
| 3 | Other additions | 24,473 | 1,635 | |
| 4 | Loss from page 1, line 21 | ( ) | | |
| 5 | Other reductions | ( 6,714) | ( 90) | |
| 6 | Combine lines 1 through 5 | 278,601 | 3,185 | |
| 7 | Distributions other than dividend distributions | 90,000 | | |
| 8 | Balance at end of tax year. Subtract line 7 from line 6 | 188,601 | 3,185 | |

¶ **111**

Form **4797**

Department of the Treasury
Internal Revenue Service (99)

## Sales of Business Property

(Also Involuntary Conversions and Recapture Amounts
Under Sections 179 and 280F(b)(2))
▶Attach to your tax return. ▶See separate instructions.

OMB No. 1545-0184

20**05**

Attachment
Sequence No. **27**

| Name(s) shown on return | Identifying number |
|---|---|
| **Douglas Plastics Company** | 31-0031258 |

**1** Enter the gross proceeds from sales or exchanges reported to you for 2005 on Form(s) 1099-B or 1099-S (or substitute statement) that you are including on line 2, 10, or 20 (see instructions). . . . . . . . . . . . . | **1** | 62,223

### Part I   Sales or Exchanges of Property Used in a Trade or Business and Involuntary Conversions From Other Than Casualty or Theft—Most Property Held More Than 1 Year (see instructions)

| (a) Description of property | (b) Date acquired (mo., day, yr.) | (c) Date sold (mo., day, yr.) | (d) Gross sales price | (e) Depreciation allowed or allowable since acquisition | (f) Cost or other basis, plus improvements and expense of sale | (g) Gain or (loss) Subtract (f) from the sum of (d) and (e) |
|---|---|---|---|---|---|---|
| **2** Land | 01-25-81 | 01-13-05 | 13,000 | | 10,000 | 3,000 |
| | | | | | | |
| | | | | | | |
| | | | | | | |

| | | |
|---|---|---|
| **3** Gain, if any, from Form 4684, line 42 . . . . . . . . . | **3** | |
| **4** Section 1231 gain from installment sales from Form 6252, line 26 or 37 . . . . . | **4** | |
| **5** Section 1231 gain or (loss) from like-kind exchanges from Form 8824 . . . . . | **5** | |
| **6** Gain, if any, from line 32, from other than casualty or theft . . . . . . . | **6** | 13,223 |
| **7** Combine lines 2 through 6. Enter the gain or (loss) here and on the appropriate line as follows: . . . . . | **7** | 16,223 |

**Partnerships (except electing large partnerships) and S corporations.** Report the gain or (loss) following the instructions for Form 1065, Schedule K, line 10, or Form 1120S, Schedule K, line 9. Skip lines 8, 9, 11, and 12 below.

**Individuals, partners, S corporation shareholders, and all others.** If line 7 is zero or a loss, enter the amount from line 7 on line 11 below and skip lines 8 and 9. If line 7 is a gain and you did not have any prior year section 1231 losses, or they were recaptured in an earlier year, enter the gain from line 7 as a long-term capital gain on the Schedule D filed with your return and skip lines 8, 9, 11, and 12 below.

| | | |
|---|---|---|
| **8** Nonrecaptured net section 1231 losses from prior years (see instructions) . . . . . . . . | **8** | |
| **9** Subtract line 8 from line 7. If zero or less, enter -0-. If line 9 is zero, enter the gain from line 7 on line 12 below. If line 9 is more than zero, enter the amount from line 8 on line 12 below and enter the gain from line 9 as a long-term capital gain on the Schedule D filed with your return (see instructions). . . . . . . . . . | **9** | |

### Part II   Ordinary Gains and Losses (see instructions)

**10** Ordinary gains and losses not included on lines 11 through 16 (include property held 1 year or less):

| | | | | | | |
|---|---|---|---|---|---|---|
| | | | | | | |
| | | | | | | |
| | | | | | | |
| | | | | | | |

| | | |
|---|---|---|
| **11** Loss, if any, from line 7. . . . . . . . . . . . | **11** | ( ) |
| **12** Gain, if any, from line 7 or amount from line 8, if applicable . . . . . . . . | **12** | |
| **13** Gain, if any, from line 31 . . . . . . . . . . . | **13** | 4,857 |
| **14** Net gain or (loss) from Form 4684, lines 34 and 41a . . . . . . . | **14** | |
| **15** Ordinary gain from installment sales from Form 6252, line 25 or 36 . . . . . | **15** | |
| **16** Ordinary gain or (loss) from like-kind exchanges from Form 8824 . . . . . | **16** | |
| **17** Combine lines 10 through 16 . . . . . . . . . . . | **17** | 4,857 |

**18** For all except individual returns, enter the amount from line 17 on the appropriate line of your return and skip lines a and b below. For individual returns, complete lines a and b below:

**a** If the loss on line 11 includes a loss from Form 4684, line 38, column (b)(ii), enter that part of the loss here. Enter the part of the loss from income-producing property on Schedule A (Form 1040), line 27, and the part of the loss from property used as an employee on Schedule A (Form 1040), line 22. Identify as from "Form 4797, line 18a." See instructions . . . . . . . . . | **18a** | |

**b** Redetermine the gain or (loss) on line 17 excluding the loss, if any, on line 18a. Enter here and on Form 1040, line 14 . . . . . . . . . . . | **18b** | |

For Paperwork Reduction Act Notice, see separate instructions.     Cat. No. 13086I     Form **4797** (2005)

¶ **111**

Form 4797 (2005)      Page **2**

### Part III   Gain From Disposition of Property Under Sections 1245, 1250, 1252, 1254, and 1255 (see instructions)

| 19 | (a) Description of section 1245, 1250, 1252, 1254, or 1255 property: | (b) Date acquired (mo., day, yr.) | (c) Date sold (mo., day, yr.) |
|---|---|---|---|
| A | Building | 01-10-81 | 01-18-05 |
| B | Machine | 01-14-02 | 01-18-05 |
| C | | | |
| D | | | |

| | These columns relate to the properties on lines 19A through 19D. ▶ | | Property A | Property B | Property C | Property D |
|---|---|---|---|---|---|---|
| 20 | Gross sales price (**Note:** *See line 1 before completing.*) | 20 | 49,223 | 5,041 | | |
| 21 | Cost or other basis plus expense of sale | 21 | 90,000 | 10,000 | | |
| 22 | Depreciation (or depletion) allowed or allowable | 22 | 57,564 | 6,252 | | |
| 23 | Adjusted basis. Subtract line 22 from line 21 | 23 | 32,436 | 3,748 | | |
| 24 | Total gain. Subtract line 23 from line 20 | 24 | 16,787 | 1,293 | | |
| 25 | **If section 1245 property:** | | | | | |
| a | Depreciation allowed or allowable from line 22 | 25a | | 6,252 | | |
| b | Enter the **smaller** of line 24 or 25a | 25b | | 1,293 | | |
| 26 | **If section 1250 property:** If straight line depreciation was used, enter -0- on line 26g, except for a corporation subject to section 291. | | | | | |
| a | Additional depreciation after 1975 (see instructions) | 26a | 3,564 | | | |
| b | Applicable percentage multiplied by the **smaller** of line 24 or line 26a (see instructions) | 26b | 3,564 | | | |
| c | Subtract line 26a from line 24. If residential rental property **or** line 24 is not more than line 26a, skip lines 26d and 26e | 26c | 13,223 | | | |
| d | Additional depreciation after 1969 and before 1976 | 26d | 0 | | | |
| e | Enter the **smaller** of line 26c or 26d | 26e | 0 | | | |
| f | Section 291 amount (corporations only) | 26f | 0 | | | |
| g | Add lines 26b, 26e, and 26f | 26g | 3,564 | | | |
| 27 | **If section 1252 property:** Skip this section if you did not dispose of farmland or if this form is being completed for a partnership (other than an electing large partnership). | | | | | |
| a | Soil, water, and land clearing expenses | 27a | | | | |
| b | Line 27a multiplied by applicable percentage (see instructions) | 27b | | | | |
| c | Enter the **smaller** of line 24 or 27b | 27c | | | | |
| 28 | **If section 1254 property:** | | | | | |
| a | Intangible drilling and development costs, expenditures for development of mines and other natural deposits, and mining exploration costs (see instructions) | 28a | | | | |
| b | Enter the **smaller** of line 24 or 28a | 28b | | | | |
| 29 | **If section 1255 property:** | | | | | |
| a | Applicable percentage of payments excluded from income under section 126 (see instructions) | 29a | | | | |
| b | Enter the **smaller** of line 24 or 29a (see instructions) | 29b | | | | |

**Summary of Part III Gains.** Complete property columns A through D through line 29b before going to line 30.

| 30 | Total gains for all properties. Add property columns A through D, line 24 | 30 | 18,080 |
|---|---|---|---|
| 31 | Add property columns A through D, lines 25b, 26g, 27c, 28b, and 29b. Enter here and on line 13 | 31 | 4,857 |
| 32 | Subtract line 31 from line 30. Enter the portion from casualty or theft on Form 4684, line 36. Enter the portion from other than casualty or theft on Form 4797, line 6 | 32 | 13,223 |

### Part IV   Recapture Amounts Under Sections 179 and 280F(b)(2) When Business Use Drops to 50% or Less (see instructions)

| | | | (a) Section 179 | (b) Section 280F(b)(2) |
|---|---|---|---|---|
| 33 | Section 179 expense deduction or depreciation allowable in prior years | 33 | | |
| 34 | Recomputed depreciation (see instructions) | 34 | | |
| 35 | Recapture amount. Subtract line 34 from line 33. See the instructions for where to report | 35 | | |

Form **4797** (2005)

| | Final K-1 | Amended K-1 | OMB No. 1545-0130 |
|---|---|---|---|

**Schedule K-1 (Form 1120S)** 2005
Department of the Treasury
Internal Revenue Service

For calendar year 2005, or tax
year beginning _____, 2005
ending _____, 20___

## Shareholder's Share of Income, Deductions, Credits, etc.
▶ See back of form and separate instructions.

### Part I — Information About the Corporation

**A** Corporation's employer identification number
31-0099009

**B** Corporation's name, address, city, state, and ZIP code
Douglas Plastics Company
2400 Lakeview Street
Fargo, North Dakota 58103

**C** IRS Center where corporation filed return
Ogden, UT

**D** Tax shelter registration number, if any _____

**E** Check if Form 8271 is attached

### Part II — Information About the Shareholder

**F** Shareholder's identifying number
555-11-6789

**G** Shareholder's name, address, city, state and ZIP code
Douglas Pratt
660 Sprinsteen Street
Fargo, North Dakota 58103

**H** Shareholder's percentage of stock ownership for tax year ... 50 %

For IRS Use Only

### Part III — Shareholder's Share of Current Year Income, Deductions, Credits, and Other Items

| # | Item | Amount | # | Item | Amount |
|---|---|---|---|---|---|
| 1 | Ordinary business income (loss) | 41,468 | 13 | Credits & credit recapture L | 1,250 |
| 2 | Net rental real estate income (loss) | 2,000 | | | |
| 3 | Other net rental income (loss) | | | | |
| 4 | Interest income | 1,731 | | | |
| 5a | Ordinary dividends | 394 | | | |
| 5b | Qualified dividends | | 14 | Foreign transactions | |
| 6 | Royalties | | | | |
| 7 | Net short-term capital gain (loss) | | | | |
| 8a | Net long-term capital gain (loss) | (957) | | | |
| 8b | Collectibles (28%) gain (loss) | | | | |
| 8c | Unrecaptured section 1250 gain | | | | |
| 9 | Net section 1231 gain (loss) | 8,111.50 | | | |
| 10 | Other income (loss) | | 15 | Alternative minimum tax (AMT) items | |
| | | | A | | 575.50 |
| | | | B | | (1,364) |
| 11 | Section 179 deduction | | 16 | Items affecting shareholder basis | |
| 12 A | Other deductions | 750 | A | | 817.50 |
| | | | C | | 1,695 |
| | | | D | | 45,000 |
| | | | 17 | Other information A | 2,125 |

\* See attached statement for additional information.

For Privacy Act and Paperwork Reduction Act Notice, see Instructions for Form 1120S. Cat. No. 11520D Schedule K-1 (Form 1120S) 2005

¶111

Schedule K-1 (Form 1120S) 2005                                                                 Page **2**

This list identifies the codes used on Schedule K-1 for all shareholders and provides summarized reporting information for shareholders who file Form 1040. For detailed reporting and filing information, see the separate Shareholder's Instructions for Schedule K-1 and the instructions for your income tax return.

| | Code | | Enter on |
|---|---|---|---|

**1. Ordinary business income (loss).** You must first determine whether the income (loss) is passive or nonpassive. Then enter on your return as follows:

| | Enter on |
|---|---|
| Passive loss | See the Shareholder's Instructions |
| Passive income | Schedule E, line 28, column (g) |
| Nonpassive loss | Schedule E, line 28, column (h) |
| Nonpassive income | Schedule E, line 28, column (j) |

**2. Net rental real estate income (loss)** — See the Shareholder's Instructions

**3. Other net rental income (loss)**

| | |
|---|---|
| Net income | Schedule E, line 28, column (g) |
| Net loss | See the Shareholder's Instructions |

**4. Interest income** — Form 1040, line 8a

**5a. Ordinary dividends** — Form 1040, line 9a

**5b. Qualified dividends** — Form 1040, line 9b

**6. Royalties** — Schedule E, line 4

**7. Net short-term capital gain (loss)** — Schedule D, line 5, column (f)

**8a. Net long-term capital gain (loss)** — Schedule D, line 12, column (f)

**8b. Collectibles (28%) gain (loss)** — 28% Rate Gain Worksheet, line 4 (Schedule D instructions)

**8c. Unrecaptured section 1250 gain** — See the Shareholder's Instructions

**9. Net section 1231 gain (loss)** — See the Shareholder's Instructions

**10. Other income (loss)**

| Code | | |
|---|---|---|
| A | Other portfolio income (loss) | See the Shareholder's Instructions |
| B | Involuntary conversions | See the Shareholder's Instructions |
| C | Sec. 1256 contracts & straddles | Form 6781, line 1 |
| D | Mining exploration costs recapture | See Pub. 535 |
| E | Other income (loss) | See the Shareholder's Instructions |

**11. Section 179 deduction** — See the Shareholder's Instructions

**12. Other deductions**

| Code | | |
|---|---|---|
| A | Cash contributions (50%) | Schedule A, line 15a |
| B | Cash contributions (30%) | Schedule A, line 15a |
| C | Noncash contributions (50%) | Schedule A, line 16 |
| D | Noncash contributions (30%) | Schedule A, line 16 |
| E | Capital gain property to a 50% organization (30%) | Schedule A, line 16 |
| F | Capital gain property (20%) | Schedule A, line 16 |
| G | Cash contributions (100%) | See the Shareholder's Instructions |
| H | Investment interest expense | Form 4952, line 1 |
| I | Deductions—royalty income | Schedule E, line 18 |
| J | Section 59(e)(2) expenditures | See the Shareholder's Instructions |
| K | Deductions—portfolio (2% floor) | Schedule A, line 22 |
| L | Deductions—portfolio (other) | Schedule A, line 27 |
| M | Reforestation expense deduction | See the Shareholder's Instructions |
| N | Preproductive period expenses | See the Shareholder's Instructions |
| O | Commercial revitalization deduction from rental real estate activities | See Form 8582 Instructions |
| P | Domestic production activities information | See Form 8903 Instructions |
| Q | Qualified production activities income | Form 8903, line 7 |
| R | Employer's W-2 wages | Form 8903, line 13 |
| S | Other deductions | See the Shareholder's Instructions |

**13. Credits & credit recapture**

| Code | | |
|---|---|---|
| A | Low-income housing credit (section 42(j)(5)) | Form 8586, line 4 |
| B | Low-income housing credit (other) | Form 8586, line 4 |
| C | Qualified rehabilitation expenditures (rental real estate) | Form 3468, line 1 |
| D | Qualified rehabilitation expenditures (other than rental real estate) | Form 3468, line 1 |
| E | Basis of energy property | See the Shareholder's Instructions |
| F | Other rental real estate credits | See the Shareholder's Instructions |
| G | Other rental credits | See the Shareholder's Instructions |
| H | Undistributed capital gains credit | Form 1040, line 70, check box a |
| I | Credit for alcohol used as fuel | Form 6478, line 4 |
| J | Work opportunity credit | Form 5884, line 3 |
| K | Welfare-to-work credit | Form 8861, line 3 |
| L | Disabled access credit | Form 8826, line 7 |

| Code | | Enter on |
|---|---|---|
| M | Empowerment zone and renewal community employment credit | Form 8844, line 3 |
| N | Credit for increasing research activities | Form 6765, line 42 |
| O | New markets credit | Form 8874, line 2 |
| P | Credit for employer social security and Medicare taxes | Form 8846, line 5 |
| Q | Backup withholding | Form 1040, line 64 |
| R | Recapture of low-income housing credit (section 42(j)(5)) | Form 8611, line 8 |
| S | Recapture of low-income housing credit (other) | Form 8611, line 8 |
| T | Recapture of investment credit | See Form 4255 |
| U | Other credits | See the Shareholder's Instructions |
| V | Recapture of other credits | See the Shareholder's Instructions |

**14. Foreign transactions**

| Code | | |
|---|---|---|
| A | Name of country or U.S. possession | Form 1116, Part I |
| B | Gross income from all sources | Form 1116, Part I |
| C | Gross income sourced at shareholder level | Form 1116, Part I |

*Foreign gross income sourced at corporate level*

| | | |
|---|---|---|
| D | Passive | Form 1116, Part I |
| E | Listed categories | Form 1116, Part I |
| F | General limitation | Form 1116, Part I |

*Deductions allocated and apportioned at shareholder level*

| | | |
|---|---|---|
| G | Interest expense | Form 1116, Part I |
| H | Other | Form 1116, Part I |

*Deductions allocated and apportioned at corporate level to foreign source income*

| | | |
|---|---|---|
| I | Passive | Form 1116, Part I |
| J | Listed categories | Form 1116, Part I |
| K | General limitation | Form 1116, Part I |

*Other information*

| | | |
|---|---|---|
| L | Total foreign taxes paid | Form 1116, Part II |
| M | Total foreign taxes accrued | Form 1116, Part II |
| N | Reduction in taxes available for credit | Form 1116, line 12 |
| O | Foreign trading gross receipts | Form 8873 |
| P | Extraterritorial income exclusion | Form 8873 |
| Q | Other foreign transactions | See the Shareholder's Instructions |

**15. Alternative minimum tax (AMT) items**

| Code | | |
|---|---|---|
| A | Post-1986 depreciation adjustment | |
| B | Adjusted gain or loss | See the Shareholder's Instructions and the Instructions for Form 6251 |
| C | Depletion (other than oil & gas) | |
| D | Oil, gas, & geothermal—gross income | |
| E | Oil, gas, & geothermal—deductions | |
| F | Other AMT items | |

**16. Items affecting shareholder basis**

| Code | | |
|---|---|---|
| A | Tax-exempt interest income | Form 1040, line 8b |
| B | Other tax-exempt income | See the Shareholder's Instructions |
| C | Nondeductible expenses | See the Shareholder's Instructions |
| D | Property distributions | See the Shareholder's Instructions |
| E | Repayment of loans from shareholders | See the Shareholder's Instructions |

**17. Other information**

| Code | | |
|---|---|---|
| A | Investment income | Form 4952, line 4a |
| B | Investment expenses | Form 4952, line 5 |
| C | Look-back interest—completed long-term contracts | See Form 8697 |
| D | Look-back interest—income forecast method | See Form 8866 |
| E | Dispositions of property with section 179 deductions | |
| F | Recapture of section 179 deduction | |
| G | Section 453(l)(3) information | |
| H | Section 453A(c) information | |
| I | Section 1260(b) information | See the Shareholder's Instructions |
| J | Interest allocable to production expenditures | |
| K | CCF nonqualified withdrawal | |
| L | Information needed to figure depletion—oil and gas | |
| M | Amortization of reforestation costs | |
| N | Other information | |

*Printed on recycled paper*

¶ **111**

# Topical Index

References are to paragraph (not page, except where indicated) numbers and correspond as follows:
Corporations 1–41; Partnerships 42–68; Estates and Trusts 71–96; S Corporations 101–111